Business and Humanities

Business and Humanities

Discovering the Human Side of Business in the Age of Globalization

Second Edition

Edited by Kristina Gibby-Wachter, Ph.D.

University of Utah

cognella

SAN DIEGO

Bassim Hamadeh, CEO and Publisher
Carrie Baarns, Manager, Revisions and Author Care
Kaela Martin, Project Editor
Susana Christie, Senior Developmental Editor
Alia Bales, Production Manager
Jess Estrella, Senior Graphic Designer
Alexa Lucido, Licensing Manager
Natalie Piccotti, Director of Marketing
Kassie Graves, Senior Vice President, Editorial
Jamie Giganti, Director of Academic Publishing

Printed in the United States of America.

cognella® | ACADEMIC PUBLISHING
320 South Cedros Ave., Ste. 400, Solana Beach, CA 92075

Contents

Introduction ix

Unit I Culture and Business 1

Reading 1.1 Attitudes, Values and Beliefs 7
Richard Pettinger

Reading 1.2 The Non-Western World 25
Pradyumna P. Karan

Reading 1.3 Intercultural Communication 41
Thomas M. Steinfatt and Diane M. Millette

Unit II Psychology and Identity of Self 51

Reading 2.1 The Psychology of Business 55
Jay J. Silverberg

Reading 2.2 Discovering the Happiness Advantage 65
Shawn Achor

Reading 2.3 The Basics About Emotions in Business 75
Richard M. Contino and Penelope J. Holt

Reading 2.4 A Reader's Guide to Using These Ideas: Selection from Smarter Faster Better: The Transformative Power of Real Productivity 81
Charles Duhigg

Unit III History and Philosophy 95

Reading 3.1 Introduction to Feminisms: A Global History 103
Lucy Delap

Reading 3.2 Genesis of the Black Working Class 115
Joe William Trotter

Reading 3.3 Conclusion: How History Impacts on Management 139
Morgen Witzel

Reading 3.4 What Is Philosophy? 161
Joseph Gilbert

Reading 3.5 Women, Gender and Feminism at Work 173
Allison Elias

Reading 3.6 Plato on Topos, Economy, and Transition 187
Janina Rosicka

Unit IV Visual Arts and Business 209

Reading 4.1 What Is Art? What Is an Artist? What Is Art History? 215
Julia C. Fischer

Reading 4.2 Directing Creativity: The Art and Craft of Creative Leadership 223
Piers Ibbotson and Lotte Darsø

Reading 4.3 Art World, Art Business, Art Market 229
Jeffrey Taylor

Reading 4.4 Arts Meets Management 237
Kurt Mayer

Unit V Sociology, Anthropology, and Business 245

Reading 5.1 Studying Work, Society and Organisation 253
Tony Watson

Reading 5.2 Sociology for Business 263
Martin Joseph
Reading 5.3 Business Anthropology: An Overview 273
Robert Guang Tian
Reading 5.4 Applied Anthropology and Change 279
Alexander M. Ervin
Reading 5.5 Cultural Anthropology and Global Business 283
Gary P. Ferraro and Elizabeth K. Briody

Unit VI Globalization and the Application of Humanities in Business 301

Reading 6.1 Culture and Globalization 307
Veronica Velo
Reading 6.2 Sustainability, Social Enterprise, and Impact Investment 317
Nader H. Asgary, Dina Frutos-Bencze, and Massood V. Samii
Reading 6.3 Introduction: Governments and Corporate Social Responsibility 331
Josep M. Lozano, Laura Albareda, Tamyko Ysa, Heike Roscher, and Manila Marcuccio
Reading 6.4 COVID-19 and World Order 339
Hal Brands and Francis J. Gavin

Introduction

> *"Great things in business are never done by one person. They're done by a team of people."*
>
> —Steve Jobs

Humanities are more relevant than ever in our technologically advanced, globalized business world. The worldwide COVID-19 pandemic and associated quarantining, expansion of remote work, and other practices that required our isolation underscores the powerful need for human connection. In fact, interpersonal connection has become widely recognized as a basic need for survival. The ability to discover the human side of business is widely recognized as the key to business success.

Previously, in our age of daily technological innovation, the essence of being human was easily overlooked. This is ironic, particularly when considering we are directly connected to human beings globally in a way that is unprecedented. Globalization requires the successful businessperson to understand what it means to be human in ways outside of their own experience. Many CEOs and other executive officers have a background in humanities.[1] Accordingly, cutting-edge business schools incorporate humanities as a vital addition to their curriculum.

Business students who graduate having studied humanities will have an edge in the competitive job market that will be advantageous in their future careers. An influx of research in academia, articles in trade journals, and a focus on the importance of humanities in business and mainstream media all demonstrate the breadth and attention given to the importance of the incorporation of humanities in today's business world.

This text examines the importance of humanities in business using a combination of related disciplines in order to uncover the essence of human thinking and patterns of behavior. Theories used within the text will provide a broader understanding of how people work and how markets are driven. In short, students and business leaders will be able to make connections from theory to practice across time and in many global regions. In this era of globalization, such an understanding is critical to the understanding of business.

In today's complex world, business professionals are required to think clearly, communicate well, and analyze a variety of situations from divergent perspectives. An ability to analyze situations from a humanities perspective provides insight into essentially everything. Humanities provide understanding from the past, insight in the present, and lucidity about the future. In addition, through the humanities, analytical thinking is sharpened by the ability to read with discernment and write effectively.[2] Business leaders with knowledge of the humanities know how to ask questions and look at problem-solving from a variety of perspectives.[3] Humanities include the following disciplines that relate to the wide spectrum of experiences in business:

1. Art and art history
2. Classics
3. Literature
4. Culture and languages
5. English
6. History
7. Jurisprudence
8. Linguistics
9. Music
10. Philosophy
11. Religious studies
12. Theatre
13. Communications

Thinking about business practices from the lived perspectives of actual people in business creates a more comprehensive view of particular situations than traditional mechanical analyses. The academic foundation for this standard is found in the basic studies of humanities and the analysis of human experiences throughout history and continuing to the present, in various time periods and diverse cultural contexts.

An understanding of the humanities provides business students and professionals with the tools needed to access the human side of business, such as research methodologies by which patterns of behaviors, trends, and economics can be measured beyond mere numbers. The study of humanities strengthens the ability to communicate, collaborate, and create positive relationships within organizations. Humanities also inspire creativity in business, resulting in original and educated problem-solving skills and advanced solutions. In addition, an understanding of the humanities provides a strong base that gives business leaders the ability to think on their feet in diverse situations and in new cultures. This type of thinking expands beyond the office and leads to enriched lives beyond work.[4] Competency in business humanities is an asset to stakeholders as well. Civic and cultural responsibilities of business leaders become part of the informed decision-making process. We learn to ask questions about our world with humanities. Further, the critical element of cultural competency in business requires solid footing in the humanities with diversity in the workforce and global business.[5]

People are saturated in culture; it is the foundation upon which patterns develop, behaviors emerge, and decisions are made. Culture is a standard in each particular setting by which actions are measured in terms of attitudes, values, and beliefs. It is the measure by which norms and acceptable behavior are perpetuated within particular societies. Culture is developed through systematic processes that may vary by segment within particular locations; therefore, elements of culture are not fixed.

Deviation from and compliance with particular norms are inevitable; accordingly, people accommodate and resist elements of their own culture in varying degrees as a means of survival. Furthermore, situations that are new are threatening, so people respond with fear or arrogance to accommodate the situation, to reach a point of comfort.[6] The repercussions of such thinking can be devastating in a business setting, where deals are buried, contracts nullified, and relationships severed. On the other hand, the competent businessperson who is culturally astute can adapt to new situations, modify their behavior to meet the circumstance, and placate misunderstandings. This is where the humanities come in: the study human of behavior in its various forms using integrated schools of thought is a systematic research-based process that opens the eyes and minds of business professionals within their organizations as well as in cross-organizational interaction.

While each of the humanities stands on its own from an academic perspective, their application is not distinct in business practice. Disciplines overlap to create an informed and practical study of contemporary business situations and problems that will ultimately result in a refined knowledge of the circumstance in question.

However, traditional humanities analyses are not enough. The study of critical theory incorporated with the humanities brings individual and particular group analysis to the table with the study of race, class, and gender in business settings. With the analysis of cultural capital, selective traditions, and systems of power, organizational leaders are better positioned to foster social justice and equality in policies, procedure, and practice.

The objective of this book is to examine the potential impact that a working knowledge of the humanities can have in solid business scholarship and successful business practice. This text will not only cover theory but also analyze these theories in practice (praxis). The topics covered provide insight into diverse cultures, philosophies, histories, arts, and so forth. The global economy is multifaceted and must be approached as such. Therefore, strong business analysis should be drawn from multiple perspectives. Rules are constantly changing, and adaptation is a part of success. Research from key disciplines in the humanities demonstrates their significance in today's business world.

Each unit will deal with a particular school of the humanities, but clearly distinct disciplines borrow from and lend themselves to others. This strategy is not meant to diminish the significance of any of the specialties but rather to point to the coherence of the subjects in business.

Unit I establishes the essence and significance of culture as the fiber that holds a society or group together. Values, attitudes, beliefs, and actions are shaped by culture, so it follows that culture varies largely from place to place. Understanding, adaptability, and empathy are required in a global economy, so it is vital for leaders to have the skills necessary to develop cultural competency based on cross-cultural analysis in order to effectively manage, develop, and communicate within their organizations as well as with stakeholders.

Psychology and self-identity are the focus of Unit II. Psychology has been integrated with business management for several decades, but the relevance persists. More recently, positive psychology has proven to be valuable in organizational management.[7] Workplaces are more productive and profitable when business leaders approach management with positive strategies. The strategies are beneficial to all involved, including the managers. Positive leaders demonstrate excellent leadership based on a strong sense of self acquired through self-reflexivity, adaptability, and a focus on possibility.

History and philosophy are grouped together in Unit III as each discipline builds upon the other. History teaches students contextual analysis rooted in events of the past. The values, priorities, and ideals within each time period are built upon specific philosophies in terms of ethics, ideals, and morality. Business practices of the past impact those in the present. Critical inquiry of historical events, policies, and so forth, in turn, require philosophical analysis to determine past mindsets and the relevance of those principles to present situations. Historical and philosophical methodology require rigorous systematic analysis that address issues of perspective, bias, privilege, failure, and success using diverse sources. The impact of the past on present and future business practices is key to success in our age.

Visual arts are addressed in Unit IV from two different perspectives. A basic working knowledge of the elements of art is first addressed to develop a basis for the relevance of aesthetics in the workplace. The next focus is on the practical application of visual arts in contemporary management strategies. Many of the tactics that employ visual arts draw on performing arts as well.

The twin studies of sociology and anthropology are covered in Unit V. Both disciplines use the scientific method in analysis, share key elements of inquiry, and look at similar issues. However, the scope and purpose of each school of thought is distinct. Sociological analysis focuses on macroanalysis in business, while anthropology focuses on microanalysis.

Unit VI looks at the application of critical theory in business with key issues that matter in today's business world. Issues related to race, class, and gender are moving to the forefront of policy making within organizations. Accordingly, the significance of each topic is considered in business settings in a diverse global market.

Unit VII places culture in the context of globalization through the analysis of cultural competency—a necessary component of corporate sustainability. Sustainability for the business, stakeholders, and environment are the goals for effective business leaders in our global marketplace. Each of the disciplines discussed in the previous units contributes to the final topic. The application of the humanities in business is a driving force in a successful business model and for successful business leaders in the 21st century.

Notes

1. Champagne, A. (2017, August 18). Liberal arts is the foundation for professional success in the 21st century. 4Humanities. https://4humanities.org/?s=UK+business+leaders
   Stanford Humanities Center. (n.d.). Why do the humanities matter? http://shc.stanford.edu/why-do-humanities-matterhttps://blogs.sciencemag.org/sciencecareers/2011/05/ten-important-r.html
2. Makovsky, K. (2013, July 3). *The difference humanities makes in business*. Forbes. https://www.forbes.com/sites/kenmakovsky/2013/07/03/the-difference-humanities-makes-in-business/#5e2db7f72e0c
   Why the humanities still matter. (2014, August 19). The New York Times. https://www.nytimes.com/2014/08/20/opinion/why-the-humanities-still-matter.html
   Here are 9 reasons why humanities matter. What's your number 10? (n.d.). http://curt-rice.com/2014/02/25/here-are-9-reasons-why-humanities-matter-whats-your-number-10/.
3. Rice, C. (2014).*Becoming women: The embodied self in image culture*. University of Toronto Press.
4. Gilbert, S. (2016, June 30). Learning to be human. The Atlantic. https://www.theatlantic.com/entertainment/archive/2016/06/learning-to-be-human/489659/
   Floor, A. (2017, Winter). Why humanities matter. Continuum. https://continuum.utah.edu/features/why-humanities-matter/
5. Heffernan, T. (2004). Trust formation in cross-cultural business-to-business relationships. *Qualitative Market Research: An International Journal*, *7*(2), 114–125; Beth Stanek, M. (2000). The need for global managers: A business necessity. *Management Decision*, *38*(4), 232–242.
   Kasemsap, K. (2016). Analyzing the roles of human capital and competency in global business. In *Project Management: Concepts, Methodologies, Tools, and Applications* (pp. 2190–2218). IGI Global.
   Demangeot, C., Adkins, N. R., Mueller, R. D., Henderson, G. R., Ferguson, N. S., Mandiberg, J. M., Roy, A., Johnson, G. D., Kipnis, E., Pullig, C., Broderick, A. J., Zúñiga, M. A. (2013). Toward intercultural competency in multicultural marketplaces. *Journal of Public Policy & Marketing*, *32*(Special Issue), 156–164.
   Ogrean, C., Herciu, M., & Belascu, L. (2009). Competency-based management and global competencies—challenges for firm strategic management. *International Review of Business Research Papers*, *5*(4), 114–122.
   Koprucu, S. (2009). Raising global citizens: Focus on cultural competency. *School Business Affairs*, *75*(4), 30–32.
   Ferraro, G. P., & Briody, E. K. (2013). *The cultural dimension of global business*. Pearson.
   Becker, G. K. (2018). Moral leadership in business. *Contemporary Issues in Leadership* (pp. 237–257).
   Amernic, J., Craig, R., & Tourish, D. (2007). The transformational leader as pedagogue, physician, architect, commander, and saint: Five root metaphors in Jack Welch's letters to stockholders of General Electric. *Human Relations*, *60*(12), 1839–1872.
   Wibbeke, E. S., & McArthur, S. (2013). *Global business leadership*. Routledge.
   Pusch, M. D. (2009). The interculturally competent global leader. *The SAGE handbook of intercultural competence* (pp. 66–84). SAGE.
   Schwarz, G. M., Kerr, S., Mowday, R. T., Starbuck, W. H., Tung, R. L., & Von Glinow, M. A. (2006). Astute foresight or wishful thinking? Learning from visions. *Journal of Management Inquiry*, *15*(4), 347–361.
   Lennick, D., & Kiel, F. (2007). *Moral intelligence: Enhancing business performance and leadership success*. Pearson Prentice Hall.
   Rosen, R. T., Rosen, R. H., Digh, P., Phillips, C., & Singer, M. (2000). *Global literacies: Lessons on business leadership and national cultures*. Simon and Schuster.

Krell, E. (2013). Exploring what it takes to lead in the 21st century. *Baylor Business Review*, *31*(2), 4.

6. Anyon, J. (1984). Intersections of gender and class: Accommodation and resistance by working-class and affluent females to contradictory sex role ideologies. *The Journal of Education*, *166*(1), 25–48.
   Olmedo, I. M. (2003). Accommodation and resistance: Latinas struggle for their children's education. *Anthropology & Education Quarterly*, *34*(4), 373–395.
   Goto, S. T. (1997). Nerds, normal people, and homeboys: Accommodation and resistance among Chinese American students. *Anthropology & Education Quarterly*, *28*(1), 70–84.
   Basas, C. G. (2008). Back rooms, board rooms-reasonable accommodation and resistance under the ADA. Berkeley Journal of Employment and Labor Law, *29*, 59.
   Davidman, L. (1990). Accommodation and resistance to modernity: A comparison of two contemporary Orthodox Jewish groups. *Sociological Analysis*, *51*(1), 35–51.
   Craith, M. N. (2007). Languages and power: Accommodation and resistance. In *Language, Power and Identity Politics* (pp. 1–20). Palgrave MacMillan.
7. Wiegand, D. M., & Geller, E. S. (2005). Connecting positive psychology and organizational behavior management: Achievement motivation and the power of positive reinforcement. *Journal of Organizational Behavior Management*, *24*(1–2), 3–25.
   Bakker, A. B., & Schaufeli, W. B. (2008). Positive organizational behavior: Engaged employees in flourishing organizations. *Journal of Organizational Behavior: The International Journal of Industrial, Occupational and Organizational Psychology and Behavior*, *29*(2), 147–154.
   Youssef, C. M., & Luthans, F. (2007). Positive organizational behavior in the workplace: The impact of hope, optimism, and resilience. *Journal of Management*, *33*(5), 774–800.
   Salovey, P., Mayer, J. D., Caruso, D., & Yoo, S. H. (2002). The positive psychology of emotional intelligence. *Handbook of Positive Psychology*, *159*, 171.

Unit I

Culture and Business

"Culture does not make people. People make culture."
—Chimamanda Ngozi Adichie

Culture defines people and their environment; therefore, the study of culture provides strategic insight pertaining to specific societies that are relevant to businesses.[1] The broad spectrum of culture is diverse and interchangeable.[2] In its many forms, culture can be broken down to both intangible and tangible elements. In its immaterial form, culture is represented by values, beliefs, standards, norms, and attitudes that shape traditional practices in everyday life and provide impetus for change. At the same time, culture is reflected in the physical objects that point to the persona of society. Culture changes shape according to societal standards; however, fundamental cultural elements remain constant from generation to generation.[3] Culture dovetails with business in relation to general societal patterns of behavior as well as internal, company-specific structures.[4] It is critical for the successful businessperson to be proficient in cultural competency for diverse situations in this age of globalization.[5]

The following terms describe provide a basic lexicon for the study of culture:[6]

- Values are preferred ideas that people share in a given society about what is good, bad, beautiful, ugly, and so on. Clearly, values are context-specific, as notions that indicate something is desirable in one situation may be undesirable in another. However, some values transcend location. For example, the value of integrity in business is consistently the ideal; therefore, it is naturally assumed to be a standard in most business transactions.

- Beliefs are shaped by values and represent personal philosophies.
- Attitudes reflect people's viewpoints in given situations.
- Norms are concepts and behaviors that constitute the normal. Normative behavior varies from place to place and evolves over time.
- Language is a system of verbal or written symbols that communicate culture-specific meaning. It provides a framework from which ideas, feelings, and experiences can be expressed.
- Social structure refers to the pattern within culture that is organized according to status and role expectations.
- Social organization is the arrangement of parts that constitute society, the organization of social positions within society, and the distribution of people within those positions.
    - Status categorizes socially defined positions.
    - Roles are clustered sets of behavior expected within status in repeated patterns of behavior.
    - Groups are collections of two or more people who interact based on a shared set of expectations. Groups can be a one-time occurrence or people regularly interacting with each other. Status and roles are interrelated in groups.
    - Institutions are patterns of behavior that are accepted, expected, and practiced over time. They are reflective of the values and norms of a given society in indeterminate form; however, physical structures referred to as institutions house and perpetuate immaterial values. For example, a university (physical institution) expedites the value of education (institution as concept).
    - Hierarchies are systems of power within specific cultures and organizations that dictate status and role expectations of people within each system.
    - Agency is the realized capacity of people to act upon their world purposefully and reflectively. In short, it is the amount of freedom afforded individuals within particular cultures.
    - Identity combines the personal world with the collective space of cultural forms and social relations, not confined to the body but spread across the social environment.
    - Inequality is reflected in cultural systems of power and subordination.
    - Social stratification is the division of people along socioeconomic lines; it is, in essence, the layering of people according to material goods and status within particular cultures.

Evidence of the components of culture are symbolized in patterns of behavior and physical elements:

- *traditions*
- *rituals*
- *lifestyles*
- *artifacts and objects*
- *foods*

The study of culture in business as a valid theoretical model is a relatively recent practice. Since the late 1990s there has been a distinct turn to culture within the world of business.[7] Organizational change, globalization, and technology require an extension of the traditional business model. Cultural business analysis challenges mechanistic models of business, looking beyond the computations of means/end analysis. Rather, it takes into consideration the players associated with the business, the impact of human actions on business, and the outcome of behaviors in business settings.[8] It provides a solid base from which to explain business practices and to provide direction based on theoretical findings. Theories are concepts and ideas designed to set forth the interrelated concepts and facts of a particular culture, and provide the foundation to validate, predict, control, or explain social behavior in a scientific and organized way.[9]

The incorporation of cultural analyses into traditional mechanistic business analysis requires the analysis of beliefs, values, and symbols that represent product, technology, business standards, and business practices.[10]

In this unit, Allen Batteau examines the evolution of the relevance of culture in the business world, moving from a soft or emotional concept on the periphery of business analysis to an integrated core concept that cannot be overlooked in any type of business. Batteau argues that cultural consciousness has become a business in the 21st century. He further categorizes corporate culture as either relationship-oriented or performance-oriented, and identifies the distinct cultural nature of each category. Batteau closes his argument by demonstrating the value of cultural analysis in business. The result is a new and more effective way of doing business.

Next, Richard Pettinger narrows the focus of cultural analysis in business with an examination of the context in which business takes place. He identifies values, beliefs, and attitudes associated with successful business practices. Further, Pettinger looks at factors that shape corporate identity on both personal and corporate levels. This article gets at the core of the person in business, showing that identity, individuality, and corporate cohesion are all essential to a success. Pettinger recognizes that it takes work to achieve those goals. Corporate practice should reflect corporate identity, notwithstanding personal issues of stakeholders. Teaching, learning, and assimilation of values and attitudes are possible when the position of the learners is taken into consideration in defining corporate identity and purpose.

The subjectivity and position of people are vital in the future of business, according to Pradyumna Karan. His article examines the dichotomy of Western and non-Western worlds. He argues that issues of power, including colonization and modernization, are contradictory along social, economic, and political lines. Further, modern practices challenge ancient belief systems. However, cross-cultural connections can be made through common belief patterns. For example, social and cultural objectives, such as poverty reduction, citizens' participation, employment, and preservation of cultural heritage, may be shared beliefs that form a common ground for positive development. Still, there are significant problems that cause culture clash between Western and non-Western societies, including development, resource management, and environmental issues. Karan suggests strategies for businesses to satisfy demands for growth in developing countries while maintaining respect for local culture.

Cultural bridges based on effective communication create cultural competency, according to the final author in this section, Swalomir Magala. He acknowledges that the complexities of evolving societies clashing or cooperating with one another challenge understandings on both sides. Magala argues that knowledge is malleable and subjective, and humans are complex beings driven by values. Because they are fed by emotion, the result is change. However, there are universal positions that provide a common ground from which decisions can be made. Magala identifies the role of language, mass media, and cultural codes specific to societies as means of creating common ground (or further conflict). His position is positive as he argues that cross-cultural competency is on the increase in the 21st century.

This unit provides theoretical insight into cultural analysis from perspectives that build upon each other. Effective cultural analysis is done on both micro and macrolevels. This takes the needs of corporate stakeholders into account while providing insight for corporate growth, innovation, and development.

Notes

1. Castro, B. (2013). *Business and society: A reader in the history, sociology and ethics of business.* Oxford University Press. See pp. 141–152.
   Caulkins, D. (2013). *Changing rhetoric of corporate culture in companion to organizational anthropology.* See pp. 56–73.
   Gregory, D., Johnston, R., Pratt, G., Watts, M., & Whatmore, S. (Eds.). (2009). Cultural economy. In *The dictionary of human geography.* Wiley Blackwell.
2. Gundling, E. (2011). *Working GlobeSmart: 12 people skills for doing business across borders.*
   Williams, R. (1958). *Culture is ordinary.* See pp. 3–18.
3. Pettinger, R. (2013). *Organizational behavior.* See Chapter 5, pp. 83–124.
   Anheier, H., Isar, Y. R., Paul, A., & Cunningham, S. (2008). *The cultural economy* (Cultures and Globalization Series 2). SAGE.
4. DuGay, P. (2013). *Production of culture/cultures of production.* See pp. 70–95.
5. Carté, P., & Fox, Chris. (2008). *Bridging the culture gap: A practical guide to international business communication* (2nd ed., Gale virtual reference library). Kogan Page.
   Amin, A., & Thrift, N. (2007). Cultural economy and cities. *Progress in Human Geography, 31*(2), 143–161.
   Deresky, H. (2013). *International management: Managing across borders and cultures,* Chapter 1.
6. Hechter, M., Nadel, L., & Michod, R. E. (Eds.). (1993). *The origin of values.* AldineTransaction.
   McClelland, D. C. (1985). How motives, skills, and values determine what people do. *American Psychologist, 40*(7), 812.
   Ferris, K., & Stein, J. (2014). *The real world: An introduction to sociology* (4th ed.).
   Back, L., Bennett, A., & Edles, L. D. (2012). *Cultural sociology: An introduction* (1st ed.).
   Hall, J., Grindstaff, L., & Lo, M. M. (2010). *Handbook of cultural sociology* (1st ed.).
   Rousseau, N. (2014). *Society explained: An introduction to sociology.*
   Birx, H. (2010). *21st century anthropology: A reference handbook.* SAGE.
   Lim, S. G., & Lim, J. H. (2014). *Culture and values in the leader, the teacher & you.* See pp. 113–143.
7. Lash, S., & Urry, J. (1994). *Economies of signs and space* (Theory, Culture & Society).
8. Amin, A., & Thrift, N. (2007). Cultural economy and cities. *Progress in Human Geography, 31*(2), 143–161.
   Adamopoulos, J., & Kashima, Y. (1999). *Social psychology and cultural context* (Cross-cultural Psychology Series, vol. 4). SAGE.
9. Sagini, M. (2013). *Organizational behavior: Challenges of the new millennium.*
   Heifetz, R., Grashow, A., & Linsky, M. (2009). *The practice of adaptive leadership: Tools and tactics for changing your organization and the world* (MRSV). Harvard Business Press.
   Halualani, R. (2019). *Intercultural communication: A critical perspective* (MRSV).
10. Du Gay, P., & Pryke, M. (2002). *Cultural economy: Cultural analysis and commercial life* (Culture, representation, and identities). SAGE.

Amin, A., & Thrift, N. (2007). Cultural-economy and cities. *Progress in Human Geography*, *31*(2), 143–161.

Attitudes, Values and Beliefs

Richard Pettinger

Richard Pettinger, "Attitudes, Values and Beliefs," *Organizational Behavior: Performance Management in Practice*, pp. 83–97. Copyright © 2010 by Taylor & Francis Group. Reprinted with permission.

Introduction

Attitudes, values and beliefs are the mental, moral and ethical dispositions adopted by individuals to others and the situations and environments in which they find themselves. Attitudes, values and beliefs can be ordered and summarized as follows.

- **Emotional:** feelings of positivity, negativity, neutrality or indifference; anger, love, hatred, desire, rejection, envy and jealousy; satisfaction and dissatisfaction. Emotional aspects are present in all work as part of the content; working relationships with other people; reactions to the environment; and the demands placed on particular occupations.
- **Professional:** the nature of identity with the work; the belief in the importance and value of the work; the contribution that the work makes, and is supposed to make; the extent of commitment to the organization; identity with the organization and the expertise delivered.
- **Social:** contribution to society; disposition towards society, and the component groups; disposition towards neighbours and others in the locality; propensity to use local organizations; propensity to be involved in social activities.
- **Personal:** religious convictions; political convictions; conduct in society (including work); participation in social institutions and clubs; contribution to the needs and wants of society.

- **Informational:** the nature and quality of the information present and the importance that it is given. Where this is known or widely understood to be wrong or incomplete, feelings of negativity and frustration arise.
- **Behavioural:** the tendency to act in particular ways in given situations. This leads to the formation of attitudes where the behaviour required can be demonstrated as important or valuable; and to negative attitudes where the behaviour required is seen as futile or unimportant.

Attitudes, values and beliefs are shaped and influenced by the following.

- **Past experience:** memories of what happened in the past affect current and future feelings.
- **Preconception:** impressions formed of something or someone in advance of meeting them, participating, or being involved.
- **Specific influences:** especially those of peer groups, work groups and key individuals—managers and supervisors. These also include family and social groups; and they may also include religious and political influences.
- **Prejudices:** which may be harmless (e.g. 'London is the best place in the world') or repugnant (e.g. prejudices against racial, religious or social groups).
- **Organizational identity:** the extent to which people have pride (or otherwise) in working for their organization; the extent to which people value their job, work and contribution; and the extent to which the organization values them, and their contribution.
- **Defence:** once formed, attitudes and values are internalized and become a part of the individual. Any challenge to them is often viewed as a more general threat to the comfort of the individual (see Box 1.1.1).

Box 1.1.1 Before going to bed ...

Peter Scott, a management consultant, was running a residential course. On one of the evenings, there was a late session, and it ran on until 10.00 pm. As the group was breaking up for the night, Peter asked them: 'If you were at home, what would you now be doing?'

Back came the responses, and there was all the usual and expected content: watching the late night news, making a cup of tea or coffee, checking on the children, taking the dog for a quick walk, putting out the cat. Peter asked: 'Why? Why do you do these things?'

Back came the usual responses: the cat needs to go out; I need to make sure that the children are comfortable and settled; I like to see the news before I go to bed.

Peter alighted on the news: Why, he asked, was it necessary for people to watch the news before going to bed? What was the attraction of knowing everything that was going on in the world immediately before 'switching off'?

The discussion developed further. Steering the discussion around the news and watching it last thing at night, Peter observed that several of the course delegates were getting agitated, and one or two were getting angry. Why shouldn't they watch the news last thing at night? What was wrong with watching the news last thing at night? Why were they even discussing it?

Peter found himself having to conduct a full debrief. Concentrating on the response to the news question, it became clear that people used this not particularly to know what was going on in the world, but as a behavioural 'full stop' at the end of the day. Many of the delegates were prepared to admit that they could not even remember what had been on the news by the time they got to bed. Nevertheless, this was how they always behaved; this was how they brought closure to every day. Questioning this (or even denying them the opportunity to watch the news) meant that you were in fact calling into question one of the fundamental behavioural points of reference for people.

Attitudes

As stated above, attitudes are the dispositions adopted by individuals and groups towards others, to their surroundings and society, to their environment and to their organization and occupations. Attitudes are shaped, formed and developed by every influence, activity and institution that people come across in their lives. People form distinctive attitudes towards each of the following:

- their family and friends;
- their occupation, profession and place of work;
- societies and institutions that they come across as they go about their lives;
- companies, organizations, societies and institutions with which they do business;
- individuals, organizations and institutions about which they have plenty of general knowledge (e.g. the Queen, the prime minister, Australia/France/China) but little, if any, direct experience or contact.

In the place of work, attitudes towards the particular organization, and the attitudes held by organizations towards their staff and other stakeholders, are of vital concern. The attitudes of the individuals are shaped by:

- the approach taken by the organization when individuals first apply to work there;
- the recruitment and selection process;

- the basis on which appointments are made;
- the induction and orientation process;
- the initial and continuing attitude and demeanour of colleagues, managers and supervisors;
- the overall management style;
- the culture and climate of the organization;
- the collective prevailing work ethic.

The attitudes held by the organization towards its staff are shaped by:

- the perspective adopted, whether adversarial, consultative, participative, positive or negative [...];
- the nature of rewards on offer, who gets them and for what (e.g. performance, conformity, obedience, loyalty);
- the approach taken to the management of discipline, grievances and disputes;
- the organization's stated priorities (e.g. sales, marketing, production, service delivery, customer satisfaction);
- the organization's actual priorities (ideally the same list as above, in practice it includes self-service and organization politics, the search for favours, patronage and influence).

Shaping and reinforcing the attitudes of people at work is therefore vital to organization staff and group harmony; personal, professional and occupational comfort and confidence; and the generation of involvement and commitment. People's capabilities and expertise have to be harnessed so as to produce a willingness to perform, as well as capability to carry out, their tasks and duties to the best of their abilities (see Box 1.1.2; Figure 1.1.1).

Positive and Negative Attitudes

Attitudes are infectious. Companies, organizations and work groups that have positive attitudes find that new starters and incomers quickly become positive also. Companies, organizations and work groups that have negative attitudes find that new starters and incomers also quickly begin to become negative themselves.

Box 1.1.2 Capability and willingness

The need to have staff who show commitment and who want to work for the particular organization has caused many managers to concentrate on attitudes rather than expertise when making staff selections. The standpoint is that, as long as people are good at (but not necessarily expert) at their job, high levels of commitment will deliver a much better long-term output than those who are expert but uncommitted, as follows:

Notes

- Levels of high capability but low willingness can be observed at the top end of the football industry (among others), where high-reputation players are engaged on excellent wages—and they then fail to deliver. They have joined the particular club for money only; otherwise, they do not want to be there.
- On the other hand, a fully committed attitude will not carry people through if they do not have at least a fundamental capability for the job. At least one CEO of one of the UK retail banks that failed was fully committed to the job and the organization, working long hours and being actively involved in everything. However, he simply did not have the capability or understanding to do the job effectively.

So, an active decision is required in all cases; it is not possible to make any form of rule that 'a positive attitude will compensate for lack in expertise at all times'. However, it does remain true that for a great many tasks and occupations a willingness to learn is the product of a positive and committed attitude.

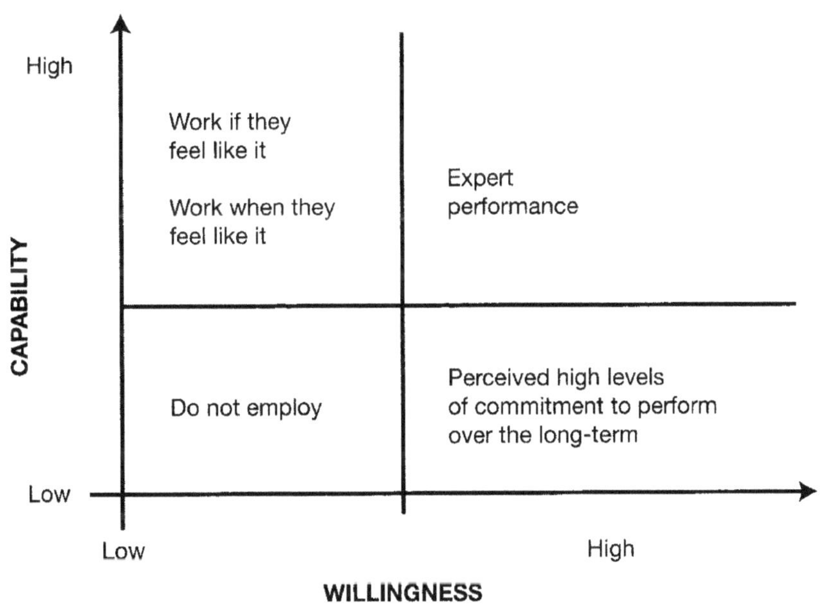

Figure 1.1.1 The balance between capability and willingness.

Clearly, the ideal is to have:

- positive attitudes on the part of all staff, resulting in collective commitment to the work, the customers, the other stakeholders and the organization;

- collective involvement so that, as well as generating high levels of team, group and organization spirit, there is an overall and understood body of commitment that can be called on at any time when necessary.

Additionally, where attitudes are positive, the word quickly gets around that this is a good organization to work for, and that the staff are friendly, kind and decent as well as expert and committed (see Box 1.1.3).

Values

Values are the absolute standards by which people order their lives. Everyone needs to be aware of their own personal values so that they may deal pragmatically with any situation. This may extend to marked differences between individuals or between an individual and the demands of the organization.

Value conflicts often arise at places of work; anything to which people are required to ascribe must recognize this and, if it is to be effective, must be capable of harmonization with the values of the individual. These values may be summarized as follows:

Box 1.1.3 Negative attitudes

'You don't have to be mad to work here, but it helps' is an urban myth posted on many an office and factory wall.

As long as that is where it stays, this is fine. However, there are various attitudes which, as stated above, can, and do, become infectious as follows:

- 'I hate it here';
- 'It's boring';
- 'That blasted manager or supervisor' (not always such a polite turn of phrase).

Recognizing that all was not quite right at his organization, one senior general manager of a corporate communications company started joining his staff either at their breaks, or when they went outside for a cigarette. The staff quickly engaged him in conversation and he found that negative attitudes were coming from a small, but influential, group of administrative staff who felt themselves to be seen as 'only the office'. Recognizing that he had been at fault in this matter, he took steps to ensure that they received exactly the same amount of attention as sales, technical and engineering staff, and so was able to both restructure the attitude of this particular group, and also enhance collective organization spirit and commitment.

- **Theoretical:** where everything is ordered, factual and in place.
- **Economic:** making the best practical use of resources; results orientated, the cornerstone of people's standards and costs of living.
- **Aesthetic:** the process of seeing and perceiving beauty; relating that which is positive and desirable or negative and undesirable.
- **Social:** the sharing of emotions with other people.
- **Integrity:** matters of loyalty, honesty, openness, trust, honour, decency; concern for the truth.
- **Political:** the ways and choices concerning the ordering of society and its subsections and strata.
- **Religious and ethical:** the dignity of mankind; the inherent worth of people; the morality—the absolute standards—of human conduct; this includes specific beliefs and requirements of particular religions.
- **Organizational:** the values espoused by the organization, and the ways in which it delivers these and reinforces them.
- **Occupational and professional:** the value placed on the occupation/profession by individuals; and the value placed on the occupation/profession by organizations.

Box 1.1.4 The Financial Services Authority

The banking crisis of 2007 and beyond in the UK was brought about by the actions of individuals working within those organizations. However, the Financial Services Authority was supposed to oversee these actions, and prevent banking and financial institutions from taking unnecessary risks, or becoming involved in markets and activities of which they had no expert knowledge.

Part of the initial inquiry conducted into the failure of the UK banking and financial services system laid the blame firmly at the door of the Financial Services Authority, which had demonstrably failed to discharge its duties, leaving banking and financial services' companies to go about their business as they saw fit. A disease of complacency, sloppiness and indifference was identified, and this prevailed among all the regulatory staff at the Financial Services Authority.

This did not prevent staff from picking up bonuses to the collective value of £20 million in 2009. Defending the decision to award these bonuses, a spokesman for the Financial Services Authority stated: 'For many years, they have tried to do their best. In particular over the past twelve months, they have worked very hard.'

Both the action in awarding the bonuses and also the statement above reflect the lack of value placed on either the work or the organization. On the basis of the story as told above, staff are simply receiving these bonuses for turning up to work.

Values have to be capable of acceptance by everyone involved. Values have therefore to be supported by a combination of known and understood organization responsibility, the managerial and supervisory style present, and the procedures and institutions of the organization. It is no use overtly espousing a positive set of values if every managerial procedure and activity is negative. It is no use espousing a collective set of organizational values and work ethics if the organization in practice rewards individual performance in isolation from the total effectiveness of overall performance (see Box 1.1.4).

Shared Values

Shared values are a clear set of values or direction offered by an organization to its people, its customers and environment that give a clear sense of identity. The adoption of shared values is central to the generation of high levels of commitment and motivation among those who work in organizations. Recognizing that people bring a diverse range of qualities to an organization is essential. Giving a clear corporate purpose that is both above individual aspirations, and also accommodates them, is a major function of the articulation of shared values. This is also instrumental in structuring particular ethical and moral stances that are taken.

Shared values are affected by:

- past experiences and interactions with the given person, people or situation;
- continuing experiences and interactions;
- perceptions and levels of general understanding;
- presence of, and understanding of, the particular rules, regulations and other limitations with which these are bounded;
- particular mental and physical aspects;
- levels of identity with the others involved and with the situation;
- the extent to which the people/situation are known or unknown;
- aspects of risks and uncertainty;
- levels of active or passive involvement;
- positive aspects—the extent to which something good and productive is certain or expected to come out;
- negative aspects—the extent to which something negative and unproductive is certain or expected to come out;
- any strong or prevailing moral, ethical or social pressures;
- general degrees of comfort—again usually based on levels of knowledge and understanding.

Each of the above elements has an effect, and so has to be taken into account when creating a work ethic to which everyone can subscribe, as well as patterns of behaviour, attendance and performance (see Box 1.1.5).

Box 1.1.5 Creating a positive work ethic

'Teams that play together, work together' is a strap-line or mantra used by outward-bound and physical training and activity centres to try to gain corporate clients. The line of reasoning is: by getting staff to engage in such things as paint-balling activities, long distance walks, orienteering and similar activities, a team spirit can be built.

In isolation, activities like this are never enough to build a genuine and lasting team spirit, *esprit de corps* and collective, positive and harmonious work ethic. This has to be formed in the organization.

The foundations of this are that everyone involved respects and values the contribution of the others, so that they can deliver their part of the activities required in the sure and certain knowledge that everyone else is doing the same.

Forming these collective attitudes and shared values depends crucially on how people are integrated into the organization, and the extent to which this integration is acceptable to:

- the present staff;
- newcomers and incomers.

In many cases, there are introductory rituals and performances that particular work groups do demand of newcomers and incomers. However, they have to be carefully structured so as to provide a basis on which the professional and occupational activities can be developed, and not so that the relationship is destroyed.

Many outward-bound activities also tend to reinforce differences rather than create harmony. For example, when the business studies department of a further education college went for a three-day residential outward-bound break at a centre in Devon, the two top managers present were able to excuse themselves from the orienteering and rock-climbing activities on the grounds that they were 'out of condition'. This simply meant that, while the rest of the staff had a nice time in general, they would rather have been at home, and not participating in an exercise which those in charge had destroyed through their own lack of participation.

Formation of Attitudes and Values

The elements indicated are adopted by individuals in their own unique ways to form their own distinctive attitudes. The main processes that are involved are:

- Their propensity to accept rather than reject those attitudes and values of the group (including the organization) to which they seek to belong; they have a high degree of potential compliance.

- Their perception of the future relationship as being productive, effective, profitable and harmonious—people do not willingly enter a situation if they have no expectational perception of this; people are more willing and likely to enter situations the greater the likelihood of this being achieved; and people will avoid situations where these elements are neither present nor apparent.
- Relating past experience to current and future situations, relationships and environment; positive experiences tend towards the formation of positive attitudes; negative experiences tend towards the formation of negative attitudes.
- Relating present experience to preconceptions and prejudgements about new situations, relationships and organizations.
- Availability and completeness of information; availability includes access and clarity; completeness includes reference to key and critical gaps; and also to the value and usefulness of that which is available.
- The general state of organizational well-being, the general state of the individual, and the relationship and interaction between the two.
- Other pressures, including the views of peers, co-workers, superiors, subordinates, family, friends; and economic, social, legal, moral and ethical pressures. These are likely to include sweeping generalizations, prevailing received wisdom, opinions and prejudices (opinions formed without full reference to available facts); and again, from the variety of sources indicated.
- Any myths and legends present in the particular group or situation. For example, the statement that 'The person who holds job X or sits in office Y always gets promoted first/never gets promoted at all' puts behavioural and psychological pressures on each situation.

Each part of the process is present in the promotion and development of all attitudes, though the mix varies between particular situations and individuals. The mix also changes as people come into, and go out of, organizations and their groups. Also, by seeking to move, individuals may require (or perceive themselves to require) to change their attitudes in order to stand any chance of being successful. Their attitude may change again, depending on whether or not they were able to make the move, and if they did, whether or not this was successful (see Box 1.1.6).

Box 1.1.6 'We always did this at my last place'

When managers (especially new managers) say to their staff 'We did this at my last place', they ought to be given a hearing, and this then ought to form the basis for a useful and productive discussion about what the matter in hand happens to be.

In practice, however, it can be (and often is) a maddening phrase because, said in the wrong way, it gives the impression to the present group of staff that their situation and circumstances do not count. This is very dangerous towards collective and shared values, and can be very destructive. For example, a sales team at one of the UK's leading double-glazing companies was used to working on its own and informing head office of their movements and whereabouts on an informal basis. When a new manager was appointed, he wanted to get everybody to use the oracle diary management system. This would enable everyone (including him) to know where everyone was at any given time. Proposing this, the manager stated: 'This is not to check up on you. It is so that I know where you are at all times. It also makes the scheduling of staff meetings very much easier.' He then went on to say: 'We did this at my last place, and it was very effective.'

Over the next two months, nobody used the system. The manager sent round a reminder, and requested that everybody become familiar with it and install their movements on it within the next six months.

In practice, of course, nothing happened. The system was easy enough to use; however, nobody saw the value of it, either to themselves or to their work. The manager's overall approach had simply ensured that the system would never be implemented (it is also entirely possible that by giving the staff six months to get themselves familiar and get their movements on to the system, he was bowing to the inevitable—that it would indeed never be used).

Adjustment of Attitudes and Values

Adjustment is the development of attitudes and values (positive and negative) in a given situation. The processes by which adjustment is achieved are similar to those above. However, they tend to reinforce what is already present—for example, the perception if the future is well understood; if the availability of information is regarded as satisfactory.

Problems occur when a radical adjustment is either required, or else is to be imposed. The first response to such an adjustment or shift is often simply to shut it out—those affected do not believe the evidence before them.

Adjustment therefore works best where the prevailing attitudes are being developed rather than radically transformed (see Figure 1.1.2). Where a radical change of attitude is required, it is much better from the point of view of generating effective organizational behaviour and interpersonal and inter-group relations if it is tackled as a major change.

Positive	Negative
Equality of opportunity and treatment Saying what is meant, meaning what is said Identifying and solving problems Clarity of purpose Unity of purpose Reward for achievement, loyalty and commitment Openness of management style Particular standards set at outset Absolute standards for everyone High and equal value placed on all staff Recognition of every contribution Pride in the organization Identity with the organization High levels of esteem and respect for staff Clarity of communications Harmony High-quality information Open personal relationships Open operational and professional relationships	Inequality of opportunity and treatment Expediency Victimization, scapegoating Lack of clarity Fragmentation of purpose Rewards based on favouritism and infighting Remoteness and distance of management style (both physical and psychological) Standards allowed to emerge Different standards for different groups, departments, divisions and individuals Different levels of value placed on different staff groups Lack of recognition Lack of pride in the organization Lack of identity; rejection of identity Low levels of esteem and respect; variations in levels of esteem and respect according to occupation, department, division and function Lack of clarity of communications Hostility Low-quality information

Figure 1.1.2 Influences on attitudes at work: summary.

Adjustment in Practice

Adjustment in attitudes and values takes place in all working situations. Once people know and understand what adjustments they need to make, the reasons and how quickly, they will normally do so. However, they will only do so if it is demonstrably in their interests. Requiring people to change their attitudes and values therefore requires full and active involvement on the part of managers and supervisors, reinforced by extensive consultation and communication, institutions and procedures that are in regular and effective use.

If all of this is present, staff normally have a good and clear understanding of specific, key and critical developments in their organization, and the implications for their own jobs and work practices and methods. Within the best-run organizations, in many cases, staff will approach their managers and supervisors concerning matters that need adjustment before they are ever raised by the organization.

However, if organizational practice is not supported by this level of communication and involvement, adjustment is much harder to achieve. When organizations and their managers try to tell staff that radical changes must take place, and the reasons for these, staff tend to resist [...]. The result is that adjustments take place more slowly, more grudgingly and with less active involvement. People see threats to their positions rather than the opportunities created by the need for advancement (see Box 1.1.7).

Box 1.1.7 Ryanair

When Michael O'Leary became chief executive of Ryanair, the Irish airline, he declared that the company was now to become a low-cost, mass-passenger carrier. When Ryanair opened up its initial route network, people were pleasantly astonished to find that the fares were as low as £1 per single journey, and anyone who was going to the right place at the right time could, from time to time, get free tickets.

The established airline industry confidently waited for Ryanair to go bankrupt. Top and senior managers at British Airways and others remained completely confident that theirs was the only 'business model' that worked.

However, Ryanair did not go bankrupt. The extreme level of fares caused people who would not otherwise normally travel by air to take an interest, and to begin to take themselves on trips.

Catches were found of course. In many cases, while the outward journey was indeed very cheap, the return fare was much higher. Hidden charges began to emerge. Ryanair charged people extra whether booking online or over the phone; and when they removed the telephone and check-in desk facility altogether, it still cost £5 to check-in online. The route network grew; and while the fares rose, they did not rise to the levels charged hitherto by British Airways, Air France, KLM and other national flag carrying airlines on short-haul routes.

And, of course, the national flag carrying airlines had to make their own adjustments. In particular, they had to bring down their fares on short-haul routes to levels which were at least comparable with those of Ryanair and other low-cost operators (especially easyJet).

This example shows adjustment in practice at each point. When it started out in this form, Ryanair believed it could adjust the whole basis of passenger air travel. It believed it could do this for its own chosen levels of fares and not those charged by the rest of the industry. It caused the rest of the industry to adjust its expectations and ways of working.

It caused passengers to adjust their expectations of how to book and what they would have to pay for.

Each of these adjustments contributed (and continues to contribute) to the development of the airline industry, and especially to this form of air travel.

Beliefs

Beliefs are the certainties of the world. They may be:

- **Absolute:** based on such things as mathematical fact; night following day, mortality and taxation.
- **Near absolute:** based on seasonal changes; the continuous development of knowledge and awareness; continuous technological and social development.
- **Acts and articles of faith:** based on the certainty of God; and often underpinned by religious allegiance and the following and adoption of the teachings of those who pronounce in the name of God; this may also extend to the adoption of social and political creeds.
- **Political beliefs:** based on the dogma and teachings of specific political leaders and thinkers.
- **Other strong ethical and moral standpoints:** relating to honesty, trustworthiness, right and wrong.
- Strong illusions and perceptions of order, permanence and stability: often founded on long steady-state factors.
- **Right and wrong:** personal judgements of what is right and what is wrong, and the ways in which right and wrong actions should be undertaken (or not).
- **Moral aspects:** related to right and wrong, but also with wider connotations (e.g. if it is wrong for a man to hit a woman, is it also wrong for a man to be as abusive as he likes towards a woman, though stopping short of hitting her?).

Beliefs are the psychological cornerstone of the lives of people. They provide the foundations and framework upon which people order and structure the rest of their lives. They are internalized to the heart and soul of the individual, providing the basis for other attitudes, values and chosen behaviour.

Everyone needs and wants to believe in something—and this 'something' includes:

- faith and religion, as above;
- political ideologies and systems;
- particular individuals.

People also need to 'believe' in the company or organization for which they work. After all, they give a large proportion of their life to their work, and so they need to know and understand (believe) that what they do is of value, worthwhile and founded on some kind of integrity. They need to have some kind of belief in the overall integrity of the organization, and in the expertise and commitment of its top and senior managers. They need to have some kind of belief in the products and services produced and delivered. They need to have some kind of comfort, security and assurance in their patterns and standards of conduct, behaviour and performance so that they are able to assume that if they, and everyone else, do their jobs properly, then the organization itself is both secure and also profitable.

People also have a strong propensity to 'believe' in the character and integrity of their colleagues, as well as the managers for whom they directly work.

It is immediately clear from this that there are different levels of belief. These levels of belief may be classified as follows.

Faith and Conviction

This is where people collectively and individually are convinced to the point of certain knowledge and understanding of the righteousness of everything that they do, say, think and believe. This occurs most strongly in religious and political beliefs; and it is reinforced by the fact that religious and political groups are composed of those who share the same beliefs and convictions.

Faith therefore comes from within, and is reinforced by those with whom people associate. This kind of faith and conviction sets a pattern for life, and has direct influences on what people will, and will not, do.

Right and Wrong

Everyone has a sense of right and wrong which they apply as they go about their daily and working lives. Right and wrong is not always absolute, however; what people are prepared and willing to do, and what they are not prepared or willing to do, comes partly from their own beliefs and convictions, and partly also from the following.

- What the law allows and does not allow.
- Levels of personal and collective comfort and discomfort.
- The particular situation in which people find themselves (see Box 1.1.8).

Box 1.1.8 Right and wrong (1)

The level of adjustment concerning right and wrong, and some of the factors which limit the absolute nature of right and wrong, can be seen from the following examples.

- A Scottish equal opportunities officer is both comfortable and also happy to engage in sectarian chanting at Celtic versus Rangers football matches.
- People are happy to take paper and pens from their place of work, or to use the office computer to book their holidays, but would not dream of stealing from

shops.
- MPs claiming large allowances for second homes and incidental expenses insist that they have worked within the rules.

In these cases, therefore, what is right and wrong is tempered by the situation, circumstances and, by implication, what is permissible and not permissible behaviour. More generally:

- everyone knows that it is wrong to jump the queue at the supermarket, but if we are in a hurry, we will all do it;
- everyone knows that it is wrong to weave in and out of traffic when driving, but again, we all do it in different sets of circumstances.

It is a complex part of human behaviour, and one that needs to be carefully managed in organizations. Otherwise, 'wrong' becomes 'not wrong', and if such behaviour is still not limited, then it becomes 'right'.

- Responsibility: people's knowledge and understanding of what is right and wrong is tempered by corporate responsibility. In the name of the organization, and when they know that they will be supported, people will therefore carry out actions that they know to be wrong because the organization has given its assurance and permission.
- Accountability: people's knowledge and understanding of what is right and wrong is tempered by the ways in which they will be held to account for their actions. If they know that no sanction is forthcoming, they will tend to act in ways that they choose. If they know that they are going to be rewarded for bad, unacceptable, morally wrong or illegal behaviour, then they will nevertheless tend to act in these ways (see Box 1.1.9).

General Expectations

This is where people make assumptions, especially about the certainty and stability of the organizations for which they work. These general expectations and assumptions are something less than utter faith. Nor do they mean that collective and individual assumptions about the organization are always right. However, these assumptions come to be ingrained, especially if people have no reason to question them.

Box 1.1.9 'We need a victim'

When things go wrong in companies and organizations, the culture and prevailing attitudes and values demand that someone is held accountable, and some visible and discernible action is taken as the result.

In many cases, this has caused companies and organizations to make specific high-profile dismissals and redundancies. For example:

- When the opening of Terminal 5 at Heathrow airport went badly wrong in 2008, British Airways very publicly dismissed two top managers who were associated with the project.
- In order to meet a budget deficit, Kent County Council very publicly reduced the range of courses on offer at its further education colleges, making 300 redundancies.
- When the Royal Bank of Scotland announced its record losses, it very publicly made 14,000 staff redundant.

Whether there is any connection between the ills of the organizations, the budget deficits or the losses and the need for redundancies is never actually made clear. It also means that those who took the decisions to (in these particular cases) implement the Terminal 5 project, expand the range of further education teaching and employ the numbers of staff at Royal Bank of Scotland are never called to account. Neither are the top managers who, in fact, did nothing about the problems until after they had occurred rather than creating conditions in which these issues could not occur in the first place.

These expectations, and the kinds of belief that they foster, apply to all the major aspects of organizational life:

- management style, attitudes, priorities, demands and expectations;
- pay and rewards, including 'the annual pay rise', and also bonuses, trappings of status and badges of office;
- interpersonal, inter-group and intra-group relations and patterns of behaviour on which these relations are based (see Box 1.1.10).

Box 1.1.10 General expectations

Just how deep people's general expectations actually are [...] can be seen from the flood of complaints that television companies receive when supposedly assured and predictable programme schedules are disrupted for a reason. For example:

- when soap opera broadcasts are cancelled or shifted in order to accommodate sporting events, there are always complaints;
- when major crises and emergencies occur, news programmes tend also to take over from light entertainment.

In 2008, Shannon Matthews, a nine-year-old girl, vanished from her home and was believed to have been kidnapped. After a three-week search, Shannon was found, and her mother and partner arrested on charges of kidnapping and conspiracy to defraud. On the day that the mother and partner were convicted, the BBC replaced an episode of 'Holby City' with a 'Panorama Special' on the Matthews' kidnapping case.

This programme change brought 19,000 complaints. It was hardly a major Issue; but it interrupted and distorted a major general expectation of people's lives.

Complacency

Complacency occurs when people come to believe, as absolute fact, in everything that goes on around them. This can, and does, happen from time to time in all organizations. The best organizations take active steps to make sure that their staff do not fall into positions of complacency, and so come to believe in the utter infallibility and immortality of everything that they do [...].

Reading 1.2

The Non-Western World

Pradyumna P. Karan

What is the non-Western world, and why it is important to learn about its peoples and cultures? When we speak of the non-Western world we are referring to the areas in which cultures developed essentially apart from the Greco-Judaic-Christian tradition of the Western culture. Thus, it includes East Asia (China, Japan, and Korea), Southeast Asia, the Indian subcontinent, the Middle East and Sub-Saharan Africa. Latin America, Russian Asia, and Oceania are excluded. The indigenous cultures of Latin America and Oceania are not Western, but they are also not non-Western in the same sense as the ancient civilizations of China and India. Moreover, the culture of the pre-Columbian settled communities in Yucatan and Andes (600 B.C.), the empire of the Mayas in Central America, the Inca civilization (1200–1535 A.D.), and the Aztec empire (1325–1521 A.D.) in the valley of Mexico were conquered.

Colonization by the West played a role in the decay of indigenous peoples and their culture. The migration of swarms of Europeans and the transplanting into the new lands of languages, religion, arts, and institutions of Europe represented a great outward growth of Western culture on the other side of the Atlantic. Where the natives were not numerous in North America, the English drove them back into wilderness beyond the pale of the European settlements. In other regions, however, where the Spaniards and Portuguese penetrated, the new Western culture was merely overlaid like a veneer upon the older, indigenous culture of the natives. Throughout the hemisphere and also later on in Australia, New Zealand, and Oceania, power—economic, social, and political—was in the hands of the settlers of European stock, and this power assured the dominance of the Western culture. Therefore, the contemporary cultural pattern in Latin America and Oceania, unlike the non-Western cultures of Asia and Africa, is based dominantly on Western traditions and values.

Culture in this book refers to the distinctive ways of life such as language and writings; value and belief systems; and forms of social, political, and economic organization that characterize human groups. It is the sum total of ways of living built by a group of human beings and transmitted from one generation to another. Often, regional cultures fused into one, creating larger cultural zones. Civilization resulted from this process of fusion into larger units such as India or China. Civilizations systematized ideas into organized stories, philosophies, and formal religions. Civilizations spread common belief patterns over wide areas as a means of linking diverse peoples. Civilization persists when these common belief patterns are maintained by a large population over a considerable period of time. Generally speaking, tribal societies or cultures are without them. In addition, tribal cultures are usually smaller and local. There are some exceptions such as the Yoruba of West Africa, whose tribe numbered hundreds of thousands, who maintained large cities and specialists, but lacked writing and large public works, which usually accompany civilizations.

The use of writing is a major clue for identifying cultures because the introduction of writing into a society improves transmission of social and cultural traits and enhances the availability of knowledge to affect and change all else in society. Likewise, the maintenance of cities and the specialization of occupation (such as blacksmiths, priests, traders, and rulers, and the technology and economic organization to support them) cannot exist without a rural hinterland to feed the city dwellers and without transport for food supplies. Once this economic basis is available, there is more effective energy and wealth for the development of culture.

There is a core of solidarity among non-Western societies of Asia and Africa that derives from non-European cultural roots, shared memories of the past, domination by Western powers, a resolve to remove the remaining traces of Western colonialism, and a feeling that they are a distinct part of humanity, long victimized and now sharing a common aspiration to protect their independence and development. Except for Japan, Singapore, South Korea, and Taiwan, the non-Western lands range from the least developed nations to some that are close to crossing the threshold that Japan and Western nations crossed during the twentieth century.

Our focus in this book is on six major non-Western culture areas: China, India, Japan, Southeast Asia, the Islamic Middle East, and Sub-Saharan Africa (Figure 1.2.1). Civilizations in China, India, and the Nile and Tigris-Euphrates valleys of the Middle East were already old when the Europeans rose out of barbarism. Sumeria, Tigris-Euphrates valleys around 4,000 B.C., Egypt (Nile Valley) five hundred years later, China (Yellow River Valley) around 3,500 B.C., and India (Indus Valley) about 2,500 B.C. all reached cultural maturity centuries before the Greeks appeared as the first civilized culture in the West (about 800 B.C.). Except for China and India, all of these ancient civilizations had lost their power by the time of Christ, and with few exceptions had been assimilated into later peoples. Distinctive cultural areas discussed in this book are delimited from one another partly by geography; partly by history; partly by cultural traits such as language, religion, political and economic organization; and most of all by value systems, behavior, and attitude.

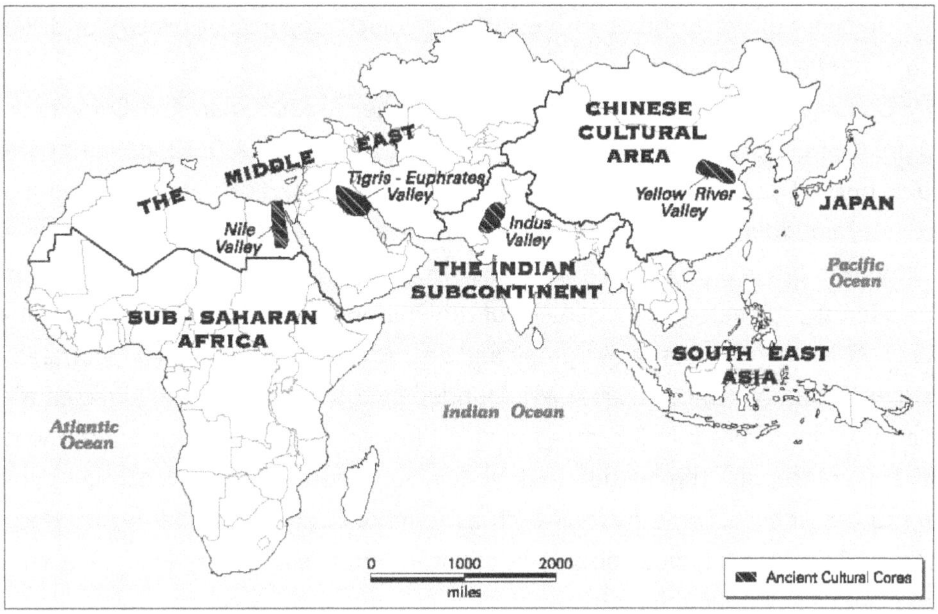

Figure 1.2.1 The non-Western world.

The non-Western cultures of China (based on Confucianism) and India (based on Hinduism) survived to our day with national cultural ideals that were substantially unchanged for twenty-five centuries. Both are now engaged in a struggle for development in a modern age. China and India are patriarchs among the world's civilizations, but they are also relatively new in the contemporary political family of nations. The experiences of the Chinese and Indians have marked similarities. China and India have each known an almost changeless civilization during two thousand years, securely based on a national belief system and an ethical code that reflects a national soul at peace with itself. Even the challenge of foreign religions—Buddhism in China and Islam in India—has not upset the basic pattern. Both nations have lived self-contained lives with relatively little curiosity about the lands beyond their borders, except in commerce. But both have been exploited for four centuries by more aggressive peoples from the West. Both countries hold immense lands and resources which still may be inadequate to support sustainable development of their large populations. As a result, both face bewildering problems of development, resource use, and environmental management.

Chinese cultural influence has been dominant in Japan and Korea since early times. Political and institutional forms were taken from China; the Chinese system of writing was adopted in Japan, which permitted the Japanese to gain ready access to the Confucian classics and to Chinese editions of the Buddhist scriptures. Buddhism was introduced in Japan about 552 A.D. from China and Korea, and has thrived alongside the indigenous Shinto religion. For several centuries Japan lived in splendid isolation under the rule of the Shoguns (1336–1868). Perry's visit in 1854 led to the opening of Japan, and initiated a period of rapid growth. Japanese borrowed first from the Chinese and later from the West those elements that fitted their needs and environment. The resulting combination has been unique, and Japan today represents a distinctive culture of great interest and of much importance. Post-World War II Japan has advanced as one of the major economic superpowers in the world.

Culturally, Southeast Asia has been a zone of convergence for Indian and Chinese cultures. People from southern areas of China migrated into Southeast Asia. About 100 A.D. Hindu states were established in the East Indies by the Dravidian Kings of South India. By the second century A.D. several Indian colonies had developed in Cambodia. Hinduism expanded with the Hindu colonization of Java and there was expansion of Buddhism between 700 and 800 A.D. Islam was introduced about 1000 A.D. The Hindu states of Southeast Asia fell shortly before the discovery of the Philippines by the Portuguese navigator Ferdinand Magellan in 1521. As a crossroad between Europe and East Asia (China and Japan), Southeast Asia attracted Europeans. Batavia (formerly named Jakarta) was founded by the Dutch in 1619; two centuries later Raffles (1781–1826), an English governor in Sumatra founded Singapore in 1819. Most of Southeast Asia became colonies of Britain, France, and the Netherlands. Today, Southeast Asia is a dynamic region ruled mostly by authoritarian governments. Some nations such as Cambodia and Thailand are making slow progress toward democracy. The region's most populous country, Indonesia, is engaged in a struggle between democratization and Islamic fundamentalism.

Torn between ancient traditions and the modern world, the Islamic countries of the Middle East search for a balance. It has become, as in ancient times, a nexus of bitter conflict. Some disputes are battles within nations, as a surging younger generation challenges autocratic regimes for opportunity and political reform. Others pit nation against nation, over issues ranging from weapons proliferation to the proper interpretation of Islam. The clash of Israelis and Palestinians over tiny parcels of land continues to make headlines around the world. In this land of crisis, oil-rich nations, and the birthplace of three great faiths—Judaism, Christianity and Islam—the United States is currently involved in establishing a foothold for democracy in Iraq. If this attempt is successful, it may change the political landscape of the region.

The political and economic development of Sub-Saharan Africa presents a major challenge in the twenty-first century. Most of its nations are among the non-Western world's youngest and poorest. Colonial inroads beginning in the sixteenth century led to the exploitation of the region's human and natural resources. By the mid-nineteenth century, European, American, and Arab slave traders had robbed the continent of perhaps as many as 25 million human beings. At the 1884 Berlin Conference, the competing European powers gerrymandered Africa with their own political boundaries. In the after math of the wind of decolonization which began to sweep across Africa in the mid-1950s, Sub-Saharan nations became independent. Arbitrary political boundaries, which often divide language and tribal groups, have resulted in ethnic fragmentation. It has helped touch off civil wars and numerous coups led by military dictators during the post-independence period. Warring factions and regimes sell off diamonds, oil, timber, and ore to build armies and buy weapons, deepening conflicts and poverty. Meanwhile, about two thirds of Africans depend on agriculture for their livelihoods. The fate of agricultural production, therefore, directly affects economic growth, social improvement, and political stability. As the region's population continues to grow, rapidly outpacing the growth rate in other regions of the non-Western world, its agricultural land is becoming increasingly degraded. Unless African governments, supported by the international community, take the lead in confronting the problems of land degradation, deteriorating agricultural productivity will undermine the foundations of sustainable development in Sub-Saharan Africa.

Sources of Ideas Shaping the Roots of Non-Western Culture

All of the six non-Western cultural areas are distinct from the West. Western culture is the product of Greco-Judaic-Christian tradition, Roman law, Greek philosophy (ideas of democracy and civil liberty), and the ideas and value systems derived from the Renaissance (1400–1650) in Europe. Writing as a part of technology has been an intellectual tool used by various cultures, and the great literary works have been a source of ideas that have shaped cultures. Writing led to achievements in astronomy, arithmetic, and geometry, and also in the accumulation of social surplus and the distinctive quality of the cultures that were established in Western and non-Western worlds. The great literature of the Western culture such as the Bible, the writings of Plato (427–347 B.C., the Greek philosopher), Homer (the eighth-century Greek epic poet), Thomas Moore (1478–1536, English humanist and statesman), Machiavelli (1469–1527, Italian philosopher and author), Martin Luther (1438–1546, German theologian and author, leader of the Protestant Reformation), Galileo (1564–1642, Italian physicist and astronomer), Voltaire (1694–1778, French philosopher and historian), Karl Marx (1818–1883, German economist, philosopher, and socialist), Charles Darwin (1809–1882, English naturalist), and Sigmund Freud (1856–1939, Austrian neurologist and founder of psychoanalysis) provide sources of ideas that helped to shape the Western culture. Literature in both Western and non-Western worlds represents reflection and refinement of thought that relates the community to the wider society and culture and often exemplifies the behavior of the people in that culture.

The ideas and values enunciated in these great books and by the authors noted in the preceding paragraph are clearly distinct from the literature of the non-Western world. Among the great literature of the non-Western world are the works by Confucius (551–470 B.C.), Li Po (701–762 B.C.), and Tu Fu (713–770 B.C.), the Vedic Hymns (2000–800 B.C.), the Upanishad (eighth to sixth century B.C.), the *Mahabharat* (about 1000 B.C.), works of Kalidasa (fifth or sixth century A.D.), the Koran (between 610 and 632 A.D.), *The Arabian Nights* (786–809 A.D.), and the poems of Omar Khayyam (eleventh century A.D.) and Hafiz (1300–1383 A.D.). These classical works tell us about sources of ideas that shaped the cultures of the non-Western world. Through the poems and essays one can capture the distinctive cultural values of the people.

Chinese literature had ethical content and its specialists influenced the people by precept and example. Li Po and Tu Fu in their poetry open a new world—a delicate, fragile world of bamboo and jade, yet inhabited by intensely human characters—revealing the distinctive aspects of the Chinese culture amd life. Confucius pointed out a sensible way of life. No others could possibly represent the great Chinese culture to the world so well as these three master spirits. Despite periodic civil wars and invasions, the cultural unity of China has reasserted itself time and again and absorbed many would-be conquerors in its long history. The Chinese have assimilated foreign ideas and political systems without losing their essential point of view.

The persistent cultural stability of China has been due to four elements: rapport with earth and nature, the family, veneration of ancestors, and the Confucian code. The identification of the Chinese peasant with the land (to a greater extent than elsewhere) strengthened stability. The Chinese learned in the family from the beginning that individual preferences must be subordinated to the welfare of the group; Chinese family members deferred to the head of the family, who was the oldest male member. The old not only retained their authority during life but also after death through the veneration of ancestors. Veneration of the past did restrain hasty changes and the disruptions that invasions brought to most other peoples. Confucius concentrated on human relationships, and his teachings codified how to get along in this life.

In India there has been more reciprocal influence between literati and common people, between sacred literature and popular tradition. The ancient hymns of the Vedas, composed anonymously between 2000 and 800 B.C., are the foundations of the Indian culture and are the oldest writings in any Indo-European language. They are the ultimate source of Hindu religion and culture. Of the four great collections, the *Rig-Veda* (verse-knowledge) is the oldest and is the source of the other three. Compiled in stages over a long period, it contains hymns to the folk gods of nature such as sky (Varuna) and fire (Agni), and later hymns to abstract concepts such as the "Origin of All Things," which lead into the philosophical discussion of the Upanishads. These lyrics project an exalted sympathy with nature through noble imagery, vivid descriptions, simple, concrete diction, and a fine reverent tone. India's greatest folk epic, the *Mahabharat,* dating back to perhaps 1000 B.C. and the longest poem in the world with 100,000 couplets, abounds in loosely connected stories and essays. The central plot of the epic concerns a great struggle between two families of royal cousins for succession to the throne. Like the Trojan War of the Greeks, the struggle has foundation in a protracted war between rival kingdoms. The most famous section of the Mahabharat is the Gita, a philosophical dialogue between the god Krishna and Arjun, hero of the epic. The subject of the Gita is the Hindu reconciliation of work and necessary activity in this world with the idea that the world is a mere illusion to be ignored. Krishna explains that disinterested performance of duty in this world involves no desire and hence no sin. This subtle interpretation of actions in terms of attitude and intention is a central feature of Indian culture.

Kalidasa, as a great playwright of India, has often been called "the Shakespeare of India," and the parallel goes far. Like Shakespeare, he was equally at home in narrative, lyric, and dramatic poetry. In the plan of his dramas, too, Kalidasa reminds us of Shakespeare, in his combination of serious and comic elements within the same play, especially in the use of clowns, and in his frequent interpolation of lyric verse in the midst of dramatic scenes. Kalidasa did not write tragedies. To the Hindu, defeat and death in this world have no tragic meaning.

The fantastic love theme of Kalidasa's *Shakuntala* attracted the German poet Goethe (1749–1832), who borrowed from the play for his *Faust,* and Goldmark's overture to Shakuntala has long been a standard concert selection. Kalidasa's work shows that all the pessimism and asceticism in the Hindu view of life do not stifle the longing for worldly beauty and love for nature, seasons, and landscape.

In contemporary times Mohandas Karamchand Gandhi's life and work provided a source of ideas that influenced Indian society and has had effects beyond the non-Western world in Martin Luther King, Jr.'s struggles for racial and political equality in America. Born in 1869, M. K. Gandhi spent twenty-one tumultuous years in South Africa resisting racism using his weapon of nonviolent *satyagarha* (pursuit of truth). He was 45 years old when he returned to India and transformed both the tactics and the purpose of India's struggle against the British. This "half naked *fakir,*" as the British called him, converted an elite struggle into a mass movement, a violent uprising into a nonviolent but nonetheless insistent struggle, and political demands into a testament of faith (Figure 1.2.2). Gandhi's ideas and life carry a remarkable message for many oppressed people who daily wrestle with the challenges of social and political reform. Gandhi's nonviolent resistance served well both Aung San Suu Kyi of Myanmar (Burma) and Nelson Mandela of South Africa during their years of arrest for demanding political and social justice.

Figure 1.2.2 Mohandas Gandhi addressing a public meeting in 1946. A nonviolent movement led by Gandhi led to the independence of India, marking the beginning of decolonization of the non-Western world. The teachings of Gandhi inspired Martin Luther King, Jr. to nonviolent resistance in the civil rights movement. (Photo: G R. Jani.).

The Koran, the first important body of Arabic prose, is the great book of authority for the morals, laws, theological doctrines, and social ethics for the Muslims everywhere from North Africa to Southeast Asia. Its 114 chapters, or suras, of varying length are accepted as the word of Allah, revealed to his only prophet, Mohammed. From the first to the last it preaches the unity and soleness of the Most High, the Most Merciful, and Most Compassionate God, Allah; to serve him and to die for him are the greatest of privileges, to neglect him and to disregard his commandments are the unforgivable sins. The imagery of the Koran is the imagery of the desert, of the lonely places of body and soul, of the unsophisticated pastoral and rural scene rather than the crowded bazaar and teeming city streets. It entertains the promise of idyllic sensual existence for the faithful after the Day of Judgment. Millions of people today live by its words in the non-Western world.

African cultures have powerful persistence through deeply rooted religious beliefs connecting Africans with their environment through worship of ancestors and gods of nature, including a creator god, combined with strong community and family ties. Transmission by story and memory, in a largely oral tradition, add to the mix and maintain the vitality of the traditional cultures.

Some of the great works of the non-Western world noted above are in part a record of the ideas and customs, the special visions and feelings of the non-Western peoples. Through these works students of the non-Western world can understand the nations and cultures that created the great books. They tell us about their past and they help us understand the context of their present society. Knowing and understanding the great books of the non-Western cultures leads us into contact with ideas that may be new to many readers in the West, but such contact frees us from provincialism in the realm of ideas and gives us respect for other points of view.

We can summarize some of the major differences between non-Western and Western cultures (Table 1.2.1). These differences center around three related issues: the relation between society and nature, the role of religion in society, and the structure and nature of cultural values and the role of individuals and groups in the society. The common elements underlie all non-Western cultural areas, but there are other elements that distinguish each culture within a major cultural cluster and each major cluster from other clusters. The non-Western world should be viewed as a mosaic of cultures rather than as a big homogenous, undifferentiated area.

Many non-Western values involve blending some of the world's intellectual traditions such as Confucianism, Buddhism, Hinduism, and Islam. As in the West, some of the non-Western values have gone wrong in parts of Asia. The attachment to the family has fostered nepotism in countries such as Indonesia and China. The importance of personal relationships rather than formal legality has become cronyism. Consensus has become wheel-greasing and corrupt politics. Conservatism and respect for authority has become rigidity and inability to innovate. Much-vaunted educational achievements have become rote learning and a refusal to question those in authority.

Table 1.2.1 Major Differences Between Western and Non-Western Cultures

Western	**Non-Western**
1. Superiority over nature	1. Adaptation to nature
2. Christianity concerned with absolute moral values, differences between good and evil, and redemption of the soul.	2. Non-Western religions focus on virtue. Confucianism provides an ethical code of behavior.
3. Society is built on legalistic contractual relationships.	3. Society is built on direct personal relationships.
4. Individualistic orientation.	4. Group orientation: clan, caste, tribe.
5. Behavior controlled by rules, punishments and rewards	5. Behavior controlled by group adaptation. Departures from the group norm are accompanied by feelings of shame.
6. Attribution groups are important (family, class, occupation).	6. Frame groups are important (village, neighborhood, company, region, and nation).
7. Weak hierarchical structure	7. Strong hierarchical structure.
8. Important values are freedom and personal conscience.	8. Important values are security and obedience.
9. Need for self-assertion.	9. Need for coordination.
10. Contractual relationships based on rights and duties.	10. Personal relationships based on mutual obligations and mutual dependence.

Interaction Between Western and Non-Western Peoples

More than 2,000 years ago, commercial interaction between the non-Western world and Europe was via the Silk Road, perhaps history's most famous highway (Figure 1.2.3). The route wound for 5,000 miles from China across vast steppes, through the mountains of Central Asia and Northern India to the open ports of the Mediterranean. Precious bales of silk from China, exotic spices, muslin, gems, and ivory from India were ferried on the backs of camels on the Silk Road to markets in Europe. Large-scale Western interaction with Asia and Africa began chiefly as a capitalist search for markets and commodities, but it soon grew into a movement of much greater scope. It intensified after 1500 A.D. following the discovery of the sea route to India by Vasco da Gama in 1498, six years after the discovery of the New World by Columbus.

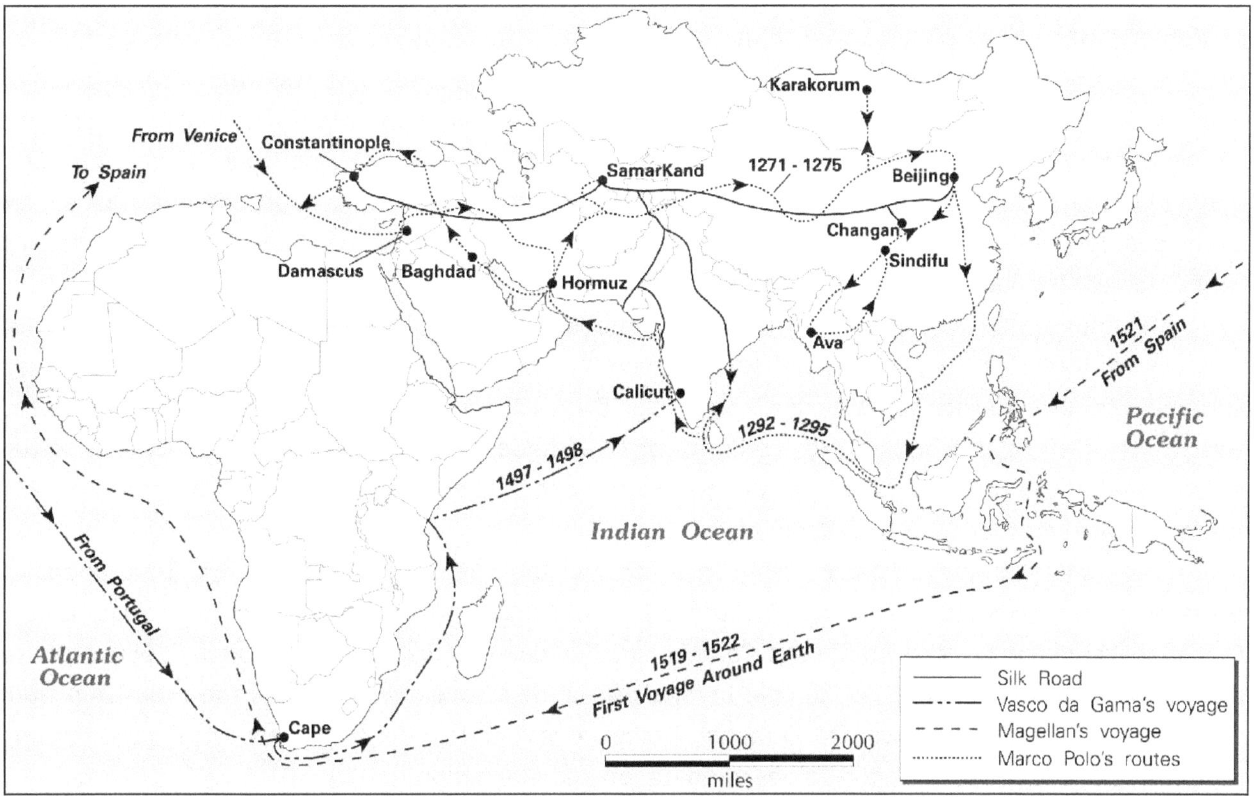

Figure 1.2.3 Early links between the Western and non-Western worlds.

Five hundred years ago, on the eve of Europe's intrusion into Asia and Africa, non-Western societies were stagnant. Many African societies were subsistence oriented and weak. Asian societies were more feudal and science and technology were "frozen." Between the feudal class and an oppressed peasantry, only a rudimentary class of merchants had arisen, except in China, among the Arabs, and perhaps in India and Japan.

Western Europe, on the other hand, rose on the strength of a dynamic economic system. An agricultural revolution in the twelfth century was followed by the growth of trade and industry, and the "rebirth of Europe" in the fifteenth century. A merchant-led middle class gradually rose to power, committed to the application of science and industry. Denied access to Eastern silk and spices, Europeans embarked on the Age of Exploration (see box on spices). Science and technology led to naval superiority and Western dominance of the non-Western world. A period of some five hundred years followed in which the Western trade and economy overwhelmed Asia and Africa.

In the Age of Colonialism (1500–1800), Europeans founded colonies all over the non-Western world and, with arrogance and inhumanity, imposed slavery on Africa, although most of Africa was colonized after 1800. Only Japan and Thailand escaped colonial rule. It was followed by the Age of Imperialism (1800–1947), which marked a period of intensified colonialism. With the evolution of West European capitalism, there was an intensified need for colonies to provide investment opportunities abroad, secure sources of raw materials, and guaranteed markets. The colonies brought profit and wealth to a substantial section of the European population. The desire for profitable trade, plunder, and enrichment were forces that led to the establishment of the imperial structure. For example, India was the main provider of employment for substantial numbers of the upper and middle classes in Britain. The Indian Empire also helped Britain to maintain its military power because the Indian Army could be shipped all over the world to fight wars on Britain's behalf, as in 1914 and 1939. Indian troops raised in the subcontinent and paid for by the people of India helped maintain Britain's global military status. The importance of economic factors varied; sometimes political factors were more important in colonial activities.

The cultural interactions between Africa and the West began following the European discovery of the New World during the fifteenth and early sixteenth centuries. Labor needs on plantations prompted Europeans to turn to Africa as a source of slave labor. Slave collection centers were established along the west coast of Africa, and during three centuries of slave trade, ships carried millions of Africans to the Americas. After the scramble for Africa was over by the end of the nineteenth century, European powers had partitioned most of the Sub-Saharan Africa.

There was widespread contact between Arabs and the West from ancient times. Translations of Greek and other texts led to an Islamic intellectual awakening in the ninth century. All of Spain except Granada—including the great libraries of Cordoba and Toledo—was lost to Islamic rule by 1250. The rise of Islam created fear in Christian Europe. European Crusaders sought to win back the Holy Land from the Muslims. Muslims often scorned European backwardness and crudeness, and when Europe became powerful, they often evaded opportunities for imitation and interaction.

The Western impact on non-Western societies varied according to the intensity of European interest and the internal strength of the Asian society concerned. Where European interest was marginal, even weakly organized societies were left more or less undisturbed. Where European interest was intense, the impact varied according to the internal strength of the victimized society. Even in the post-independence period (since 1947), the interaction between the Western and the non-Western worlds is taking place within the constraints of a strongly entrenched global capitalist system.

Geography of Spices

In 1992 America, Spain, and Italy celebrated the 500th anniversary of Columbus's voyage; they also should have paid tribute to spices. After all, when Columbus bumped into America, he was on a mission for the King and Queen of Spain to locate a new and speedier route to a place called the Spice Islands, now part of Indonesia.

In the fifteenth century, any country that dominated the market in spices from Asia—the equivalent of controlling massive oil reserves today—was rich. Today, the effect of spices on the balance of trade is inconsequential, at least in the United States, and competition in the spice market is between companies, not countries. But the fortunes in spices are still substantial. Their use has more than doubled in the last 20 years, to over 762 billion pounds in 2000, when Americans spent an estimated $2 billion on dried herbs and spices for cooking, according to the American Spice Trade Association in New York.

Elite Europeans 500 years ago needed spices to mask the taste and aroma of food that was often putrid; Americans are now using spices to add zest to dishes that are underseasoned, having little or no salt. The increased interest in highly seasoned ethnic cuisines such as Cajun, Mexican, Indian, and Chinese has also boosted demand. To further pump up usage, manufacturers are coming out with new varieties of blended spices such as special concoctions for microwave cooking. Some manufacturers also are trying to tap the fastest-growing segment of the market, the food processing industry.

In the trade, spices include all the plant material used as seasonings in dried or shelf-stable form. That includes the spices derived from tropical trees and plants such as black pepper, cinnamon, cloves, turmeric, ginger, nutmeg, cardamom, and allspice, in addition to dehydrated onion and garlic, and capsicums such as dried chilies and paprika.

Historically, the quest for rare tropical spices led to the quest for the most efficient trade routes. Cutting a few months from a two-year voyage or reducing the likelihood of shipwreck could give the spice merchant an advantage, and at various times, Venice, Portugal, and the Netherlands all reaped fortunes from trading in spices.

In early times, black pepper was the most valued spice; at one point, it accounted for 25 percent of the world's trade. When Alaric, the king of the Visigoths, first arrived at the walls of Rome in 408 A.D., he demanded not only gold and silver as a tribute, but also 3,000 pounds of precious pepper. In Antwerp, Belgium, by the mid-1500s, the price of pepper had become the Dow Jones of the day.

With few exceptions such as the Mediterranean spices, virtually all aromatic spices used in the United States are still imported from the tropics in the non-Western lands, some directly by companies, others through brokers. America's biggest spice companies are also the oldest. McCormick, Schilling, and the Durkee brand date back to the late nineteenth century. McCormick & Company, the nation's biggest spice maker, bought Schilling in 1947 and has since marketed the McCormick brand east of the Mississippi and Schilling to the west. The R.T. French Company bought Durkee Famous Foods of Cleveland in 1985; today, its Durkee-French division is the number two producer. Besides McCormick and Durkee-French, the other major spice marketers include Spice Islands, Lawry's, and such supermarket chains as Kroger, Safeway, and Winn-Dixie, which are believed to control 17 percent of the market.

The memory of colonial rule by Western countries—Britain, France, Belgium, the Netherlands, Germany, Italy, Portugal, and, briefly, the United States—is still vivid in the non-Western world; so are the consequences of colonial rule's end. It is hard to imagine so comprehensive a change as decolonization in so little time. Suddenly, in Asia and Africa the colonial rule was a thing of the past by the end of 1950s. The very word *imperialism* acquired a strong overtone of condemnation, as did *colonialism*. This was true not only in the former colonies, but also in the former imperial or colonial powers in the West.

Why did imperialism and colonialism come so suddenly, so dramatically, to an end? Of course, the people of the former colonial territories actively sought independence. Some non-Western countries ceased to be governed because they had become ungovernable by outside authority. Self-assertion and self-determination was too strong. This was undoubtedly true in India, where dissent had sophistication and a resulting force far in excess of what could be mobilized in opposition by the Western colonial power. Here, *Satyagraha* (which literally means "the force for truth") was shaped into a powerful political philosophy by M. K. Gandhi to assert and advance civil and political rights. Drawing on the ancient Indian tradition that evil could best be countered by nonresistence, *Satyagraha* became associated with noncooperation and nonviolent civil disobedience. The protestors used techniques such as nonpayment of taxes and refusal to cooperate with authority. It became a potent weapon in Gandhi's hands, a nonviolent means of confronting the big battalions of imperial [supremacy]. This step may be viewed as an important watershed in the history of resistence to imperialism and in the development of peaceful techniques to assert nationalism. There was organized military resistance to the colonial power in Indo-China against the French, in Indonesia against the Dutch, and in Malaya against the British. The rise of nationalism emerged as the most effective Asian and African response to Western colonialism.

Nationalism arrived late in Africa, in part because European conquest came late, and in part because most of the colonial units were arbitrary, with no relationship to political tradition. John Sarbah (1865–1910) from the British Gold Coast colony (now Ghana) argued for customary laws and virtues. In the 1920s and 1930s a larger number of Africans trained in the West led a more sweeping nationalistic agitation. The first meeting of the Pan-African Congress was held in 1919.

The British encouraged Arab and Jewish nationalism in the Middle East in the early twentieth century, hoping to undermine the Ottoman Empire. A steady increase of nationalistic agitation and identification has persisted in Asia and Africa.

Often nationalism was fueled by mounting repression and aided by a common language (the colonial ruler's), the mass media, and the new network of roads and railroads. In much of the colonial world, the Western powers were allowed to go in peace. In the United States there was no thought of keeping the Philippines by force.

There was also another important reason for sudden decolonization. After World War II colonialism no longer served any important economic interest. Economic factors joined hands with idealism and became a vital force for rapid decolonization. Once, the acquisition of colonial territory brought revenues and exploitable resources that benefited the merchant and industrial interests within the governments of colonial powers. With colonial possessions went a national monopoly of trade centered on import of raw materials from colonial lands and export of industrial factory products. After World War II economic development became centered internally rather than externally; it was from domestic economic growth that nations prospered. Trade between the industrial countries became dominant; economic relations with the colonial world became marginalized. The colonies could depart without major economic cost to the Western colonial powers. Few in the United States suffered financial loss from the liberation of the Philippines.

In the years following decolonization, the extension of superpower influence of the United States and the Soviet Union over the newly independent and poorer nations of the non-Western world was seen as the new form of imperialism during the decades of the Cold War. The superpower rivalry had disastrous military aspects in Afghanistan, Vietnam, and other places in the non-Western world. The end of the Cold War, the downfall of communism, and the break-up of the Soviet Union in 1991 brought this to an end.

As we enter the twenty-first century there are great economic powers (the United States, Japan, and Germany) and lesser ones (such as China and India) with varying military strengths, but imperialism and colonialism belong to the past. The non-Western nations must now deal with the imperial legacy of grave, indeed intolerable, human suffering left in its wake. When the former colonial [possessions] achieved independence, they were forced to take on the most demanding of human tasks—the provision of honest, reliable, and responsible government. Many non-Western countries have failed in this regard. From this, in turn has come economic failure, for economic success depends on the support and supervision of a stable, efficient, and effective governmental structure. Instability, incompetence, corruption, and the dictatorship of the favored few have been all too frequent in the non-Western world during the last fifty years. In extreme, but not exceptional instances, there is civil disorder and conflict. Cambodia, Afghanistan, Nigeria, Congo, and Burma are recent examples. Even where things are better, the routine tasks of the state—the collection of taxes, the rendering of essential services, and the provision of a firm legal basis for economic progress—are poorly performed or not performed at all (Figure 1.2.4).

Figure 1.2.4 "Down with pro-imperialist new economic policies" written on the wall of a government building in Patna, India. Many people in the non-Western world are still concerned with neocolonial economic policies that have led to the economic domination of the non-Western world by the West. (Photo: P. P. Karan.).

Without stable and efficient government, the essential requirement for social and economic development is unrealized. In most of the non-Western nations, stark poverty is still endemic. The West cannot set itself apart from this poverty and feel comfortable and content in its affluence while its former colonies are poor; it must be on the conscience of the former colonial powers. Since decolonization, the poor non-Western countries have received attention from the West. During the Cold War period (1950–1989) most of this attention was the result of the hope or fear of Communism. An influential constituency in the Western countries, and recently in Japan, has consistently expressed sympathy and supported aid for the poor lands, as have the World Bank and other international agencies. In recent years, the United States has spent $12 to $15 billion for bilateral and multilateral international development and security assistance. As the leader in an increasingly integrated global order, the United States has a vital stake in promoting sustainable development, political stability, and democracy in the non-Western world.

In the early days of development, assistance agriculture was frequently neglected. Emphasis was on the cities and their inhabitants, and that was where development occurred. Food prices were often fixed to favor the urban population, and this had a depressive effect on agricultural production. There are exceptions, the leading example, as is so often the case, being in India. Since independence, the Indian population has more than doubled, but, supported by grain hybrids, fertilizer, irrigation, other soil and water management, and assured prices for fanners, so has food production. In more recent times, the role of agricultural and rural development has become evident and accepted, and the importance of good education—particularly the education of women—environment, and infrastructure for effective development has been appreciated.

Most of the non-Western nations have followed the West's frontier economics model of development, in which the environment has been treated as an infinite supply of physical resources (raw materials, energy, water, soil, and air) for use. At the same time, the environment has been viewed as an infinite sink for the by-products of development in the form of various types of pollution (waste) and ecological degradation. Some countries such as Japan have moved to the environmental protection model of development, in which the focus is on clean-up and repair of ecological damage resulting from development activities. A sustainable development program will involve three dimensions: economic, environmental, and sociocultural. These three dimensions must be addressed by the non-Western countries with equal emphasis to ensure sustainability. The economic dimension involves achieving the maximum flow of income while maintaining the stock of assets (or capital—environmental, human, and industrial) that yields these benefits. The focus of the environmental dimension is on the maintenance of the stability of biological and physical ecosystems. The sociocultural dimension involves maintenance of the stability of social and cultural systems, particularly reduction of destructive social conflicts and preservation of cultural diversity. These three dimensions of sustainable development form a closely integrated triangle with interactions among them (Figure 1.2.5).

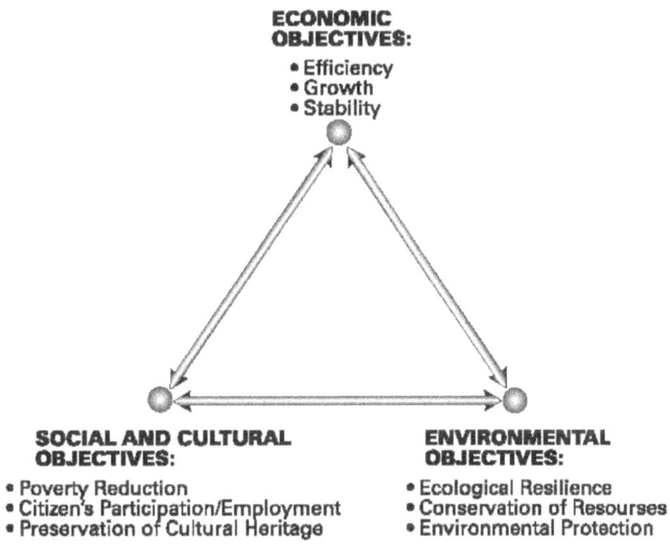

Figure 1.2.5 Model of Sustainable Development

Intercultural Communication

Thomas M. Steinfatt and Diane M. Millette

Thomas M. Steinfatt and Diane M. Millette, "Intercultural Communication," *An Integrated Approach to Communication Theory and Research*, pp. 1–8, 299–322.

The study of intercultural communication is important in any society or culture. This is especially true in the United States, which has made *intercultural openness* a central feature of its cultural persona. The United States is currently experiencing the greatest period of immigration in its history. Although the late 19th and early 20th centuries witnessed a greater *proportional* population increase due to immigration, the actual *number* of legal immigrants entering the United States since 1980 was greater per decade than in any previous time in history. When illegal immigration is factored in, the current period of immigration is unsurpassed in American history, yielding a nation whose cultural heritage is changing, and, as a corollary, its communication is changing as well.

Communication

Following Langer (1942), we believe that communication in its most fundamental form is intrapersonal. Communication begins as an attempt by human beings to come to know their environment through symbols. This occurs through a gradual recognition by the child that symbols, objects, and ideas, and internal mental representations of them, can be related to each other in a meaningful fashion. To paraphrase Langer, children first use communication to bring objects into their minds, not into their hands. Once children learn that this is possible, then symbol-object-mind relationships are possible. Only after such relationships are learned can communication evolve to a social stage where people recognize that others also make similar symbol-object-mind inferences, and that these related networks of inferences can be used to interact with others. At the social stage, communication can be used for social tasks, such as making requests or transmitting cultural information. In all stages of human development, communication involves the assignment of meaning by the individual to external stimuli, including symbolically encoded messages from other persons. Communication is inherently a meaning assignment process within the individual. Since meaning is assigned to messages based on the beliefs, attitudes, and values of the individual, and since persons from different cultures often have different beliefs, attitudes, and values, the normal human misunderstandings which occur in same-culture interactions are often magnified by the wider differences in cultural assumptions and belief systems inherent in cross-cultural interactions.

Culture

The diversity of the concept "culture" is illustrated by Kluckhohn's (1949) 12 meanings for the term, from the way of life of a people, their social legacy, pooled learning, way of thinking, feeling, and believing, through their mechanism for normative regulation of behavior and techniques for adjusting to the environment and other people, to theories about the way these people behave. Citing Max Weber as inspiration, Geertz (1973, p. 5) holds that "man is an animal suspended in webs of significance he himself has spun, I take culture to be those webs, and the analysis of it to be therefore not an experimental science in search of law but an interpretative one in search of meaning."

We conceive of culture in its broadest sense as the accumulated knowledge and beliefs of specific portions of humanity. Thus defined, the fundamental nature of culture is phenomenological: culture exists fundamentally in the hearts and minds of people. Cultural artifacts such as paintings, sculpture, machinery, and construction projects are products of the knowledge and beliefs that constitute culture. While cultural artifacts provide clues to culture, culture itself can be passed on to other persons and future generations only through communication. No study of culture's artifacts, no matter how deep or extensive, can describe, explain, predict, or even transmit culture from one person or generation to another without communication about cultural meaning. Intercultural communication involves communication between people from different cultures, leading to several questions: What constitutes a "different" culture? Do intercultural differences necessarily involve different languages? Different ways of thinking? Different world-views? Different beliefs, attitudes, and values?

Intercultural Communication

While there is little disagreement that communication between a Karen hill tribesman in northern Thailand and an American college student involves intercultural differences, we might ask if communication between any two persons with different attitudes, beliefs, and values also involves intercultural differences. For example, while the value system espoused by a given corporation is commonly referred to as corporate culture, does that mean that communication between workers at IBM and Microsoft necessarily involves intercultural differences? Perhaps. Between someone at IBM and a farm worker?

Possibly. To study such interactions from an intercultural perspective might raise different questions and produce different answers from those found in a more standard organizational communication analysis. But rather than attempt to give final answers, we prefer to discuss the central thrust of intercultural communication, as opposed to attempting to delineate intercultural communication's absolute boundaries.

Thus, we regard the study of intercultural communication as the study of communication between people with different mind-sets and ways of looking at and perceiving the world that go beyond the differences normally found among people who regard themselves as culturally similar. Since communication occurs through cognitive processing, we might ask whether Eastern and Western ways of thinking are different. Does such a notion imply different cognitive structures or communication processes, or, can the observations which lead people to infer a different way of thinking be explained simply through different content in beliefs, attitudes, and values within the cultures? Though commonly applied to communication between persons who are each embedded in a different cultural group, intercultural communication also has heuristic utility when applied to the examination of two persons, ostensibly from the same culture, gender, age, ethnic group, and socioeconomic status, whose assumptions about the nature of the world and ways of relating to it are sufficiently divergent to produce the forms of misunderstanding commonly found in intercultural analysis. *The central thrust of intercultural communication is in the analysis of meaning assignment in interactions between persons whose attitudes, beliefs, and values differ due to a corresponding difference in their cultural or co-cultural backgrounds.* These attitudes, beliefs, and values represent, in part, the individual's theories of what others in the same culture believe, as well as how this differentiates persons of that culture from persons of other cultures.

Four Major Areas of Intercultural Communication Study

The term *Intercultural Communication* has both a broad and a narrower referent. The broad sense is that of an encompassing term for four major areas of intercultural communication defined by their intent: I. *Cross-cultural Communication*; II. *International Communication;* III. *Development Communication;* and intercultural communication's narrower referent, IV. *Intercultural Communication proper.* These areas are not fixed and independent. Studies in each area often have relevance to studies in others, and some research traditions, linguistic relativity, for example, might be classified in several different areas. We will spend more time discussing some areas than others.

Cross-Cultural Communication

Borrowing terminology from descriptive linguistics, Pike (1966) developed his *etic* and *emic* distinction from *phonetic* and *phonemic*. He observed that phonetics studies sound and symbol production as observed by others outside the person being studied, while phonemics examines meaning, which is inside the person. Thus *emic* approaches look at a single culture, often from the perspective of a person thinking, communicating, and behaving within that culture—so their idiosyncrasies as cultures may be determined. This is the approach of ethnology and cross-cultural communication. And *etic* approaches to intercultural communication examine cultures from the outside—so their commonalities may be determined. The *etic* approach is that of intercultural communication proper.

Cross-cultural communication concerns the comparison of communication across two or more specific cultures or ethnicities, such as Japanese communication styles compared with U.S. communication styles, or African-American, Hispanic, and Anglo styles within the United States. Studies of linguistic relativity and of ethnography are also forms of cross-cultural communication so defined. Scholars concerned with multicultural education and cultural diversity are often interested in both cross-cultural communication and intercultural communication proper. Many works on cross-cultural communication are heavily weighted in the comparison, focusing on one presumably unfamiliar culture almost to the exclusion of the culture presumed to be familiar. In such cases the cross-cultural study becomes more a uni-cultural study.

Communication Across Cultures and Ethnicities

The single cross-cultural interaction which has generated the most in-depth, book-length communication research concerning intercultural communication with its members is Japanese-American communication. Barnlund (1989), Goldman (1990, 1994), Gudykunst (1993), Gudykunst and Nishida (1994), and Sato (1992) each discuss Japanese-American communication from different perspectives. Goldman (1990) and Sato (1992) focus on Japanese communicating with Americans, while Barnlund (1989), Goldman (1994), and Gudykunst and Nishida (1994) are oriented toward the American perspective in interacting with Japanese. Gudykunst (1993) contrasts the study of communication in Japan with that in the United States, and Stewart and Bennett (1991) discuss the cultural patterns of Americans.

Kim (1986) summarizes research on interethnic communication to the mid-1980s. Hecht, Jackson, and Ribeau (2003) provide an example of research on ethnic styles, delineating African-American communication patterns as contrasted with other common U.S. forms. Other views representative of a multicultural and cultural diversity approach to intercultural communication are provided in Andersen and Collins (1992) and Gonzalez, Houston, and Chen (1994). Central to these essays are concerns with the concepts of racism, sexism, prejudice, self-concept, and power differences which enter into interethnic interactions.

Gannon (2004) provides an introduction to the study of various cultures in his book *Understanding Global Cultures*, which is popular within the business community for persons whose work takes them to unfamiliar cultures. Gannon employs cultural metaphors to help those unfamiliar with a given culture attain a notion of the dominant mind-set found in that country or culture. Whether such dominant unified mind-sets exist, and whether the use of such metaphors actually assists in cross-cultural communication or simply provides comfort to prospective travelers, has not been sufficiently studied.

Linguistic Relativity

Another cross-cultural area is the study of linguistic relativity, which can be traced to Aristotle's speculations on whether doing philosophy while using Greek as a symbol system would make the knowledge discovered different if, say, Latin were the symbol system (Steinfatt,1989). Aristotle's answer was that the language in use would not make a substantial difference in the final result—that any thought could be expressed equally well in any language.

This view held sway until the late 19th century, when Cassirer (1953) suggested that the language used to conduct philosophical analyses could influence the resultant knowledge. Cassirer's work was not widely accepted in philosophy, but a young Yale anthropologist, Edward Sapir, began to write and lecture on topics in linguistic anthropology in the late 1800s. Sapir (1921) suggested that thought was potentially relative to language. Prior to 1920 Benjamin Lee Whorf, an undergraduate student in engineering at MIT who was working his way through college as an inspector for an insurance company, began to study Hopi and Mayan cultures. In the 1920s he lectured extensively on his thesis, developed independently of Sapir's ideas, that the language of thought influences its content. Though not Sapir's student at this point, he had heard of Sapir and attended one of Sapir's lectures at Yale late in that decade, eventually joining Sapir's graduate program in anthropology as a student. From this simple meeting was born what has come to be called the *Sapir–Whorf hypothesis,* that language structures thought. Mandell (1931) presents an early view of linguistic relativity; reviews of experimental research may be found in Gibson and McGarvy (1937), Woodworth (1938), Heidbreder (1948), Johnson (1950), Humphrey (1951), (1951), Diebold (1965), and Steinfatt (1988, 1989). Lee's (1996) *The Whorf Theory Complex: A Critical Reconstruction,* provides an excellent discussion of Whorf's intercultural work.

Sapir (1921), Whorf (1956), and Cassirer (1953) are perhaps the best known advocates of the notion that language influences thought. They treated linguistic relativity as an interlanguage phenomenon, a process attributable to differences between languages. Sapir and Whorf's thesis involves both "linguistic determinism" and "linguistic relativity." Linguistic determinism holds that language shapes thought, but allows that people who speak different languages could still have the same thoughts and think in similar ways. For example, a counterfactual conditional (e.g., "I would take you if I were going that way but I'm not so I can't") is very difficult to express in Chinese. But while the language makes such thoughts difficult to express, linguistic determinism suggests that such thoughts could occur in Chinese, although they would be difficult. Linguistic relativity, a more radical version of linguistic determinism, holds that different languages actually shape thought differently (Glucksberg & Danks, 1975). Linguistic relativity would argue that speakers of Chinese would have great difficulty thinking in counterfactual conditional terms and that thought processes in Chinese would have to follow the structure of the language.

As initially proposed, the *Weltanschauung*—world *view*—thesis of linguistic relativity was very general and thus almost impossible to test. Greenberg (1956), Lenneberg and Roberts (1956), Henle (1958), Fishman (1960), Osgood and Sebeok (1965), and Slobin (1979) all have suggested different ways of organizing the hypothesis. Steinfatt (1989) proposed that three groups of independent variables—phonological, syntactical, and semantic—are possible causative sets in linguistic relativity as the basis for any proposed differences in thought. At least one variable from at least one of these sets must influence at least one dependent measure in one of three variable sets—the logic of thought itself, the structure of cognition and worldview, or perception and areas of cognition—in order for a linguistic relativity effect to be claimed. Beyond looking at differences between natural languages as a source of linguistic relativity effects, Steinfatt (1989) also suggested that substantial phonological, syntactical, or semantic differences in any natural language would have to be regarded as a potential source of linguistic relativity effects. Thus, dialects such as Black-American English, compound bilingualism, aphasics relearning a language, and the deaf, should provide examples of linguistic relativity effects if such effects actually occur. Linguistic relativity should not be limited to the natural language differences proposed by Whorf (1956) and others. Additionally, Steinfatt (1989) suggested that knowledge of the methods by which language is acquired should provide insight into whether linguistic relativity effects are likely to exist.

Traditional Ethnography

The traditional referent of ethnography is the branch of anthropology dealing with the scientific description of specific human cultures, both the fieldwork and the writing that it engenders. Barfield (2001) defines ethnography as systematic description of a single existing culture that can be observed in the present. In Malinowski's (1922) classic definition, ethnography is the endeavor of describing a culture, "to grasp the native's point of view, his relation to life, to realize *his* vision of *his* world" (1922, p. 25). Kaplan (1964, p. 31) refers to this as the "act meaning," as opposed to the "action meaning" that is taken as data by many social scientists. This apprehension of the act meaning was usually accomplished through personal immersion in the object culture involving a lengthy process of participation, participant observation, and interview, often by a single observer, producing highly detailed and descriptive notes that became the raw data for later analysis. The observation process and note creation were the fundamental method, and were seen as largely devoid of theory, though they were often guided by notions of kinship systems and other important areas and classifications. No specific characteristics of culture were to be defined *a priori,* and the researcher was to ignore all preconceived notions of the culture to be studied. The important characteristics, relationships, and patterns would emerge naturally during the research, so that notes had to be very detailed as the observer would not know what would later emerge as important. This form of ethnography became a well-established method for the study of human cultures in the late 19th and early 20th centuries.

Aside from potential concerns with ethnography regarding validity and reliability—since *one* person from an *outside* culture was to assign meaning producing a single known reality—traditional cultures so described were often viewed in isolation from each other and from the world. The methods of traditional ethnography were also vulnerable to political attack since they were associated from the outset with imperialism and the colonial subordination of non-Western peoples by European powers. The observations of ethnographers necessarily occur within the form of ethnocentricity of the times, and most ethnographers believed it was possible for a single "scientific observer" to create detailed interpretations of other cultures from a detached point of view (Vidich & Lyman, 1994). Little consideration was given to the observer's role as observer, nor to the possible impact of an observer on the research, particularly as an outsider from a ruling power. Nor was consideration given to the need for a diverse set of views from multiple observers, with multiple voices speaking from within the community to be studied, who might be heard differently by different observers.

By the early 1960s these criticisms of the traditional ethnographic method were regularly taught as such in U.S. graduate programs in anthropology. This occurred in most programs, but not in all of them. By the 1970s Geertz's (1973) emphasis on "thick description," influenced by Ryle's (1968) discussion of the meaning of a wink, suggests that the descriptions within ethnography must consider the context of the behaviors described, to the point that the description of the behavior makes the behavior in its context meaningful to an outsider. Thin description results from the outside observation of behaviors with little interpretation, and thick description includes the interpretation of the behavior from the point of view of the cultural actor. Beginning with his 1960s work on Javanese religion, Geertz (1960, 1973, 1983, 1988) was one of ethnography's principal proponents. Wolcott (1994) provides a clear description of the use of ethnography in multiple settings, where researchers are especially interested in studying the ways in which people embedded in a culture make decisions. Gladwin (1989) discusses the use of "decision trees" in this process.

The Variance Within is of the Same Order as the Variance Between

Certainly a note of caution is in order whenever a given culture is being described. When discussing a culture and defining its important communication features, abstraction involves searching for what is central within the culture and ignoring the peripheral. Yet central to any culture is cultural variation often involving the peripheral. When we apply intercultural communication to specific situations as communication between, say, Vietnamese and American cultures, or Black and White cultures within American society, this conceptualization implies a certain unity of culture for Vietnamese, Americans, Whites, and Blacks. The assumption often is that people within a culture are relatively similar and the major differences are to be found between those of one culture and those of another. Naturally, nothing is further from the truth. To employ a statistical analogy from the analysis of variance, we may say that the variation within a given culture is normally of the same order of magnitude as the variation between cultures. There is often as much variation in a given culture between its social classes as there is between that culture and any other culture. In fact, ethnic variations within a given culture can easily be greater than the average variation between that culture and another. Learning how a particular cultural group thinks and communicates does not guarantee that such findings will hold for a specific member of a cultural group, especially when the cultural interaction situation is factored in. At a minimum, if the social class and ethnicity of the specific individuals involved is not considered, knowledge of the culture alone is often of little use in predicting interactional outcomes, though this is not always the case (e.g., Jones, 1979).

Postmodernism

The methods of ethnography came under further attack by postmodernism in the 1980s and beyond, an attack that in large part simply echoed the known criticisms of ethnography, emphasizing some criticisms over others, and attempting to fuse them into a postmodern critique. In general, this attempt was neither coherent and well thought out, nor worth exploring further. The most distinguishing and consistent new features of postmodernist attacks were the invention of a non-existent "modernism," allowing postmodernism's straw man attack on it, and the apparent inability of many of its major proponents to write competently in their native language. Its proponents consider this a strong point.

References

Andersen, M. L., & Collins, P H. (1992). *Race, class, and gender.* Belmont, CA: Wadsworth.

Barfield, T. (Ed.). (2001). *The dictionary of anthropology.* London: Blackwell.

Barnlund, D. C. (1989). *Communicative styles of Japanese and Americans.* Belmont, CA: Wadsworth.

Cassirer, E. (1953). *The philosophy of symbolic forms: Vol. 1. Language* (R. Manheim, Trans.). New Haven, CT: Yale University Press.

Diebold, A. R. (1965). A survey of psycholinguistic research, 1954–1964. In C. E. Osgood & T. A. Sebeok (Eds.), *Psycholinguistics* (pp. 205–291). Bloomington: Indiana University Press.

Fishman, J. A. (1960). A systematization of the Whorfian hypothesis. *Behavioral Science, 5,* 323–339.

Gannon, M. J. (2004). *Understanding global cultures: Metaphorical journeys through 28 nations* (3rd ed.). Thousand Oaks, CA: Sage.

Geertz, C. (1960). *The religion of Java.* Chicago/London: University of Chicago Press

Geertz, C. (1973). *The interpretation of cultures.* New York: Basic Books.

Geertz, C. (1983). *Local knowledge: Further essays in interpretive anthropology.* New York: Basic Books.

Geertz, C. (1988). *Works and lives: The anthropologist as author.* Stanford, CA: Stanford University Press.

Gibson, E. J., & McGarvy, H. R. (1937). Experimental studies of thought and reasoning. *Psychological Bulletin, 34,* 327–350.

Gladwin, C. H. (1989). *Ethnographic decision tree modeling.* Thousand Oaks, CA: Sage.

Glucksberg, S., & Danks, J. H. (1975). *Experimental psycholinguistics.* Hillsdale, NJ: Erlbaum.

Goldman, A. (1990). *For Japanese only: Intercultural communication with Americans.* Tokyo: Japan Times.

Goldman, A. (1994). *Doing business with the Japanese: A guide to successful communication, management, and diplomacy.* Albany, NY: State University of New York Press.

Gonzalez, A., Houston, M., & Chen, V. (1994). *Our voices: Essays in culture, ethnicity, and communication.* Los Angeles: Roxbury.

Greenberg, J. H. (1956). Concerning inferences from linguistic to nonlinguistic data. In H. Hoijer (Ed.), *Language in culture* (pp. 3–19). Chicago: University of Chicago Press.

Gudykunst, W. B. (1983a). Intercultural communication theory. In *International and intercultural communication annual.* Thousand Oaks, CA: Sage.

Gudykunst, W. B. (1983b). Toward a typology of stranger–host relationships. *International Journal of Intercultural Relations, 7,* 401–413.

Gudykunst, W. B., & Nishida, T (1994). *Bridging Japanese/North American differences.* Thousand Oaks, CA: Sage.

Hecht, M. L., Jackson, R. L., II, & Ribeau, S. A. (2003). *African American communication: Exploring identity and cultural interpretation* (2nd ed.). Mahwah, NJ: Erlbaum.

Heidbreder, E. (1948). Studying human thinking. In T. G. Andrews (Ed.), *Methods of psychology* (pp. 96–123). New York: Wiley.

Henle, P. (1958). Language, thought, and culture. In P. Henle (Ed.), *Language and culture* (pp. 1–24). Ann Arbor: University of Michigan Press.

Humphrey, G. (1951). *Thinking: An introduction to its experimental psychology.* New York: Wiley.

Johnson, D. M. (1950). Problem solving and symbolic processes. *Annual Review of Psychology, 1,* 297–310.

Jones, S. E. (1979). Integrating etic and emic approaches in the study of intercultural communication. In M. K. Asante, E. Newmark, & C. A. Blake (Eds.), *The handbook of intercultural communication* (pp. 57–74). Thousand Oaks, CA: Sage.

Kaplan, A. (1964). *The conduct of inquiry.* San Francisco: Chandler.

Kim, Y. Y. (1986). *Interethnic communication current research.* Thousand Oaks, CA: Sage.

Kluckhohn, C. (1949). *Mirror for man: The relation of anthropology to modern life.* New York: Whittlesey House.

Langer, S. K. (1942). *Philosophy in a new key.* Cambridge, MA: Harvard University Press.

Lee, P. (1996). *The Whorf theory complex: A critical reconstruction.* Philadelphia: J. Benjamins.

Lenneberg, E., & Roberts, J. M. (1956). *The language of experience.* Bloomington: Indiana University Publication in Anthropology & Linguistics.

Malinowski, B. (1922). *Argonauts of the Western Pacific: An account of native enterprise and adventure in the archipelagoes of Melanesian New Guinea.* London: Routledge & Kegan Paul.

Mandell, S. (1931). The relation of language to thought. *Quarterly Journal of Speech, 17,* 522–531.

Osgood, C. E., & Sebeok, T A. (1965). *Psycholinguistics.* Bloomington: Indiana University Press.

Pike, K. L. (1966). Etic and emic standpoints for the description of behavior. In A. G. Smith (Ed.), *Communication and culture* (pp. 152–163). New York: Holt, Rinehart & Winston.

Ryle, G. (1968). *The thinking of thoughts: What is "Le Penseur" doing?* (University Lectures, no.18). University of Saskatchewan. http://lucy.ukc.ac.uk/CSACSIA/Vol14/Papers/ryle_1.html

Sapir, E. (1921). *Language: An introduction to the study of speech.* New York: Harcourt, Brace, & World.

Sato, A. (1992). *Understanding Japanese communication.* Tokyo: Japan Times.

Slobin, D. T (1979). *Psycholinguistics.* Glenview, IL: Scott Foresman.

Steinfatt, T. M. (1988, November). *Language and intercultural differences: Linguistic relativity.* "Top Three" paper, Intercultural Communication Division, Speech Communication Association, New Orleans, LA.

Steinfatt, T. M. (1989). Linguistic relativity: Toward a broader view. In S. Ting-Toomey & F. Korzenny (Eds.), *International and intercultural communication annual: Vol. 13. Language, communication and culture* (pp. 35–75). Thousand Oaks, CA: Sage.

Stewart, E. C., & Bennett, M. J. (1991). *American cultural patterns: A cross-cultural perspective.* Yarmouth, ME: Intercultural.

Vidich, A. J., & Lyman, S. M. (1994). Qualitative methods: Their history in sociology and anthropology. In N. K. Denzin & Y. S. Lincoln (Eds.), *Handbook of qualitative research* (pp. 23–59). Thousand Oaks, CA: Sage.
Whorf, B. L. (1956). *Language, thought, and reality.* Cambridge, MA: MIT Press.
Wolcott, H. F. (1994). *Transforming qualitative data.* Thousand Oaks, CA: Sage.
Woodworth, R. S. (1938). *Experimental psychology.* New York: Holt.

Unit II

Psychology and Identity of Self

"The greatest discovery of my generation is that human beings can alter their lives by altering their attitudes of mind."
—William James

Stripped down to basics, psychology is the scientific study of mind and behavior, coming from the Greek words "psyche," meaning life, and "logos," meaning explanation.[1] Applied psychology provides scientific explanations for social behavior, based on scientific methodology.[2] Psychology has been recognized as a legitimate player in business since the 1970s, with the introduction of business psychology courses in business schools. In addition, the practice of business leaders borrowing concepts from sports psychology was commonly used in the late 1970s to develop stronger work ties among employees and to develop an understanding of work environment, based on the team mentality and principles of good sportsmanship.[3] In addition, employers drew from sports psychology to deal with clients: psychological factors interact with other factors to influence behavior. The companies had gained an understanding that psychologists offer businesses a wide range of helpful and unique services.[4]

Today, psychology has evolved from the study of intangible thought and consciousness to the study of quantifiable matter made available through technological advances such as MRIs, EEGs, and so on.[5]

Business psychology provides insight into the thoughts, feelings, and behaviors of employees; consequently, managers who apply psychological principles to work relationships have insight into the lives and motivations of people who work for them. This connection fosters a positive climate of trust that contributes to the overall well-being and profitability of organizations. For example, psychology in the treatment and prevention of stress-related, lifestyle-related, chronic, and terminal health problems has been proven to improve employee health as well as work environments.[6] In addition, the analysis of cognitive skills and cognitive development in the workplace provides guidance for business leaders in terms of training, development, and educational programs, as well as developing empathy for their employees and other stakeholders.

Two branches of psychology are applied to business settings in order to develop perspectives that are used to understand human behavior:[7]

- Research psychologists use scientific methods to create new knowledge about the causes of behavior and the implications for business on a large scale.
- Psychologist practitioners, such as those providing clinical, counseling, and industrial-organizational psychological services, deal with mind and behavior on individual bases.

Both address issues related to consciousness, sensations, perceptions, thinking, communicating, motivations, and emotions.[8] Psychology provides a framework, based on scientific research, to deal with workplace issues driven by the state of mind(s). Business psychologists recognize people's ability to learn from their environment, and further recognize the importance of context and culture, in that growth and development are improved by a positive environment; conversely, they argue, growth and development are stifled in a negative environment.[9] Ultimately, business psychologists provide business leaders and their employees with the tools to cope with everyday organizational life, in periods of calm as well as in crisis situations. Leaders are able to apply principles of psychology to manage stress and other negative issues that impact the bottom line in the long run. This improves working conditions for all parties. Further, illness is reduced when employees are able to adapt to change and negotiate on-the-job stressors using psychological skills related to their working environment. The ability to do so is critical to the corporate bottom line in productivity and profitability.[10]

The following are broad theoretical frameworks or meta-theories of psychology that pertain to business psychology:

- **Biological:** Centers on the biological underpinnings of behavior, including the effects of evolution and genetics.
- **Psychoanalytic/psychodynamic:** Emphasizes the importance of unconscious mental processes, early child development, personality, the self, attachment patterns, and relationships.
- **Behaviorism:** Most human traits are learned; this approach emphasizes the role and influence of a person's environment and previous learning experiences on understanding behavior.
- **Cognitive:** Centers on the mental processing of information, including the specific functions of attention, concentration, reasoning, problem-solving, and memory.
- **Humanistic and existential:** Emphasizes that each person is unique and that humans have the ability and responsibility to make choices in their lives.

- **Sociocultural:** Focuses on the social and cultural factors that affect behavior.

Basic psychological terms related to business psychology

- **The information processing model:** A framework used by cognitive psychologists to explain and describe mental processes; likens the thinking process to how a computer works.
- **Short-term/working memory:** The reproduction, recognition, or recall of a limited amount of material after a period of about 10 to 30 seconds.
- **Long-term memory:** A relatively permanent information storage system that enables one to retain, retrieve, and make use of skills and knowledge hours, weeks, or even years after they were originally learned.
- **Mental acuity:** Sharpness of mind in terms of memory, focus, and concentration.
- **Content validity:** The extent to which a test measures a representative sample of the subject matter or behavior under investigation.
- **Cohort effect**: Any outcome associated with being a member of a group whose members all undergo similar experiences.
- **Primacy effect**: The tendency for facts, impressions, or items that are presented first to be better learned or remembered than material presented later in the sequence.
- **Recency effect**: A memory phenomenon in which the most recently presented facts, impressions, or items are learned or remembered better than material presented earlier.

The readings in this unit focus on the importance of psychology and the identity of self for business students as well as business leaders. First of all, based on a decade of research at Harvard and case studies from his work with Fortune 500 executives in 42 countries, Achor explains that we can reprogram our brains to become more positive, and ultimately more successful, at work. He identifies seven practices to improve performance and maximize potential that apply to business and personal lives alike. Next, based on his findings in neuroscience, Goleman argues that people are wired to interact with each other. He defines social intelligence on the basis that our interactions with other people shape our minds. Ultimately, he argues, a high level of social intelligence improves our standard of living, personal performance, and organizational success.

Notes

1. Piotrowski, N. A. (2005). *Psychology basics* (Rev. ed.). Salem Press.
2. Gawronski, B., & Bodenhausen, G. (2014). *Theory and explanation in social psychology*. Guilford Publications.
3. Tod, D. (2014). *Sport psychology: The basics*. Routledge.
   Foxhall, K. (July/August 2001). A spark to the business-psychology connection. *The Monitor*, 32(7).
4. Foxhall, K. (July/August 2001). A spark to the business-psychology connection. *The Monitor*, 32(7).
5. Cash, A. (2013). *Psychology for dummies*. John Wiley & Sons.
6. Piotrowski, N. A. (2005). *Psychology basics* (Rev. ed.). Salem Press.

7. [Author removed at the request of original publisher]. (n.d.). *Introduction to psychology*. https://open.lib.umn.edu/intropsyc/
8. Cash, A. (2013). *Psychology for dummies*. John Wiley & Sons.
9. Bonoma, T. V., & Johnston, W. J. (1978). The social psychology of industrial buying and selling. *Industrial Marketing Management*, 7(4), 213–224.
10. Van Kippenberg, D. *(2011). Advancing theory in organizational psychology*. Organizational Psychology Review, 1(1), 3–8.
    Nichols, R. (2013). *Listening to people.*

Reading 2.1

The Psychology of Business

Jay J. Silverberg

> *Sometimes being the only one that isn't desperate to be noticed is what makes them pay attention.*
>
> Morley, LA Street Artist

Psychology, as it applies to business, identifies how and why people make decisions. Applied psychology helps you quantify the hierarchy of relationships; determine the most effective strategies in marketing, selling, and dealmaking; and identify how to effectively communicate with your team, your clients, and your network connections. It allows you to motivate others and maneuver people to act in your best interest.

Understand and appeal directly to what the potential customer is getting out of dealing with you, and what triggers them to respond positively to you. If, for example, you are selling a service that makes that person's job easier, gives them more free time, or more time to do what they enjoy or do best, or makes them look good to their superiors, they will more than likely deal with you. Those motivators are called the "hot buttons." Good entrepreneurs identify and use them effectively.

A Behavioral Psychology Quickie

Here are two examples whereby psychology very subtly plays such an important part of everyday decision making. The ramifications to business are pretty compelling.

Question: Two cookie jars. One is full. The other jar has only three cookies left. The subjects are offered a cookie from either jar. Which do people choose?

Answer: The one with three cookies. It is perceived as having something special that others are reaching for. How does that apply to your marketing? Are you offering anything special? Different? Is it a question of supply and demand?

Question: Why do waiters who bring customers candies with their bill get 23 percent higher tips? Answer: Because in the customer's mind, they show they are caring, even if they really don't. How's your customer service?

You Really, Truly Need to Know What Motivates Others

> *A concern about appearing honest may outweigh our desire to actually be honest even in situations where it will cost us money to lie.*
>
> Shoham Choshen-Hillel, "General Lying to Appear Honest," *Journal of Experimental Psychology*, January 30, 2020

It is important to recognize the patterns of motivation in order to fully comprehend how to manipulate the people you will be dealing with in the business world.

Understand these and you will master how to control people in every conceivable business situation. Once you tune in to what they want and need from you, then play into them.

These are the "hot buttons," that is, what motivates people to act, in order of priority within each category. Use these motivators to your full advantage. They are your source of power and advantage. (Note: Some items appear on more than one list, but in a different hierarchy of importance.)

Ambition

- climbing the social ladder
- wealth, greed
- promotions
- power
- recognition by peers
- career path (long-term planning)
- building a following
- status
- contacts and connections
- favors (IOU's for cashing in later)
- survival
- greed (ambition gone berserk)

*PYA (Protect Your ***)*

- caution
- fear of doing anything wrong that can be blamed on them
- longevity
- acceptance by peers
- recognition by management
- stability (status quo)
- promotion
- wealth

Status Quo

- ego, pride
- fear of change
- timidity, that is, lack of conviction

Unpredictable

- revenge against company or "the system"
- apathy
- incompetence

Aside from "unpredictable," all the others are clearly identifiable motives which you absolutely must learn to recognize in people and situations, in order to fully capitalize on every opportunity and in each and every encounter. You must also learn to "play" on people's needs and motives. Role-play to fine-tune those skills. Everybody does something for a reason. Nothing is by accident.

Don't believe everything you don't hear.

Dan Waldschmidt

The Three Most Influential Motivational "Hot Buttons"

- **Ego**—people like to be made to feel important, or special. It is human nature. When you buy a pair of Nike sneakers and you see the bold check mark on the side of the shoe, that is appealing to your ego. It is telling you that you are great and you are strong. Is it unethical to appeal to people's ego?
- **Flattery/Pride**—how often have you walked into a clothing store, tried something on, and been told that it makes you look younger or slimmer? Does the store owner mean it, or are they bending the ethical rules slightly and harmlessly to get the sale?
- **Greed**—everyone likes to feel that they are getting a deal. That is why stores have markdowns, sales, suggested list prices slashed, Boxing Day sales, two-for-one sales, and more. Are the

sellers losing money? Lost leaders bring in more traffic.

The Psychology of Influencing People: Play the Head Games Effectively

Get people to buy, change attitudes, build excitement, enhance your image, build loyalty, and extract referrals—these are all doable by applying the principles of psychology into business.

- **Reciprocity:** the equitable exchange of valued assets, namely ideas, contacts, favors, and leads.
- **Commitment and Consistency:** Try to assure that the prospective client agrees with what you are proposing. That early commitment has a greater chance of leading to a contract or sale. Newsletter sign-ups are one type of extracting an early commitment.
- **Social Proof:** Work to establish a comfort level for the customer. Where somebody else likes the product, as expressed in a testimonial or commercial, that is validation. For example, in the travel and accommodation industry, the host will often ask you to post a positive comment on Trip Advisor, Travelocity or Lonely Planet.
- **Liking:** Whoever represents the company needs to be likeable. This improves the chances of doing business.
- **Authority:** People respond to authority and celebrities. Companies use "pitchmen" who are well recognized, such as sports figures or recognized actors (or pretend doctors) to influence decision makers.
- **Scarcity:** Based on "supply and demand," limited-time offers and limited availability are two techniques promoting scarcity.

Influencing people is also the cornerstone of every business book on marketing and selling. "The influence of yes" highlights how the behavioral building blocks of psychology can be applied in the business world. These are powerful tools for you to apply in all your business dealings.

Human Need: Another Psychological Business Trigger

Human need governs decision making. Everybody has needs, but, if you can catalog, in broad strokes, what those needs are, and build them into your products or business behavior, you can then influence people to act to your advantage by triggering any of the following:

- Avoidance of pain
- Comfort, both physical and emotional
- Gaining pleasure
- Need for new stimuli
- Feeling of closeness

- Ability to be involved
- Personalization

Just as important is our "perception of need." That is, creating need in the minds of the client.

One such additional psychological influencer is novelty. People have a curiosity about the unknown. Novelty, it is said, activates the brain. Apple is the master of novelty, introducing new innovative products that we didn't even know we needed.

Finally, using business psychology in everyday situations such as team building, leadership, and human resources can also be explored at https://www.fundera.com/blog/psychology-101-can-help-run-better-business (Meredith Wood, Fundera).

The Fine Art of Gentle and Subtle Persuasion

If and when you tell people what to do, they can often become defensive. That's human nature. We are territorial beasts. But, if you lead them to arrive at the same conclusion as yours all by themselves, they are far more likely to buy what you're selling. The key action here is "lead."

Think of it like a parent–child relationship where you don't command your youngster to eat the oatmeal. Instead you make it fun, show them you are eating it too, make a game of it, and watch them dig in. You lead. Think of it that way and you can't lose.

There are a few tricks to changing somebody's mind without force-feeding them.

- Ask questions that lead the other party toward the decision that you want. Stop selling. Start directing.
- Give people options to choose from. And while you focus moreso on the option you want them to choose by also giving the person alternatives, that makes it seem like the decision is theirs alone.
- The person you are dealing with will have a need, that is, what they want or desire to achieve, and where they are at now, that likely being at a shortfall to filling their need. That is the "gap," and that is your primary target.
- Be empathetic and understanding, and listen. Just be quiet and hear what is being said, or asked of you, and respond in a thoughtful manner. In the end, you will get what you want, and so will the other party.

Why People Deal with You

Why do people deal with you? They are not necessarily being "nice." That's a false comfort. They are being selfish. What you do for them is their primary motivation. Never lose sight of that. They may "like" you, but it's your usefulness to them that they like even more.

Why Winners Win

Winners win because they want to. They are driven to and are oblivious to any distractions or weaknesses. They are always "on." They impress the heck out of everyone, and often themselves as well. Winners win because they make things happen regardless of what others may say. At the risk of sounding like a sports product cliche, they "just do it".

Why Losers Lose

Losers visualize the penalties of failure and associate failure with pain. Winners visualize the rewards of success. Your attitude and outlook dictate everything.

Maslow's "Hierarchy of Needs" Applied to Business

Abraham Maslow[1] developed a motivational pyramid model of human needs, from the most basic needs like food, shelter, and safety at the bottom of the pyramid to the highest, most elite needs including emotional satisfaction. It is a stepped process, whereby each lower tier need must be achieved before the person can advance to the next highest step. This process is called "self-actualization." Here is the **Hierarchy of Needs** adapted to a business perspective.

1. **Physiological** needs (the lowest achievable need on the pyramid) demand the person to seek water, sleep, and food. Business parallels encompass meeting physiological needs with items such as training materials, accounting software or business planning tools.
2. Next on the pyramid is **Safety**, generally described as security, shelter, and protection. The business analogy includes insurance, alarm systems, retirement security, and investments.
3. **Belongingness** is the third tier and includes basic emotional needs such as love, friendship, and acceptance by others. Its business partners might well be clothing, grooming products, entertainment, clubs and resorts, bars, and even dating sites and services.
4. Reaching toward the top, we find **Ego** as the next need. This need caters to prestige, status, and accomplishment. Appropriate business offerings include money, luxury cars, credit cards, houses/ condos, country club memberships, and other status possessions. This need is targeted by a plethora of products and services, particularly in our western greedy and relentless need for social prominence. Do you want a Honda Fit or an Acura? Hmm, tough choice.
5. Finally, sitting at the top of the pyramid is the much sought after **Self-actualization**, as depicted by self-fulfillment and enrichment (sigh, don't we all seek this level). This is fulfilled with travel, education, and spiritual experiences. The euphoria of success!

This begs the question that knowing where your product or service fits in, how you will fulfill those human needs, and is there an awareness in the market that you are playing in that tier? As well, understand that the higher your product or service caters within that pyramid, the smaller and more "elite" your market becomes.

Don't live the same year 75 times and call it a life.

Robin Sharma

"The Selfish (Business) Gene": We Are All Selfish

The Selfish Gene (Richard Dawkins, 1976) builds on the principal theory expounded by George C. Williams's *Adaptation and Natural Selection* (1966). While it discusses the predominance of dominating genes in our DNA makeup, it has morphed into "the survival of the fittest" among us. It is competition focused, even "dog-eat-dog," which is a further bastardization of The Selfish Gene theory. The essence, then, can be distilled into a key principle of behavior that can be directly applied to business.

People act of their own self-interest. Everything we do is inherently selfish. When we give to a charity, we do it because it makes us feel good about ourselves. When someone purchases a product or contracts your service, they do it to satisfy their personal interests. Make sure you flatter people and tell them how wonderful, smart, and successful you think they are (whether you mean it or not), and, coincidentally, that they will become increasingly moreso when they deal with you.

From an entrepreneurial perspective, that "selfish gene" needs to also be in your DNA makeup. That means doing for you, not just for others. Become "business-selfish" to cope, survive, grow, and succeed. Let others worry about themselves. You take care of you.

When you go into business for yourself, you do it for you, first and foremost, and that is fine too. If others around you benefit from your efforts, that's a rewarding secondary effect. Don't go into business just for everybody else except yourself. Martyrdom is not fashionable in the business milieu.

Greed and Revenge

Greed and revenge are two of the most destructive reasons to do anything in business. Yet, time and again, I have seen these cited by clients as a motive in price undercutting, negative advertising and, even worse, inflating a contract/sale with no consideration to repeat business. Each contract/sale should not be your last one with a client, but instead, the first of many. Worship your existing and critically important repeat clients.

And Pavlov Had His Dogs

Pavlovian conditioning demonstrated the ability to trigger dogs to salivate when they learned to recognize a repeatable stimulus, such as the sound of a bell. It became a behavioral reflex.

So how do we humans react when we are continuously bombarded by "in-your-face" product logos or the image of a well-recognized actor hawking whatever? We salivate. Anybody else hear that bell?

Even Socrates Understood Selfishness

In Plato's *Republic*, Socrates's older brother, Glaucon, acknowledges that people's behavior is rooted in their own self-interest. "Even the most 'just' man would act purely for themselves and not care if they harmed anyone in the process."[2] Further, Glaucon went on to theorize that people only do the right thing because they fear being punished if they get caught.

Selfishness is age-old and a psychological principle, whereby you appeal to the selfish nature of your audience. It is a readily applied business tactic.

Psychological Egoism and Hedonism: More Selfish Behavior

Now we are into the somewhat outlandish, but still useful motivational drivers that entrepreneurs should be aware of.

Psychological Egoism dictates that people are motivated not only by their own self-interest, but also by helping others fulfill their self-interest because it makes them look good or feel good, or, more importantly, be perceived favorably by others. So much for the purity of altruism!

Psychological Hedonism states that "the ultimate motive for voluntary action is the desire to experience pleasure or to avoid pain ... Immediate gratification can be sacrificed for a chance of greater, future pleasure."[3]

What Does All This Mean?

In reviewing this particular [reading], I would be somewhat remiss in not apologizing to the reader. You have been bombarded with every conceivable motivator and driver that can direct business to your company. You have been exposed to the doctrine of self-interest, greed, pride, ego, hedonism, egoism, and every other "-ism" in the book of pushing people's hot buttons to act.

In doing so, there was a concerted effort to present everything so that you could find something, some psychological thread, that you can comfortably build into your company, your offerings, and even your business persona. You now have a great deal of food for thought and tons of mind games and psychobabble to choose from.

The takeaway here is that selfishness rules supreme, be it physical or emotional, and that at the end of the day, people are people. Knowing how and why they act greatly enhances your chances to score on everything from controlling people and dealmaking to closing sales. It's all a matter of exploiting the rules of human nature and becoming somewhat of an empath to tune in to people and deliver what they need.

This Is How It Works in Real Life

I had a client in the chemical business. Pretty dull, but highly profitable. His plant was old and located in an area that was undergoing urban sprawl. He discussed with me the opportunity to move to a newer location. He wanted me to do a business case study.

I asked him why, since he was not being forced to move. I told him he was crazy, and then started questioning him about the "real" reasons behind the relocation. I knew my client well and sensed there were other circumstances at play.

Apparently, 40 years earlier, his uncle, ready to retire, had handed the business over to him for $1. Now that uncle's son was employed at the company, and my client, reaching retirement age, wanted to do the same for his nephew with a clean succession.

We worked out a plan for succession with the continuity of remaining in the existing facility, thereby avoiding moving costs, which would have included prohibitive regulatory/environmental issues due to the nature of the business. Everyone was pleased.

I may have lost a contract for a business case study, but by knowing my client, listening, and understanding his decision making "hot buttons," I became his trusted business adviser forever.

Notes

1. Cherry, K. March 16, 2020. "Biography of Abraham Maslow (1908–1970)." *History and Biographies*. https://www.verywellmind.com/biography-of-abrahammaslow-1908-1970-2795524, (date accessed June 10, 2020).
2. Pappas, S. March 27, 2017. "Are Humans Inherently Selfish?" *Wellness*. https://www.huffpost.com/entry/are-humans-inherently-selfish_n_58b4544ee4b0780bac2bccf0, (date accessed June 10, 2020).
3. Wikipedia. "Psychological Egoism." https://en.wikipedia.org/wiki/Psychological_egoism, (date accessed June 10, 2020).

Reading 2.2

Discovering the Happiness Advantage

Shawn Achor

I applied to Harvard on a dare.

I was raised in Waco, Texas, and never really expected to leave. Even as I was applying to Harvard, I was setting down roots and training to be a local volunteer firefighter. For me, Harvard was a place from the movies, the place mothers joke about their kids going to when they grow up. The chances of actually getting in were infinitesimally small. I told myself I'd be happy just to tell my kids someday, offhandedly at dinner, that I had even *applied* to Harvard. (I imagined my imaginary children being quite impressed.)

When I unexpectedly got accepted, I felt thrilled and humbled by the privilege. I wanted to do the opportunity justice. So I went to Harvard, and I stayed ... for the next twelve years.

When I left Waco, I had been out of Texas four times and never out of the country (though Texans consider anything out of Texas foreign travel). But as soon as I stepped out of the T in Cambridge and into Harvard Yard, I fell in love. So after getting my BA, I found a way to stay. I went to grad school, taught sections in sixteen different courses, and then began delivering lectures. As I pursued my graduate studies, I also became a Proctor, an officer of Harvard hired to live in residence with undergraduates to help them navigate the difficult path to both academic success and happiness within the Ivory Tower. This effectively meant that I lived in a college dorm for a total of 12 years of my life (not a fact I brought up on first dates).

I tell you this for two reasons. First, because I saw Harvard as such a privilege, it fundamentally changed the way my brain processed my experience. I felt grateful for every moment, even in the midst of stress, exams, and blizzards (something else I had only seen in the movies). Second, my 12 years teaching in the classrooms and living in the dorms afforded me a comprehensive view of how thousands of other Harvard students advanced through the stresses and challenges of their college years. That's when I began noticing the patterns.

Paradise Lost and Found

Around the time that Harvard was founded, John Milton wrote in *Paradise Lost,* "The Mind is its own place, and in itself can make a heaven of hell, a hell of heaven."

Three hundred years later, I observed this principle come to life. Many of my students saw Harvard as a privilege, but others quickly lost sight of that reality and focused only on the workload, the competition, the stress. They fretted incessantly about their future, despite the fact that they were earning a degree that would open so many doors. They felt overwhelmed by every small setback instead of energized by the possibilities in front of them. And after watching enough of those students struggle to make their way through, something dawned on me. Not only were these students the ones who seemed most susceptible to stress and depression, they were the ones whose grades and academic performance were suffering the most.

Years later, in the fall of 2009, I was invited to go on a month-long speaking tour throughout Africa. During the trip, a CEO from South Africa named Salim took me to Soweto, a township just outside of Johannesburg that many inspiring people, including Nelson Mandela and Archbishop Desmond Tutu, have called their home.

We visited a school next to a shantytown where there was no electricity and scarce running water. Only when I was in front of the children did it dawn on me that none of the stories I normally use in my talks would work. Sharing the research and experiences of privileged American college students and wealthy, powerful business leaders seemed inappropriate. So I tried to open a dialogue. Struggling for points of common experience, I asked in a very clearly tongue-in-cheek tone, "Who here likes to do school work?" I thought the seemingly universal distaste for school work would bond us together. But to my shock, 95 percent of the children raised their hands and started smiling genuinely and enthusiastically.

Afterward, I jokingly asked Salim why the children of Soweto were so weird. "They see schoolwork as a privilege," he replied, "one that many of their parents did not have." When I returned to Harvard two weeks later, I saw students complaining about the very thing the Soweto students saw as a privilege. I started to realize just how much our interpretation of reality changes our experience of that reality. The students who were so focused on the stress and the pressure—the ones who saw learning as a chore—were missing out on all the opportunities right in front of them. But those who saw attending Harvard as a privilege seemed to shine even brighter. Almost unconsciously at first, and then with ever-increasing interest, I became fascinated with what caused those high potential individuals to develop a positive mindset to excel, especially in such a competitive environment. And likewise, what caused those who succumbed to the pressure to fail—or stay stuck in a negative or neutral position.

Researching Happiness at Hogwarts

For me, Harvard remains a magical place, even after twelve years. When I invite friends from Texas to visit, they claim that eating in the freshman dining hall is like being at Hogwarts, Harry Potter's fantastical school of magic. Add in the other beautiful buildings, the university's abundant resources, and the seemingly endless opportunities it offers, and my friends often end up asking, "Shawn, why would you waste your time studying happiness at Harvard? Seriously, what does a Harvard student possibly have to be unhappy about?"

In Milton's time, Harvard had a motto that reflected the school's religious roots: *Veritas, Christo et Ecclesiae* (Truth, for Christ and the Church). For many years now, that motto has been truncated to a single word: *Veritas,* or just truth. There are now many truths at Harvard, and one of them is that despite all its magnificent facilities, a wonderful faculty, and a student body made up of some of America's (and the world's) best and brightest, it is home to many chronically unhappy young men and women. In 2004, for instance, a *Harvard Crimson* poll found that as many as 4 in 5 Harvard students suffer from depression at least once during the school year, and nearly half of all students suffer from depression so debilitating they can't function.[1]

This unhappiness epidemic is not unique to Harvard. A Conference Board survey released in January of 2010 found that only 45 percent of workers surveyed were happy at their jobs, the lowest in 22 years of polling.[2] Depression rates today are ten times higher than they were in 1960.[3] Every year the age threshold of unhappiness sinks lower, not just at universities but across the nation. Fifty years ago, the mean onset age of depression was 29.5 years old. Today, it is almost exactly half that: 14.5 years old. My friends wanted to know, Why study happiness at Harvard? The question I asked in response was: Why *not* start there?

So I set out to find the students, those 1 in 5 who were truly flourishing—the individuals who were above the curve in terms of their happiness, performance, achievement, productivity, humor, energy, or resilience—to see what exactly was giving them such an advantage over their peers. What was it that allowed these people to escape the gravitational pull of the norm? Could patterns be teased out of their lives and experience to help others in all walks of life to be more successful in an increasingly stressful and negative world? As it turns out, they could.

Scientific discovery is a lot about timing and luck. I serendipitously found three mentors—Harvard professors Phil Stone, Ellen Langer, and Tai Ben-Shahar—who happened to be at the vanguard of a brand new field called positive psychology. Breaking with traditional psychology's focus on what makes people *un*happy and how they can return to "normal," these three were applying the same scientific rigor to what makes people thrive and excel—the very same questions I wanted to answer.

Escaping the Cult of the Average

The graph below may seem boring, but it is the very reason I wake up excited every morning. (Clearly, I live a very exciting life.) It is also the basis of the research underlying this book.

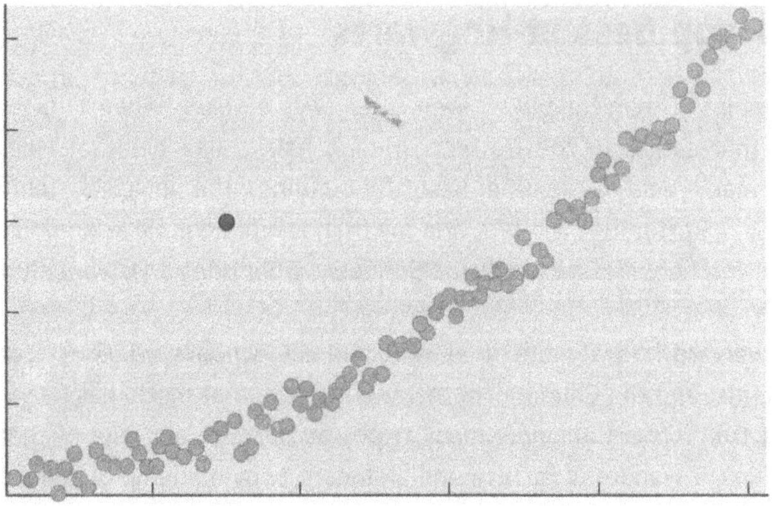

Image 2.2.1

This is a scatter-plot diagram. Each dot represents an individual, and each axis represents some variable. This particular diagram could be plotting anything: weight in relation to height, sleep in relation to energy, happiness in relation to success, and so on. If we got this data back as researchers, we would be thrilled because very clearly there is a trend going on here, and that means that we can get published, which in the academic world is all that really matters. The fact that there is one weird red dot—what we call an outlier—up above the curve is no problem. It's no problem because we can just delete it. We can delete it because it's clearly a measurement error—and we know that it's an error because it's screwing up our data.

One of the very first things students in intro psychology, statistics, or economics courses learn is how to "clean up the data." If you are interested in observing the general trend of what you are researching, then outliers mess up your findings. That's why there exist countless formulas and statistics packages to help enterprising researchers eliminate these "problems." And to be clear, this is not cheating; these are statistically valid procedures—if, that is, one is interested only in the general trend. I am not.

The typical approach to understanding human behavior has always been to look for the average behavior or outcome. But in my view this misguided approach has created what I call the "cult of the average" in the behavioral sciences. If someone asks a question such as "How fast can a child learn how to read in a classroom?" science changes that question to "How fast does the *average* child learn to read in the classroom?" We then ignore the children who read faster or slower, and tailor the classroom toward the "average" child. This is what Tai Ben-Shahar calls "the error of the average." That's the first mistake traditional psychology makes.

If we study merely what is average, we will remain merely average.

Conventional psychology consciously ignores outliers because they don't fit the pattern. I've sought to do the opposite: Instead of deleting these outliers, I want to learn from them. (This concept was originally described by Abraham Maslow as he explains the need to study the growing tip of the curve.)

Too Focused on the Negative

True, there are psychology researchers out there who don't just study what is average. They tend to focus on those who fall only on one side of average—below it. According to Ben-Shahar in *Happier,* this is the second mistake traditional psychology makes. Of course, the people who fall below normal are the ones who tend to need the most help—to be relieved of depression or alcohol abuse or chronic stress. As a result, psychologists understandably have spent considerable effort studying how they can help these people recover and get back to normal. Valuable as such work is, it still only yields half the picture.

You can eliminate depression without making someone happy. You can cure anxiety without teaching someone optimism. You can return someone to work without improving their job performance. If all you strive for is diminishing the bad, you'll only attain the average and you'll miss out entirely on the opportunity to exceed the average.

> You can study gravity forever without learning how to fly.

Extraordinarily, as late as 1998, there was a 17-to-l negative-to-positive ratio of research in the field of psychology. In other words, for every one study about happiness and thriving there were 17 studies on depression and disorder. This is very telling. As a society, we know very well how to be unwell and miserable and so little about how to thrive.

A few years back, one event in particular really drove this home for me. I had been asked to speak at the "Wellness Week" at one of the most elite New England boarding schools. The topics to be discussed: Monday, eating disorders; Tuesday, depression; Wednesday, drugs and violence; Thursday, risky sex; and Friday, who knew? That's not a wellness week; that's a sickness week.

This pattern of focusing on the negative pervades not only our research and schools but our society. Turn on the news, and the majority of airtime is spent on accidents, corruption, murders, abuse. This focus on the negative tricks our brains into believing that this sorry ratio is reality, that most of life is negative. Ever heard of Medical School Syndrome? In the first year of medical school, as students listen to all the diseases and symptoms that can befall a person, many aspiring doctors become suddenly convinced that they have come down with ALL of them. A few years ago, my brother-in-law called me from Yale Medical School and told me that he had "leprosy" (which even at Yale is extremely rare). But I had no idea how to console him because he had just gotten over a week of menopause and was very sensitive. The point is, as we will see throughout this book, what we spend our time and mental energy focusing on can indeed become our reality.

It is not healthy nor scientifically responsible only to study the negative half of human experience. In 1998, Martin Seligman, then president of the American Psychological Association, announced that it was finally time to shift the traditional approach to psychology and start to focus more on the positive side of the curve. That we needed to study what works, not just what is broken. Thus, "positive psychology" was born.

Going Hungry at Harvard

In 2006, Dr. Tai Ben-Shahar asked if I would serve as his head teaching fellow to help design and teach a course called Positive Psychology. Tai was not yet internationally well-known; his best-selling book *Happier* wouldn't be published until the following spring. Under the circumstances, we thought we'd be lucky to lure in a hundred undergraduates brave enough to risk a hit on their transcripts by foregoing a credit in, say, advanced economic theory for one in happiness.

Over the next two semesters, nearly 1,200 Harvard students enrolled in the class—that's one in every six students at one of the most hard-driving universities in the world. We quickly began to realize that these students were there because they were hungry. They were starving to be happier, not sometime in the future, but in the present. And they were there because despite all the advantages they enjoyed, they still felt unfulfilled.

Take a moment to imagine one of these students: By age one, many were lying in their cribs wearing a onesie saying "Bound for Harvard" or maybe a cute little Yale hat (in case something terrible happened). Since they were in pre-pre-kindergarten—which in some cases they were enrolled in even before being conceived—they were in the top 1 percent of their class, and then the top 1 percent of those who took standardized testing along the way. They won awards, they broke records. This kind of high achievement was not just encouraged, it was expected. I know one Harvard student whose mother would keep every handwriting exercise and restaurant placemat drawing he ever did, because "this is going to be in a museum someday." (That was a lot of pressure on me, Mom.)

And then they get into Harvard, walk confidently into that Hogwarts-like freshman dining hall on the first day of college, and have a terrible realization: *50 percent of them are suddenly below average.*

I like to tell my advisees: If my calculations are correct, 99 percent of Harvard students do not graduate in the top 1 percent. They don't find that joke very funny.

With so much pressure to be great, it is no surprise to find that when these kids fall, they fall hard. To make matters worse, this pressure—and the depression that follows—pulls people inward, away from their friends, families, and social supports, at a time when they need the support most. They skip meals, shut themselves in their rooms or the library, emerging only for the occasional kegger (and then in an attempt to blow off steam they get too drunk to even enjoy themselves—or at least remember enjoying themselves). They even seem too busy, too preoccupied, and too stressed to reach out for love. Based on my study of Harvard undergraduates, the average number of romantic relationships over four years is less than one. The average number of sexual partners, if you're curious, is 0.5 per student. (I have no idea what 0.5 sexual partners means, but it sounds like the scientific equivalent of second base.) In my survey, I found that among these brilliant Harvard students, 24 percent are *unaware* if they are currently involved in any romantic relationship.

What was going on here was that like so many people in contemporary society, along the way to gaining their superb educations, and their shiny opportunities, they had absorbed the wrong lessons. They had mastered formulas in calculus and chemistry. They had read great books and learned world history and become fluent in foreign languages. But they had never formally been taught how to maximize their brains' potential or how to find meaning and happiness. Armed with iPhones and personal digital assistants, they had multitasked their way through a storm of resume-building experiences, often at the expense of actual ones. In their pursuit of high achievement, they had isolated themselves from their peers and loved ones and thus compromised the very support systems they so ardently needed. Repeatedly, I noticed these patterns in my own students, who often broke down under the tyranny of expectations we place on ourselves and those around us.

Brilliant people sometimes do the most unintelligent thing possible. In the midst of stress, rather than investing, these individuals *divested* from the greatest predictor of success and happiness: their social support network. Countless studies have found that social relationships are the best guarantee of heightened well-being and lowered stress, both an antidote for depression and a prescription for high performance. But instead, these students had somehow learned that when the going gets tough, the tough get going—to an isolated cubicle in the library basement.

These best and brightest willingly sacrificed happiness for success because, like so many of us, they had been taught that if you work hard you will be successful—and only then, once you are successful, will you be happy. They had been taught that happiness is the reward you get only when you become partner of an investment firm, win the Nobel Prize, or get elected to Congress.

But in fact, as you will learn throughout this book, new research in psychology and neuroscience shows that it works the other way around: We become more successful *when* we are happier and more positive. For example, doctors put in a positive mood before making a diagnosis show almost three times more intelligence and creativity than doctors in a neutral state, and they make accurate diagnoses 19 percent faster. Optimistic salespeople outsell their pessimistic counterparts by 56 percent. Students primed to feel happy before taking math achievement tests far outperform their neutral peers. *It turns out that our brains are literally hardwired to perform at their best not when they are negative or even neutral, but when they are positive.*

Yet in today's world, we ironically sacrifice happiness for success only to lower our brains' success rates. Our hard-driving lives leave us feeling stressed, and we feel swamped by the mounting pressure to succeed at any cost.

Listening to Positive Outliers

The more I studied the research emerging from the field of positive psychology, the more I learned how wrongheaded we are (not just the Harvard students, but all of us) in our beliefs about personal and professional fulfillment. Studies conclusively showed that the quickest way to high achievement is *not* a single-minded concentration on work, and that the best way to motivate employees is *not* to bark orders and foster a stressed and fearful workforce. Instead, radical new research on happiness and optimism were turning both the academic and corporate worlds upside down. I immediately saw an opportunity—I could test these ideas out on my students. I could design a study to see if these new ideas indeed explained why some students were thriving while others succumbed to stress and depression. By studying the patterns and habits of people above the curve, I could glean information about not just how to move us up to average, but how to move the entire average up.

Luckily, I was in a unique position to conduct this research. As a freshman proctor, I'd been blessed for a dozen years with an incredible close-up view of these students—what their habits are, what makes them tick, and what we can learn from their experiences to apply to our own lives. I'd been able to read all the admissions files, see the admissions committee's comments, watch the students progress intellectually and socially, and see what jobs they received after college. I also ended up grading a large percentage of them in the classroom as a teaching fellow for sixteen different courses. To get to know the students beyond just their exams and transcripts, I began meeting with students at my "coffice" in Starbucks to hear their stories. By my calculation, I have sat for more than a half hour individually with over 1,100 Harvard students—enough caffeine to get an entire Olympic team disqualified for decades.

I then took these observations and used them to design and conduct my own empirical survey of 1,600 high achieving undergraduates—one of the largest studies on happiness ever performed on students at Harvard. At the same time, I continued to steep myself in the positive psychology research that was suddenly exploding out of my own institution and out of university laboratories all around the world. The result? Surprising and exciting conclusions about what causes some to rise to the top and thrive in challenging environments while others sink down and never become what they have in them to be. What I found, and what you're about to read, was revealing, not just for Harvard, but for all of us in the working world.

The Seven Principles

Once I'd finished gathering and analyzing this massive amount of research, I was able to isolate seven specific, actionable, and proven patterns that predict success and achievement.

The Happiness Advantage—Because positive brains have a biological advantage over brains that are neutral or negative, this principle teaches us how to retrain our brains to capitalize on positivity and improve our productivity and performance.

The Fulcrum and the Lever—How we experience the world, and our ability to succeed within it, constantly changes based on our mindset. This principle teaches us how we can adjust our mindset (our fulcrum) in a way that gives us the power (the lever) to be more fulfilled and successful.

The Tetris Effect—When our brains get stuck in a pattern that focuses on stress, negativity, and failure, we set ourselves up to fail. This principle teaches us how to retrain our brains to spot patterns of possibility, so we can see—and seize—opportunity wherever we look.

Falling Up—In the midst of defeat, stress, and crisis, our brains map different paths to help us cope. This principle is about finding the mental path that not only leads us up out of failure or suffering, but teaches us to be happier and more successful because of it.

The Zorro Circle—When challenges loom and we get overwhelmed, our rational brains can get hijacked by emotions. This principle teaches us how to regain control by focusing first on small, manageable goals, and then gradually expanding our circle to achieve bigger and bigger ones.

The 20-Second Rule—Sustaining lasting change often feels impossible because our willpower is limited. And when willpower fails, we fall back on our old habits and succumb to the path of least resistance. This principle shows how, by making small energy adjustments, we can reroute the path of least resistance and replace bad habits with good ones.

Social Investment—In the midst of challenges and stress, some people choose to hunker down and retreat within themselves. But the most successful people invest in their friends, peers, and family members to propel themselves forward. This principle teaches us how to invest more in one of the greatest predictors of success and excellence—our social support network.

Together, these Seven Principles helped Harvard students (and later, tens of thousands of people in the "real world") overcome obstacles, reverse bad habits, become more efficient and productive, make the most of opportunities, conquer their most ambitious goals, and reach their fullest potential.

Out of the Ivory Tower

While I loved working with students, what I really wanted was to see if these same principles could also drive happiness and success in the real world. To bridge the gap between academia and business, I formed a small consulting firm, called Aspirant, to deliver and test this research at companies and nonprofit organizations.

A month later, the global economy began to collapse.

References

Kaplan, K. A. (January 12, 2004). College faces mental health crisis. *The Harvard Crimson.*
U.S. Job Satisfaction at lowest level in two decades. (January 5, 2010). *The Conference Board.*
Seligman, M. E. P. (2002). *Authentic Happiness.* New York: Free Press, at 117.

Notes

1. Kaplan, K. A. (January 12, 2004). College faces mental health crisis. *The Harvard Crimson.*
2. U.S. Job Satisfaction at lowest level in two decades. (January 5, 2010). *The Conference Board.*
3. Seligman, M.E.P. (2002). *Authentic Happiness.* New York: Free Press, at 117.

The Basics About Emotions in Business

Richard M. Contino and Penelope J. Holt

Richard M. Contino and Penelope J. Holt, "The Basics About Emotions in Business," *Emotional Intelligence at Work: A Personal Operating System for Career Success*, pp. 19-25.

The Powerful Role Emotions Play in Business

We're all driven in our personal lives, sometimes unknowingly, uncontrollably and irrationally, by our emotional needs. The same is true in our business lives. If you're in business and cannot see the powerful grip that emotions, particularly destructive or nonproductive ones, have on everyone around you, including yourself, then lost income, lost opportunity, and lack of progress are guaranteed.

Unhealthy emotional needs drive a whole range of counterproductive behaviors from people who might:

- Impulsively quit jobs;
- Kill business deals;
- Chronically miss deadlines;
- Show up late for work;
- Fail to return phone calls;
- Become argumentative;
- Refuse overtime;
- Renege on promises;
- Dominate meetings;

- Criticize others; and
- Talk too much.

And the list goes on.

BEQ Case Study: An Inability to Listen

Jeremy was an expert business strategist. More than that, he was typically the hardest-working person on any team he joined. He unfailingly crunched data and thought long and hard about how to design effective solutions. But Jeremy had a fatal flaw that almost killed his career: he was incapable of really listening to others. In almost every meeting, Jeremy interrupted and stepped on others when they spoke, seemingly oblivious to their contributions.

Colleagues could see in his eyes that Jeremy was barely listening to them, no matter how qualified or senior they might be. He was simply waiting for his chance to speak again, and the sooner the better. Some saw his behavior as arrogance. Others saw it as anxiety. Jeremy seemed so eager to share the valuable content he had worked hard to develop that he literally couldn't take in what others were saying. The outcome of this bad habit was always the same: Although Jeremy was smart, others felt disrespected by him, and few managed to develop a productive rapport with him, aside from leveraging his necessary input for a given project.

Throughout his career, numerous bosses gave Jeremy important feedback on changing his bad habit. And later, after he went into business for himself, clients and associates delivered the same message. "For heaven's sake, can you stop interrupting and let someone else speak?" one client scolded Jeremy during a tense conference call. Jeremy was momentarily silent, but soon returned to his familiar ways.

An overriding impulse to talk and not adequately listen hurt Jeremy in business, costing him relationships and revenue. But Jeremy was either unwilling or unable to change. Dominating every conversation and meeting, as though he were the smartest and most worthy person involved, remained Jeremy's primary driver and need, no matter the cost to his professional well-being or bank account.

Ringing any bells? Starting to recognize the stranglehold that counterproductive motivations might have?

A Ground Floor Insight

The need for big a pay-day, power, attention, the spotlight, recognition, and control, all acted out in the business arena, are driven by emotional needs. Think about it. And if you find yourself continually losing to other people's office politics, or emotionally manipulative business tactics, you're not applying BEQ correctly. Unfortunately, in business, the statement "Nice guys finish last" is often true, in a sense. It really should be "Unaware guys finish last."

BEQ Awareness Challenge: Often business or staff meetings run according to a published agenda, and most of us tend to assume that all participants are there to follow this agenda. The next time you attend a meeting, stop and ask yourself if you have any underlying or hidden motivations: perhaps to be noticed by a supervisor? To get even with a colleague who undermined you? To make sure you get rightful credit for an idea that is working well, but few are aware you initiated.

How about other attendees? Go around the room and silently try to guess what each person is preoccupied with, or might be trying to accomplish in terms of a personal agenda. It matters little whether your guesses are right or wrong. What counts is that you challenge your assumptions and prescribed thinking to understand that business objectives always sit side by side with the emotional needs of the people involved in achieving them.

Managing Your Process

Reaching your business goals, whether negotiating a deal, setting up a branding strategy, building a business, or getting promoted, requires recognizing the emotional undercurrents at play within the people and situations you encounter. And you must assess and manage your own emotional process, making sure you unblock yourself by removing the filters, received opinions, attitudes, and incorrect beliefs about business that have been passed on to you and which often contradict real-world experience. Learning to view yourself and others more honestly, despite built-in resistance, demonstrates high BEQ.

There is no surefire way to change the emotionally driven actions of people who may be thwarting you. Confronting their bad behavior will not be met with open arms or even acknowledged. The hard truth is that you can change only how you think and how you act. Think of business as a card game. If you suspect someone is cheating, you have only two choices: get out of the game, or play absolutely no-holds-barred, within the limits of your personal integrity, to win.

BEQ Case Study: Fear of Being Honest

Robert was head of finance at a struggling mid-sized distributor of medical equipment. After the turnover of two CEOs in just two years, the company's board hired yet another CEO, on a three-month trial, to make sure the fit was right. "I trust your feedback," the board sponsor told Robert. "If you think this guy is a bad match, I want you to tell me before we convert him to the permanent CEO role."

John, the new CEO, was talented, but displayed a thinly veiled ego that was more about command and control than respecting and nurturing the management team he had joined. This egotism and several other traits did not sit well with Robert, but he felt guilty for holding such a negative opinion of the new CEO. It's a tough job, Robert thought. I should cut the guy some slack as he tries to get the company back on the right track.

Even though he felt uneasy, Robert gave the thumbs up on John's permanent appointment to CEO, when the board asked him for his final verdict and feedback. No sooner was the ink dry on John's permanent contract than he threw off the façade of agreeableness and revealed himself to be the self-dealing tyrant his previous behavior had suggested. Within six months, Robert and several other key managers had their resumes out, seeking new positions.

Robert mentally reviewed the last few months. If he were honest with himself, he could see that he had correctly read the writing on the wall in strongly suspecting that John was not an effective leader. But he had been unwilling or unable to trust his instincts and be brutally honest in his feedback to the board. Robert had wanted to be "fair" to John, who in turn showed himself to be ruthless and self-serving.

The Challenge of Hidden Emotions

Identifying and acknowledging hidden emotional motivations or unhelpful tendencies is hard and sometimes painful. In the beginning, it takes a persistent effort.

BEQ Awareness Challenge: We are seldom awake or brave enough to confront the true motivations and games being played by those around us. Neither are we fully aware of our own unconscious needs, which often includes acting out what we, like Robert in the previous example, mistakenly think we should be doing in business, versus what is actually in the best interests of ourselves and others.

Most of us want to avoid disappointment at all costs, and yet we may find ourselves expecting or bracing for it. Unconsciously anticipating disappointment or failure distracts us from focusing single mindedly on achieving success. A tendency to hedge can undermine our efforts and rob us of victory.

A solution: Where possible, adopt the absolute conviction that you will succeed. If you can't do this, at least try to remain relaxed, curious and open minded, rather than fearful and negative, about potential outcomes. Embrace fearlessness as a way to stay open to new paths and possibilities, even the ones that intimidate you. As Eleanor Roosevelt famously advised, "Do one thing every day that scares you."

One successful real estate entrepreneur shared his approach to acting boldly and decisively:

> Every day, I build my fear muscle. I take well calculated risks that often feel too big and daring and outside my comfort zone. Nevertheless, I strive to remain convinced that any new deal will work out. If I can't sustain optimism, I at least try to adopt an attitude of curiosity instead of fear or dread. Being curious, instead of worrying, is how I keep at bay the anxiety that would otherwise stop me from taking action and making progress. If a project fails, at least I get to learn an important lesson about what does or does not work.

Why We Turn a Blind Eye to Destructive Emotional Issues

Facing the truth about hidden agendas is not only uncomfortable, but it can also even be frightening, particularly when our financial security is at stake. All of us know it's virtually impossible to deal with an irrational person, so is it any wonder that we want to look away from those who are irrational, when our livelihood or well-being is in some way dependent on what they do and how they act. And what about when we are being irrational and getting in our own way?

The party line that emotions have no place in business is self-serving denial. Who, after all, wants to admit that hard work, common sense, talent, and logic may not be enough to guarantee success? But it's undeniable that those driven by emotion and ego needs over reason often control a deal, a department, or even the whole show. Take Mr. Doomsday for example.

Doomsday Thinkers

Have you ever worked with someone who continually criticizes everyone and everything? Or been in a meeting where someone, let's call him Mr. Doomsday, finds endless reasons why a solid new business idea won't work? If so, did you notice how these negative types often succeed in killing a viable idea or bringing the business discussion to an absolute and frustrating halt? More importantly, did you wonder why such people are allowed to push their negative views and get away with it, because others typically don't push back? The answer is that negative players often infect groupthink.

It's difficult to remain optimistic and open minded in the face of relentless skepticism and negativity. Teams sense that when there is not universal commitment to making an idea work, it will fail. Another version of this is when those team players, who do not support an idea, only pay lip service to implementing it in meetings, while actively undermining the strategy in their ongoing efforts.

Several years ago, the *Harvard Business Review* cited this behavior of playing along, without sincere effort and commitment, as a key indicator of business failure: Teams might appear to reach consensus and commit to implementing a business strategy, only to have it fail, because skeptical, resentful, or negative team members don't back up their reluctant agreement with the effort required for success. In fact, they often work secretly to sabotage teamwork and undermine those who champion the project.

So what motivates the doomsday types? Sometimes they may genuinely disagree with the consensus opinion or the validity of a business idea. In other instances, a Mr. Doomsday is anxiety ridden, cripplingly risk-averse, and afraid of failure. It's easier to shoot down a viable idea than to live with the persistent worry that it might fail. The doomsday types may look good on paper, with the right education and resume, but in reality, they hobble their own career prospects and stymie the hard chargers around them.

Another reason we may be reluctant to call out another's negative behavior is that they are doing our dirty work for us. Maybe we too are afraid of failure, and so it is easy to hide behind the person who speaks up and voices the doubts and fear we secretly harbor. Now we have a partner in the crime of not trying or risking. We don't have to question our own fear of failure. We can take refuge in other doomsday complainers, who are sure that a good idea won't work. Congratulations! That's one more business risk or opportunity to succeed that you don't have to take up!

A Reader's Guide to Using These Ideas

Selection from *Smarter Faster Better: The Transformative Power of Real Productivity*

Charles Duhigg

Charles Duhigg, "Appendix: A Reader's Guide to Using These Ideas," *Smarter Faster Better: The Transformative Power of Real Productivity*, pp. 269-286.

A few months after I reached out to Atul Gawande—the author and physician from the introduction who helped spark my interest in the science of productivity—I began reporting this book. For almost two years, I conducted interviews with experts, read piles of scientific papers, and tracked down case studies. At some point, I began to imagine that I had become something of a productivity expert myself. When it came time to start writing, I figured, translating all those ideas onto paper would be relatively easy. The words would fly from my fingertips.

That is not what happened.

Some days I would sit at my desk and spend hours jumping from website to website looking for new studies to read, then organize my notes. I would get onto airplanes, my carry-on bag stuffed with scientific papers I intended to read, and spend the flight returning emails, writing to-do lists, and ignoring the big, important tasks I needed to complete.

I had a goal in mind—I wanted to write a book about how we can apply these discoveries in productivity to our own lives—but it seemed so far off, so overwhelming, that I kept focusing on easier-to-accomplish objectives. A few months went by, and all I had to show for it was a series of outlines, but no chapters.

"I feel like a failure," I wrote my editor during one particularly dispiriting moment. "I don't know what I'm doing wrong."

When he wrote back, he pointed out the obvious: Maybe I needed to take what I was learning from the experts and apply it to my own life. I had to live by the principles described in this book.

Motivation

One of my hardest challenges, for instance, concerned my motivation, which seemed to flag at exactly the wrong times. While I was working on this book, I was still also a reporter at *The New York Times*. What's more, I was out promoting my previous book, and trying to be a good father and husband. In other words, I was exhausted. After a long day at the *Times,* I would come home and need to start typing up notes, or draft a chapter, or help put my kids to bed, or clean up the dishes, or reply to emails—and I'd find that self-motivation was in short supply. Emails, in particular, were a small form of daily torture. My in-box was constantly stuffed with questions from colleagues, queries from other authors, correspondence from researchers whom I hoped to interview, and other miscellaneous questions that required a thoughtful response.

However, all I wanted to do was watch TV.

As I struggled each night to find the drive to reply to emails, I began thinking about the key insight from chapter one and the ideas that Gen. Charles Krulak used to redesign Marine Corps boot camp by strengthening recruits' internal locus of control:

- Motivation becomes easier when we transform a chore into a choice. Doing so gives us a sense of control.

On any given day, for instance, I had—let's say—at least about fifty emails that needed responses. Every evening, I would resolve to sit down at my computer and deal with them as soon as dinner was over. And, every evening, I would find ways to procrastinate—by reading the kids one more story, or cleaning up the living room, or checking Facebook—in order to avoid the drudgery of typing response after response. Or, I would sweep through my in-box, hitting the reply key again and again, and then, confronted with a screen full of responses awaiting my words, feel overwhelmed.

General Krulak had told me something that stuck with me: "Most recruits don't know how to force themselves to start something hard. But if we can train them to take the first step by doing something that makes them feel in charge, it's easier to keep going."

I realized that Krulak's insight could help me motivate. And so one night, after putting the kids to bed, I sat at my laptop and hit the reply button, creating a series of responses. Then, as fast as I could, I typed a sentence within each email—any sentence at all—to get me going. For instance, a co-worker sent a note asking if I could join him at a meeting. I had put off replying because I didn't want to attend. I knew the meeting would be long and boring. But I couldn't completely ignore him. So I wrote one sentence in my response:

I can attend, but I'll need to leave after twenty minutes.

I went through two dozen replies just like that, writing a short sentence in each one, hardly thinking about it. And then, I went back and filled in the rest of each email:

Hey Jim,

Sure, I can attend, but I'll need to leave after twenty minutes.

I hope that's okay.

Thanks,

Charles

I noticed two things: First, it was much easier to reply to an email once I had at least one sentence on the screen. Second, and more important, it was easier to get motivated when that first sentence was something that made me feel in control. When I told Jim that I could only stay for twenty minutes, it reminded me that I didn't have to commit to his project if I didn't want to. When I drafted a reply to someone asking me to come speak at a conference, I began by typing:

I would like to leave on Tuesday and be back in New York by Thursday night.

Which reinforced that I was in control of whether I attended or not.

Put differently, as I typed a series of short replies, each reminded me that I was in control of the choices being put before me. (As a psychologist might say, I used those sentences to amplify my internal locus of control.) Within thirty-five minutes, I had cleared out my in-box.

But what about other kinds of procrastination? What about when you're confronting a bigger, more involved task, like writing a long memo or having a hard conversation with a colleague? What if there isn't an easy way to prove to yourself that you're in control? For those, I remember the other key lesson from the motivation chapter:

- Self-motivation becomes easier when we see our choices as affirmations of our deeper values and goals.

That's why Marine Corps recruits ask each other "why": "Why are you climbing this mountain?", "Why are you missing the birth of your daughter?", "Why are you cleaning a mess hall, or doing push-ups, or running onto a battlefield when there are safer, easier ways to live?" Forcing ourselves to explain *why* we are doing something helps us remember that this chore is a step along a longer path, and that by choosing to take that journey, we are getting closer to more meaningful objectives.

To motivate myself to read studies on airplanes, for instance, I began writing at the top of each manuscript *why* it was important for me to get that task done. When I pulled a study out of my bag, then, it became a little easier to dive in. Something as simple as jotting down a couple of reasons *why* I am doing something makes it much simpler to start.

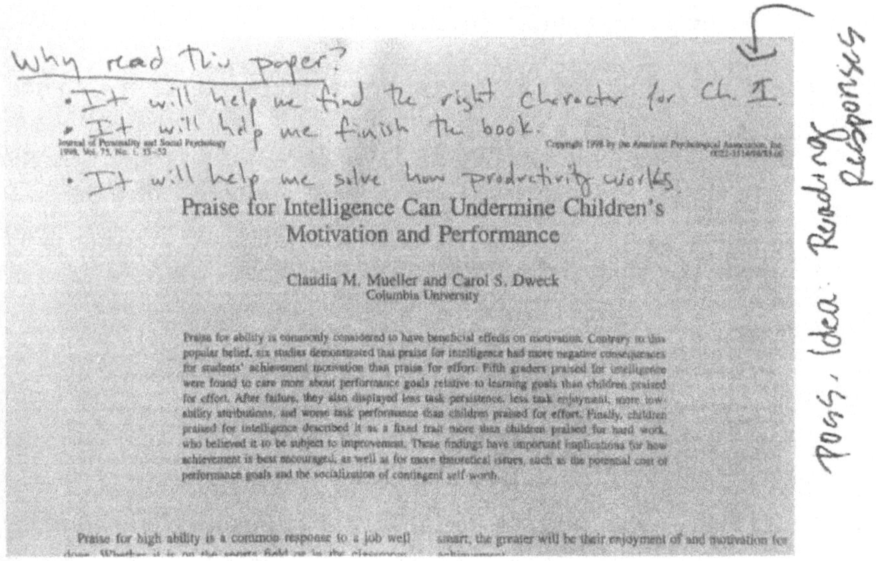

Why read this paper?
- It will help me find the right character for Ch. I.
- It will help me finish the book.
- It will help me solve how productivity works.

Reading Responses

Posts: Idea

Journal of Personality and Social Psychology
1998, Vol. 75, No. 1, 33–52

Copyright 1998 by the American Psychological Association, Inc.

Praise for Intelligence Can Undermine Children's Motivation and Performance

Claudia M. Mueller and Carol S. Dweck
Columbia University

Praise for ability is commonly considered to have beneficial effects on motivation. Contrary to this popular belief, six studies demonstrated that praise for intelligence had more negative consequences for students' achievement motivation than praise for effort. Fifth graders praised for intelligence were found to care more about performance goals relative to learning goals than children praised for effort. After failure, they also displayed less task persistence, less task enjoyment, more low-ability attributions, and worse task performance than children praised for effort. Finally, children praised for intelligence described it as a fixed trait more than children praised for hard work, who believed it to be subject to improvement. These findings have important implications for how achievement is best encouraged, as well as for more theoretical issues, such as the potential cost of performance goals and the socialization of contingent self-worth.

Praise for high ability is a common response to a job well ... smart, the greater will be their enjoyment of and motivation for ...

Image 2.4.1

Motivation is triggered by making choices that demonstrate (to ourselves) that we are in control—and that we are moving toward goals that are meaningful. It's that feeling of self-determination that gets us going.

To Generate Motivation

- Make a choice that puts you in control. If you're replying to emails, write an initial sentence that expresses an opinion or decision. If you need to have a hard conversation, decide where it will occur ahead of time. The specific choice itself matters less in sparking motivation than the assertion of control.
- Figure out how this task is connected to something you care about. Explain to yourself why this chore will help you get closer to a meaningful goal. Explain *why* this matters—and then, you'll find it easier to start.

Goal Setting

Simply figuring out how to motivate myself wasn't always enough, however. Writing a book is a big goal—too big, in many ways, to grasp the entirety of it at first. In trying to figure out how to wrap my head around the objective, I was helped enormously by the reporting I conducted regarding goal setting. The big takeaway was that I needed two kinds of aims:

- needed a stretch goal, something to spark big ambitions.
- *AND* I needed a SMART goal, to help me form a concrete plan.

One of the most effective ways to formulate both objectives, experts told me, is through a specific kind of to-do list. I needed to write out my goals—but in a way that forced me to identify my stretch objectives and my SMART aims. So I began writing to-do lists, and at the top of each one, I wrote my overarching ambition, what I was working toward in the long term. (That helped me avoid the need for cognitive closure that can force us to become obsessed with short-term, easy-to-achieve goals.) And then underneath, I described a subgoal and all its SMART components, which forged me to come up with a plan—which, in turn, made it more likely that all my goals would be achieved.

One of my stretch goals in reporting this book, for instance, was to find a story that illustrated how mental models worked. I knew that aviation experts felt that mental models played an important role in how pilots responded to emergencies, and so, at the top of my to-do list for this chapter, I wrote:

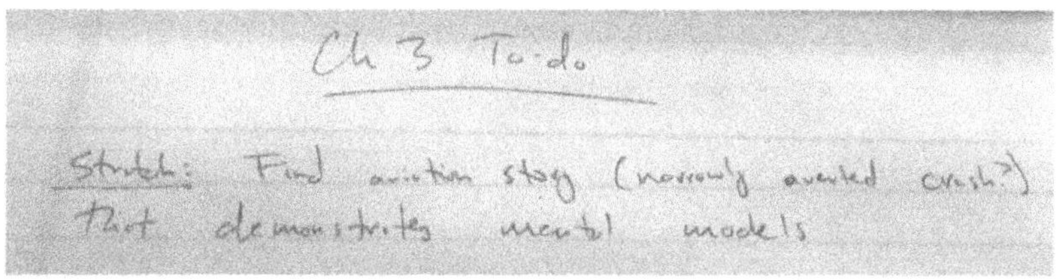

Image 2.4.2

Then, below that stretch goal, I wrote my SMART goals related to that big ambition:

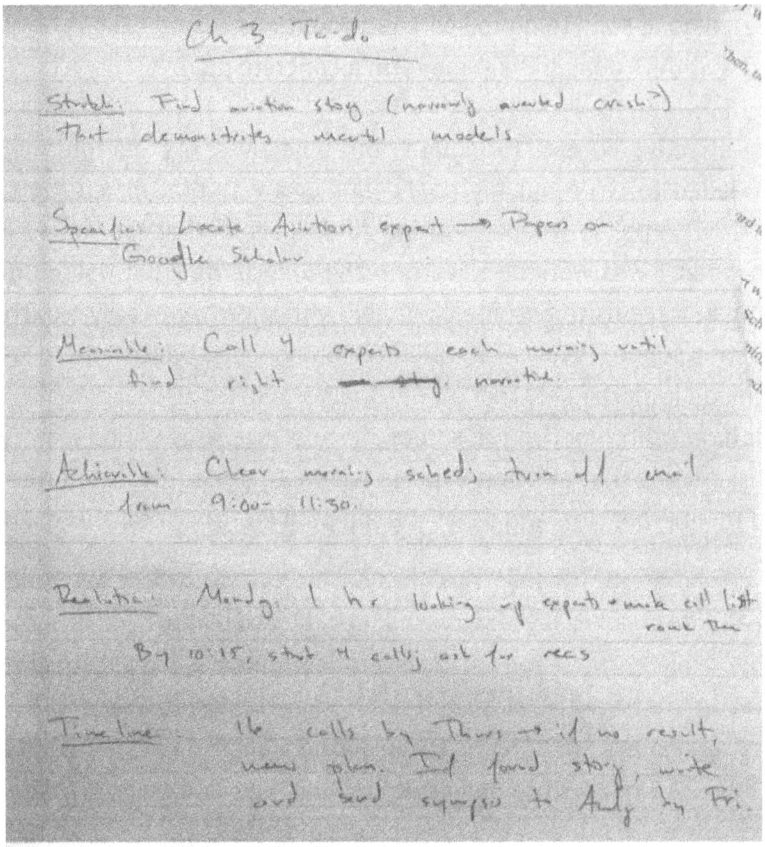

Image 2.4.3

In case that's hard to read, here's what I wrote:

Stretch: Find an aviation story (a narrowly averted crash?) that demonstrates mental models.

Specific: Locate an aviation expert by researching academic papers on Google Scholar.

Measurable: Call four experts each morning until I find the right person/story.

Achievable: Clear my morning schedule to focus on this task, and turn off email from 9:00 to 11:30.

Realistic: On Monday, spend an hour researching aviation experts and creating a call list; rank those experts and, by 10:15, begin my four calls of the day. At the end of each conversation, ask them to recommend other experts to call.

Timeline: If I do four calls a day, then I should have made at least sixteen calls by Thursday. If I haven't found the perfect story by Thursday, I'll come up with a new plan. If I *do* find the right story, I'll send a synopsis to my editor on Friday.

It took only a few minutes to jot down these stretch and SMART goals—but it made a huge difference in how much I got done that week. Now I create a similar to-do list for every big task—and as a result, I know exactly what to do when I sit at my desk each morning. Instead of having to make decisions—and running the risks of distraction—I have a clear sense of how to proceed.

In addition, because I'm always being reminded of my stretch goal, I don't get easily sidetracked, or captured by the need to simply check things off of my list. As scientists might say, I've muted my craving for cognitive closure. I don't stop working merely because I had a good interview, or because I found a helpful study, or because I found an interesting narrative that *might* go in the book. Instead, I'm always reminded that I'm chasing SMART goals for a bigger reason: to find the perfect story, or finish a chapter, or write a book. In fact, I have a whole series of stretch goals to remind me of my grander ambitions:

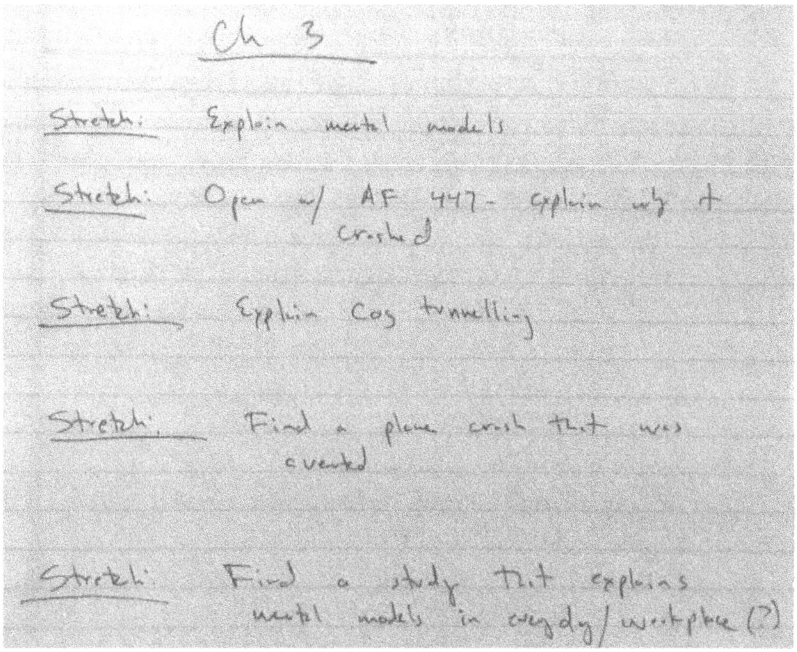

Image 2.4.4

To Set Goals:

- Choose a stretch goal: an ambition that reflects your biggest aspirations.
- Then, break that into subgoals and develop SMART objectives.

Focus

This being real life, however, there are always distractions and other demands competing for my attention. And so, in addition to having a plan, I needed to work on maintaining my focus. There's a key insight from the chapter about the averted aviation disaster of Qantas Flight 32 that I have tried to keep in mind:

- We aid our focus by building mental models—telling ourselves stories—about what we *expect* to see.

To make sure I stayed focused on my stretch and SMART goals, I had to envision what I *expected* to happen when I sat down at my desk each morning. And so, every Sunday night, I got into a habit of taking a few moments with a pad and pen to imagine what the next day and week *ought* to look like. I usually chose three or four things I wanted to make sure happened, and made myself answer a series of questions:

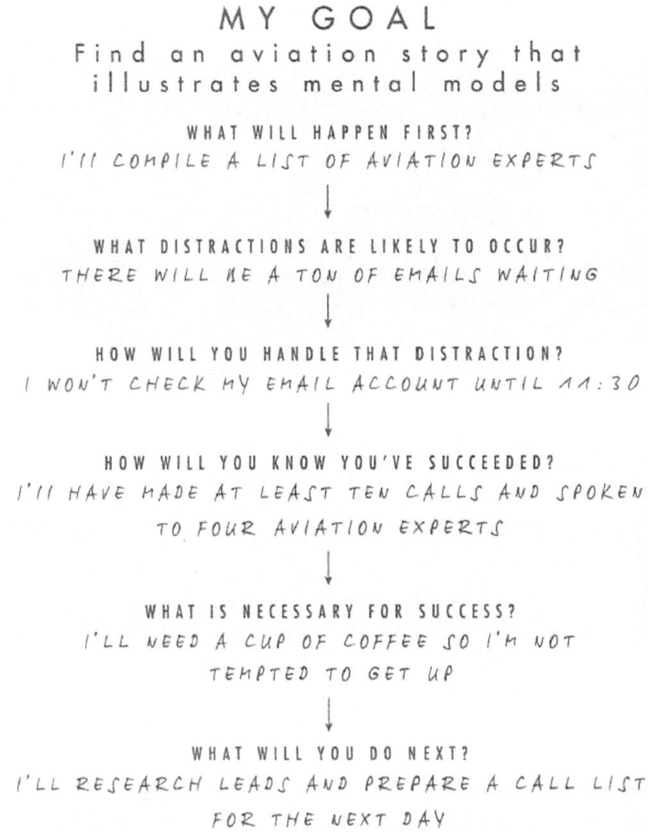

Image 2.4.5

It typically takes only a few minutes to envision what I hope will occur. But by the end of this exercise, I have a story in my mind—a mental model of how my morning should proceed—and, as a result, when distractions inevitably arise, it's easier to decide, in the moment, whether they deserve my focus or can be ignored.

If my email account says there are thirty new messages, I know that I should ignore them until 11:30, because that's what the story inside my head tells me to do. If the phone rings and caller ID indicates it's an expert I'm trying to contact, I'll take the call, because that interruption has a place within my mental model.

I have a stretch goal and a SMART goal that give me a plan—and a picture inside my head of how that plan is supposed to unfold, so making the choices that shape focus is much easier.

To Stay Focused:

- Envision what will happen. What will occur first? What are potential obstacles? How will you preempt them? Telling yourself a story about what you *expect* to occur makes it easier to decide where your focus should go when your plan encounters real life.

Decision Making

I had worked on coming up with stretch goals and SMART objectives. I had a mental model to stay focused. I had found ways to improve my motivation. Despite all that, however, every so often something came along that would blow my well-crafted intentions apart. Sometimes it was small, like my wife asking if I wanted to get lunch together. Sometimes it was big, like an editor asking me to take on an exciting, but unplanned, assignment.

So how should I make a decision when confronted with the unexpected? Perhaps there was a valuable insight in the chapter on probabilistic thinking:

- Envision multiple futures, and then force myself to figure out which ones are most likely—and why.

For a simple decision like whether I should meet my wife for lunch, the calculus is easy: In one potential future, I take an hour for lunch and come back happy and relaxed. In another, lunch goes long and we spend most of it discussing family logistics and babysitter problems, and when I get back to my desk I'm fried—and behind schedule.

By thinking through potential futures, I was better prepared to influence which of those futures would actually occur. When choosing a restaurant to meet my wife, for instance, I suggested one close to my office so I could make it back to my desk quickly. When family logistics came up during lunch, I asked my wife to wait until that evening to talk calendars. By anticipating the future, I was better prepared to make wiser decisions.

But bigger decisions—such as whether to take on an exciting new writing assignment—require a bit more analysis. Midway through writing this book, for instance, a production company asked if I was interested in developing a TV show. To decide if I should pursue that opportunity—which would delay my reporting, but might pay off in the long run—I wrote out a few potential futures of what might happen if I worked on writing a show:

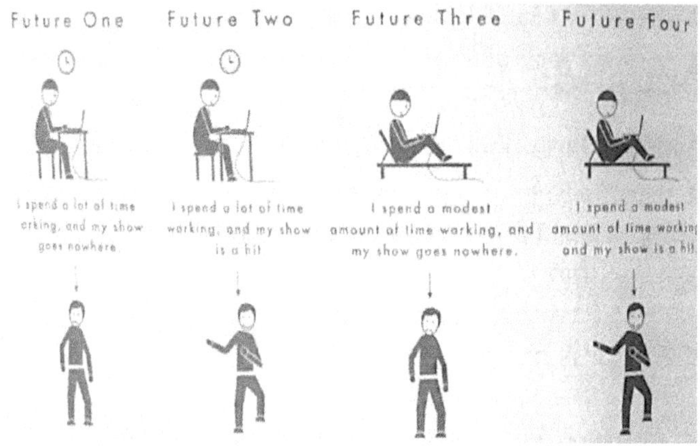

Image 2.4.6

I had no idea how to evaluate these potential futures. I knew there were dozens of other possibilities I should be considering but couldn't anticipate. And so I called some friends in television. Based on those conversations, I assigned each scenario a rough probability:

Image 2.4.7

Based on the estimations of professionals, it seemed most possible that if I invested a lot of time, it wasn't likely to pay off. But if I invested a modest amount of time, there was a likelihood I would learn something, if nothing else.

At that point, I wanted to let my Bayesian instincts guide me, and so I spent a few days letting my imagination play with various outcomes. In the end, I decided that there was another potential future I was ignoring: That even if this show never materialized, I might have a lot of fun. So I decided to commit—but I specified, up front, that I wanted my participation to be modest.

It was a great decision. All told, my involvement in the project was small—probably the equivalent of two weeks. But the payoffs have exceeded my expectations. The show will premiere this fall and I've learned a lot working on it.

What's most important, however, is that I made this decision in a deliberate way. Because I had anticipated various possibilities about what might occur—and, in fact, had drawn up some stretch and SMART goals before joining the project—I was able to manage my involvement.

To Make Better Decisions:

- Envision multiple futures. By pushing yourself to imagine various possibilities—some of which might be contradictory—you're better equipped to make wise choices.
- We can hone our Bayesian instincts by seeking out different experiences, perspectives, and other people's ideas. By finding information and then letting ourselves sit with it, options become clearer.

The Big Idea

This appendix offers a quick overview of a few key concepts that have been meaningful in my own day-to-day life. If you can become more motivated, more focused, better at setting goals and making good decisions, then you're a long way down the path to becoming more productive. There are, of course, other ideas in this book that also help when we are managing other people, when we are trying to learn faster, when we need to innovate faster. Each of those areas of productivity have their own insights, as well:

To Make Teams More Effective:

- Manage the *how,* not the *who* of teams. Psychological safety emerges when everyone feels like they can speak in roughly equal measure and when teammates show they are sensitive to how each other feel.
- If you are leading a team, think about the message your choices reveal. Are you encouraging equality in speaking, or rewarding the loudest people? Are you showing you are listening by repeating what people say and replying to questions and thoughts? Are you demonstrating sensitivity by reacting when someone seems upset or flustered? Are you showcasing that sensitivity, so other people will follow your lead?

To Manage Others Productively:

- Lean and agile management techniques tell us employees work smarter and better when they believe they have more decision-making authority and when they believe their colleagues are committed to their success.
- By pushing decision making to whoever is closest to a problem, managers take advantage of everyone's expertise and unlock innovation.

- A sense of control can fuel motivation, but for that drive to produce insights and solutions, people need to know their suggestions won't be ignored and that their mistakes won't be held against them.

To Encourage Innovation:

- Creativity often emerges by combining old ideas in new ways—and "innovation brokers" are key. To become a broker yourself and encourage brokerage within your organization:
- Be sensitive to your own experiences. Paying attention to how things make you think and feel is how we distinguish clichés from real insights. Study your own emotional reactions.
- Recognize that the stress that emerges amid the creative process isn't a sign everything is falling apart. Rather, creative desperation is often critical: Anxiety can be what often pushes us to see old ideas in new ways.
- Finally, remember that the relief accompanying a creative breakthrough, while sweet, can also blind us to alternatives. By forcing ourselves to critique what we've already done, by making ourselves look at it from different perspectives, by giving new authority to someone who didn't have it before, we retain clear eyes.

To Absorb Data Better:

- When we encounter new information, we should force ourselves to *do something* with it. Write yourself a note explaining what you just learned, or figure out a small way to test an idea, or graph a series of data points onto a piece of paper, or force yourself to explain an idea to a friend. Every choice we make in life is an experiment—the trick is getting ourselves to see the data embedded in those decisions, and then to use it somehow so we learn from it.

What's most important, throughout all these concepts, is the foundational idea undergirding these lessons, the tissue that connects the eight insights at the heart of this book: Productivity is about recognizing choices that other people often overlook. It's about making certain decisions in certain ways. The way we choose to see our own lives; the stories we tell ourselves, and the goals we push ourselves to spell out in detail; the culture we establish amount teammates; the ways we frame our choices and manage the information in our lives. Productive people and companies force themselves to make choices most other people are content to ignore Productivity emerges when people push themselves to think differently.

When I was working on this book, I came upon a story that I loved, one of my favorite bits of reporting. The tale involved Malcom McLean, the man who essentially created the modem shipping container. McLean died in 2001, but he left behind videotapes and numerous records, and I spent months reading about him, as well as interviewing members of his family and dozens of his former colleagues. They described a man who had relentlessly chased an idea—that shipping goods inside of big metal boxes would make docks more productive—and how that insight eventually transformed manufacturing, the transportation industry, and the economies of whole continents. They explained that McLean was so productive because he was fanatically obsessed with a single idea.

I devoted many, many hours to learning about McLean. I wrote several drafts of his story, determined to fit it into this book.

In the end, however, none of them worked. The lesson he offered—that a single-minded devotion to an idea can spur massive change—turned out not to be as universal and important as the other concepts I wanted to explain. McLean's story was interesting but not vital. What worked for him doesn't work for everyone. There're lots of examples where fanatical devotion has backfired. His insight wasn't big enough to be included among the other eight ideas in this book.

And yet the time I spent researching McLean was worth it, because discarding that work helped me understand the mechanics of focus. My mental model of this book kept conflicting with what I was learning about McLean. My SMART plan for the McLean story didn't match up with my stretch goal of describing universally applicable lessons. In other words, researching McLean helped me figure out what this book was *supposed* to be about. It served as a valuable reminder of how productivity actually functions: Productivity doesn't mean that every action is efficient, it doesn't mean that waste never occurs. In fact, as Disney learned, sometimes you have to foster tension to encourage creativity. Sometimes a misstep is the most important footfall along the path to success.

But in the end, if you learn how to recognize certain choices that, to many, might not be obvious, then you can become smarter, faster, and better over time. Anyone can become more creative, more focused, better at framing their goals and making wise decisions. Schools can be transformed by changing how people absorb data. Teams can be taught how to learn more from mistakes, or use tension to their advantage, or make what seems like misspent hours into lessons getting them closer to their goals. Schools can be remade by empowering the people closest to a problem. The lives of senior citizens can be remade by teaching them to become subversives.

We can all become more productive. Now you know how to start.

Unit III

History and Philosophy

History

> *"The work of today is the history of tomorrow, and we are its makers."*
>
> —Juliette Gordon Law

The backbone of an organization is found in its story—the story of the business itself as well as that of the people who have made the business what it is today. Regardless of lifespan, an understanding of the history of a business is central to analysis. The most effective historical analysis incorporates social elements with hard data, thus making it a social history. Correspondingly, a large picture of events beyond reports and statistics provides insight into what makes an organization tick. This is accomplished with historical analysis, using concrete methodology in theoretical development. It is a multifaceted approach using both primary and secondary documents and, when possible, oral histories. Effective historiography draws from a wide range of sources to form an overarching understanding of the business from a perspective beyond documented technical procedures. The viewpoints of employees, ordinary consumers, and other stakeholders inform the analysis, thus making it a history of people.[1] Social history establishes the context, background, relevant players, and implications of corporate practice in historical analysis.[2]

Two basic categories are used as references in historical research. First, secondary sources are taken from formal or official documentation related to an organization's practices and procedures. In our information age, these are often easily accessible. On the other hand, primary sources, the second category, come directly from specific participants and are more difficult to obtain. These sources provide personal perspectives of events and may be found in personal notes, diaries, and so forth, or from oral histories based on interviews of participants.[3] Social roles and ideologies are not necessarily consistent with lived behavior, so a behind-the-scenes aspect of events fills in the gaps.[4] Ideally, both primary and secondary sources are used to paint a more comprehensive picture of the past. For example, in economic history, economic processes can best be understood by systematically comparing experiences across time, regions, and countries. The investigation, then, becomes a comparative economic history, taking into account the impact of environment on people. A shift toward this methodology is inevitable in our information age, with the vast amount of data now available to cover a wide range of experience.[5] Researchers who look beyond the surface of official records are able to address the impact or relevance of the contents of the documents when the lives of the players are connected to the writing.

Regardless of the types of sources used, historians take care to draw sound inferences using solid research, and they take into account events and behaviors beyond their particular subject during the time period in question to establish causal relationships.[6] In particular, historians need to view the past through the lens of the people who lived the experience, to gain appropriate perspective through empathetic consideration that reaches beyond the personal biases of researchers.[7] Further, contextual and interpretational investigations of the past provide insight into the character and practices of institutions and organizations.[8] Motivations, biases, and other issues that lurk beneath the surface are integral to historiography—beyond the obvious.[9] For instance, questions that target power relationships and legitimate forms of knowledge, such as rationale for pay increases, who benefitted from certain policy changes, the long-term implications of certain business practices for particular employees, and so forth, provide critical insight for the historian's investigation.[10] The analysis of complex phenomena helps us to develop a rich understanding of the past and better enables us to predict future trends.[11]

Theoretical development hinges on the traceability of rationale, particularly in terms of validity, reliability, credibility, sample, and transferability.[12] Even so, continuity and the lack of uniformity among historical findings is inevitable due to the subjectivity of researchers.[13] Historians need to be aware of the influence that they carry in analysis because a key part of an inquiry, inference, is shaped by their interpretation. For that reason, as many resources as possible need to be examined to create the best possible picture. As an example, the analysis of a bootlegger's notes during the Great Depression of the 1930s would need to be considered against the backdrop of economic and social events of the time, as well as other people and groups involved in the line of distribution. Also, the authenticity of written primary sources must be verifiable. Similarly, oral histories must be collected from viable and relevant sources. Biographical techniques assist situation-specific understanding.

Historical analysis is done through either situational *reconstruction* or *deconstruction* of an event. With reconstruction, facts normally precede interpretation, whereas the method of deconstruction is a process of deduction whereby researchers deliberately look for inherent bias through analysis of style, genre, and narrative structure.[14] Deconstruction requires identification of all stakeholders, their interests, and their motivations to act in specific ways that influence organizations. In addition, patterns and trends of the time period must be drawn along with contextualization of the event and material used in research.[15] The process of deconstruction enables researchers to avoid pitfalls of monolithic research from their sources. However, the researcher needs to be aware of their potential bias in order to avoid anachronisms, reading the present into the past.[16] In addition, the position and bias of interviewed subjects and authors of documents are to be considered to achieve the most comprehensive analysis possible using available materials.

Bias, the practice of favoring one group or person over another, is inevitable. After all, our circumstances typically motivate our actions. Social historians look for evidence of bias to find clues to power dynamics.[17] This comparative analysis reveals underlying patterns of behavior and issues using macrolevel theory in research.[18] Six interrelated examples of bias found in historical research are listed as follows:[19]

1. **Linguistic bias:** Choice of words/identifiers that privilege one group or person over another group or person.
2. **Stereotyping:** Consistently portraying people of a certain gender, age, race, and so on, with one set of values, behaviors, and roles.
3. **Invisibility:** The omission or exclusion of people or groups.
4. **Imbalance:** The presentation of only one perspective on an issue, situation, or group of people.
5. **Unreality:** The presentation and unrealistic portrayal of history or contemporary life made by glossing over controversial subjects such as discrimination and prejudice.
6. **Fragmentation:** The depictions and contributions of certain individuals or groups are seen as isolated from the main body of the text or curriculum.

The ability to think historically is an integral part of business. It is the method by which business leaders find out what went right within organizations and what mistakes were made.[20] It further helps establish a competitive advantage with the ability to influence behavior, market creation, and growth activities based on past patterns of behavior that hold immediate relevance to contemporary circumstances.[21] The evolution of markets, changing business strategy, and the formation of firms and companies are highly interrelated phenomena that rely on historical analysis.[22] Business history deals with businesses and enterprises in a dynamic process of change (top down), compared to the history of work, which investigates the effects of such changes with regard to work carried out in the workplace (bottom up).[23] Experts in both business and academia agree that business leaders who hold a working knowledge of historical analysis and apply the concepts to their organizations are able to influence the success of the business, incorporating methods that they would not otherwise have access to.[24]

The following concepts are used in historical methodology:

1. **Ahistorical thinking** occurs when researchers interpret material from the perspective of present conditions rather than taking circumstances of the past into consideration.
2. **Historical analysis** is the collection of evidence from legitimate sources, and its interpretation is based on critical thinking and rigorous evaluation of data.

3. **Historical synthesis** is the development of a solid line of argumentation typically based on a large, shared body of research by multiple historians.
4. **Political economy** measures the social climate of a society based on political and economic factors that shape societal management and governance.
5. **Ideologies** are systems of ideas and ideals that shape the thinking of groups.
6. **Historical causation** is the analysis of cause-and-effect relationships of the past.
7. **Periodization** is the practice of dividing history into segments of time based on generalized or shared characteristics of particular years.
8. **Comparison** is a critical tool used by historians involving various points of view in regard to an issue or event.
9. **Contextualization** is the placement of historical figures and events during the time in which they lived, based on location, time period, and social standards.
10. **Interpretation** is the ability to analyze and describe the past through evidence, reasoning, multiple perspectives, and frames of reference.

This unit begins with an introduction to historical analysis that demonstrates the necessity of divergent perspectives in formulating inclusive records in the interpretation of the past. Delap probes the global perspective of women's history, finding patterns of behavior of women from different time periods and multiple backgrounds that are contradictory yet have some similarities. Her international analysis comes from a grassroots level that points to the striation of women's experiences and influence from vastly divergent perspectives.

Next, Trotter analyzes economic and industrial history from the viewpoints of African Americans over a 400-year period, from 1619 to the present. He establishes the integral role of African American workers in the making of America. Trotter validates the participation of African Americans in the formal economy according to social norms, and in spite of hegemonic customs that narrowly defined specific roles and expectations of African Americans. He further demonstrates the impact of ideology on behavior, standards, and policies through his insightful analysis.

Finally, Witzel demonstrates the relevance of historical analysis to business in terms of learning from the past to predict the future—both connected to profitability and progress for contemporary business. He argues that while managers spend a significant amount of time analyzing the future, it is inevitable that they draw from the past as they do so. Memory, he says, plays a key part in the actions and decisions of people. Purposefully incorporating historical analysis in business management provides business leaders with a type of freedom of action in the present. Self-examination with consideration of past events, policies, and so forth provide insight into methods in use and whether or not they are appropriate for the time and place. While there has been a lot of change in the centuries of management practice, there has also been a lot of continuity, adapted and re-adapted for the times. Witzel supports his position with team research projects in various industries.

Philosophy

"The important thing is not to stop questioning. Curiosity has its own reason for existing."
—Albert Einstein

Philosophy is the study and love of wisdom. Naturally, philosophical inquiry begins with asking questions about the nature of life and living, beginning with basic universal mysteries and questions that are natural for all people to ask. Philosophers are in a constant state of inquiry, asking questions related to the following concepts:

1. **What is the nature of reality?**
2. **How do we know what we know?**
3. **How should society be organized?**
4. **Why do we suffer?**
5. **How can we find happiness?**

Philosophy is organized thought established through rational reflection shaped by reason rather than experimentation; accordingly, it is timeless and malleable. It is a process of asking questions and developing answers systematically—not an arbitrary or abstract method of inquiry. Rather, it requires analysis that is built and rebuilt over time and in varying circumstances. Philosophy draws from varied knowledge, including experiential, intuitive, and some empirical knowledge, all of which must come from credible sources that are able to withstand rigorous scrutiny.

Because questions never cease, philosophy evolves according to the philosophers seeking answers—connected to their time period and influenced by their location. Even so, philosophy is based on values above time that are worth being known for their own sake.[25] Philosophy relies on some historical analysis to establish a foundation from which to build. There are multiple factors that influence the development of particular ideologies that shape conceptual frameworks. For example, the consideration of time period, political economy, and contextual analysis places philosophers where they lived and identifies circumstances that shaped their development of thought. Further, the discipline of philosophy requires authenticity in analysis; therefore, similar to the historian, the philosopher has to examine themselves in relationship to values and normative behavior.

The schools of philosophy are interrelated, though each has characteristics specific to itself:[26]

1. **Metaphysics:** Studies the nature of being, with two major questions: What is being? What are its fundamental features and properties?
2. **Epistemology:** The analysis of theories of knowledge and ways of knowing.
3. **Ethics:** The philosophical study of moral judgments, which includes the question, Are moral judgments correct?
4. **Social philosophy:** The philosophical study of society and its institutions, concerned with what determines the features of the ideal or best.

5. **Political philosophy:** Focuses on one institution, the state, and seeks to determine its justification and organization.
6. **Aesthetics:** The philosophical study of art along ethical lines, value judgments about art, and beauty, in general.
7. **Logic:** The theory of corrective reasoning, which seeks to investigate and establish the criteria of valid inference and demonstration.
8. **Skepticism:** Self-defined.

Philosophy shapes the image of a business and is evident in policies, practices, mission statements, and alliances. Ethics in business are philosophy-based and should be consistent with the values of stakeholders in defining a corporate image and identity. There are separate schools of philosophy shaped by location and time (e.g., Western v. Eastern intellectual thought). However, there are some key terms that generally apply to the use of philosophy in business, as follows:[27]

- **Analysis:** Solving or dissolving a problem.
- **Attribute:** The essential characteristics of a substance.
- **Contingency:** The nature of that which happens accidentally.
- **Deduction:** Start with a set of possibilities, and reduce it until a smaller subset remains.
- **Existence:** The act and reality of being.
- **Fallacy:** An erroneous logical inference.
- **Freedom:** Untied from any previous constraint.
- **Induction:** Begin with a limited number of observations, and *increase* that number by generalizing.
- **Inference:** Drawing conclusions based on evidence.
- **Intuition:** The kind of cognition or knowledge that comes from within.
- **Obligation:** An ethical term that means what is morally right and points to what one ought to do.
- **Perception**: An intuition, an immediate knowledge obtained through our senses.
- **Phenomenon:** Something which appears.
- **Reality:** The characteristic of being; signifies existence.
- **Relativism:** The view that standards of reasoning and procedures of justification are confined to context.
- **Understanding:** An epistemological concept and the human faculty of recognizing the truth of a knowledge in form of judgement. Understanding is rational and is, indeed, a part of cognitive reason or reason itself in the wider sense.

The philosophical readings for this unit provide both theory and the application of philosophy to business practices, which has been taking place for centuries. Gilbert introduces basic concepts and ways of thinking along philosophical lines. He points to basic questions about human existence and purpose that we have considered universally. These questions shape the nature of other fields of study in his perspective. Gilbert frames philosophy first as a field of study and then as a means of clear thinking and proper naming.

In business, philosophy not only holds a place in ethics but in the daily decisions made by managers. He further argues that workers and other employees also benefit from philosophical inquiry, although his emphasis is on the role of philosophy for managers and business leaders. Philosophical inquiry makes managers aware of the ethical implications of their actions and can provide them with tools for thinking through ethical problems that they face in the course of their work.

Next, Rosicka provides an avenue on which to put philosophical theory into practice based on an aspect of Plato's economic theory that she terms "philosophy of economy space." Her analysis of Plato's theory of *topos* is placed within the economic cycles of prosperity and scarcity, and the transitionary periods between the two, referred to as deluge. Rosicka provides insight into Plato's argument that there needs to be a balance between time and space as well as the balance that is necessary for all aspects of our lives. She provides further elucidation regarding Plato's ideal society in terms of roles individuals play through their patterns of behavior. People fall short of the ideal and then draw closer to that ideal in periods of prosperity associated with the lowlands and scarcity associated with mountains. Our behaviors disrupt our lives, sending us into transitional periods of deluge. Rosicka develops Plato's theory with a concise approach, showing that the argument Plato made over 2,500 years ago is still relevant. His theory can be tested against both historical and contemporary economic cycles.

Notes

1. Schwarzkopf, S. (2015). Marketing history from below: Towards a paradigm shift in marketing historical research. *Journal of Historical Research in Marketing*, *7*(3), 295–309.
2. Faire, L. (Ed.). (2016). *Research methods for history*. Edinburgh University Press.
3. Dayton-Wood, A., Hammonds, L., Matherson, L., & Tollison, L. (2012). Bridging gaps and preserving memories through oral history research and writing. *English Journal*, 101(4), 77–82.
4. Blau, F. D., Ferber, M. A., & Winkler, A. E. (1992). *The economics of women, men, and work*. Prentice-Hall.
5. Hatton, T. (2013). *New Comparative Economic History*.
6. Lieberman, E. S. (2001). Causal inference in historical institutional analysis: A specification of periodization strategies. *Comparative Political Studies*, *34*(9), 1011–1035.
7. Gatrell, C. (2008). *Embodying women's work*. McGraw-Hill Education (UK).
8. Friedman, W. (2017). Recent trends in business history research: Capitalism, democracy, and innovation. *Enterprise & Society*, *18*(4), 748–771.
9. Decker, S., Kipping, M., & Wadhwani, R. (2015). New business histories! Plurality in business history research methods. *Business History*, *57*(1), 1–11.
10. Tadajewski, M. (2012). History and critical marketing studies. *Journal of Historical Research in Marketing*, *4*(3), 440–452.
11. Porra, J. S., Parks, M., & Hirschheim, R. (2014). The historical research method and information systems research. *Journal of the Association of Information Systems*, *15*(9), 536–576.
12. Jóhannesson, I. Á. (2010). The politics of historical discourse analysis: A qualitative research method? *Discourse: Studies in the Cultural Politics of Education*, *31*(2), 251–264.
13. Smith, R., & Lux, D. (1993). Historical method in consumer research: Developing causal explanations of change. *Journal of Consumer Research*, *19*(4), 595–610.
    Spirkin, A. (1975). Dialectical materialism. In *Themes in Soviet Marxist philosophy* (pp. 5–47). Springer.

Shimomissé, E. (1996). *Stanford philosophical reference.*

14. Munslow, A. (1997). *Deconstructing history.* Routledge.
15. Turner, K. (1998). *Doing rhetorical history: Concepts and cases* (Studies in rhetoric and communication). University of Alabama Press.
16. Fullerton, R. A. (2011). Historical methodology: The perspective of a professionally trained historian turned marketer. *Journal of Historical Research in Marketing, 3*(4), 436–448.
17. Jones, J. (2009). *Labor of love, labor of sorrow: Black women, work, and the family, from slavery to the present.* Basic Books.
18. Layton, R. A. (2015). Formation, growth, and adaptive change in marketing systems. *Journal of Macromarketing, 35*(3), 302–319.
19. Sadker, M., Sadker, D., & Long, L. (1993). Gender and educational equality. *Multicultural Education: Issues and Perspectives*, 111–128.
20. Dearlove, D. (2013). *Business history.*
21. Fillis, I. (2015). Biographical research as a methodology for understanding entrepreneurial marketing. *International Journal of Entrepreneurial Behavior & Research, 21*(3), 429–447.
22. Magnusson, L. (2013). *Business history and the history of work.*
23. Hatton, T. (2013). *New comparative economic history.*
24. Dearlove, D. (2013). *Business history.*
25. Moore and Bruder, *Philosophy the power of ideas* (2nd ed.).
26. Moore and Bruder, *Philosophy the power of ideas* (2nd ed.).
27. Spirkin, A. (1975). Dialectical materialism. In *Themes in Soviet Marxist philosophy (pp.* 5–47). Springer.
    Eiichi Shimomissé, 1996; *Stanford Philosophical Reference.* Relativism. (2015, September 11). Stanford Encyclopedia of Philosophy. https://plato.stanford.edu/entries/relativism/
    https://philosophyterms.com/inference/

Introduction to Feminisms: A Global History

Lucy Delap

[...]

Feminism seeks an alliance that spans more than half of humanity. There may have never been such an ambitious movement in human history. But what do feminists want? All share the insight that being a woman means disadvantage vis-à-vis men, and that this can be addressed through struggle. But the resulting political claims have varied dramatically over time and proceeded under many different names. Feminism is best understood as an overlapping, internally complex set of actions, questions and demands that has been in formulation since the eighteenth century or even earlier. Its concerns change over time. A century ago, British socialist-feminist Ethel Snowden described feminism as a project seeking the purity of men and women through harnessing 'those instinctive feminine forces which make for the protection of the race'. Twenty-first-century feminists are unlikely to identify with this rhetoric, and Snowden's race politics would have been contested by the anonymous Gold Coast letter-writer. There is nonetheless remarkable freshness and relevance to the feminist debates of the past when viewed through the lens of contemporary feminist concerns. Snowden's insistence, for example, that women have an equal right to fight in the military resonates with today's hard-fought campaigns to gain equality in battlefield operations.

Feminists have been motivated by the terrible realities of women's lack of control over their bodies—the rapes, sexual abuses, unwilling pregnancies and the relentless pressures of the male gaze. They have drawn attention to women's poverty, their exclusion from safer and better-paid jobs, their vulnerabilities through marriage or motherhood, their illiteracy. They have shown the cost of women's lack of legal rights, that have taken the form of loss of custody of their children, forced labour, lack of medical resources and land rights, and women's vulnerability in conditions of occupation, war and famine. The costs and human misery of gender inequalities have been and remain incalculable. Yet feminist activism has also been creative and empowering, creating coalitions and inspiring commitment to change. Ideas and dreams have taken shape as campaigns and protests; individuals have found hope, resilience and justice.

Feminism has been repeatedly written off as a political movement that has achieved its aims—only to come back with renewed force as another generation of women angrily name their malaise. Today's campaigners have deep interest in what some ambivalently term 'the F word'. But many are uncertain as to how their activism relates to feminist history: some embrace 'foremothers' such as Concepción Arenal, Mary Wollstonecraft or Funmilayo Ransome-Kuti. Others repudiate the past and stress the uniqueness of 'their' feminism.

The ambivalence about the term, and the content of the feminist past, is unsurprising. The historical organizing frame of 'feminist waves' has not proved up to the job of making sense of the complexities of feminist history. Talk of first, second, third and fourth waves of feminism, or variants such as 'new feminism' or riot grrrl, have not always mapped easily onto women's experiences. And for many women, their activism has been so bound up in other movements—socialist, nationalist, anti-colonialist—that the term 'feminism' has been rejected as too divisive, too Euro-American, too white, too middle-class.

There will be some familiar stories in what follows, of suffrage militancy and stone-throwing protests; of radical feminist celebration of women's power and solidarity. But there is no assumption that feminism looks the same in each place or time. A theme running through the book will be a central paradox of feminism: as a movement, feminism insists on women's inclusion in all areas of social and political life and demands the radical transformation of those exclusionary structures; but feminism has its own forms of marginalization and has struggled to extend its boundaries to all women on equal terms. Black, working-class, lesbian, trans and bisexual, disabled, non-Western and non-Christian women have often been shut out of what theorist Chela Sandoval has termed 'hegemonic feminism'.[1] Despite its cosmopolitan origins, [...] 'feminism' has often been associated with a Western model of emancipated womanhood. The voices of those with different backgrounds or goals have not always been listened to, and feminist campaigning has not always met their needs. Archival materials, where they document feminism at all, tend to lean towards the story that more powerful and privileged feminists have wanted to tell. As Adele Murdolo comments, 'very few documents exist in the feminist archive that readily reveal a conflictual and racially or ethnically divided movement.'[2]

Feminist battles have sometimes been regarded as already won, victories realized at the moment of enfranchisement, or where pioneering women finally achieved rights to practise medicine, to have custody of their children or to drive. In the 1990s, there was much talk of a 'post-feminist world' in which political power, economic success and cultural riches were all for women's taking. But this confidence that feminism had done its work has diminished considerably in the last decade of economic austerity, brutal wars and authoritarian politics. In 2013, prominent Nigerian novelist Chimamanda Ngozi Adichie gave a TED Talk which declared, 'We should all be feminists.' She published this clarion call in 2014, and her words were also sampled by pop icon Beyoncé, who had toured under a giant projection of the word 'feminist' in 2013. The published version of 'We Should All Be Feminists' was given to every sixteen-year-old in Sweden shortly after it came out. Yet anti-feminist and misogynist rhetoric has dominated recent political debates. In 2016, Hillary Clinton failed to win the American presidential election, having faced intense negative coverage over her appearance. She and other female politicians faced vitriol from their opponent Donald Trump, who declared of Carly Fiorina in his own Republican Party: 'Look at that face!' and 'Would anyone vote for that?' His words prompted millions of women across the world to march in early 2017. They were incensed by Trump's boasts of having 'grabbed women by the pussy', and coined the slogan 'pussy grabs back'. Across the globe, the pink 'pussy hat' became ubiquitous at protests and marches, echoing the red 'liberty cap' or *'bonnet rouge'* of republican *citoyennes* during the French Revolution. 2017 was also the year that a major American dictionary, Merriam-Webster, declared 'feminism' to be its most looked-up word. A global poll showed that only in Japan did a majority of respondents disagree with the statement: 'I advocate and support equal opportunities for women—I do more than just think about these things, I actually speak up and out to change things for women in my country.'[3] Talk of post-feminism seems unconvincing in the face of these social and political trends.

Coined in the late nineteenth century, 'feminism' has always been a controversial term. An American comic newspaper called it the 'New Name for Masher' and pictured a man making unwelcome advances to a woman while declaring, 'Pay no attention to me, mademoiselle, I'm only a feminist.'[4] It took some time to gain a more stable meaning as a person campaigning against injustice to women. Rebecca West, who began writing for a feminist journal, *The Freewoman,* at the age of twenty in 1911, defined being a feminist as what people called her 'whenever I express sentiments that differentiate me from a *doormat*'. But she nonetheless wrote under a pseudonym, for fear of embarrassing her family.

It has not only been women who have been inspired by ideas of equality, 'gender justice' and living different lives. Throughout this book, we will meet men who have worked to advance women's rights, often through deep personal investment in feminist goals as also benefiting men. Indeed, the very term 'feminist' became used in the late nineteenth century to replace the idea of 'the women's movement' with a more open-ended identity that was open to both sexes. In 1906, at a meeting of the International Council of Women in Paris, a Monsieur Legendre interrupted the meeting, declaring himself to be the feminist candidate in a recent local election; participants were not impressed, and newspapers reported him as being 'ruthlessly expelled' from this women-only gathering.[5] He was not the only man to stand on a feminist ticket in twentieth-century elections. George Lansbury, who went on to lead the British Labour Party, stood as a women's suffrage candidate in Middlesbrough in 1906, and in Bow and Bromley in 1913. Accused of seeking 'petticoat government', Lansbury lost both elections, but his commitment was undiminished. He was imprisoned for inciting violence in the women's suffrage cause later in 1913, where he joined the hunger strike which was widely used by women prisoners to protest their incarceration. In more recent years, campaigners have produced t-shirts for all, including in men's sizes, emblazoned with 'This is what a feminist looks like'. This slogan was taken up by United States former president Barack Obama in 2016, though for many men, being a feminist is still something they approach with ambivalence and anxiety.

For some women and men, feminism has proved a transformative, explosive, life changing way of seeing the world. For others, it has elicited responses of visceral repudiation, laughter, ambivalence and irony. Impoverished women claiming welfare rights, Black women protesting police violence and housing conditions, working-class women in labour unions calling for equal pay and safe workplaces, or men meeting in men's groups have often opted for other labels, such as 'anti-sexist', 'womanist' and 'social justice campaigner'. Those who preferred other names for their activism should not be claimed as 'feminists'. But their motivations, and why they avoided this label, are important to historians of feminisms, who must cast their net widely in documenting activism against gender injustice.[6]

The 'When' of Feminism

Being a feminist has been projected back into past centuries with mixed success. There have been efforts to claim figures such as the late-medieval writer Christine de Pizan, or even the ancient Alexandrian philosopher Hypatia, as 'feminists'. Of course, these historical actors did not think in these terms, and it is misleading to approach them through our much later ideological concerns. Instead, we should ask what terms and concepts they used to think about men and women. A division of the world into two sexes cannot be taken for granted. In some parts of the world, it is not clear that there was a clearly recognizable concept of 'woman'. As historians of China have argued, the category of 'female persons' (*funü*) was a relatively late invention and related directly to family status. In many contexts, female persons were profoundly subdivided—into 'wives' and 'courtesans' in Qing China. The same might be said about the class divide of 'women' and 'ladies' in nineteenth-century Britain.

Local diversity has meant that the emergence of organized demands for change happened in very different ways all over the world. Where they existed, 'feminists' spoke for different groups and in diverse registers. 'The women's movement' or 'woman question' was the terminology of nineteenth-century Europe and the Americas, while 'women's awakening' was widely debated in Middle Eastern and North African countries in the early twentieth century. Others in this period preferred to talk of the 'new woman' as a symbol of new forms of economic and cultural opportunity for women. Chinese radicals variously made demands in the name of women's rights (*funüjie*) and gender equality (*nannü pingdeng*). Feminism does not map in any straightforward way onto these terrains, and historians of feminism must take care not to erase the local specificity of struggles and activism. However, it would be a mistake to simply look at all these debates and movements in isolation; they often shared key ideas or drew inspiration from each other's struggles. We can chart the rich interweaving of global debates on the relationship between gender and power, at the same time as recognizing feminism as a deeply historical and context-specific phenomenon.

Though it was often defined in highly various ways, 'feminism' as a term was adopted globally in the early twentieth century. It might refer to women's 'rights' as well as to campaigns of women's advancement, protection and equality. A single issue of a magazine titled *La Aurora Feminista* (*The Feminist Dawn*) was published in Chile in 1904, the same year that Rosika Schwimmer (1877–1948) founded the Feministák Egyesülete (Feminist Association) in Hungary; a Centro Feminista was founded the following year in Buenos Aires, Argentina. An Asociación Feminista Filipina was founded in the Philippines in 1905; Filipina women saw feminism as carving out a civic role for women, attempting to improve the regulation of women's work and preventing early marriage.[7] In the same year, Argentina hosted the first International Feminine Congress, and saw the publication in La Plata of the journal *La Nueva Mujer* (*The New Woman*). The motto of the Congress had been 'Let Us Work', and the emphasis of Latin American feminism in these early years was on social service and the protection of women by the state. Its critics accused feminists of being *marimacho*—half man, half woman. But the term 'feminism' was flexible enough to be adopted by religious conservatives such as Laura Correa de Bustos, who published an account of '*feminismo Christiano*' (Christian feminism) in the Uruguayan capital Montevideo in 1907.[8]

In Britain, the suffrage movement is often assumed to speak for feminist concerns of the period. However, contributors to the first British magazine that called itself 'feminist', *The Freewoman,* used 'feminism' in 1911 to distinguish their beliefs from the suffrage campaign for votes for women. By 'feminist', its avant-garde editors indicated a term open to both sexes, and one which rejected conventional political institutions. They sought revolutionary change; one editor, Dora Marsden, declared controversially that 'rebels armed with rifles' would be most likely to gain respect. Other terms were also available—French radicals experimented with '*éclaireuse*' ('trailblazer') to capture a sense of pioneering women, 'liberated from all that still burdens the bulk of their companions'.[9] German-speaking activists wavered between '*Feminismus*' (feminism) and '*Frauenbewegung*' (women's movement), fearing that the former term had implications of 'free love' or British suffrage militancy.[10] Feminism has often been a 'loanword', deployed in a wide variety of places to label different kinds of gender politics; there was talk of feminism as '*feminizumu*' in Japan in 1910. Russian activists however preferred the term '*ravnopravki*' or 'equal righters' when, in the heady revolutionary days of 1905, they founded the Union of Equal Rights for Women.[11] Across the world, there was fascination with this new concept, as well as suspicion of European or American influences.

Sometimes external labels stuck. The British media mocked early-twentieth-century militants by terming them 'suffragettes', but this name was embraced with enthusiasm by those throwing stones for the right to vote. 'Bra burners' was an insult of the 1970s, but activists came up with their own puns and subversive reappropriations: Harpies Bizarre, Hags, Lavender Menace, the Monstrous Regiment, the Society for Cutting Up Men.

The meaning of 'feminist' has continued to evolve, and to be controversial. Activists in the 1970s and 80s often preferred to talk of 'women's liberation', since they associated 'feminist' with reformist 'liberal' politics of parliamentary rights and suffrage. Feminists in France associated with the 'Psych et Po' (Psychoanalysis and Politics) grouping disliked 'feminist' as an American import connoting confrontation. They preferred to talk of '*femmes en lutte*' ('women in the struggle') as a means of capturing their distinctive stress on feminine difference and maternal qualities. Late-twentieth-century Japanese activists have preferred to talk about a 'gender-free' society. By the twenty-first century, many activists across the world have felt the need to routinely preface their feminism with other flags, resulting in labels such as 'intersectional feminism' or 'trans-friendly feminism'.

Despite the many varieties of feminisms, one of the overarching feminist dreams has been of a movement that could span all women: 'Helping each other, all of one mind', as the Chinese banner declared at the 1913 conference of the International Woman Suffrage Alliance. This fantasy has carried with it the paradox of an abstract political agenda that, in its very inclusivity, ignores concrete exclusions. Talk of 'black feminism' or 'Chicana feminism' has sometimes attempted to solve this problem, but critics have argued that this simply foregrounds the exclusion of black or Chicana women from the ethnically unmarked feminist 'mainstream'. African American writer Alice Walker coined the term 'womanism' in 1984, and this has been taken up by some black women. 'Womanist' (or 'womynist' for those who preferred to entirely excise the 'man' lurking in 'woman') runs the same risks as 'feminist' of universalizing its claims. But it does provide a useful reminder of the limits and exclusions of feminism as an affiliation. As the African American activist Frances Watkins Harper (1825–1911) put it succinctly as far back as 1866: 'You white women speak here of rights. I speak of wrongs.' Harper wanted the women's movement to challenge the racial segregation of streetcars, but her white peers were reluctant to take on issues of racial exclusion. As an African American woman and a former domestic servant, she continued: 'I, as a colored woman, have had in this country an education which has made me feel as if I were in the situation of Ishmael, my hand against every man, and every man's hand against me.'[12] She and her fellow African American activists formed the National Association of Colored Women in 1897, preferring, in an environment of growing racial exclusion, to organize separately from white women and without embracing 'feminism' as a platform.

These debates over naming and belonging suggest the need to look closely at the historically variable labelling of gender activism, and to think hard about the work different names do. We need not engage in a competitive struggle to identify the first, or the truest, feminists. Instead, we can trace out experiences of exclusion and difference amongst gender and social justice activists, and chart their passionate, painful or strategic coalitions.

Despite the renewed interest in what feminism 'means' in the present day, it is important to recognize that its meaning has been mobile. Feminist symbols and slogans have been malleable, reshaped in formats that were useable for different audiences. *Feminisms: A Global History* will explore traditions that include Islamic, black, indigenous and lesbian feminisms. More controversially, it will also explore men's identification with feminism, in order to probe long-standing tensions over who is being addressed by feminism, and who can be part of the movement.

Why Global?

Why should we approach feminism from a global perspective? Histories of feminisms have often been organized around a 'civilizational' and Eurocentric model. In these stories, feminism can be dated back to the European writers of the seventeenth century, such as Aphra Behn, François Poullain de la Barre and Sarah Fyge, who began to think about women as an 'enslaved class'. Such writers were inspired by ideas of women's spiritual equality within mostly Protestant religious traditions. When they talked of 'enslavement', they rarely considered women who were literally enslaved on the plantations and estates of the Americas and Caribbean. They began to find ways to name and renounce experiences of rape and forced marriage—though again, without reference to the prevalence of such experiences for the enslaved. These intellectuals have often been viewed as significant 'foremothers' for the history of feminisms.

In older histories, the baton was usually then passed to women who experienced the American and French revolutions in the late eighteenth century, such as Abigail Adams and Olympe de Gouges. De Gouges, who proclaimed the rights of women in her *Declaration of the Rights of Woman and the*

Female Citizen (1791), is often named with the British writer Mary Wollstonecraft as the initiators of ideas and polemics that are recognizably feminist. Their influence is then traced onwards, through the more activist nineteenth century, during which campaigns flourished on women's education, property rights and suffrage, and into the twentieth century. Only recently have figures such as former slave and poet Phyllis Wheatley (*c.* 1753–84) been added to this story. Feminist history has often been structured around a limited cast of mostly white and educated foremothers. This has led to lineages of inheritance that not only risk misreading earlier versions of feminist thought and action, but have also been organized around the desire to show 'who was first'. Simply put, the earliest texts that can be read as 'feminist' have been used to establish a national priority, where white citizens of imperial powers such as France, Britain or the United States came to be taken as originating points.

The writing of global or world history has for decades now challenged this kind of account. Historians have proposed ways of understanding the global that take alternative starting points and new thinkers. We might take as an originating feminist moment the 1799 Rasheed (Rosetta) Women's Conference, where a group of Egyptian women, radicalized by protesting the 1798 French invasion at Alexandria, met to discuss the conditions of women's employment and family status. Alternatively, a starting point might be the rights given to indigenous female householders to vote in Sierra Leone in 1792—a right lost when their country became a British Crown Colony in 1808. Indigenous and settler women gained voting rights in New Zealand from 1893, well ahead of their European and American counterparts. These perspectives help challenge the assumed priority of European feminisms.

Global histories of feminism have focused on the large-scale structures that underpinned ideas about the 'woman question', women's rights and women's emancipation. There has been deep attention to the role of empires, for example, in shaping the nineteenth- and twentieth-century women's movements and producing a world in which liberty and citizenship were denied to colonized populations. Colonized peoples underwent mass migrations within systems of indentured and forced labour. Women in many settings found their access to land and trading rights curtailed. Women of imperial powers used the rhetoric of racial and civilizational advancement to become authorities on colonized women. They used the roles of missionary, settler and wife to travel, describe the lives of non-Western women, and intervene in how they were treated, sometimes in the name of equality or feminism. For later decades, when empires began to be dismantled, it was the geopolitical contests of the Cold War that helped to authorize and shape women's and feminist activism.

The nineteenth and twentieth centuries were also dominated by the development of nationalism, and this meant that women's status and freedoms were often tied to debates about national progress. Within such debates, the problematic idea of 'backwardness' as a means to capture local discontent with women's circumstances features prominently. In Brazil, for example, the imagined European or North American emancipated, educated woman was used to make claims for the advancement of the nation or region. The editor of the Brazilian women's rights newspaper, *O Jornal das Senhoras* (*The Ladies' Journal*), noted in the journal's first editorial in 1852:

> in France, England, Italy, Spain, the United States, and in Portugal itself, cases abound of women dedicated to literature who contribute to various newspapers. Perchance shall

> South America alone stay stationary in its ideas when the entire world marches toward progress and moves toward the moral and material improvement of society?

O Jornal das Senhoras had been founded in Rio de Janeiro and was edited by the Argentinian-born Juana Paula Manso de Noronha (1819–75). Manso saw *O Jornal das Senhoras* as a platform to work for the 'social betterment and the moral emancipation of women'. While it was rhetorically useful for Manso to draw a contrast between 'advanced' and 'backward' regions, in reality the kinds of reforms actually (or imagined to be) taking place in nations such as Britain, France and the United States were also evident in Brazil. The first university college for women in Britain, Girton College in Cambridge, opened in 1869. Women were given the right to enter higher education only a decade later in 1879 in Brazil—in the same year that the French state resolved to provide *lycées* (secondary education) for French girls. Women's suffrage was seriously debated in the Brazilian Constitutional Congress of 1891, paralleling similar debates in Britain and the United States. And despite her rhetoric of backwardness, Manso was convinced that Europe need not take the lead, since 'the banner of enlightenment waves gracefully in the perfumed breeze of the tropics'.[13]

Manso's mobility across national borders reminds us that histories of feminism cannot be located only within single nation states, regions or empires. Global influences have been based on the migration of individuals, as refugees, students, exiles and workers. An early women's suffrage petition in Britain, for example, was organized by Anne Knight of the Sheffield Female Political Association in 1851 after she had spent time with French activist Jeanne Deroin in Paris during the revolutionary days of 1848; in turn, Deroin published Harriet Taylor Mill's 1851 essay 'The Enfranchisement of Women' in her journal *L'Almanach des Femmes* in 1852. With the rise of technologies of travel and communications in the nineteenth century, some women were peripatetic across multiple nations—historian Bonnie Anderson, for example, tracks the Jewish abolitionist and suffragist Ernestine Rose (1810–92) across Poland, Berlin, Paris, London and New York as she fled an arranged marriage and immersed herself in socialist and feminist activism.[14]

Historians have become newly attentive to the deliberate cultivation of transnational spaces, in the pages of globally circulating periodicals, in conventions, conferences, alliances and federations. Sometimes transnationalism was a deliberate tactic, witnessed in the global mobilization undertaken by bodies such as the Women's Christian Temperance Union in the nineteenth century. International organizations such as the International Council of Women helped foster important elements of global governance, such as the League of Nations Commission on the Legal Status of Women (1937). The 'left-feminist' Women's International Democratic Federation built up similar networks of campaigning and mobility in the second half of the twentieth century, which later helped inform the influential United Nations (UN) World Conferences on Women in Mexico City (1975), Copenhagen (1980), Nairobi (1985) and Beijing (1995).[15]

A global history approach also allows us to see the interactions between globally famous texts and local intellectual or activist traditions.[16] John Stuart Mill's important book, *The Subjection of Women,* for example, was published in Britain in 1869, in the context of Mill's recent attempts to get a women's suffrage bill through the Houses of Parliament, where he sat as the Member for the City and Westminster. It was quickly translated into many languages, including into Spanish by a Chilean woman, Martina Barros Borgaño, in 1872, and published in the Chilean journal *Revista de Santiago* as *La Esclavitud de la Mujer*. The Chilean women's movement drew on European texts but retained its own distinctive emphases. In

Chile, where few men voted, the most pressing question was not suffrage but the economic exploitation of women drawn into industry, and this perspective reshaped the meaning of Mill's ideas about the 'slavery' of women.

Feminism is better understood as a conversation rather than an import; but a conversation with many registers. It has taken place under unequal conditions, where some voices are amplified and some are routinely ignored.[17] The idea of 'entangled histories' has been used by global historians to capture the ways in which ideas, people and texts crossed and re-crossed borders to create multiple 'intersections'; historian Kathryn Gleadle invites us to think of feminist history as a non-linear rhizome root structure, full of unexpected growth points, dead ends and patterns of influence.[18] Some of this patterning stretched over time; feminists and others sustained critical dialogue with earlier texts and reworked their ideas. The assumed priority of white, educated Euro-American women has turned out to be a myth.[19] [...] There may sometimes be faint lines of influence, but there is just as likely to be repudiation and innovation. Rather than trying to find origins in Europe, I work with a more diffuse idea of 'mosaic feminism', built up from inherited fragments but offering distinctive patterns and pictures. Like mosaics, the view from afar and the close reading of feminisms may give a very different picture. And like mosaics, feminist coalitions were built up from the bits and pieces available—other movements, committed individuals, actions and ideas. Some mosaics have been long-lived; others have crumbled, and their tiles have been reused, or have disappeared from view.

The familiar centring of Europe is displaced and 'provincialized' by telling the histories of other networks and sites, such as the importance of Japan in hosting Chinese exiles in the early twentieth century, creating a site of powerful exchange. International campaigners and writers on suffrage, temperance, anti-colonialism and peace questions are also brought into view, displacing those located firmly within the nation state. Throughout the book, I alternate between wide-angle summaries of different feminist beliefs or campaigns, and close scrutiny of the lives of individual women who fought against gender inequities. In doing so, I hope to draw out some important new ways of reading feminist practices and ideas across historical time. Influenced by Kimberly Springer's concept of 'politics in the cracks', I suggest that we look not only at the shards and fragments that make up a mosaic, but also at the gaps between the pieces. Springer's work on black feminist organizations such as the Third World Women's Alliance describes a politics created in 'the cracks'—snatched moments between the demands of everyday work and care. Black women's organizing also fell between the civil rights and the women's movements, awkwardly or creatively showing up the intersections of class, gender and race.[20] Springer's 'interstitial' politics draws our attention to concerns that did not fit easily into existing feminist politics, and the opportunities and dislocations that resulted. In a similar spirit, we might ask what makes the mosaic stable, or what erodes its patterns. Or investigate how dreams, campaigns, spaces and places, emotions and songs could provide a kind of feminist 'cement', embedding a politics into its historical shape, and giving way over time so that mosaic pieces might drop out and new patterns can emerge.

Metaphors of mosaics and conversations give a sense of the richness of feminist debates. But it is important also to maintain in view the discord, violence and trouble that have also characterized feminism. As the feminist philosopher bell hooks has observed, 'women can and do participate in politics of domination, as perpetrators as well as victims.'[21] Some of the global systems that emerged around the same historical moment as the 'woman question' and feminism—systems such as imperialism, missionary and settler colonialism, indentured labour, nationalism—were projects that relied on violence and subordination. The world is not, historically, a freely traversed space for all. While we as twenty-first-century observers might take a global perspective on the feminist past, this privilege was not available to the historical actors themselves. A global history of feminism, as historian Mrinalini Sinha has insisted, will not simply pluralize our picture so that we think in terms of 'feminisms'.[22] Instead, our account of feminisms must acknowledge what Sinha terms the 'discrepant histories of different women's movements', marked by contests, conflicts and power-play.

Theory, Activism and Useability

What have feminisms been used for? What uses might they have today? The idea of 'useable history' offers a means of thinking about history in dialogue with the present—a history which can help clarify questions of feminist strategy, priority and focus in the contemporary moment by showing how dilemmas and campaigns were shaped in the past. Feminist ideas and campaigns have been used to redistribute domestic labour, to transform how children are raised and educated, how art and music are created, how 'work' is categorized and rewarded, how legal systems operate. Without wanting to claim that history offers direct repeats or recapitulations, we can look back to feminisms past and find precursors to problems today. We might ask, historically who could reside in the category 'feminist'? Who gets left out? What kinds of differences did feminism make to individuals, to societies or to nations?

Thinking about useability does not mean that we should explore the feminist past only for contemporary inspiration. Instead, we can also grasp the specificity and distinctiveness of how, say, religion informed feminism in the late eighteenth century, or how nation-building provided a specific context to the development of women's movements in early-twentieth-century China or the Middle East. A useable history is not one that judges the past by today's standards. Instead, useability reminds us of the variable ways in which feminisms have been put to use, rhetorically, intellectually and materially, in the lives of historical actors.[23] And inevitably, each reader will bring their own questions and determine what is useable for them. Useable feminisms must be non-doctrinaire and open-ended, shaped but not determined by the encounter between past and present.

There may be aspects of the feminist past that make us uncomfortable today. But the idea of useability acknowledges the need for a historical underpinning to today's activism.[24] Feminists have long been caught in an awkward position in relation to their history; moments of rejection of what mothers or grandmothers believed in are motivated by a need to rebel, to declare a new era and to shake off inheritances. Novelties such as social media platforms can make contemporary feminists feel that the #CuéntaLo (Tell It) or #MeToo moments are very different from preceding feminist upsurges. But at the same time, there has always been a strongly historical aspect to feminist movements, sometimes imbued with nostalgia for the past. And only a brief look back reveals strong shared themes, around sexual harassment at work and in the street, and challenges to male violence, impunity and disrespect for women.

For many, a book about feminist history will be at least partly an intellectual journey. Feminism has always been, amongst other things, an invitation to think hard about how and why society is organized, and why (some) men have louder voices, more resources and more authority than women. Feminist thinkers have been engaged with the big ideas of modern times—they have challenged the liberal self, the social contract, accounts of democratic citizenship, state and nation, as well as socialist ideas of revolution. Feminism has intersected with and contributed to anarchist critiques, as well as ecological, theological and critical race scholarship. Indeed, as higher education has expanded in the late twentieth century, feminism has become an established part of the academic landscape across much of the world. Yet theory was also produced at the cutting edge of protest, consciousness-raising and campaigning. It has often been intended to be useable in activism, as well as in personal life transformation.

The ways in which history is written have changed and pluralized over the past twenty years. There has been a flourishing of work in cultural history, as well as the development of new approaches to the study of material culture, space, capitalism and the emotions, to name but a few recent growth areas. [...]

These new perspectives root feminist history to some of the most innovative areas of historical research and shake up our sense of the uses of feminism. They take us across continents, and show why universal definitions of feminism, spanning time and place, aren't going to work. Instead, I invite us to examine 'feminisms' across a global canvas, spanning 250 years. The resulting stories are less about gender equality than about gender justice—demands for an environment in which all can thrive. This could mean paying a fair wage, kicking out colonial occupiers or embracing Goddess spirituality. It sometimes meant conflicts between different feminist goals and dreams. I argue that we can find inspiration in the feminist past, as well as a fuller understanding of why Chimamanda Ngozi Adichie's invitation for 'us' to all 'be feminists' is never going to be a straightforward task.

Notes

1. Chela Sandoval, *Methodology of the Oppressed* (University of Minnesota Press, 2000).
2. Adele Murdolo, 'Safe Homes for Immigrant and Refugee Women: Narrating Alternative Histories of the Women's Refuge Movement in Australia', *Frontiers: A Journal of Women Studies* 35:3 (2014), 146.
3. https://www.ipsos.com/sites/default/files/2017-03/global-advisor-feminism-charts-2017.pdf.
4. *Emporia Daily Gazette,* Kansas, USA (27 November 1897), vol. 7.
5. *The Times* (18 June 1906), 6.
6. For a video introducing some of the concepts of feminism, see https://www.youtube.com/watch?v=H_GBrIntUq8.
7. Mina Roces, 'Is the Suffragist an American Colonial Construct? Defining "the Filipino Woman" in Colonial Philippines', In Louise P. Edwards and Mina Roces (eds.), *Women's Suffrage in Asia: Gender, Nationalism and Democracy* (Routledge, 2005), 29.
8. Asunción Lavrín, *Women, Feminism, and Social Change in Argentina, Chile, and Uruguay, 1890–1940* (University of Nebraska Press, 1995), 26–36.
9. Mary Louise Roberts, *Disruptive Acts* (University of Chicago Press, 2002), 39.
10. Johanna Gehmacher, 'In/Visible Transfers: Translation as a Crucial Practice in Transnational Women's Movements around 1900', *German Historical Institute London Bulletin* 41:2 (2019), 3–44.
11. Natalia Novikova, 'Early Historical Accounts of the Russian Women's Movement: A Political Dialogue or a Dispute?', *Women's History Review* 20:4 (2011), 509–19.

12. Frances Watkins Harper, 'We Are All Bound Up Together': speech at the 11th National Woman's Rights Convention in New York, May 1866.
13. June Edith Hahner, *Emancipating the Female Sex: The Struggle for Women's Rights in Brazil, 1850–1940* (Duke University Press, 1990), 26–30, 209–10.
14. Bonnie S. Anderson, *Joyous Greetings: The First International Women's Movement, 1830–1860* (Oxford University Press, 2001).
15. Francisca de Haan, 'Writing Inter-Transnational History: The Case of Women's Movements and Feminisms', in Barbara Haider-Wilson, William D. Godsey and Wolfgang Mueller (eds.), *Internationale Geschichte in Theorie und Praxis/ International History in Theory and Practice* (Verlag der Österreichischen Akademie der Wissenschaften, 2017), 501–36.
16. Kathy Davis, *The Making of Our Bodies, Ourselves: How Feminism Travels across Borders* (Duke University Press, 2008).
17. Nancy Hewitt's metaphor of radio waves has brilliantly signalled this idea of feminist voices of varying volumes: Nancy A. Hewitt (ed.), *No Permanent Waves: Recasting Histories of U.S. Feminism* (Rutgers University Press, 2010).
18. Kathryn Gleadle, 'The Imagined Communities of Women's History: Current Debates and Emerging Themes, a Rhizomatic Approach', *Women's History Review* 22:4 (2013), 524–40.
19. Kathryn Gleadle and Zoë Thomas, 'Global Feminisms, *c.* 1870–1930: Vocabularies and Concepts—A Comparative Approach', *Women's History Review* 27:7 (2018), 1209–24.
20. Kimberly Springer, *Living for the Revolution: Black Feminist Organizations, 1968-1980* (Duke University Press, 2005).
21. bell hooks, *Talking Back: Thinking Feminist, Thinking Black* (Sheba Feminist, 1989).
22. Mrinalini Sinha, 'Mapping the Imperial Social Formation: A Modest Proposal for Feminist History', *Signs* 25:4 (2000), 1077–82
23. 'Use' is critically explored by Sara Ahmed, *What's the Use? On the Uses of Use* (Duke University Press, 2019).
24. Kathleen A. Laughlin *et al.*, 'Is It Time to Jump Ship? Historians Rethink the Waves Metaphor', *Feminist Formations* 22:1 (2010), 97.

Genesis of the Black Working Class

Joe William Trotter

By the late eighteenth century, the enslaved African population had increased to well over a thousand in each of five cities: New York, Boston, Philadelphia, Charleston, and New Orleans. In the wake of the American Revolution, the free wage-earning black population had also expanded alongside the enslaved black working class. These black workers, both enslaved and free, fueled the rise of the early American city as they also enhanced the wealth and power of urban slaveowners and employers. Working as general laborers, domestic servants, building and construction laborers, deckhands, sailors, ship pilots, artisans, and factory workers, African people were indispensable to the growth and development of the new nation. Despite their crucial contributions to the rise of preindustrial America, however, free workers of color were not rewarded with increased opportunities and rights. In the first half of the nineteenth century, they encountered sharp competition from rising numbers of European immigrants, mostly from Germany and Ireland. At the same time, they lived and worked under the burden of racially restrictive labor legislation; a vigorous, white-led African recolonization movement; and mob violence. As a result, free blacks lost access to increasing numbers of jobs in the skilled craft s as well as the most coveted general labor and household-service occupations. Still, they were active participants in the making of their own lives as well as the New World social order.[1]

The Colonial Generation

The first urban black workers and their children cleared and leveled land, cut firewood, and prepared ground for the erection of buildings, for crop cultivation, and for burying the dead.[2] In 1723, among 88 survivors of one slave voyage to New Orleans, 50 enslaved men dug drainage ditches along the Mississippi River and constructed levees; 35 raised buildings on the company's plantation; and another 3 returned to work in the seafaring transatlantic trade system.[3] France may have founded New Orleans and Louisiana, "but it was slaves from Senegal to Congo who laid the foundation," historian Lawrence Powell concludes in his study of the city's history.[4] Similarly, within months of Charlestown's founding in 1670, the demand for enslaved blacks became so intense that buyers sometimes came "very nearly to Blows" wrangling over "who should get the good Slaves." Enslaved people toiled "in the streets of Charles Town, in the Anglican church and in the market, and in gentry dining rooms, kitchens, and stableyards."[5] For their part, early Afro–New Yorkers worked on the establishment and maintenance of the Dutch bouwerys (farms), Fort Amsterdam, and public roads. They also burned limestone and oyster shells for use in outhouses and for interring the dead. Only "a great deal of money," promises, and "bribe[s]," the Dutch West India Company declared, would induce white workers to perform such labor on behalf of the colony's survival and development.[6]

In Philadelphia, the *Pennsylvania Gazette* regularly advertised for slaves suited for both rural and urban labor, including household service. As indentured white servants increasingly "reneged on their contracts" and searched for "less restrictive employment" opportunities, one of Philadelphia's most active slave traders vigorously urged the "more general use of Slaves" over free white workers.[7] Bostonians, too, hoped to recruit "slaves sufficient to doe" all their general labor and household work. In 1740, an English visitor observed the use of black men as servants: When the Boston "ladies ride out to take the air in a chaise or chair ... they have a negro servant drive them. The gentlemen [also] ride out here as in England ... with their negroes to attend."[8]

African people helped to build and service the colonial city not only as general laborers and household and domestic workers but also as skilled craftsmen and craftswomen. Wealthy European merchants, artisans, and diverse business owners purchased, trained, and employed Africans as brick masons, carpenters, cabinetmakers, sailmakers, bakers, coopers, and tailors, among other trades. By the eve of the American Revolution, slaveholders encouraged black Philadelphians to learn trades and placed a large "share of the ordinary trades of the city in their hands." The *New York Gazette* as well as the *Boston News Letter, Boston Chronicle,* and *Boston Gazette* regularly carried ads for the purchase of slave coopers, carpenters, joiners, tailors, bakers, blacksmiths, and sometimes printers. In 1719, when a New York colonial court sentenced an African American blacksmith to death for theft, his owner, also a blacksmith, asked the court to spare the slave's life, arguing that he himself was a "very poor Lame and Antient man" and that he had "nothing whereby to sustain himself but what is procured by the Labour of the said Negro man."[9]

Blacks worked in an even broader range of skilled craft s in the urban South than in the North. New Bern, Petersburg, Richmond, and other smaller southern towns and cities employed significant numbers of enslaved craftsmen, but skilled blacks found their greatest opportunities for artisan labor in New Orleans, Charleston, and later to some extent Baltimore. Between 1750 and 1779, Charleston probate records revealed that no less than 73 percent of the city's artisans owned slaves upon their death. White artisans worked and cooperated "with slaves on a daily basis as blacks and whites learned their trades together." On one occasion, a carpenter, Thomas Bennett, sought "immediately a handy white lad and two negro boys as apprentices to carpenter's trade." Between 1770 and 1799, Charleston's white artisans placed twice as many newspaper advertisements for black as for white workers. In 1728, the governor of Louisiana reported "placing negroes as apprentices with all the workmen who we think are good and honest men, and if the same practice had been followed when they were first sent to the colony, we could at present do without several white men." By 1732, numerous New Orleans tradesmen and merchants owned blacks "whom they housed and trained in their shops." An estimated 15 percent of the city's enslaved people resided in artisan households, and some 25 percent of all the city's tradesmen "lived with slaves."[10] Enslaved African people not only cultivated the land and built the levees, but also "framed the houses, plastered the walls, and shingled the roofs. As well they forged the tools that made the barrels that stored the tobacco and indigo, which were then carried to market in wagons and carts that their hands built and kept in repair."[11]

In 1790, Baltimore's craftsmen and craftswomen accounted for one quarter of the city's slaveholders as well as a quarter of all enslaved blacks. Two decades later, Baltimore's artisans and manufacturers had increased to 35 percent of slaveowners, with 30 percent of the city's enslaved population. Significant numbers of Baltimore's enslaved blacks had gained skills as carpenters, blacksmiths, and lumber-mill hands in surrounding rural areas before moving to the city. At the turn of the nineteenth century, historian Charles Steffen notes, two-thirds of Baltimore's wealthiest fifty-two craftsmen owned one or more slaves. Enslaved skilled workers stood at the "top of the slave occupational hierarchy," and shipbuilders claimed the lion's share of enslaved blacks, "with a mean average" of about six slaves per firm among them.[12]

Artisans deployed a wide range of skills and know-how within the context of specific crafts. They took pride in their specialized tools, higher earnings, greater autonomy in the workforce, and "mastery of the expertise required to produce material objects their communities needed and valued." Before the advent of woodworking machinery of various types, especially planing machines, African American carpenters performed this work by hand much like their West African kinsmen. In precolonial West Africa, canoe builders had carved out "massive tree trunks, larger even than the giant cypress that boat slaves would hollow in South Carolina." According to historian and urban sociologist W. E. B. Du Bois and his co-author Augustus Dill, in the American colonies these artisans could thus take a "single-tree" from the forest and carve out "a hundred other things too numerous to mention." The African American carpenter "in those days was also the 'cabinet maker,' the woodturner, coffin maker, generally the pattern maker, and the maker of most things made of wood." Similarly, the African American blacksmith "in the days of slavery was expected to make any and everything wrought of iron. He was to all intents and purposes the 'machine blacksmith,' 'horseshoer,' 'carriage and wagon ironer and trimmer,' 'gunsmith,' [and] 'wheelwright.'"

Before their forced migration to South Carolina, some enslaved Africans had worked on the construction of the Barbadian city of Bridgetown. African artisans not only constructed the city's buildings but also "crafted their ornamental embellishments." More than those of any other North American city, Charleston's eighteenth-century buildings showed the distinct imprint of West African–influenced Barbadian culture, including intricate "wrought ironworks" on the galleries of buildings, gates, and "garden walls flanking the street."[13] While some contemporary observers described black artisans as "tolerable good," other observers used such terms as "first rate" and "excellent," especially in advertisements for the return of runaway craftsmen.[14]

While most black artisans were men, women also worked in the skilled trades. As early as July 1763, the *Providence Gazette* advertised for the return of a 38-year-old runaway named Dinas, described as a "skilled seamstress." The owner of another runaway female slave described her as a skilled "needlewoman." In New York, according to historian Leslie Harris, enslaved African American women, "like the white women of artisan families, assisted the men in their skilled tasks as necessary." Free black women were also prominent among the hardworking "artisans and tradespersons who lived above their own shops" in Charleston by the late eighteenth century. Moreover, similar to male migrants from surrounding farms and plantations across the early American North and South, large numbers of black women (some fugitives) migrated to cities from the countryside, where they had learned to spin thread, weave cloth, and sew. In Georgia, the state not only mandated that landowners plant five hundred acres of mulberry trees for every five hundred acres of land for the development of the silk culture but required that black slave women be sent to Savannah "at the proper season every year" to gain training in the craft of "reeling and winding silk." According to one scholar, revolutionary and early America represented a kind of "golden age" of the black artisan, including to some extent women as well as men.[15]

Able-bodied adult men and women carried out the bulk of slave labor, but colonial cities quickly incorporated enslaved children into established work routines. In 1721, one New York slaveholder, Cadwallader Colden, instructed his agent to buy two "well made" black males "about eighteen years of age" and "a negro Girl of about thirteen years old." Colden wanted the young men for general labor and the female to assist his wife, "chiefly to keep the children & to sow." In 1730, the *New York Gazette* advertised "a Likely Negro Girl about 18 Years of Age, and a likely Negro Boy about 16 Years, both born in this City, they can speak good English and Dutch and are bred up to all sorts of House-work." When Phillis Wheatley arrived in New England during the early 1760s, she also embarked upon a well-worn path of domestic slavery for young children in the household of a Boston family. And in 1766, the *South Carolina Gazette* described one 12-year-old as a "handy" girl with experience "waiting in a house and attending children." By hiring young people out, their owners could also earn more than enough to cover their keep. General and household labor of enslaved people, young and old, men and women, freed white men and, to some extent, white women for engagement in alternative professional, skilled, and entrepreneurial activities.[16]

Although poor and working-class whites also labored in such general and household service jobs and buoyed the wealth of colonial elites, enslaved people enriched cities through both their labor and their sale as commodities on the open market. Slaveowners used this distinction to help discipline the enslaved labor force and sharpen the divide between free and slave labor. As historian Daniel Walker notes, the threat of sale was one of the most effective "social-control mechanisms available to slave regimes throughout the Americas, both rural and urban." Enslaved blacks themselves would later recall how some owners "used to say that if we didn't suit him he would put us in his pocket quick—meaning he would sell us."[17]

While their numbers would remain small, the free black population nonetheless slowly increased by the beginning of the American Revolution, rising to 600 in Charleston and to just over 1,000 in Philadelphia and New York. Compared to their plantation counterparts, urban black workers gained substantial access to long-distance travel, informal commercial networks, wage labor, and opportunities for emancipation. At the core of this cluster of forces was the "hiring-out" system, including the Dutch system of "half freedom" in New Amsterdam. This arrangement enabled some enslaved people to find their own jobs, negotiate wages, and, through overwork, earn their own money to purchase their freedom and the freedom of loved ones. This system of labor was by no means limited to the city. Historian Dylan Penningroth estimated that 6 percent of enslaved rural blacks and 31 percent of urban slaves worked under hiring-out agreements by the late antebellum years, and "over a lifetime, their chances of being hired out increased."[18]

Sailors and river pilots figured prominently among the gradually expanding free black population. By the mid-eighteenth century, black men, slave and free, constituted as much as 25 percent of the muster for vessels departing Atlantic port cities for the high seas. Black and white sailors endured an exceedingly hierarchical, violent, and repressive shipboard environment. They weathered the same storms, shipwrecks, and "the same infernally leaking ships." But black sailors worked disproportionately as cooks and stewards and encountered frequent day-to-day assaults on their persons. One sailor, John Jea, later recalled how his white shipmates "used to flog, beat, and kick me about, the same as I had been a dog." Another free black sailor, John Dean, related to Thomas Clarkson, a young British scholar and social activist, how the captain of one ship punished him for a "trifling" infraction "for which he was in no-wise to blame." The captain "fastened him with his belly to the deck, and that in this situation, he had poured hot pitch upon his back, and made incisions in it with hot tongs." Yet despite this context of violent inequality, the open sea nonetheless offered enslaved blacks opportunities to breach the racial divide emerging in the urban Atlantic world, including engagement in interracial working-class mutinies and piracy.[19]

The sailor Olaudah Equiano spent the bulk of his life "either in ports or on ships sailing between ports." Equiano not only learned to read, write, and cipher while still enslaved but obtained permission to hire himself out as an experienced sailor on the high seas. He soon took advantage of the "working" and hiring-out system to accumulate sufficient funds to purchase his freedom. Somewhat similar to Equiano, the enslaved Charlestonian Thomas Jeremiah learned the pilot's trade and obtained his freedom by the eve of the Revolution. All oceangoing vessels appearing in Charleston Harbor depended on skilled pilots like Jeremiah, "who guided vessels over the bar through the harbor's narrow ship channel." Jeremiah became an experienced pilot, thoroughly acquainted with "the time and direction of the tide, knowledge of the reigning winds; of the different depths of the water." He became a stellar example of how one enslaved African not only became a free wage earner but also transformed himself into an influential member of the free black elite. On one occasion, he was convicted and sentenced to the stocks to receive ten lashes, but he appealed his sentence and received a pardon from the lieutenant governor and commander in chief.[20]

Figure 3.2.1 African people not only entered colonial North America in the holds of slave ships. They also worked as deckhands on numerous vessels that plied the Atlantic during the era of the slave trade. Here, the eighteenth-century Anglo-American artist included an African among white shipmates during a rescue at sea in Havana, based on a real-life event. Watson and the Shark, 1778 by John Singleton Copley. Courtesy, National Gallery of Art, Washington, DC.

The piloting skills of early American blacks were closely intertwined with knowledge acquired in the Old World. Along with canoe-building, carpentry, and blacksmithing skills, African people brought river navigational skills to the Americas. On the inland and coastal waters of West Africa and the New World, Europeans depended on the skills of African boatmen, and ship pilots connected enslaved people and Europeans to emerging capitalist markets on both sides of the Atlantic. Thus, according to historian Kevin Dawson, "privileged exploitation" marked the lives and labor of enslaved pilots. They exchanged their specialized knowledge for opportunities to cultivate "semi-independent lives within the boundaries of bondage." Although European captains of ships proved competent to steer vessels across the Atlantic, they recognized the expertise of the African boatmen and "willingly entrusted" their lives to these skilled black rivermen. In August 1778, an enslaved pilot steered a fifty-gun British warship through the dangerous passage called Hell Gate, near Harlem, New York. When the white commander countered his orders during a particularly perilous moment in the journey, the black pilot firmly retorted, "You no speak here!" The captain complied and the African successfully guided the ship to safety.[21]

Rivermen and sailors occupied a pivotal place in the development of African American trade networks. As he moved from port to port around the globe, Equiano supplemented his wages through the sale of quantities of rum and sugar. In 1765, when his ship docked in Philadelphia, he quickly engaged the local trade network of enslaved and free blacks and sold a few of his own products "chiefly to the Quakers." On another occasion, Equiano sailed into Charleston Harbor. He hired a crew of enslaved black rivermen to ferry him across the harbor to conduct business. Charleston's black river pilots helped Equiano dispose of his wares. Unlike white Philadelphians, however, Charleston's white men purchased Equiano's sugar and rum, as he later reported, "with smooth promises and fair words" but paid him in debased copper dollars. According to Equiano, one white Charlestonian "took advantage of my being a negro man, and obliged me to put up with those [copper coins] or none, although I objected."[22]

Trade networks, wage labor, and employment on the high seas and inland waterways all contributed to the growing number of free people of color, which in turn broadened opportunities for other enslaved blacks to escape bondage and become free wage earners. Charleston slaveowners complained that runaways hired themselves out to free people of color. Aft er successfully hiding out for eight months, Harry, a carpenter, was finally sighted on King Street in Charleston. He had apparently secured employment with free black carpenters, "as he is intimate with numbers of them." One low-country resident reported that his Angolan washerwoman "sometimes hires herself to free negroes." Another Angolan slave, a skilled needlewoman, also received employment from "free Negroes and others" during her time away "without permission."[23]

While some free blacks provided significant opportunities for their enslaved counterparts to obtain freedom, others insisted that their own freedom included the right to purchase, own, and employ slave labor on equal terms with their white counterparts. Both New Orleans and Charleston exhibited elements of this process, described by some scholars as a "three-tier" or "three-caste" society, where mixed-race free people of color stood between the large majority of enslaved blacks and their white owners. In this system, the most well-to-do free blacks not only became slaveowners themselves but also allied with white slaveowners to discourage and even help to squash slave rebellions. "Libres," as historian Kimberly Hanger notes, justified the enslavement of most black people in exchange for an opportunity to manumit their own kinsmen and women.

While late eighteenth- and early nineteenth-century Savannah is often treated as a three-tier city, recent scholarship uncovers a greater measure of racial solidarity among free and enslaved blacks in Savannah than in Charleston and New Orleans. Nonetheless, slaveholding was an important indicator of increasing social stratification among blacks in all three of these cities.[24]

Revolution, the New Republic, and the Free Black Proletariat

Under the impact of the American Revolution, the end of the international slave trade in 1808, and passage of the Northwest Ordinance in 1787 prohibiting slavery north of the Ohio River, the free black population dramatically increased during the early nineteenth century. Free people of color rose from no more than about 1,000 at the outset of the period in each city to nearly 2,000 in Boston by the 1830s and 1840s, 10,000 in Philadelphia, 14,000 in New York, 2,000 in Charleston, 3,000 in Washington, DC, 11,600 in New

Orleans, and 14,800 in Baltimore (the largest concentration of free blacks in the nation at that time). The majority of urban blacks, free and enslaved, men and women, migrated to southern cities from surrounding rural areas within the South, while northern black communities expanded through the arrival of increasing numbers of southern-born black migrants, particularly from the Upper South and border states of Virginia and Maryland.[25]

By the early nineteenth century, black women outdistanced men in most cities across the urban North and South. In 1850, only Richmond among major antebellum cities reported an excess of black men over women. Antebellum slaveowners increasingly sold able-bodied and skilled black men to the booming cotton-growing regions of the Deep South, leaving cities with disproportionately large black female populations. This phenomenon was not limited to adolescent boys or adult males, but also included young boys under ten years of age. Although New Orleans enacted a law against the sale of children under ten, the greater numbers of female than male children in this group suggest that the law against selling young children was not systematically enforced.[26]

Enslaved and free black women shouldered the twin burdens of reproductive and productive labor. As recent scholars note, the colonial and early national eras witnessed the gradual emergence of the "Atlantic service economy," characterized by the increasing "commodification of reproductive labor." Middle class and elite families turned to poor and working-class women to perform labor that "ladies" of the household increasingly viewed as beneath their station in life. In their detailed analysis of black women's lives in colonial Boston and other New England towns, historians Catherine Adams and Elizabeth H. Pleck underscore the pursuit and use of enslaved women to perform what they describe as "household drudge" work. Among the wealthiest households, enslaved black women and girls polished furniture and the family silver and assisted the "lady" of the house with her clothes and hair, drew her bath, and mended her clothes. Some elite men also preferred "the servant girl to shave them rather than going to a barber." The vast majority of mistresses nonetheless used enslaved women "not as their personal attendant" but rather as heavy-laden domestic laborers—black women were "put to work sweeping, emptying chamber pots, carrying water, washing the dishes, brewing, looking aft er children, cooking and baking, spinning, knitting, carding, and sewing."[27]

Household labor not only entailed long hours and tedious work—cleaning, cooking, washing, ironing, sewing, or whatever employers demanded—but it also made black women vulnerable to widespread physical and sexual abuse. In Charleston, some slaveowners realized a "superordinate level of accumulation" by forcing enslaved women household workers to perform "sexual acts for money" in addition to their washing, cleaning, and other domestic tasks. In some cases, slaveowners ordered enslaved women to have sex with enslaved men to increase the slave workforce. Among free people of color, live-in single women servants faced the brunt of such sexual and labor exploitation on the job, while married women made up the bulk of washerwomen—a low-paying and exceedingly labor-intensive but preferred job. In 1817, black women made up nearly 80 percent of all washerwomen listed in the Baltimore city directory. Among black female heads of households, laundrywomen accounted for 194 of 231 female heads of households in 1822 and 440 of 526 in 1840. The advantage of this job was that washerwomen worked within their own homes while supervising and caring for young children. Nonetheless, washing entailed carrying heavy buckets of water from hydrants or streams to backyards and kitchens, where the women boiled the water and carried out the heavy labor of scrubbing and lifting water-soaked garments. This work resulted in "aching backs, ... burning hands from lye soaps and rough washboards." Next, washerwomen hung the clothes out in backyards to dry and then "heated irons on the fire to press the clothes and delivered bundles of clean and pressed laundry to the owners."[28]

Although women increasingly outnumbered men in the urban North and South, employers continued to value men over women in the wage-earning labor market. While enslaved and free black women labored almost exclusively as household workers, enslaved and free black men worked as artisans, general laborers, and factory hands as well as household and personal servants. Some southern industrial promoters hoped to end the region's dependence on northern industrial firms for consumer goods. They looked to African American men as a source of industrial labor "in cotton and woolen factories, ... in iron furnaces, ... factories and work shops, ... in the manufacture of such articles as are now made almost exclusively in the Northern states."

While slave labor gradually disappeared from the northern workforce by mid-century, free and enslaved blacks continued to labor side by side in the industrializing urban South. In most instances, the preference was for enslaved labor. In 1845, the governor of South Carolina wrote to the British abolitionist Thomas Clarkson that "we are beginning to manufacture with slaves."[29] A few years later, in Charleston, April 10–15, 1854, the Southern and Western States Convention passed a resolution affirming that "experiments have fully proven that slave labor can be profitably employed in manufacturing establishments." By 1850, enslaved blacks made up a majority of the laborers at the city's Gibbes and Williams Steam Saw Mill, the Bennett Mill, and the Chisholm Mill. Other industrial firms that hired enslaved workers included West Point Rice Mills, Horlbeck's Brickyard, and the Charleston Bridge Company. Located on the Ashley River, the West Point Rice Mills employed African American engineers, blacksmiths, carpenters, and coopers among its 160-member slave workforce. Further, the Savannah, Ogeechee, and Altamaha Canal Company, chartered in 1824, leased hundreds of enslaved men from Georgia slaveowners to clear land, dig the channel, and construct the canal locks that connected the Savannah River with the Ogeechee. Savannah's enslaved black men also worked for the Georgia Central Railroad Company, the Upper Steam Rice Mill, the Steam Boat Company of Georgia, and the Savannah Brick Company, to name a few. Historian Whittington Johnson notes, "Nearly all the crew of the Georgia Central Railroad, except the conductors, was composed of slaves; the engineers, firemen, other workers, and construction crews were slaves." In New Orleans, during the 1790s, an estimated 20 percent of "libres," or free people of color, worked in the "manufacturing" sector, mainly as shoemakers and carpenters.[30]

The enthusiasm for slave labor in the manufacturing and other sectors of the urban economy meant that free black men and women almost uniformly worked in jobs defined as less skilled and at lower pay than their enslaved and free white counterparts. At the same time, however, the South's black workers as a whole often occupied a broader range of skilled and manufacturing jobs than their counterparts farther north. This phenomenon was not limited to the Deep South as suggested by the above examples. Baltimore's Maryland Chemical Works employed predominantly adult male black workers to manufacture some thirty different "medicines, pigments, dyes, and industrial chemicals." But the firm was "best known for its alum, used by cloth manufactures as a mordant to set dyes in cloth," characterized by an exceedingly tedious labor process. "Throughout the six-to-eight-month process, laborers stoked furnaces, agitated alum broth, raked up drying alum heaps, and shoveled alum from furnace to cistern and back again, day and night, seven days a week." In Louisville, even though most enslaved and free blacks occupied jobs as janitors, handymen, and household servants, by 1850 over 13 percent of black men occupied jobs as craftsmen compared to 8.2 percent in Cincinnati and about 4 percent in Pittsburgh. More so than their northern counterparts, southern employers often blurred the line between African American male and female laborers and adult and child laborers. One Louisville firm advertised for "100 women and boys for brickyards, draymen, etc., 40 men and boys for ropewalk, 40 men and boys for hotel waiters, and 50 boys and girls for tobacco stemmeries."[31]

Richmond emerged as the premier employer of blacks in the manufacturing sector of the urban economy. It claimed a reputation as "the manufacturing heart of Dixie" and the principal employer of black industrial workers. At the outbreak of the Civil War, the city's enslaved population had increased from fewer than 5,000 in 1820 to over 11,600 in 1860; only 2,500 free people of color lived in Richmond. Moreover, as noted above, Richmond was the only city to consistently count more black men than women. Black men took the lion's share of jobs in the city's expanding manufacturing economy. The city employed black workers in its flour mills, stone quarries, and nearby coal fields as well as in the construction of buildings, canals, and railroads. Most important, as the South's premier tobacco- and iron-producing center, Richmond employed large numbers of enslaved black workers in its leading industrial sector. At Joseph Anderson's renowned Tredegar Iron Company, African Americans performed all available skilled jobs—as puddlers, heaters, and rollers—as well as general labor. In a letter to the editor of a leading Charleston, South Carolina, newspaper, Anderson proudly advertised his firm's reliance on slave labor. He rented and hired enslaved blacks but "preferred to own them." At the core of his workforce were a "lot of 35 men and boys he had specially trained to handle key operations." Black workers also fueled the labor force at the James H. Grant, T. S. Hardgrove, and Talbott Brothers tobacco-manufacturing plants.[32]

Tobacco manufacturing involved enslaved men, women, and children in an intricate and arduous system of production. The tobacco industry revolved around the production of smoking and especially chewing tobacco. Each process entailed lots of heavy lifting, packaging, and repackaging of hogsheads; labor-intensive preliminary work in the tobacco stemmeries, where women worked on the roof of buildings as "pickers" sorting and resorting dried tobacco leaves; and the actual manufacturing of the final product itself. Tobacco manufacturers focused mainly on supplying the huge market for chewing tobacco. By the beginning of the Civil War, Richmond reported some fifty tobacco factories employing no fewer than 3,400 African American workers. Antebellum tourists to the city viewed a visit to a tobacco factory as a high point of their journey, "drawn by the unusual sight [and sound] of black industrial workers coordinating their repetitive motions through song." In the making of chewing tobacco, once women had stemmed and dried the leaves, "skilled black men would mix huge vats of a black, syrupy compound of licorice and sugar into which they would dip the stemmed leaves. ... In the lump-making room, two-men teams—the lumper (or twister) and his helper, usually a child—jointly labored."[33]

Across the urban industrial South, in Richmond and elsewhere, employers of slave labor reported large annual profit margins, reaching between 7 and 10 percent in most cases and as high as 42–65 percent in other instances.[34]

Immigration and the Limits of Free Labor

In addition to the use of enslaved workers in southern industry, free wage earners of color encountered new and more daunting challenges in the urban North and South during the antebellum years. For one thing, Deep South cotton planters required increasing numbers of skilled blacks "to construct quarters for master and slaves and to build and repair barns, presses, and a variety of agricultural machinery." In their seminal essay on the subject, labor historians Ira Berlin and Herbert Gutman concluded, "Slave artisans may have been the first to go west, pulled out of the cities in large numbers by the rapid spread of plantation agriculture across the South. In a time of great economic growth, artisan standing provided scant protection from sale ... to distant rural workplaces, a process that reduced the number of slave artisans in cities."[35] At the same time, the estimated 3.7 million European immigrants who entered the United States between the American Revolution and 1860 took an expanding range of jobs in the artisan field, the newly developing manufacturing sector, and the most lucrative segments of household, general labor, and personal service employment.[36]

Massive European immigration had its most profound impact on the development of the northern black working class. By 1850, black men holding skilled jobs stood at only 8.3, 5.4, and 5.7 percent, respectively, in Philadelphia, New York, and Boston. In Pittsburgh and Cincinnati, respectively, only 4 and 8 percent of blacks gained jobs as carpenters, shoemakers, masons, and other skilled artisans. Although the South attracted relatively fewer immigrants, significant numbers moved to Richmond, Baltimore, New Orleans, Charleston, Savannah, and other southern cities. By the onset of the Civil War, immigrants had increased to over 20 percent of the total population in Charleston and over 25 percent in Savannah. Predominantly adult men, immigrants made up over 30 percent of the working class in Richmond and 42 percent in Charleston. In 1829, when the Chesapeake and Ohio Canal Company built a waterway just above Georgetown in the District of Columbia, it initially employed African Americans but quickly replaced them with Irishmen.

Nonetheless, despite heightened competition with immigrant workers, southern free wage earners of color held on to a uniformly higher ratio of skilled jobs than their northern counterparts. In 1850, between 12 and 18 percent of free black men reported employment as artisans in Washington, Baltimore, and Louisville. These figures reached over 60 percent in New Orleans and Charleston, where the size of the free black population remained exceedingly small compared to the number of enslaved African American workers.[37]

In the urban North, black carpenters, plasterers, masons, and other skilled workers found few opportunities for employment even among their white abolitionist supporters. As skilled black artisans moved into the urban North in rising numbers, they repeatedly complained that they "found every door closed against the colored man in a free state, excepting the jails and penitentiaries," and they described themselves as little better off than their brothers and sisters in Virginia. And as their parents encountered these barriers, black youth gained few opportunities to enter the skilled crafts. In 1836, a convention of the New England Anti-Slavery Society reported, "The colored people are almost altogether deprived of bringing up their children to mechanical employments, to commercial business, or other more lucrative occupations, whereby so many of our white laborers are enabled to rise above the drudgery in which they commence their ... life."[38]

Across the early nineteenth-century economy, free black workers faced increasing confinement to a narrow range of jobs described as general labor and household and personal service. "Competition of the foreigners," Du Bois concluded, pushed Philadelphia's black artisans "more and more to the wall."[39] At the same time, as master craftsmen increasingly expelled blacks from the artisan trades, new northern manufacturing firms hired white over black labor. These included cotton textile mills, machine foundries, and boot and shoe manufacturing firms in New York, Philadelphia, Providence, and Boston, as well as booming iron, shipbuilding, and milling industries in the urban Midwest, most notably Cincinnati and Pittsburgh. By 1850, an estimated 70 percent of Pittsburgh's African American men worked as general laborers, coachmen, and waiters, and in other household service jobs, while 66 percent of Cincinnati's black men occupied only five job categories: boatmen, barbers, laborers, cooks, and waiters.[40]

Increasing numbers of black artisans put the tools of their trade aside and turned to any general labor job that they could find. Frederick Douglass recalled, "Finding my trade of no immediate benefit, I threw off my calking habiliments, and prepared myself to do any kind of work I could get to do." Douglass took jobs sawing wood, carrying hods for bricklayers, sweeping chimneys, and transporting heavy oil casks, among others.[41] In seaports across the country, enslaved and free black dockworkers put in long hours lifting and transporting 500-pound bales of cotton and heavy barrels of rice, sugar, and other bulk products at low pay. In some cases, black dockworkers "would turn three hogsheads ... upon their ends at once, each ... weighing one thousand pounds net weight." While black and white seamen earned about the same rate for the same job in northern ports, blacks received lower wages than whites for identical work in southern ports.

As black labor became further devalued, sailing jobs on the high seas as well as the prestigious piloting jobs on the inland rivers became less available to black workers. On the Mississippi, Missouri, and Ohio Rivers, the new steamboat owners and captains excluded blacks from jobs as officers, pilots, captains, engineers, clerks, and mates during the antebellum heyday of steamship travel. The preponderance of both enslaved and free black rivermen worked as laborers, dockhands, roustabouts, cooks, and cabin-cleaning crews. They also labored under harsh conditions. Riverside slaveowners themselves sometimes complained about the "overzealous driving" of enslaved blacks leased to the steamboat companies.[42]

Contemporary elite travelers and observers regularly commented on the growing concentration of blacks in what they called "menial service." A New Orleans doctor summed up this perspective when he observed black people "ever at the elbow ... behind a table, in hotels and steamboats, ever ready, brush in hand, to brush the coat or black the shoes, or to perform any *menial service* which may be required" (my italics). As early as 1815, a Cincinnati physician described blacks as "disciplined to laborious occupations ... and menial drudgery."[43] In the minds of white workers, according to a Cincinnati editor, it was largely the evils associated with human bondage that confined free blacks to a limited range of jobs "despised as being the work of slaves."[44] And this perspective proved largely immune to change. In 1793, when the Philadelphia yellow fever epidemic took the lives of some 4,000 whites and 250 blacks, African Americans worked for their distressed white neighbors as "nurses, gravediggers, and drivers of death carts." By carrying out the most dangerous and arduous work associated with the epidemic, black Philadelphians hoped not only to counter white racial hatred against the rising numbers of free people of color but also to secure much needed employment during their early transition from enslaved to free workers. But their sacrifices did little to stem resistance to African American movement up the job hierarchy into skilled artisan positions and the nascent urban manufacturing sector as the nineteenth century got under way.[45]

Martin R. Delany, a migrant from Virginia, observed growing limits on African American employment in Pittsburgh and other expanding antebellum cities. In his famous black nationalist manifesto, issued in 1852, Delany complained, "Our fathers are their coachmen, our brothers their cookmen, and ourselves their waiting men. Our mothers their nurse-women, our sisters their scrub-women, our daughters their maid-women, and our wives their washer-women." Similarly, the early nineteenth-century woman activist Maria Stewart pointedly asked, "How long shall the fair daughters of Africa be compelled to bury their minds and talents beneath a load of iron pots and kettles?"[46] Douglass also chimed in. He described the barber trade as a viable livelihood for significant numbers of blacks, while nonetheless treating it as a lowly craft that exceedingly able blacks sometimes pursued for lack of other, more remunerative and professional alternatives. Describing the barber J. M. Whitfield as "the Colored Poet of America," Douglass lamented that Whitfield's talents were confined to his barbershop. It "is painfully disheartening," Douglass said, "that talents so commanding, gifts so rare, poetic powers so distinguished, should be tied to the handle of a razor and buried in the precincts of a barbershop." Douglass, Delany, Stewart, and other free people of color did not decry domestic service labor per se, but they believed that it should not be the primary station of an entire people. Delany explained that the occupation of servant was not necessarily degrading "to one or a few people of a kind; but a whole race of servants are a degradation to that people."[47]

Even as blacks protested limits on their access to skilled jobs, they denounced the displacement of blacks from their previous strongholds in low-wage and low-prestige jobs. The barbering trade had emerged as one of the most lucrative among early nineteenth-century black men. Following the Revolution, increasing numbers of white men had abandoned it as a "servile" trade, inimical to the values of the new republican nation. African Americans soon took the lion's share of barbering jobs in the urban North and South, securing the niche by developing an elaborate system of apprenticeships for young men and opening innovative "first class" barbershops. Catering to an exclusively elite white clientele, these establishments emerged in the heart of expanding business districts in Baltimore, Charleston, Philadelphia, New York, and other cities. Black barbershops not only provided "expert" shaves and haircuts but also sold wigs and diverse personal care items, while also providing a social and political gathering place for white men of substantial influence in the urban political economy. Historian Douglas Bristol notes in his pioneering study of the black barber that these black workers envisioned themselves as skilled "knights of the razor" and transformed a job that whites perceived as "servile" into a badge of accomplishment and even "superiority" rather than "inferiority."[48]

THE ILLUSTRATED LONDON NEWS.

No. 1078.—VOL. XXXVIII. SATURDAY, MARCH 9, 1861. [WITH A SUPPLEMENT, FIVEPENCE

DEBATING IN FRANCE.

Figure 3.2.2 Urban blacks worked in a broad range of household services, general labor, and skilled crafts. The barber trade emerged as one of the most lucrative jobs open to free people of color before the onset of the Civil War. Here, a black barber is shaving a white customer in his shop in Richmond, Virginia. Courtesy, Albert and Shirley Small, Special Collections Library, University of Virginia, Charlottesville.

Soon, however, large numbers of Irish and to some extent German immigrants took jobs as house servants, cooks, stewards, barbers, and laborers. In 1853, in a famous editorial, "Learn Trades or Starve," penned following a national black convention in Rochester, New York, Douglass observed, "The old avocations, by which colored men obtained a livelihood, are rapidly, unceasingly and inevitably passing into other hands. Every hour sees the black man elbowed out of employment by some newly arrived emigrant whose hunger and whose color are thought to give him a better title to the place. ... White men are becoming house servants, cooks and stewards of vessels, at hotels, they are becoming porters, stevedores, woodsawyers, hodcarriers, brickmakers, whitewashers and barbers." "A few years ago," Douglass concluded, "a white barber would have been a curiosity—now their poles stand on every corner." In New York, municipal officials routinely rejected black applications for licenses to engage in the carrying trade. When black workers ignored such regulations and continued to work despite white resistance, white carters used physical force to drive black men out of this job. As early as the 1830s, New York's *Colored American* magazine protested discrimination against black carters and urged the mayor to use his influence to end the practice. In letters on the condition of the African race, one antebellum "southern lady" reported that legions of "foreigners" of New York had not only pushed blacks out of "all mechanical trades but even out of the most menial labors."[49]

In addition to the challenge of immigration, the place of blacks in the urban economy was further undermined by a plethora of statutes enacted by states and municipalities in the antebellum period. In 1818, the Kentucky legislature prohibited the immigration of free blacks into the state from elsewhere. In 1834, another state law required free black residents to post a bond in order to avoid expulsion from the state. Charleston passed a statute prohibiting the training of slaves for "any mechanic or handicraft trade." The Charleston city council reported that low-grade or what it called "menial" occupations were "necessarily confined to coloured persons." In 1822, the South Carolina legislature had outlawed the practice of "self-hiring" and imposed a penalty on violators, including the possible "forfeiture of the slave" involved. Savannah not only enacted laws that discriminated against free blacks but also levied special burdens on free women of color. The city required any free person of color who settled in the city to pay a fee of $100. Conviction under the law required men to work 100 days to meet the requirements of the law, but women had to labor 125 days before they were released from forced labor on public projects. In New Orleans, the city council enacted a statute in 1822 restricting municipal jobs to white laborers only, although by the 1850s nearly 50 percent of free black men would still be working in skilled jobs.[50]

Federal law prohibited slavery north of the Ohio River, but midwestern state constitutions and legislation nevertheless discriminated against free blacks and limited their access to free territory. Ohio, Indiana, Illinois, and Michigan required free blacks to post bonds (as much as $500) before they could become legal residents in these states. White migrants and immigrants were not required to post such bonds. In New York, whereas white men had unrestricted access to the state's franchise, black New Yorkers had to demonstrate ownership of $250 worth of property to qualify to vote. In order to repeal this restriction, New York blacks formed suffrage committees throughout the state. But by 1860, only Maine, New Hampshire, Vermont, and Massachusetts allowed free blacks full access to the franchise. Both northern and southern states limited the rights of free blacks to testify in court against whites, serve in the militia, marry across racial lines, attend public schools, gain access to public accommodations on an equal footing with white patrons, and even petition their government. In 1839, the Ohio legislature proclaimed that blacks and mulattoes "have no constitutional right to present their petitions to the General Assembly for any purpose whatsoever, and that any reception of such petitions on the part of the General Assembly is a mere act of privilege or policy and not imposed by any expressed or implied power of the constitution."[51]

The Assault on Free Blacks: Colonization and the Fugitive Slave Act

Efforts to curtail the presence of free black workers gained increasing elite and working-class white support with the formation of the American Colonization Society (ACS) in 1816. Under the leadership of northern and southern white elites, the ACS established headquarters in the nation's capital and spearheaded a vigorous campaign to recolonize free people of color (presumably with their consent) on African land "or such other places as Congress shall deem most expedient." The organization's constitution expressed the belief that colonization would not only rid the country of free blacks but also prepare "the way for getting rid of slaves and of slavery" within the borders of the continental United States. But the ACS's motives were far from support for the dignity of African Americans. In its publication, the *African Repository,* the ACS repeatedly articulated colonization in racist terms, describing free people of color as "notoriously ignorant, degraded and miserable, mentally diseased, broken-spirited, acted upon by no motive to honourable exertions, scarcely reached in their debasement by the heavenly light." Poor and working-class whites enthusiastically endorsed colonization as a way to remove a major competitor from the labor force, bid up the price of their own labor, and secure a place in the economy and politics of the city and nation alongside white elites. But African Americans viewed colonization, alongside the institution of slavery itself, as the greatest threat to the development of a viable free wage-earning black working class and citizenry.[52]

The African colonization movement had begun well before the incorporation of the ACS. As early as 1787, colonizationist William Thornton arrived in Philadelphia to promote a scheme for returning emancipated slaves to West Africa. He offered African Americans glowing promises of "free land" as well as self-government, schools, and "free trade" with the United States, Britain, and France. Nearly a decade later, Thomas Branagan, an Irish Catholic immigrant and former overseer on a West Indian sugar plantation, also moved to Philadelphia and pushed for the removal of free people of color to an all-black state. Rather than Africa as a destination, Branagan advocated the emigration of blacks to the western edges of the Louisiana Territory. Despite their lofty rhetoric about the possibilities of a free black state, both Branagan and Thornton described free black workers on American soil as "hopelessly degraded," "inferior," and incapable of succeeding in a free society by virtue of white prejudice against free people of color as well as their own deficiencies brought on by generations of enslavement and "degradation."[53]

In his bid to gain cross-class white support for the "repatriation" of black people, Branagan also played on white fears of interracial sex and marriage. In his 1805 anti-slave trade pamphlet, *Serious Remonstrances,* Branagan identified free black men of Philadelphia as a threat to white "racial purity." Upon gaining their freedom, he said, free men of color avidly pursued sex with white women, including by rape and the entrapment of some "white women into the bonds of matrimony." He urged white working-class and poor men to "imagine" their daughters "who have been deluded, and are now married to negroes, living in little smoaking huts, despised and scorned by both blacks, and whites." Similarly, early nineteenth-century white men denigrated enslaved and free black women and treated them as a danger to the sexual morality of white men and boys, although they nonetheless believed that black women "could be mastered and controlled [that is sexually exploited] by white American men."[54]

These ideas gradually helped to create the foundation for the formation of the ACS as a national organization. In 1817, Robert Goodloe Harper, a Baltimorean, originally from South Carolina, published a public letter urging support for the ACS. He declared free blacks permanently scarred by their "habits of thoughtless improvidence," which they presumably "contracted" while slaves, and he exhorted white Baltimoreans to halt this "idle, worthless race." While postrevolutionary northern white allies and some southern whites had supported the gradual emancipation of African people on U.S. soil, following the War of 1812 they elevated recolonization to the center of their programs for the "uplift" of African people. New York City's Manumission Society stimulated the formation of state and local chapters of the ACS, adopted its agenda, and finally disbanded as a separate entity in 1849. ACS chapters had spread to Pittsburgh, Boston, and other northern cities by the 1820s. Influential political, religious, and economic elites formed the Pittsburgh chapter of the ACS in 1826. Founding members included local Presbyterian ministers, lawyers, and cotton-mill owner Rev. Charles Avery. As late as 1852, Pittsburgh colonizationists urged the federal government to use surplus revenue to help recolonize free people of color on African soil. When ACS headquarters opened an office in Boston during the early 1830s, the popular minister Lyman Beecher quickly gathered "a host of New England clergymen in proclaiming the merits of African colonization and asking God to prosper the cause." In 1835, when the ACS encountered increasing difficulties funding its repatriation projects, the Pennsylvania and New York City chapters broke from the parent body and jointly sponsored their own African resettlement projects.[55]

Finally, passage of the Fugitive Slave Law of 1850, kidnappings, and the reenslavement of fugitives and free people of color alike further weakened the position of black workers in late antebellum cities. Black Bostonians lamented the sight of soldiers and policemen marching black fugitives over the grounds of the Boston Massacre, where Crispus Attucks and his white comrades had lost their lives in the fight for independence, and down to Boston Harbor for transport to a life of slavery in the southern states. F. H. Pettis, a Virginian with a law practice in New York, boldly advertised his fugitive-catching services as "important to the south." According to Pettis's ad, New York City contained an estimated "5,000 Runaway Slaves." Furthermore, the ad stated that the new federal law "renders it easy for the recovery of such property." Slave catchers regularly passed through the Ohio Valley cities of Cincinnati and Pittsburgh and other northern cities in search of prey.

In the wake of the Fugitive Slave Law, free blacks and their white supporters repeatedly complained that "unscrupulous whites" jailed free people of color on false pretenses; others claimed these free blacks as their own slaves and then sold them "into perpetual slavery." In the meantime, southern legislators increased their campaign to obliterate the free black population. In 1859, Maryland's Eastern Shore planter and legislator Curtis Jacobs introduced a bill calling for the complete removal of the state's free black population, declaring before the state's House of Delegates, "Nothing short of an ultimate extinguishment of the free negro element ... will cure the evils we labor under." A similar bill had been introduced into the South Carolina legislature the previous year, expressing the desire of white South Carolinians to "purge our community" of free people of color.[56]

Remarkably, the number of free wage earners of color in the United States continued to increase through the early nineteenth century in the face of kidnappings, reenslavement, and intensifying competition and conflict with white workers. But their proportion of the cities' total populations dramatically declined over time. African Americans dropped from just over 10 percent of New York's total population in 1800 to only 1.5 percent in 1860. Boston's black population also slipped, from its comparatively small 4 percent of the total in 1800 to less than 2 percent by 1860. In 1830, the African American percentage of Philadelphia's total population peaked at 12 percent, Baltimore's at 23 percent, and Charleston's at 57 percent. New Orleans had reached its highest proportion of blacks (63 percent) two decades earlier. At the outbreak of the Civil War, Charleston and New Orleans were no longer majority-black cities.[57] These declines reflected the increasingly oppressive racial conditions that confronted free and enslaved blacks during the turbulent 1850s.

Conclusion

Free and enslaved black workers helped to build, develop, and maintain the preindustrial city. Without them, no doubt, economic productivity, infrastructure development, and wealth creation would have slowed considerably in the major cities of the North and South. And, in turn, their efforts also created the beginnings of the African American working class. By the onset of the Civil War, slavery had gradually disappeared in the northern states and much of the urban Upper South, reinforcing the rise of the free wage-earning black working class. Like their enslaved counterparts, increasing numbers of free people of color took jobs as general laborers and domestic and personal servants in a variety of households, the military, and business establishments. Significant numbers of enslaved and free people of color also worked in the skilled craft s as brick masons, carpenters, blacksmiths, dressmakers, and other tradesmen and tradeswomen. Their work experiences represented a complicated blend of Old World knowledge and New World training in the artisan trades.

Yet massive European immigration, mob violence, and the African "repatriation" movement undercut these significant steps toward economic emancipation and citizenship for black people. Hostility toward wage-earning free men and women intensified with the passage of the Fugitive Slave Law of 1850, further dimming prospects for full citizenship. [...] [E]arly African American workers and their families would not take these limits on their freedom without a fight. Some would draw on an African vision of liberation and move to Canada, Haiti, or Africa to create their own independent homeland outside the United States. But most free people of color would stay and fight for emancipation, economic equality, and full citizenship rights as workers on American soil.

Notes

1. African American urban life unfolded within the larger context of plantation slavery and the development of rural America. See Jorge Cañizares-Esguerra, Matt D. Childs, and James Sidbury, eds., *The Black Urban Atlantic in the Age of the Slave Trade* (Philadelphia: University of Pennsylvania Press, 2013); Ira Berlin, *The Making of African America: The Four Great Migrations* (New York: Viking 2010); Ira Berlin, *Many Thousands Gone: The First Two Centuries of Slavery in North America* (Cambridge: Belknap Press/Harvard University Press, 1998), 12, 83–84, 145; Ira Berlin, "From Creole to African: Atlantic Creoles and the Origins of African-American Society in Mainland North America," in *Origins of the*

Black Atlantic: Rewriting Histories, ed. Laurent Dubois and Julius Scott (New York: Routledge, 2010), 116–18; Alexander X. Byrd, *Captives and Voyagers: Black Migrants across the Eighteenth Century British Atlantic World* (Baton Rouge: Louisiana State University Press, 2008), 32–85; Jacqueline Jones, *American Work: Four Centuries of Black and White Labor* (New York: W. W. Norton, 1998); W. Jeffrey Bolster, *Black Jacks: African American Seamen in the Age of Sail* (Cambridge: Harvard University Press, 1997); Marcus Rediker, *The Slave Ship: A Human History* (New York: Viking, Penguin Group [USA], 2007); Ras M. Brown, *African-Atlantic Cultures and the South Carolina Lowcountry* (New York: Cambridge University Press, 2012); James Horton and Lois Horton, *In Hope of Liberty: Culture, Community, and Protest among Northern Free Blacks, 1700–1860* (New York: Oxford University Press, 1997); William D. Piersen, *Black Yankees: The Development of an Afro-American Subculture in Eighteenth-Century New England* (Amherst, MA: University of Massachusetts Press, 1988); Edward Baptist, *The Half Has Never Been Told: Slavery and the Making of American Capitalism* (New York: Basic Books, 2014); Walter Johnson, *River of Dark Dreams: Slavery and Empire in the Cotton Kingdom* (Cambridge: Belknap Press/Harvard University Press, 2013); Sven Beckert, *Empire of Cotton: A Global History* (New York: Knopf, 2014); Christopher Clark, Nancy Hewitt, Joshua Brown, and David Jaffee, *Who Built America? Working People and the Nation's History, American Social History Project,* vol. 1, 3rd ed. (Boston: Bedford/St. Martin's, 2008). These African sources of Louisiana labor dissipated after about 1731. The French imperial government took the colony out of the hands of the Company of the Indies and disrupted its connections to the transatlantic slave trade. Under subsequent Spanish control, however, the traffic in enslaved Africans accelerated, creating what some scholars describe as the "re-Africanization" of Louisiana during the final decades of the eighteenth century.

2. Gary Nash, "The Social Evolution of Preindustrial American Cities, 1700–1820," in *The Making of Urban America,* ed. Raymond A. Mohl, 2nd ed. (Wilmington, DE: Scholarly Resources, 1997), 18–20; Howard P. Chudacoff, Judith E. Smith, and Peter C. Baldwin, *The Evolution of American Society,* 7th ed. (Boston: Prentice Hall, 2010), 4, 7, 17–20; Reynolds Farley, "The Urbanization of Negroes in the United States," *Journal of Social History* 1 (1968): 242–44; Gary B. Nash, *Forging Freedom: The Formation of Philadelphia's Black Community 1720–1840* (Cambridge: Harvard University Press, 1988), 9–10; Horton and Horton, *In Hope of Liberty,* 13; James O. Horton and Lois E. Horton, *Black Bostonians: Family Life and Community Struggle in the Antebellum North* (New York: Holmes and Meier, 1979), xiii–xv; Robert J. Cottrol, *The Afro-Yankees: Providence's Black Community in the Antebellum Era* (Westport, CT: Greenwood Press, 1982), 14–16; Piersen, *Black Yankees,* 6–7; Leslie M. Harris, *In the Shadow of Slavery: African Americans in New York City, 1626–1863* (Chicago: University of Chicago Press, 2003), 18–19, 29–30; Thelma W. Foote, *Black and White Manhattan: The History of Racial Formation in Colonial New York City* (New York: Oxford University Press, 2004), 23–40, 65; Robert Olwell, *Masters, Slaves, and Subjects: South Carolina Low Country, 1740–1790* (Ithaca, NY: Cornell University Press, 1998), 1–2, 11, 27–29; Emma Hart, *Building Charleston: Town and Society in the Eighteenth-Century British Atlantic World* (Charlottesville: University of Virginia, 2010), 25, 32–33; James A. McMillin, "The Transatlantic Slave Trade Comes to Georgia," in Leslie M. Harris and Daina R. Berry, eds., *Slavery and Freedom in Savannah* (Athens: University of Georgia Press, 2014), 12–13; Phillip D. Morgan, *Slave Counterpoint: Black Culture in the Eighteenth-Century Chesapeake and Lowcountry* (Chapel Hill: University of North Carolina Press, 1998), 59–62; Shannon L. Dawdy, *Building the Devil's Empire: French Colonial New Orleans* (Chicago: University of Chicago Press, 2008), 83, 156–58, 175–76; Lawrence N. Powell, *The Accidental City: Improving New Orleans* (Cambridge: Harvard University Press, 2012), 53–54, 70–71; Daniel H. Usner, "Colonial Projects and Frontier Practices: The First Century of New Orleans History," in *Frontier Cities: Encounters at the Crossroads of Empire,* ed. Jay Gitlin, Barbara Berglund, and Adam Arenson (Philadelphia: University of Pennsylvania Press, 2013), 36–40; Daniel H. Usner, Jr., "From African Captivity to American Slavery: The Introduction of Black Laborers to Colonial Louisiana," *Louisiana History* 20 (1979), quote, 25, 25–29; Daniel H. Usner, Jr., *Indians, Settlers, and Slaves in a Frontier Exchange Economy: The Lower Mississippi Valley before 1783* (Chapel Hill: University of North Carolina Press, 1992), 25, 33, 41; Gwendolyn Midlo Hall, *Africans in Colonial Louisiana: The Development of Afro-Creole Culture in the Eighteenth Century* (Baton Rouge: Louisiana State University Press, 1992), 29, 57–60; Kimberly S. Hanger, *Bounded Lives, Bounded Places: Free Black Society in Colonial New Orleans, 1769–1803* (Durham, NC: Duke University Press, 1997), 10–11. For the notion of a "charter generation" among early African Americans, see Berlin, *Many Thousands Gone,* 12–13, 83–84; Berlin, *The Making of African America,* quote, 71.

3. Usner, "From African Captivity to American Slavery," 26; Hall, *Africans in Colonial Louisiana,* 29, 57–60, 127; Dawdy, *Building the Devil's Empire,* 157, 177–79.

4. Powell, *The Accidental City,* 73–74.

5. Olwell, *Masters, Slaves, and Subjects,* quote, 1–2, 11; Hart, *Building Charleston,* 32–33; Morgan, *Slave Counterpoint,*

75–76. For an innovative study of both the environmental and social construction of New Orleans over nearly two hundred years of its history, see Ari Kelman, *A River and Its City: The Nature of Landscape in New Orleans* (Berkeley: University of California Press, 2003), 1–17.

6. Harris, *In the Shadow of Slavery,* 14–31, 32; Foote, *Black and White Manhattan,* 36; Joyce Goodfriend, *Before the Melting Pot: Society and Culture in Colonial New York City, 1664–1730* (Princeton, NJ: Princeton University Press, 1992), 119, 124; Christopher Moore, "A World of Possibilities: Slavery and Freedom in Dutch New Amsterdam," in *Slavery in New York,* ed. Ira Berlin and Leslie M. Harris (New York: New Press, 2005), 35–45; Horton and Horton, *In Hope of Liberty,* 10.
7. Erica A. Dunbar, *A Fragile Freedom: African American Women and Emancipation in the Antebellum City* (New Haven, CT: Yale University Press, 2008), quote, 16; Nash, *Forging Freedom,* 10–12 (quote, 10); Gary B. Nash, "Slaves and Slave Owners in Colonial Philadelphia," *William and Mary Quarterly,* 3rd ser., 30 (1973): 223–56.
8. Horton and Horton, *Black Bostonians,* 74–75; Piersen, *Black Yankees,* 43–44; Lorenzo J. Greene, *The Negro in Colonial New England, 1620–1776* (1942; repr. New York: Atheneum, 1968), 34–35, 60, 150, 111.
9. Cañizares-Esguerra, Childs, and Sidbury, *Black Urban Atlantic,* 1–3; W. E. B. Du Bois, *The Philadelphia Negro: A Social Study* (1899; repr. Philadelphia: University of Pennsylvania, 1996), 17–18; W. E. B. Du Bois and Augustus Dill, eds., *The Negro Artisan* (Atlanta: Atlanta University Conference Publications no. 17, 1912): 35ff.; Leonard Stavisky, "The Origins of Negro Craftsmanship in Colonial America," *Journal of Negro History* 32, no. 4 (October 1947): 417–29; Philip S. Foner and Ronald L. Lewis, eds., *The Black Worker to 1869,* vol. 1 (Philadelphia: Temple University Press, 1978), 9; Moore, "A World of Possibilities," 35–38, 41–45; Nash, "Social Evolution of Preindustrial American Cities," 19; Goodfriend, *Before the Melting Pot,* 112–13, 119; Harris, *In the Shadow of Slavery,* 14, 16–17, 20, 28–31.
10. Catherine W. Bishir, *Crafting Lives: African American Artisans in New Bern, North Carolina, 1770–1900* (Chapel Hill: University of North Carolina Press, 2013), 6–18; L. Diane Barnes, *Artisan Workers in the Upper South: Petersburg, Virginia, 1820–1865* (Baton Rouge: Louisiana State University Press, 2008); Hart, *Building Charleston,* 102, 103; Usner, "From African Captivity to American Slavery," 31–35; Hanger, *Bounded Lives, Bounded Places,* 57–70; Dawdy, *Building the Devil's Empire,* 177–78.
11. Powell, *The Accidental City,* 70.
12. Christopher Phillips, *Freedom's Port: The African American Community of Baltimore, 1790–1860* (Urbana: University of Chicago Press, 1997), 16–17; Charles G. Steffen, *The Mechanics of Baltimore: Workers and Politics in the Age of Revolution, 1763–1812* (Urbana: University of Illinois Press, 1984), 36–44; T. Stephen Whitman, *The Price of Freedom: Slavery and Manumission in Baltimore and Early National Maryland* (Lexington: University Press of Kentucky, 1997), 16–28; Mariana L. R. Dantas, *Black Townsmen: Urban Slavery and Freedom in the Eighteenth-Century Americas* (New York: Palgrave/Macmillan, 2008), 75–80, 145–47; Powell, *The Accidental City,* 70.
13. Du Bois and Dill, *The Negro Artisan,* 35; Bolster, *Black Jacks,* 48–49; Hilary McD. Beckles, *White Servitude and Black Slavery in Barbados, 1627–1715* (Knoxville: University of Tennessee Press, 1989), 104, 108; Pedro L. V. Welch, *Slave Society in the City: Bridgetown, Barbados 1680–1834* (Kingston, Jam.: Ian Randle, 2003), 43. See also Constance M. Green, *American Cities in the Growth of the Nation* (New York: J. De Graff, 1957), 19; Peter H. Wood, *Black Majority: Negroes in Colonial South Carolina From 1670 Through the Stono Rebellion* (New York: W. W. Norton, 1974), xiv, 45–46, 132, 146–47, 219–21; Catherine Coquery-Vidrovitch, *The History of Cities South of the Sahara: From the Origins to Colonization* (Princeton, NJ: Markus Wiener, 2008), 1–26, 49–52, 155–69; Rebecca Shumway, *The Fante and the Transatlantic Slave Trade* (Rochester, NY: University of Rochester Press, 2011), 40–42; A. G. Hopkins, *An Economic History of West Africa* (New York: Columbia University Press, 1973), 4–8; Sandra Barnes, *Ogun: An Old God for a New Age* (Philadelphia: Institute for the Study of Human Issues, 1980).
14. Bolster, *Black Jacks,* 48–49; Bishir, *Crafting Lives,* 6, 9, 38, 51; Barnes, *Artisan Workers in the Upper South,* 143–46.
15. Cottrol, *The Afro-Yankees,* 37, 44; Harris, *In the Shadow of Slavery,* 14, 20, 30–31; Morgan, *Slave Counterpoint,* 494–95; Betty Wood, *Slavery in Colonial Georgia, 1730–1775* (Athens: University of Georgia Press, 1984), 84; Catherine Adams and Elizabeth H. Pleck, *Love of Freedom: Black Women in Colonial and Revolutionary New England* (New York: Oxford University Press, 2010), 32–35; Hanger, *Bounded Lives, Bounded Places,* 57–60, 63–66; Suzanne Lebsock, *The Free Women of Peters-burg: Status and Culture in a Southern Town, 1784–1860* (New York: W. W. Norton, 1984), 97–98; Jacqueline Jones, *Labor of Love, Labor of Sorrow: Black Women, Work, and the Family from Slavery to the Present* (New York: Basic Books, 1985), 18; Bishir, *Crafting Lives,* 19 (on notion of an artisan "golden age").

16. Harris, *In the Shadow of Slavery,* 28–31; Goodfriend, *Before the Melting Pot,* 119, 124; Sharon B. Sundue, *Industrious in Their Stations: Young People at Work in Urban America, 1720–1810* (Charlottesville: University of Virginia Press, 2009), 112–14; Joanne P. Melish, *Disowning Slavery: Gradual Emancipation and "Race" in New England, 1780–1860* (Ithaca, NY: Cornell University Press, 1998), 8, 20–21.

17. See Robert E. Desrochers, Jr., "Slave-for-Sale Advertisements and Slavery in Massachusetts, 1704–1781," *William and Mary Quarterly,* 3rd ser., 59, no. 3 (July 2002): 623–64; Greene, *The Negro in Colonial New England,* 15, 23–50; Du Bois, *The Philadelphia Negro,* 14; Nash, *Forging Freedom,* 9–11; Baptist, *The Half Has Never Been Told,* 1–37; Walter Johnson, *Soul By Soul: Life Inside the Antebellum Slave Market* (Cambridge: Harvard University Press, 1999), quote, 19; Daniel E. Walker, *No More: Slavery and Cultural Resistance in Havana and New Orleans* (Minneapolis: University of Minnesota Press, 2004), quote, 85–86.

18. Goodfriend, *Before the Melting Pot,* 119, 124; Piersen, *Black Yankees,* 43–44; Harris, *In the Shadow of Slavery,* 14–31; Moore, "A World of Possibilities," 35–45; Nash, *Forging Freedom,* 36, 218; Shane White, *Somewhat More Independent: The End of Slavery in New York City, 1770–1810* (Athens: University of Georgia Press, 1991), 26–27; Leonard P. Curry, *The Free Black in Urban America, 1800–1850: The Shadow of the Dream* (Chicago: University of Chicago Press, 1981), 250; Wood, *Black Majority,* 206; Ira Berlin, *Slaves without Masters: The Free Negro in the Antebellum South* (New York: Free Press, 1974), 55; Whitman, *Price of Freedom,* 50–58, 61, quote, 77–78; Seth Rockman, *Scraping By: Wage Labor, Slavery, and Survival in Early Baltimore* (Baltimore: Johns Hopkins University Press, 2009), 45–46, 62–67; Dantas, *Black Townsmen,* 87–89; Steffen, *The Mechanics of Baltimore,* 41–42; Phillips, *Freedom's Port,* 67; Dylan C. Penningroth, *The Claims of Kinfolk: African American Property and Community in the Nineteenth-Century South* (Chapel Hill: University of North Carolina Press, 2003), 53.

19. Bolster, *Black Jacks,* 69, 95, 101; Peter Linebaugh and Marcus Rediker, *The Many-Headed Hydra: Sailors, Slaves, Commoners, and the Hidden History of the Revolutionary Atlantic* (Boston: Beacon Press, 2000), 243; Rediker, *The Slave Ship,* 41–72; Morgan, *Slave Counterpoint,* 238–39.

20. Olaudah Equiano, *The Interesting Narrative of the Life of Olaudah Equiano, Written by Himself,* ed. and introduction, Robert J. Allison (1791; repr. Boston: Bedford Books/St. Martin's Press, 1995), 2–3; Vincent Caretta, "Olaudah Equiano or Gustavus Vassa?: New Light on an Eighteenth-Century Question of Identity," *Slavery and Abolition,* 20, no. 3 (1999): 96–105; Cañizares-Esguerra, Childs, and Sidbury, *Black Urban Atlantic,* 1–5; Julius Scott, "Negroes in Foreign Bottoms: Sailors, Slaves, and Communication," in Dubois and Scott, eds., *Origins of the Black Atlantic,* 69–70; J. William Harris, *The Hanging of Thomas Jeremiah: A Free Black Man's Encounter with Liberty* (New Haven, CT: Yale University Press, 2009), 61.

21. Kevin Dawson, "The Cultural Geography of Enslaved Ship Pilots," in Cañizares-Esguerra, Childs, and Sidbury, *Black Urban Atlantic,* 163–84, quotes, 164, 167; Bolster, *Black Jacks,* 49; Harris, *Hanging of Thomas Jeremiah,* 61.

22. Bolster, *Black Jacks,* 3–4, 16, 25–36, 131–57, 258–66; Cañizares-Esguerra, Childs, and Sidbury, *Black Urban Atlantic,* 1–5; Equiano, *Interesting Narrative of the Life,* 2–3; Dubois and Scott, *Origins of the Black Atlantic,* 43–71.

23. Morgan, *Slave Counterpoint,* 494–95.

24. Walker, *No More,* 2–3; Hanger, *Bounded Lives, Bounded Places,* 1–2, 11–12, 21–23, 145–47, 163; Dawdy, *Building the Devil's Empire,* 4–12, 146–54; Whittington B. Johnson, *Black Savannah, 1788–1864* (Fayetteville: University of Arkansas Press, 1996), 39, 59–65, 70–71, 81–82; Janice L. Sumler-Edmond, "Free Black Life in Savannah," in *Slavery and Freedom in Savannah,* ed. Harris and Berry, 130–31; Bernard E. Powers, Jr., *Black Charlestonians: A Social History, 1822–1885* (Fayetteville: University of Arkansas Press, 1994), 48–50; Amrita Chakrabarti Myers, *Forging Freedom: Black Women and the Pursuit of Liberty in Antebellum Charleston* (Chapel Hill: University of North Carolina Press, 2011), 122–35; Cynthia M. Kennedy, *Braided Relations, Entwined Lives: The Women of Charleston's Urban Slave Society* (Bloomington: Indiana University Press, 2005), 65–66.

25. Stephen Middleton, *The Black Laws: Race and the Legal Process in Early Ohio* (Athens: Ohio University Press, 2005), 7–41; Wilma King, *The Essence of Liberty: Free Black Women during the Slave Era* (Columbia: University of Missouri, 2006), 64–65; Berlin, *Slaves without Masters,* 21–23; Horton and Horton, *In Hope of Liberty,* 71–76; Melish, *Disowning Slavery,* 86–88; Leon Litwack, *North of Slavery: The Negro in the Free States, 1790–1860* (Chicago: University of Chicago Press, 1961), 7–15; Arthur Zilversmit, *The First Emancipation: The Abolition of Slavery in the North* (Chicago: University of Chicago Press, 1975), 113–16, 124–37, 176–84, 208–14; Curry, *Free Black in Urban America,* 247–48, 250–55.

26. King, *Essence of Liberty,* 64–65; Walker, *No More,* 86–87; Curry, *Free Black in Urban America,* 252–53; Richard Wade, *Slavery in the Cities: The South, 1820–1860* (New York: Oxford University Press, 1964), 329–30; Jennifer Morgan, *Laboring Women: Reproduction and Gender in New World Slavery* (Philadelphia: University of Pennsylvania Press, 2004); Rockman, *Scraping By,* 101–3, 111; Horton and Horton, *Black Bostonians,* 25; Nash, *Forging Freedom,* 136–37, 142–43.

27. Adams and Pleck, *Love of Freedom,* 32–35, quote, 34; Rockman, *Scraping By,* 100–03; Jane E. Dabel, *A Respectable Woman: The Public Roles of African American Women in Nineteenth-Century New York* (New York: New York University Press, 2008), 6–7, 15–16, 78, 82–83; King, *Essence of Liberty,* 61–72; Lebsock, *Free Women of Petersburg,* 97–98; Kennedy, *Braided Relations, Entwined Lives,* 66.

28. Adams and Pleck, *Love of Freedom,* 32–35, 37; Kennedy, *Braided Relations, Entwined Lives,* 120–21; Dabel, *A Respectable Woman,* 6–7, 15–16, 78, 82–83; Lebsock, *Free Women of Petersburg,* 97–98; King, *Essence of Liberty,* 66–69; Rockman, *Scraping By,* 129–30.

29. Morgan, *Slave Counterpoint,* 352–53; Curry, *Free Black in Urban America,* 33–36, 260–66; Powers, *Black Charlestonians,* 41–43; Charles H. Wesley, *Negro Labor in the United States, 1850–1925: A Study in American Economic History* (1927; repr. New York: Russell and Russell, 1967), 13; Johnson, *Black Savannah,* 96–97; Wade, *Slavery in the Cities,* 37; Robert S. Starobin, *Industrial Slavery in the Old South* (New York: Oxford University Press, 1970), 10–18, 28–33, 63–65; Ronald L. Lewis, *Coal, Iron, and Slaves: Industrial Slavery in Maryland and Virginia, 1715–1865* (Westport, CT: Greenwood Press, 1979), 35, 88.

30. Powers, *Black Charlestonians,* 41–43; Myers, *Forging Freedom,* 57–63; Harris and Berry, *Slavery and Freedom in Savannah,* 45–46; Johnson, *Black Savannah,* 96–97.

31. Whitman, *Price of Freedom,* 33–39; Dantas, *Black Townsmen,* 81–88; Joe William Trotter, Jr., *River Jordan: African American Urban Life in the Ohio Valley* (Lexington: University Press of Kentucky, 1998), 27–29.

32. Midori Takagi, *"Rearing Wolves to Our Own Destruction": Slavery in Richmond, Virginia, 1782–1865"* (Charlottesville: University of Virginia Press, 1999), 16–36, 71–95; Wade, *Slavery in the Cities,* quote, 12–13, 32, 35, quote, 36, 37, 327; Gregg D. Kimball, *American City, Southern Place: A Cultural History of Antebellum Richmond* (Athens: University of Georgia Press, 2012), 161–62, quote; Peter Rachleff, *Black Labor in Richmond, 1865–1890* (1984; repr. Urbana: University of Illinois Press, 1989), 5–6; Starobin, *Industrial Slavery in the Old South,* 10–18, 28–33, 63–65; Claudia D. Goldin, *Urban Slavery in the American South, 1820–1860: A Quantitative History* (Chicago: University of Chicago Press, 1976), 26, 45–46, 52–54.

33. Takagi, *"Rearing Wolves to Our Own Destruction,"* 24–30; Rachleff, *Black Labor in Richmond,* 6–7; Joshua D. Rothman, *Notorious in the Neighborhood: Sex and Families across the Color Line in Virginia, 1787–1861* (Chapel Hill: University of North Carolina Press, 2003), 92–94; Kimball, *American City, Southern Place,* quote, 65.

34. Kimball, *American City, Southern Place,* 23, quote, 65; Starobin, *Industrial Slavery in the Old South,* 148–49; Lewis, *Coal, Iron, and Slaves,* 179–80.

35. Wesley, *Negro Labor in the United States,* 62; Ira Berlin and Herbert G. Gutman, "Natives and Immigrants, Free Men and Slaves: Urban Workingmen in the Antebellum American South," *American Historical Review* 88, no. 5 (December 1983): 1178, 1180, 1181–82, quote, 1193; Phillips, *Freedom's Port,* 195–96; Wade, *Slavery in the Cities,* 29–30, 273–74; Starobin, *Industrial Slavery in the Old South,* 136–37; Curry, *Free Black in Urban America,* 25–26.

36. Paul Spickard, *Almost All Aliens: Immigration, Race, and Colonialism in American History and Identity* (New York: Routledge, 2007), 102, 481; Berlin and Gutman, "Natives and Immigrants, Free Men and Slaves," 1181–82; Aaron S. Fogleman, "From Slaves, Convicts, and Servants to Free Passengers: The Transformation of Immigration in the Era of the American Revolution," *Journal of American History,* 85, no. 1 (1998): 43–76; Christopher Clark, *Social Change in America: From the Revolution through the Civil War* (Chicago: Ivan R. Dee, 2006), 60–88, 110–19; Phillips, *Freedom's Port,* 195–96.

37. Curry, *Free Black in Urban America,* 260–61; Nikki M. Taylor, *Frontiers of Freedom: Cincinnati's Black Community, 1802–1868* (Athens: Ohio University Press, 2005), 16–18.

38. Curry, *Free Black in Urban America,* 260; Trotter, *River Jordan,* 14, quote, 27, 29; Gilbert Osofsky, "Enduring Ghetto," in *Harlem: The Making of a Ghetto: Negro New York, 1890–1930* (1963; repr., New York: Harper and Row, 1971), quote, 263n44.

39. Du Bois, *The Philadelphia Negro,* 33; Horton and Horton, *In Hope of Liberty,* 117; Sterling D. Spero and Abram L. Harris, *The Black Worker: The Negro and the Labor Movement* (1930; repr., New York: Atheneum, 1968) 11–15; Harris, *In the Shadow of Slavery,* 80; Cottrol, *The Afro-Yankees,* 151–53.

40. Horton and Horton, *In Hope of Liberty,* 117; Spero and Harris, *The Black Worker,* 11–15; Harris, *In the Shadow of Slavery,* 80; Cottrol, *The Afro-Yankees,* 151–53.

41. Curry, *Free Black in Urban America,* 260; Osofsky, "Enduring Ghetto," in *Harlem: The Making of a Ghetto,* quote, 263n44. See also Frederick Douglass, *Narrative of the Life of Frederick Douglass: An American Slave* (New York: New American Library, 1968), 117–18.

42. Horton and Horton, *In Hope of Liberty,* quote, 110; Bolster, *Black Jacks,* 161; Taylor, *Frontiers of Freedom,* 27–29; Nancy Bertaux, "Structural Economic Change among Black Workers in Nineteenth Century Cincinnati," in *Race and the City: Work, Community, and Protest in Cincinnati, 1820–1970,* ed. Henry Louis Taylor, Jr. (Urbana: University of Illinois Press, 1993), 132–41, 133, 134; Thomas Buchanan, *Black Life on the Mississippi: Slaves, Free Blacks, and the Western Steamboat World* (Chapel Hill: University of North Carolina Press, 2007), 53–86.

43. Taylor, *Frontiers of Freedom,* 16–18; Trotter, *River Jordan,* 14, 29.

44. Quoted in Bertaux, "Structural Economic Change," in Taylor, *Race and the City,* 133. See also Curry, *Free Black in Urban America,* 21–22, 25–26, 258–66; Wade, *Slavery in the Cities,* 30–33; Goldin, *Urban Slavery in the American South,* 42–47; Litwack, *North of Slavery,* 153–62; Lebsock, *Free Women of Petersburg,* 97–100; Wade, *Slavery in the Cities,* 31.

45. Nash, *Forging Freedom,* 121–25; Horton and Horton, *In Hope of Liberty,* 90–92.

46. Martin R. Delany, "A Black Nationalist Manifesto, 1852," in *Let Nobody Turn Us Around: An African American Anthology,* ed. Manning Marable and Leith Mullings (Lanham, MD: Rowman and Littlefield, 2000), 70–82; King, *Essence of Liberty,* 59.

47. Douglass, quoted in Wesley, *Negro Labor in the United States,* 54–55; Douglas W. Bristol, Jr., *Knights of the Razor: Black Barbers in Slavery and Freedom* (Baltimore: Johns Hopkins University Press. 2009), 114–15; Delany, "A Black Nationalist Manifesto, 1852," in Marable and Mullings, *Let Nobody Turn Us Around,* 70–82; King, *Essence of Liberty,* 59.

48. Bristol, *Knights of the Razor,* 4–5, 61–69, 204.

49. Frederick Douglass, "Learn Trades or Starve," quoted in Harris, *In the Shadow of Slavery,* 240–41; Graham R. Hodges, *New York City Cartmen, 1667–1850* (New York: New York University Press, 1986), 4–5, 157–59; George E. Walker, *The Afro-American in New York City, 1827–1860* (New York: Garland, 1993), 30–35, quote, 35n18; Curry, *Free Black in Urban America,* 18–19; Harris, *In the Shadow of Slavery,* 217–18; Wesley, *Negro Labor in the United States,* 62–63.

50. James M. Campbell, *Slavery on Trial: Race, Class, and Criminal Justice in Antebellum Richmond, Virginia* (Gainesville: University Press of Florida, 2007), 11–12; Trotter, *River Jordan,* 25; Powers, *Black Charleston,* 10–15; Johnson, *Black Savannah,* 40–41, 45, 52; Curry, *Free Black in Urban America,* 17.

51. Stephen Kantrowitz, *More Than Freedom: Fighting for Black Citizenship in a White Republic, 1829–1889* (New York: Penguin, 2012), 14–33; Middleton, *Black Laws,* 3–12; David A. Gerber, *Black Ohio and the Color Line, 1860–1915* (Urbana: University of Illinois Press, 1976), 3–12; Trotter, *River Jordan,* 24–26; Harris, *In the Shadow of Slavery,* 80, 116–19; Litwack, *North of Slavery,* 64–93; Taylor, *Frontiers of Freedom,* 63–64; Curry, *Free Black in Urban America,* quote, 87.

52. Ousmane K. Power-Greene, *Against Wind and Tide: The African American Struggle against the Colonization Movement* (New York: New York University Press, 2014), 1–2; Claude A. Clegg III, *The Price of Liberty: African Americans and the Making of Liberia* (Chapel Hill: University of North Carolina Press, 2004), 30–31; P. J. Staudenraus, *The African Colonization Movement, 1816–1865* (New York: Octagon Books, 1980), 234–39, 196–97; James Campbell, *Middle Passages: African American Journeys to Africa, 1787–2005* (New York: Penguin, 2006), 40–46; C. Peter Ripley, Roy E. Finkenbine, Michael F. Hembree, and Donald Yacavone, eds., *Witness for Freedom: African American Voices on Race, Slavery, and Emancipation* (Chapel Hill: University of North Carolina Press, 1993), quote, 2; Kantrowitz, *More Than Freedom,* 27.

53. Staudenraus, *African Colonization Movement,* 5–8; Nash, *Forging Freedom,* 101–3, 177–79, 246–47; Julie Winch, *Philadelphia's Black Elite: Activism, Accommodation, and the Struggle for Autonomy, 1787–1848* (Philadelphia: Temple University Press, 1988), 176n11; Nicholas Guyatt, "'The Outskirts of Our Happiness': Race and the Lure of

Colonization in the Early Republic," *Journal of American History,* 95, no. 4 (2009): 992–93.

54. Clare A. Lyons, *Sex among the Rabble: An Intimate History of Gender and Power in the Age of Revolution, Philadelphia, 1730–1830* (Chapel Hill: University of North Carolina Press, 2006), 356; Emily Clark, *The Strange History of the American Quadroon: Free Women of Color in the Revolutionary Atlantic World* (Chapel Hill: University of North Carolina Press, 2013), 6.

55. Harris, *In the Shadow of Slavery,* 134–35; Melish, *Disowning Slavery,* 76, 193; Clegg, *Price of Liberty,* 145–46; Staudenraus, *African Colonization Movement,* 234–38; Trotter, *River Jordan,* 34; Phillips, *Freedom's Port,* 185–86.

56. Middleton, *Black Laws,* 201–3; R. J. M. Blackett, *Making Freedom: The Underground Railroad and the Politics of Slavery* (Chapel Hill: University of North Carolina Press, 2013), 32, 51–53; Graham Russell G. Hodges, *David Ruggles: A Radical Black Abolitionist and the Underground Railroad in New York City* (Chapel Hill: University of North Carolina Press, 2010), 199–200; Fergus M. Bordewich, *The Underground Railroad and the War for the Soul of America* (New York: HarpersCollins, 2005), 169–72; Kantrowitz, *More Than Freedom,* 1–7, 176–98; Ari Kelman, *A River and Its City: The Nature of Landscape in New Orleans* (Berkeley: University of California Press, 2003), 82–84; Wilbur Siebert, *The Underground Railroad from Slavery to Freedom* (1898; repr. New York: Arno Press and *New York Times,* 1968), 17–40, 308–9; Clegg, *Price of Liberty,* 171–77; Ripley et al., *Witness for Freedom,* 179–84; Harris, *In the Shadow of Slavery,* 271–73.

57. Middleton, *Black Laws,* 215–16; Harris, *In the Shadow of Slavery,* 271–73; Curry, *Free Black in Urban America,* 244–51, 261; Wade, *Slavery in the Cities,* 325–30; Berlin, *Slaves without Masters,* 136–37; Goldin, *Urban Slavery in the American South,* 51–60; Powers, *Black Charlestonians,* 267–68; Johnson, *Black Savannah,* 151–52; Philips, *Freedom's Port,* 236–37; Barbara Jean Fields, *Slavery and Freedom on the Middle Ground: Maryland during the Nineteenth Century* (New Haven, CT: Yale University Press, 1985), 47–48, 62.

Conclusion

How History Impacts on Management

Morgen Witzel

Morgen Witzel, "Conclusion: How History Impacts on Management," *Management History: Text and Cases*, pp. 404-445. Copyright © 2009 by Taylor & Francis Group. Reprinted with permission.

The function which distinguishes the manager above all others is his educational one. The one contribution he is uniquely expected to make is to give others vision and the ability to perform. It is vision and moral responsibility that, in the last analysis, define the manager.

—Peter Drucker, *The Practice of Management*

Worthiness in the industrial sphere can have reference to one thing only, namely the contribution of industry to the sum total of human welfare. On this basis only must industry and all its works finally be judged ... The lessons of history teach us that no efficiency of procedure will save from ultimate extinction those organizations that pursue a false objective; on the other hand, without such efficient procedure, all human group effort becomes relatively futile.

—James D. Mooney, 'The Principles of Organization'

Kings are the slaves of history.

—Leo Tolstoy, *War and Peace*

Introduction

[...] [O]ne of the purposes of this [reading] is to use the past experience and past practices of management to help people think in new ways about management as it is done in the present, and even perhaps as it might be done in the future. We have not tried to cover the whole history of management practice; indeed, we have barely scratched the surface of this huge and complex subject. Instead, the purpose has been to use past experience and practice as a mirror or a lens with which to view the present from a different angle. That means that, out of necessity, we have been selective in our choice of examples. We have tried to indicate the breadth and variety of views and practices and show how some of the most important have evolved over time, until we have reached the present day.

What can we learn from this picture, however incomplete, of the past? Another purpose of this book was to create a forum for discussion and to encourage people to draw their own lessons from the material. In keeping with that spirit, we will not set out any hard conclusions here. Instead, let us concentrate on some of the key themes that have run through this book.

One theme that emerges is that, for all that managers spend much of their time concentrating on and thinking about the future, the past still exercises a powerful influence over what they do. Some of the management practices and theories that we think of as 'new' actually have deep roots in the past. Others, while genuinely new in themselves, are nonetheless the product of social and environmental forces that in some cases go right back to the birth of civilisation. Memory, even sub-conscious memory, still plays a part in our decisions and actions. Tradition and innovation often go hand in hand. Perhaps the most important theme of all is the way that past actions and decisions can constrain those that we take in the present, narrowing our options and reducing our scope for action.

Yet the past can also enable greater freedom of action in the present, if we use it in the right way. The past is just one of many sources of inspiration and knowledge that managers have available to them. Further, examination of the past helps us to understand *why* we do things the way we do them now. This enables self-examination, and if necessary self-criticism, and these in turn can be first steps to improvement.

The Force of the Past

There is evidence, sometimes patchy and indistinct but evidence nonetheless, of people doing things we would now describe as managerial tasks as far back as the beginning of recorded history. Some of them ran businesses, small by comparison with today's global giants but large by the standards of the time, serving not just local markets but sometimes establishing locations hundreds of miles apart. Some of these managers were in government bureaucracies, some were priests in temples; some were all three of these things at once. Awareness of the importance of management is to be found in the *Duties of the Vizier*, written three and a half thousand years ago, and in many other writings of antiquity, from China, India, the Middle East and Europe. By the Middle Ages there is evidence of rudimentary forms of management training in some places, and more complex forms of financial management were emerging. In the nineteenth century the Industrial Revolution led to further advances, and at the very end of the nineteenth century, in response to both the changing needs of businesses and changing social trends, a coherent body of management theory began to emerge.

Over these centuries and millennia there has been a great deal of innovation and change. Management methods and practices have come and gone, discarded when they no longer fit the needs of the time. Yet at the same time, there has been a great deal of continuity.

For example, two of the oldest forms of organisation are the family and the bureaucracy. Both have been adapted and re-adapted and used as the basis of new forms, time and time again. We saw [...] how du Pont produced a flexible version of the bureaucratic form of organisation which enabled first his family firm Du Pont and later General Motors to expand rapidly. But most business organisations today are still, at heart, either familial-type organisations or use some version of bureaucracy—or both. Something about these forms of organisation is clearly deeply satisfying to us as human beings. Do they fulfil some latent need for organisation and structure? It is fashionable today to castigate both family organisations and bureaucracies as being old fashioned and out of date. But it may be that, at least as basic models, they still have a purpose. It would appear that both are usable as bases, from which firms can adapt, innovate and find the best organisational model that fits their purpose.

Talk of purpose brings us to strategy, the means by which purposes are achieved. Strategy in the past was a matter of principle rather than rule. There were certain things that strategists had to do if they desired success, such as gathering sufficient resources to achieve their aim, gathering knowledge of the competition and the environment, and understanding the capabilities of their own organisation. Those things are as true as when Sunzi and Vegetius first wrote about them more than two thousand years ago. Yet, as Machiavelli identified, strategists also have to be flexible and adaptable, able to respond to whatever problems emerge; and problems, as Clausewitz noted, always will emerge, this is inevitable. So strategists have to be able to innovate, respond, think and react quickly while at the same time planning for the future. Strategists, in other words, have to be very good at managing paradox. We discussed some examples of successful strategists who were both proactive and reactive, and looked at some of the options strategists have used in the past. Some of these options looked very similar to the strategic options companies use today; some did not. Strategy, it turns out, is a matter of adaptation and innovation, but often harks back to the same basic principles.

Organisations are made up of people, and strategies are carried out by people. We know far more today than our ancestors ever did about how to manage people, but for all that, human resource management continues to face many problems. Not the least of these is the continued distinction between 'managers' and 'workers', 'them' and 'us', and the tensions this creates. Is there a solution to this problem? The distinction has its roots in social hierarchies and class distinctions, which are universal and which go back to the beginnings of civilisation, if not further. Is it realistic to expect people in an organisation to put aside all thought of them and us, and to become completely egalitarian overnight? Some managers try to behave as if it were, and although this might be laudable from the point of view of those who believe in egalitarianism and democracy, this attitude creates problems of its own. At a fundamental level, the problems and tensions involved in human resource management have not changed much for thousands of years. Society has moved on, the class distinctions have become less pronounced, but the problem of 'them' and 'us' remains.

Marketing is another of those fundamental business activities for which there is evidence of practice for a very long time. Marketing practice has, unsurprisingly, evolved and changed in response to the environment and changing needs of consumers. Marketers—or what we would now call marketers—have on the whole proved fairly adept at reading both sets of changes and responding. Impressive too is the way in which marketers in earlier times, prohibited or at least restricted from competing on price and forced to use the same distribution methods, evolved other ways of distinguishing themselves from competitors, using branding and quality, for instance. Quality was an extremely important issue during the Middle Ages when there were stiff price restrictions. During the Industrial Revolution, when prices were free, the emphasis on quality sometimes declined. Early marketers were aware of all the elements of the marketing mix, but not all of them understood how those elements fitted together and interacted with each other. One of the achievements of early marketing scholarship and research was to make that relationship more clear.

Today, financial markets and financial instruments are far more complex than they were even two hundred years ago, and financial management has accordingly become much more complex. Yet it is still fundamentally a matter of managing money. The basic tasks of safeguarding the organisation's assets, raising new capital when required, directing cash inflows and outflows and managing risk, remain at the heart of financial management. It is also interesting to look at the factors that have driven innovation and development in this field. In the Middle Ages, the technological advances of the twelfth and thirteenth centuries enabled new kinds of businesses, and expansion of existing ones, but taking advantage of this technology required capital investment. As a result, there was an expansion of the financial system and developments in lending in credit which enabled the required capital to be found. The costs of overseas exploration and the increasing complexity and expense of war drove further changes in the early eighteenth century. Mirroring almost exactly the situation in the Middle Ages, technological advances and the growth of new, capital-intensive industries such as the railways in the nineteenth century resulted in still more expansion, and so on. Innovations in financial management have had their costs, and have helped to contribute at times to market instability; but while the need for innovation persists, innovation is likely to go on.

We see the same trend when we come to look at technology. Technological innovations more than not have been driven by societal needs; the need for more food or better health, the need for faster and better communications, the demand for a greater variety of goods, and so on. Looking back to the past we can see frequent examples of both entrepreneurs and existing firms identifying a need and innovating new products to fill that need. Along the way there have also been innovations in process and communications technologies that have made businesses more efficient and more effective. If innovation itself is nothing new, then neither is the importance of knowledge, the importance of which has always been recognised by a well-managed firm. What is particularly noticeable is how knowledge begets knowledge; the more knowledge we have, the easier we find it to learn and to innovate. Thus the speed at which knowledge generation and innovation happen is constantly increasing.

For centuries, the idea that businesses existed as part of society and that there were strong relationships between the two was not even a subject for discussion. It was an accepted fact. Around the time of the Industrial Revolution, for reasons we can only hypothesise, that understanding broke down and some business owners and managers began to behave as if no relationship existed. This in turn generated a great deal of tension, between managers and workers and between business owners and society. Today, we are struggling to come to a new understanding of that relationship. Again, though, it needs to be noted that the relationship changes over time. Businesses evolve and grow in response to social needs, and how well the business can satisfy those needs. Marketing logic says that businesses that cannot meet the needs of customers will fail. The logic of business and society says that businesses that do not meet the needs of society will fail too; in some cases, society will deliberately drive them out of business. This has implications for how we think about the relationship between managers and stakeholders.

The nature of leadership has changed too, and has emerged in varied forms in different cultures. Is it possible that leadership, like organisation, adopts the profile it does in response to deeper demands? Do people ask for a certain kind of leadership: authoritarian or democratic, responsive or autocratic, heroic or submissive to the needs of the people? Do people always get the leadership they want, or need? What we can see of the changing ways in which leadership is exercised and understood suggests that there is support for situational leadership theory, but there do also seem to be constants. Although the nature of leadership changes, there are similarities in the things that people have always demanded of their leaders: courage being one example.

The Persistence of Memory

When we look at the continuities in management, things that have remained basically the same even though their outward form may have changed, we are at once confronted by the question of why. What makes these things—the persistence of certain organisational forms, similar ways of thinking about leadership and strategy, the problem of class division when managing people—endure?

It is tempting to think that these are eternal verities, core concepts of management which have endured unchanging from the beginning, and will endure to the end. That is one possibility, but there are others. Consciously or sub-consciously, we inherit a great deal from the past. Our concepts of society and relationships, our own basic needs—for food, shelter, pleasure, love, self-fulfilment and so on—our concepts of value, our morals and ideas of right and wrong are all part of the basic fabric of our lives, and those of our parents and ancestors. We inherit these things for the most part without questioning them. These things are not part of management theory; but they do have an immense impact on how we do management in practice. So it may be that the features we see coming up over and over again in management are a result of memory or inheritance, rather than having some fundamental truth-value of their own.

The reinforcing of past practice may also be a feature of the way managers have traditionally been trained and educated. The apprenticeship system undoubtedly contributed to the reinforcing of existing practice. In some cases apprentices would train with more than one firm, which broadened their horizons, and in some cases people were able to train at external institutions such as the Italian abacus schools or the nineteenth-century commercial colleges, but we do not know enough about the curricula of these to know if they encouraged innovation. The advent of business schools did not necessarily solve the problem; most business schools still use the case study method pioneered at Harvard Business School which teaches managers how to face the present and future by looking at how problems have been solved in the past (a practice of which this book, of course, is fundamentally guilty as well). Of course it is possible to learn from the past, but when this becomes a matter of mere rote learning—see what they did in the past, then repeat it—there is a danger that the practices of the past will become enshrined as the dominant logic, whether they are good or bad.

And finally, there is the possibility that we imitate the past because we see this as fundamentally less risky than trying to innovate. We tend to fall back on the things we know, rather than venture into the unknown. Doing what has always been done might be imperfect, but at least we know it works most of the time; trying something new could result in things going disastrously wrong. There is also a tendency [...] to forget what has gone on before and re-invent the wheel. In their excellent book on management innovation, *Giant Steps in Management*, Mol and Birkinshaw (2008: 2) comment that 'rather like the propensity of Hollywood directors for remaking classic movies in contemporary settings, management thinkers are very good at reconceptualizing old ideas, giving them a new twist and packaging them for an audience that wasn't exposed to the original idea'.

Tradition and Innovation

Mol and Birkinshaw go on to comment that

> today's management practices are all built on prior practices. A useful analogy is the process of sedimentation in a lake or river estuary: new layers of sediment get laid down on top of old ones, but the old layers still influence the contours of the river bed, and they occasionally poke their way through to the surface. It's the same with management practices. Despite all the rhetoric about hierarchies disappearing in the workplace, we still litter our conversations with military-style terminology.
>
> (Mol and Birkinshaw 2008: 3)

The twelfth-century philosopher Bernard of Chartres had another metaphor: 'We are like pygmies seated on the shoulders of giants. We can see further than our ancestors could, and to that extent our knowledge is greater than theirs; yet without their accumulated knowledge to guide us, we would know nothing.'

The argument is often made that organisations should try to break with the past: tradition is a hindering force which inhibits creativity. Tradition, it is said, gives us reasons *not* to do things, rather than reasons to do things. But this all depends on tradition itself, and how it is managed. If tradition gives way to slavish imitation, of the sort that says, 'we do things this way because that is how we have always done them', then yes, the danger exists. But recourse to tradition should not be used to answer 'how' questions; its purpose is to answer 'why' questions. If we want to understand the purpose behind a particular way of doing business, and understand why it was adopted in the first place, we must go back to the past. Reference to the past may show that there is valid reason why this practice was adopted and it must remain, or equally that the reasons why it was adopted are no longer valid and the practice should be discarded; either way, the question cannot be answered without historical inquiry.

When firms cut themselves off from tradition in the belief that by discarding the past they are enabling themselves to better concentrate on the future, they are actually doing quite the opposite. They are cutting off an important source of knowledge about themselves. Again [...], knowledge breeds knowledge. Without prior knowledge of what *has* happened, the task of understanding what *will* happen becomes much harder and more complex. Without its foundations, the river bed will erode and the course of the river itself may change. Without the shoulders of giants to lift us up and give us a view of the far horizon, we can only see what little is immediately around us. Tradition does not necessarily hamper innovation; it can be an important source of knowledge which enables innovation, if used wisely.

The Past Constrains the Present—and Enables It

When Tolstoy wrote in *War and Peace* that 'kings are the slaves of history', he meant that no leader ever has quite the freedom of action that they imagine they have. Tolstoy believed in the inevitability of history. He thought that events piled on top of other events created an unstoppable momentum of their own, and that human beings are simply carried along by events as if being swept out to sea by a tide.

Although Tolstoy presents a picture which many might think is exaggerated, it does seem that past events can constrain and limit action in the present. Decisions made in the past have consequences, often unintended ones, that can hamper present actions (see Teece 1987; Pavitt 1990 for discussions of how past decisions constrain future strategy).[1] Take for example a company at the moment of its foundation. It might have a choice of three or four different product markets it could move into, but having limited resources it chooses just one. It invests in capacity, marketing and so on to support that market. That decision is now made, and made irrevocably. If at some point in the future the company wishes to abandon that market and move into another, then it can do so; but that decision will have costs and consequences of its own.

For a practical example, we can look at the early years of the car industry in America. Cars were seen as high-priced luxury items, and the early car makers concentrated on designs for that market, using essentially craft-based methods of production. Their choice meant that they did not seek out the mass market or invest in mass production. Ford decided to do both of these things. By the time Ford began to dominate the market, it was too late for many of the original firms to change their minds. Some were unwilling to do so, believing that they had made the right decision in the first place and/or being unwilling to abandon their original investment (and of course in some cases they were right to do so, some of these luxury brands went on to be successful). Some, like Durant's original General Motors, were unable to do so. Durant's attempts to compete with Ford met with failure, for thanks to decisions taken earlier, he had the wrong structure and the wrong products to match Ford's recipe for success.

But when Pierre du Pont and Alfred Sloan took charge of General Motors, things changed. General Motors moved onto a new competitive footing. Now it was Ford's turn to be caught in the trap of its own past decisions. Ford had concentrated on just one brand and one segment, the mass market for cheap cars. General Motors offered a range of brands that appealed to different segments. Ford could have chosen to differentiate sooner than it did, but again its top managers were unwilling to do so. Abandoning the original Model T and developing new lines would be costly, but it would have also meant sacrificing a brand that, emotionally, meant a great deal to Ford himself in particular. So the original path was adhered to, until eventually General Motors overtook Ford in terms of market share and change was forced.

Economists refer to this as 'path dependency'. A commonly cited example is the QWERTY keyboards that nearly all of us use on computers today. This keyboard was originally invented for typewriters, and became the standard design around the world. Despite experiments which have shown that this is by no means the most efficient layout for a keyboard, its use continues. The costs of replacing every keyboard with a more efficient design and retraining millions of people who have learned to touch-type using it would be far higher than the inefficiencies the present keyboard creates. So, a decision taken long ago about keyboard layout continues to affect the way we type and input information, and we are unable to break out of this trap without great cost in time and money.

But—as the example of General Motors shows—path dependency is not inevitable. The past itself shows this. Companies do reinvent themselves, like the Finnish forestry products company Nokia turning itself into a global mobile phone maker, or they can enter completely new markets, like Japanese soap maker Kao suddenly turning into the world leader in the computer floppy disks market. How do they do this? One thing we can observe from past practice is that companies that leave their options open are less prone to path dependency, while those that focus tightly are more likely to be caught out. In other words, the narrower the path, the greater degree of dependency. Ford was—at first—a well-managed company but with just one core market. General Motors was an organisational shambles but with a variety of brands and markets. Theoretically, it had a greater range of choices open to it, and was fortunate to have in du Pont and Sloan leaders who were able to assess those choices, make the right ones and then drive the firm forward accordingly.

The diversified firms we found in Italy in the Middle Ages, which were highly flexible and traded in many different markets, were certainly less prone to path dependency than the chartered trading companies that followed them a couple of centuries later. The Hudson's Bay Company, which chose to concentrate on just one product, fur, became moribund and nearly succumbed to competition; only the energy and drive of its new governor, John Simpson, turned things around [...]. The East India Company descended into being a bureaucratic manager of land and revenue, losing all its dynamism, and without support from the British government would have collapsed long before it did, in 1858.

The other factor required to break out of path dependency is will; not just on the part of leaders, but on the part of the whole organisation. (Leaders who urge change when the rest of the organisation does not wish to change have a very hard task in front of them.) The will to change is not enough to make change happen successfully; in late Imperial China the powerful mandarin Li Hongzhang certainly desired change, but was prevented from making it happen [...]. It is not just the investment and time required that create barriers to change; change also takes people out of their comfort zone and creates the impression of risk. Strong leadership and strong commitment from below are both required, as we saw in the example of William McKnight and 3M [...], or the radical change in direction at Oneida [...].

Using the Past for Competitive Advantage

Firms which fall into the trap of strategic path dependency often do not see it coming until it is too late. For all their earlier successes, both General Motors and Ford fell into this trap in the opening years of the twenty-first century by committing themselves to certain markets and brands and backing these with heavy investments. When market conditions changed as a result of high energy prices and the economic downturn a few years later, they were unable to respond quickly.

One of the key lessons of the past, therefore, is that this trap exists. The second is that there are ways it can be avoided, or at least ways to lesson its impacts. We know that flexibility and keeping options open help to lessen the danger. But this is not just a matter of strategic planning; it is also a matter of strategic *thinking*, of understanding and knowing and recognising the signs (and here again, examples taken from the past can help us to recognise those signs). And the response has to go beyond strategy. A new form of organisation may be required, as Pierre du Pont discovered when he took over at General Motors. A new approach to managing people may be required so as to secure workforce commitment. Not only new markets but new methods of marketing may be needed. New sources of finance and a new approach to financial management may be in order. Innovation and new knowledge become crucial, and the firm's links to society may make the difference between success or failure. And last of all, the firm needs leaders to provide vision and guidance and ensure everyone works towards the required goals.

Some managers are good at some of these things. But as we have seen in the past, some—Cosimo dei Medici, Pierre du Pont, William Lever, William Pirrie, Henry Heinz, the Boucicauts, Thomas Jackson, Hans Renold, Sarah Breedlove Walker, J.R.D. Tata, just to name some from the case studies in this book—were good at all of them.

Here is one lesson from the past that would seem to be incontrovertible. The firm that does a few things well will be beaten by the firm that does everything well. Genuine all-round competence at everything will succeed; genius in one area but lack of competence in others might succeed, but the odds become higher with each weak area identified. Of course it is hard to find individuals who are good at everything, which is why all the people mentioned above concentrated on their own strengths and spent a great deal of time and energy finding, training and mentoring people whose strengths were complementary to their own.

We cannot simply reach into the past and pull out ideas that will give us competitive advantage. What we can do is look at the past and understand why things are done as they are done, and then use that knowledge to either reinforce and strengthen existing ways of doing things, or innovate and create new ones.

Summing Up: Why We Manage As We Do

In some ways, the structure of this [reading] is artificial. It follows now standard divisions into managerial functions: organisation, strategy, HRM, marketing, finance and so on. This is how management is studied and taught, and especially in large firms, increasingly this is how it is practised.

There are real advantages to specialisation. Arguably, the need for specialist knowledge in areas like finance in particular has never been greater. But we need to remember that until a little over a hundred years ago—with the partial exception of finance, which in large firms was managed by specialists—these divisions did not exist. Most managers were in effect general managers. And the model was not ineffective. Some very large and powerful businesses, by the standards of the day, were built using this method. Some of them spanned continents. Some operated and traded right around the world.

There is a tendency to believe that the management methods we use now are the best that there are. The best practices we use in marketing and HRM, for example, are exactly that: the best ways of doing things, tried and proven through both theoretical analysis and practical observation. It may be that they are. Or it may be that they are relics, even if cleverly disguised ones, old wine poured into new bottles, old methods recycled and given new names. Why do we manage as we do? Why do we use the methods that we do, and not other ones? The question needs to be asked, and asked repeatedly, as to whether the ways we manage are indeed the ways best suited to the time and place. Sometimes we will find that the answer is yes, and that is comforting for we know we are on the right track. Sometimes the honest answer will be no, and then the real test comes, for we must challenge ourselves and organisations to find another way. This is hard. But the final lesson of the past is this: that unless these questions are asked, the company risks falling into the path-dependency trap. Escaping that trap will be even harder and more painful. There is more than one way to do management, more than one way to go forward. Remember the past, as you think of the future.

Research Projects

The second half of this [reading] consists of notes for research projects. The MBA module on which this book was based featured team research projects in which students used some of the learning they gained from the module to examine management practices in particular industries, how practice evolved over time, and how methods developed in certain industries impacted on management more generally. These can be used as formal research projects or simply as research exercises by teams or individuals.

The notes for each are intended as starting points for research; they suggest questions for analysis and give a brief list of possible sources. They are not complete discussions of each topic, nor are they meant to be. Their purpose is to illustrate some of the ideas in this book, and serve as the basis for yet further discussion and analysis.

Once again, there are no right or wrong answers. Readers are encouraged to use the projects as means of enhancing their own knowledge and understanding of what management is. Provided that end is achieved, the actual projects and their outputs can take any form that is desired. At the University of Exeter Business School, we asked teams to produce a 10–15-minute presentation in class, followed by a short 2,000–3,000-word report. But it should be possible to configure the outputs in any way that is desired. Again, I very much welcome comments on the utility of these projects, how well they work and what people are able to learn from them.

The Steel Industry

Steel has been manufactured on a small-scale basis since ancient times, but only became an industry of importance during the Industrial Revolution. The advent of new blast furnace technology and new methods such as the Bessemer process in the early nineteenth century meant it was now possible to mass produce steel and steel products. Simultaneously, the invention of the steam locomotive and the railway building boom greatly increased the demand for steel in the nineteenth century; the development of modern artillery also had an impact, though a little later. One of the first modern steel makers, Krupp, grew to prominence through making steel rails and steel cannon. Later, the car industry and shipbuilders became major markets for steel producers.

American steel making got off to a late start, and the first American railways were built using rails made by Krupp or by British firms. However, the gap was quickly filled by Andrew Carnegie and then other producers such as Charles Schwab at Bethlehem. By 1900, American steel makers were the largest in the world, with most production concentrated in the conglomerate United States Steel, headed by Judge Elbert Gary and backed by the money of J.P. Morgan.

Steel making on a large scale required a large amount of technology and manpower. Early steel plants were vast places employing tens of thousands of people. It became quickly apparent that these big enterprises were not being run efficiently. Some sort of managerial system was needed to make them more efficient and profitable. It is no accident that the first attempts at systematising management—scientific management—came in engineering, and that steel plants were among the first companies to employ the methods of scientific management. Elsewhere in the world, attempts at developing management systems often appeared first in the iron and steel industries.

Approaches to the Project

The steel industry was an incubator for many modern management methods, including quite a few still in use today. One starting point could be to look at the industry itself, the technological changes and the growth in demand in steel. How far did demand drive the evolution of the industry?

Second, how did that evolution require a management response? Why and how did management change? What were the key drivers of change? What forms did the change take? Here you may well find you need to get into a discussion of scientific management and similar systems, in terms of organisation and technical/people management.

Third, consider an evaluation of that system (or indeed, systems). How well did it/they work? What were the strengths? What were the weaknesses?

Fourth, what if any lasting effects have there been? What influences can you still see in modern management methods and theory, either in steel and engineering or more generally? Again, feel free to criticise these influences and developments.

Sources

Biographies of figures like Carnegie, Krupp, Schwab, Frick and other major players in the industry are a good place to start, and if you choose to explore scientific management in detail there are both the original works of Taylor, Gantt, the Gilbreths and others to choose from, and a rich secondary literature. Be sceptical about some of this; Taylor is blamed for a good many things which were properly the responsibility of the people who put his system into practice.

Other works that might be useful include:

Ashton, T.S., *Iron and Steel in the Industrial Revolution.*
Birch, Alan, *The Economic History of the British Iron and Steel Industry, 1784–1879.*
Temin, Peter, *Iron and Steel in Nineteenth-Century America.*

You should find plenty of other sources as you go along, but these and the biographies noted above will help you get started.

The Railway Industry

The railways revolutionised transport, in a way that earlier systems such as canals had not managed to do. For their time, the railways were very technologically sophisticated, relying on a range of new technologies, notably the steam engine (improved by Boulton and Watt in the late eighteenth century), new steel processes that allowed for stronger rails able to bear the weight of locomotives and rolling stock, and most critically of all, the telegraph, which enabled operations to be coordinated over long distances.

The first railways appeared in the 1830s and 1840s, and were mostly short-haul lines dedicated to particular cargoes, shipping goods from a factory or group of factories to a seaport, for example. Gradually in Europe the lines became linked, and passenger travel became more common. Thomas Cook started organising railway excursion parties in the 1840s, and by the 1860s was introducing the beginnings of mass tourism based on railway transport.

In North America, railways had been developing along the Eastern Seaboard before the Civil War, but the big boom in long-distance railway building came after the war with the drive to the west in both the USA and Canada. Long-distance routes like the Union Pacific and Canadian Pacific were built rapidly, although at a terrible cost in lives.

The advent of the railways meant it was possible to transport goods quickly over long distances, much more quickly than by water. (Consider the relative speeds of a nineteenth-century train versus those of a sailing ship or canal barge.) This meant it was possible to integrate businesses over large geographical spaces, and the railways played a major role in pulling together the emerging large corporations of America such as Carnegie Steel, Standard Oil and the meat packers such as Armour and Swift.

However, the real importance of the railways for our purposes may well be in the management methods they were forced to develop. Instead of concentrating thousands of workers at one point, as in a steel mill, the railways spread their workers over large areas, often across countries or continents. How could their operations be coordinated? Even time itself had to be re-organised; the builders of the Great Western found that time in Bristol was eight minutes behind time in London, which could have catastrophic results for scheduling. Alfred Chandler in his book *The Visible Hand* credits the railways with inventing many of the coordination and communications methods we still use today.

But the early railways were costly in terms of money and lives to build—and to run. Many companies went bankrupt. Many lives were lost in building the railways, and as late as 1888, over 1,000 people a year were being killed in railway accidents in Britain, and many more in America. Were the railways really as efficient as Chandler suggests?

Approaches to the Project

Initially, you will need to look at the history of the industry. Think about the advances in technology and the needs of growing economies. Did the railways drive economic growth, or were they driven by it?

Second, why and how did management and organisation change? What were the key drivers of that change? What forms did the change take? How were railways different from other forms of organisation? Who were the 'managers'?

Third, consider an evaluation of railway management. How well did it work? What were the strengths? What were the weaknesses?

Fourth, what if any lasting effects have there been? What influences can you still see in modern management methods and theory, either in transport management or more generally? Again, feel free to criticise these influences and developments.

Other elements are up to you. You might consider criticising or evaluating Chandler's approach, or you might want to look at special features such as coordination and communication. This is a big subject with lots of scope, so be sure to target your investigations closely.

Sources

Company histories of the big railways will be useful, and Chapters 3–6 of Alfred Chandler's *The Visible Hand* will probably be essential reading. Be aware that Chandler has been criticised, however. You might also look at changes in railway travel, in which case you might want to have a look at works on Pullman and Nagelmackers/Orient Express.

There are plenty of histories of the railways. Some are for 'train spotters' rather than serious students, so be careful not to get bogged down. Look for works which talk about the economics and organisation of railways, and then sift through these looking for details of how the railways were managed.

Other works that might be useful include:

Chandler, Alfred D., *The Railroads: The Nation's First Big Business.*
Cochran, Thomas C., *Railroad Leaders, 1845–1890.*
Grodinsky, Julius, *Transcontinental Railway Strategy.*
Reed, Malcolm C., *Railways in the Victorian Economy.*

The Textiles Industry

Textiles were big business in Europe since the Middle Ages, and were, after agriculture, the largest sector by proportion of GDP until the nineteenth century. With the exception of a few big cloth-making centres, most production was craft production, with various steps in the process farmed out to local spinners, weavers and so on, most of whom worked at home, or in small independent workshops. Each stage of cloth production, and there were many, was handled by a different person or group of people working in effect as subcontractors.

In the second half of the eighteenth century, however, there were a number of rapid technological advances, including the spinning jenny, the water frame and the mule, to name just a few of the most famous. These enabled mechanised production, and some of the first true factories began to appear, notably Arkwright's mill at Cromford in Derbyshire. Originally driven by animal power, they were then powered by water, and by the end of the century the advances in the steam engine pioneered by Boulton and Watt saw the introduction of steam power. Steam remained the main motive power in factories for many decades thereafter.

The first factories were primarily for spinning cotton into yarn, but later inventions allowed mechanised weaving and fulling as well. By the mid-nineteenth century, most of the important stages of cloth manufacturing could be done by machine. Although the putting-out or contract system did not disappear overnight, it began to decline. Meanwhile, other technological innovations allowed the new system to be applied to woollen cloth, muslin and other fabrics, and eventually the development of new synthetics such as rayon. More importantly, the utility of the factory system was appreciated by businesses in other sectors.

The factory system was widely adopted but heavily criticised. Working conditions were often very poor and unsanitary, and campaigners in Britain and elsewhere tried repeatedly to make factories safer and healthier places. Marxists saw the factory system as an effort by capital to concentrate and therefore to control labour. Others saw it as a response to rising demand levels, given growing populations and increasing prosperity in much of Europe. More recently, transaction costs theorists have seen the factory system as reducing transaction costs and therefore making production cheaper, more efficient, and even of better quality.

Approaches to the Project

A natural focus for this project would be the development of the factory system and associated methods of management, a system for which the textile industry was the primary incubator. Other focuses may occur to you, of course.

Initially, you will need to look at the history of the industry and how it evolved. Second, how did that evolution require a management response? Why and how did management change? What were the key drivers of change? What forms did the change take? What were the defining features of the new organisation? Who were the 'managers' as such?

Third, consider an evaluation of that system (or indeed, systems). How well did it/they work? What were the strengths? What were the weaknesses? In this context, I suspect you will have to look at the social impacts and the problems of health, safety and so on that were so widely criticised at the time, and since.

Fourth, what if any lasting effects have there been? What influences can you still see in modern management methods and theory, either in textiles or more generally? Again, feel free to criticise these influences and developments.

Other elements are up to you. You might consider looking at some of the different interpretations of the factory system alluded to above, or you might feel that a closer examination of some of the key entrepreneurs is in order to look at changing patterns of entrepreneurship. This is a big subject with lots of scope, so be sure to target your investigations closely.

Sources

It may be hard to find, but Andrew Ure's *The Philosophy of Machinery and Manufactures* or his *History of the Cotton Industry* may be quite helpful. Richard Fitton's biography of Arkwright may also be valuable, as might Ian Donnachie's biography of Robert Owen. Richard Donkin's book *Blood, Sweat and Tears* has at least one chapter on working under the factory system. Generally, the textile industry has been well studied, so you should not lack sources.

Other works that might be useful include:

Baines, Edward, *History of the Cotton Manufacture in Great Britain.*
Copeland, Melvin T., *The Cotton Manufacturing Industry of the United States.*
Edwards, M.M., *The Growth of the British Cotton Trade.*
Jenkins, D.T. and Ponting, K.G., *The British Wool Textile Industry, 1770–1914.*
Kerridge, Eric, *Textile Manufactures in Early Modern England.*
Wadsworth, A.P. and de Mann, Julia de L., *The Cotton Trade and Industrial Lancashire, 1600–1780.*

The Automotive Industry

It is not uncommon for particular industries to be described as having 'transformed' society, but in the case of the automobile industry in the first half of the twentieth century, the term can be fairly used. Cars went from being expensive luxuries to mass market goods within a few decades, and in doing so changed the way many people lived their lives, how companies did business, and how war was waged, among other things.

Even simple early cars were complicated pieces of machinery, and the early automotive entrepreneurs faced a constant challenge: how to build a reliable car at an affordable price. The initial reaction was to build for the luxury market and adopt a price-skimming strategy, but following the appearance of Ford and, to a much lesser extent, Louis Renault and William Morris, this became increasingly difficult as prices were forced down and the techniques of mass production applied.

Ford introduced not just one but a whole series of revolutions. The first was a design for a cheap, mass-produced car that could be afforded by the middle classes, thus opening up a huge new market sector. The second was a mass production system, based around the purpose-built assembly plant at Highland Park, that actually worked and was able to deliver the marketing promise. The third was that promise, the idea that owning a car could change your life and give you mobility and freedom, hooking into the American Dream. All these combined into an ideology known as Fordism.

Attention has focused on the struggle between Ford and his rivals, first Willys Overland and then, much more seriously, General Motors, which ultimately dethroned Ford as king of the auto makers. Quite a lot can be done just by comparing their approaches and seeing how each firm approached management, their marketing and their strategy, their organisations and their leadership.

Approaches to the Project

First, get to grips with the history of the industry itself. Material on this should be plentiful, possibly even too plentiful. Nevins and Hill needed three volumes for their history of Ford alone. The main thing you will need to understand is the nature of the technical challenges and the nature of the market.

Second, think about how and why management within the industry changed as the car industry developed. The first car makers worked on a craft production basis, or something close to it, rather like specialist sports car makers such as Morgan do today. What had to change? What were the production, operational, marketing and other requirements? How would you describe the system that evolved to meet these requirements?

Third, consider an evaluation of that system (or indeed, systems). How well did it/they work? What were the strengths? What were the weaknesses?

Fourth, what if any lasting effects have there been? What influences can you still see in modern management methods and theory, either in the car industry or more generally? Again, feel free to criticise these influences and developments.

Sources

Biographies of the people mentioned above, and on other early car makers too, are a good start. Again, there is plenty of material on Ford, although much of it is either too admiring or too harshly critical. But be sure to go beyond Ford.

Other works that might be useful include:

Bardou, J.-P *et al.*, *The Automobile Revolution.*
Cusumano, Michael A., *The Japanese Automobile Industry.*
Epstein, Ralph C., *The Automobile Industry.*
Richardson, Kenneth, *The British Motor Industry, 1896–1939.*
Whipp, Richard and Clark, Peter, *Innovation and the Auto Industry.*
Wood, Jonathan, *Wheels of Misfortune: The Rise and Fall of the British Motor Industry.*

The Financial Services Sector

In 1800, banks in the West, at least, were small affairs, usually family owned and run, although there were a few joint-stock institutions like the Bank of England and the Bank of Scotland which fulfilled an important role in state finance (though still in the private sector). Gold and silver were still the primary circulating medium, and although there were a bewildering variety of credit instruments for financing state and private debt, capital markets were still comparatively small. The world financial market was dominated by London until around 1900 when New York began to overtake it.

Capital markets grew rapidly. There were both push and pull factors here. First, rising prosperity meant that there was more liquidity and thus more push for investment. Second, the Industrial Revolution and subsequent capital-intensive projects like the railways required huge—for the time—injections of finance. Although the London markets grew rapidly, those of New York grew more rapidly still. Wall Street was little more than a genteel row of trading houses in 1860; by 1900 it was an economic powerhouse, if an occasionally shaky one. Increasing globalisation, especially around and after the First World War, led to further changes, with international banking and finance increasingly expanding, and the first steps being taken towards the foundation of true international capital markets.

At the same time, the problems of financial control grew more acute. Accountants, formerly merely clerks who added up figures in ledgers, became more important. Not only did they devise new methods of cost control and cashflow management, but they were also important in preventing abuses and fraud. Two of the great forensic accountants in history, William Deloitte and Edwin Waterhouse, helped to put in place some of the financial control measures we still use today.

This is a very big subject indeed, and you will want to narrow it down. You could look at the growth of capital markets and the impact this had on management; you might want to focus on either London or New York, but you should be able to do a brief survey of both. Or you could forget about the markets and look at financial management, corporate finance in our terms, and how the treasury function developed and how accounting became increasingly essential. Or, you could look at banking specifically and developments within that industry, at how banks were managed and how banks affected management. Other options may occur to you.

Approaches to the Project

Initially, you will need to look at the history of the subject. Think about the changes that took place. What drove those changes, and why? What was the broader impact on economies, companies, managers?

Second, how did that evolution require a management response? Why and how did management change? What were the key drivers of change? What forms did the change take?

Third, consider an evaluation of that change. What opportunities were created, what threats were posed? How well did companies respond, and how and why did they fail?

Fourth, what if any lasting effects have there been? What influences can you still see in modern management methods and theory? Feel free to criticise these influences and developments and state what you think should have happened.

Other elements are up to you, and will depend on your ultimate focus. This is a big subject with lots of scope, so be sure to target your investigations closely.

Sources

If you are going down the capital markets route, there is a wealth of material on the City of London, including David Kynaston's multi-volume work, and on Wall Street. Look for institutional histories too, of key organisations: Salomon Brothers, Goldman Sachs, J.P. Morgan, Chase, Lloyds, Barings, Warburgs, Gibbs, the Stock Exchange, the Bank of England and so on. There are also plenty of histories of New York capital markets, though you might have to resort to inter-library loans.

If you are looking at banks, much the same applies. If you want to look at accountancy and financial controls, you might find it harder; there are several journals of accounting history which should also be available online.

Other works that might be useful include:

Born, Karl Erich, *International Finance in the Nineteenth and Twentieth Centuries.*

Carosso, Vincent P., *Investment Banking in America: A History.*
Jones, Geoffrey, *Banks as Multinationals.*
Kindleberger, Charles Poor, *A Financial History of Western Europe.*
Redlich, Fritz, *The Molding of American Banking: Men and Ideas.*

Retailing

Retailing developed from a business of largely family-owned single-outlet enterprises in the early nineteenth century into many of the forms we see today; department stores, chain stores, remote ordering and so on. There were both push and pull factors involved in this change. Growing populations and rising affluence meant that more people could afford more, and better, goods. The Boucicauts' famous phrase 'the democratisation of luxury' was intended to convey the notion that the benefits of the Industrial Revolution were now available not just to the wealthy but also the middle classes and even the more affluent working classes. At the same time, new technologies such as the telegraph and telephone enabled better transport and communications, meaning more goods could be offered, and at more outlets. Finally, of course, these same technologies enabled the development of catalogue retailing, or mail order.

Taking advantage of such technologies, however, involved changing the mindset of the retail manager. The early department store retailers, especially the Boucicauts in Paris, the developers of Au Bon Marché, created not only a new kind of business but also developed a new approach to the customer. The mail order pioneers, Sears and Montgomery Ward, similarly were able to think outside the box; if the customer cannot come to the store, we will send the store to the customer. The chain store developers like Woolworth and J.C. Penney also looked for new ways of satisfying customers.

We are often accustomed to thinking of the development of marketing in terms of formal theory, the 4Ps and the like. However, the retail industry shows that managers have been capable of working out for themselves the best way to do business without necessarily having any formal guidelines or theories to work to. Three important new forms of retail outlet, all three still thriving, were developed before the term 'marketing' had really been invented, or at least before it was in widespread use.

Approaches to the Project

Initially, you will need to look at the history of the industry. Oddly enough, general histories of the retail industry are quite hard to come by, but there are biographies of individuals and firms. Try to build up a composite picture of the changes. You might also want to focus on just one aspect: department stores, mail order, etc. rather than trying to cover them all, but that is up to you.

Second, why and how did management and organisation change? What were the key drivers of that change? What forms did the change take? How were retail business different from other forms of organisation? Who were the 'managers'?

Third, consider an evaluation of retail management as it changed. How well did management systems work? What were the strengths? What were the weaknesses?

Fourth, what if any lasting effects have there been? What influences can you still see in modern management methods and theory, either in retail management or more generally? Again, feel free to criticise these influences and developments.

Other elements are up to you. You might want to compare the practice you observe with the formal marketing theory you have learned, noting similarities and discrepancies. Or you could think about whether any of the practices you observed should be given more prominence in modern retail management, or any other kind of management. These are some possibilities; you may think of others.

Sources

As mentioned, there are not that many general histories, but search for material on firms that interest you; you should be able to put your composite picture together from these specific sources. Beware of claims to have 'invented' concepts; almost everyone claims to have 'invented' the department store, for example. Be sure to check dates.

Other works that might be useful include:

Benson, J. and Shaw, G., *The Evolution of Retail Systems, c. 1800–1914.*
Mahoney, Tom and Sloane, Leonard, *The Great Merchants: America's Foremost Retail Institutions and the People Who Made Them Great.*
Strasser, Susan, *Satisfaction Guaranteed: The Making of the American Mass Market.*
Tedlow, Richard S., *New and Improved: The Story of Mass Marketing in America.*

If you are looking specifically at department stores there is a small body of literature on these, plus most major store chains have produced a history at some point.

Computers and Electronics

The development of the computer and its ancestor, the electric calculating machine, is arguably one of the most significant technological advances of the twentieth century. In this project, you will be looking at the development of the industry that made the exploitation and diffusion of that advance possible. You could begin with the pioneers, Charles Babbage and Hermann Hollerith, and then look at some of the early firms like IBM before turning to the postwar period.

The early period under consideration begins with the relatively crude electric calculating machines, which became increasingly important to business as time went on. During the Second World War, there were great advances in computer technology, and after the war it was only a matter of time before those were exploited. The first steps forward came in the 1950s, when the technological advances made by the likes of Wang An and Jay Wright Forrester began to be exploited. The two giants of the industry, IBM and Hewlett-Packard, began to grow and were challenged by the likes of Ken Olsen's DEC. Other entrepreneurs like Robert Noyce served as incubators for new businesses, in his case first Fairchild and then Intel.

There are two facets to this subject, and you may wish to choose one or the other, or combine the two. First, the nature of this industry meant that traditional command-and-control style organisations were often not appropriate. People began experimenting with new forms and new philosophies of management, and often those spilled over into management in other sectors. Second, the computer of course changed the working practices of virtually every other type of business. You might want to explore the course of that change and development and the relations between these high-tech industries and their target markets. How has this relationship affected how we use computers at work today?

Approaches to the Project

Initially, you will need to look at the history of the industry. Think about the advances in technology itself, but particularly about the management of technology. Did computers drive economic growth, or was their rapid development driven by the more general need for growth?

Second, why and how did management and organisation change? What were the key drivers of that change? What forms did the change take? You could even indulge in some counterfactual speculation if you like, and think about what management might be like if the computer had not been invented. You might want in that case to take a closer look at Babbage and the importance of knowledge.

Third, consider an evaluation of management within the industry. How well did it work? What were the strengths? What were the weaknesses? If you are going down the 'impact of the computer' route, look instead at what good and bad points have emerged in current managerial and working practice.

Fourth, related to the above, what have the lasting effects been? Did computers utterly revolutionise management, or did they just create paper blizzards and information overload? Have a look at some current theory on the subject and then decide what you think.

Other elements are up to you. One issue that you may decide is worth a look is communications. The computer industry by and large—or at least, best practice within the industry—sets great emphasis on internal communications within firms; why is this, and is that idea transferrable? This is a big subject with lots of scope, so be sure to target your investigations closely.

Sources

Generic histories of the industry are thin on the ground, but a few are given below. You may have better luck with histories of firms and individuals; there is a lot of literature on IBM, and Apple, DEC and others have been studied. The journal literature is fairly rich in works on the impact of IT going back some years. Your main problem should be to work out the scope of your project fairly early on and then target your search for materials.

Other works that might be useful include:

Anchordoguy, Marie, *Computers Inc: Japan's Challenge to IBM.*
Cortada, James W., *The Computer in the United States: From Laboratory to Market, 1930–1960.*
Flamm, Kenneth, *Creating the Computer.*
Morris, P.R., *A History of the World Semiconductor Industry.*

Select Bibliography

Mol, Michael and Birkinshaw, Julian (2008) *Giant Steps in Management: Innovations That Change the Way We Work*, London: FT-Prentice Hall.
Pavitt, Keith (1990) 'What We Know About the Strategic Management of Technology', *California Management Review* (Spring), 17–26.
Teece, David J. (1987) *The Competitive Challenge*, New York: Harper & Row.

Notes

1. My thanks to Professor Steve Brown of the University of Exeter Business School for drawing Keith Pavitt's article to my attention.

What Is Philosophy?

Joseph Gilbert

Philosophy as a Field of Knowledge

What makes a human different from other living things? Are we really free to choose different actions? What is the good life for humans? These are philosophical questions. One can try to answer them using facts known from biology, or psychology, or literature, but the attempts to answer them usually involve philosophy. Isaiah Berlin has described philosophy as dealing with those questions for which there is no clear agreement on where to look for answers. We know how to determine whether a certain drug cures a certain medical condition, or how far it is from Los Angeles to New York, or who won the World Series in 2005. We do not have clear agreement on how to decide whether universities should prepare good workers or informed citizens, or when a cause is worth dying for, or how much freedom individuals should have while living in society.

Philosophy is sometimes described as a discipline or a science or a field of knowledge. The Greek origins of the term involve two words meaning friend of or love of wisdom. In the Western intellectual tradition, we have fragments of philosophical writing that date back more than 2,500 years. The first complete writings (as opposed to fragments) that we have are from Plato and Aristotle, Greek philosophers who lived in Athens in the fourth century B.C.[1]

At least in a limited way, at one time or another, we all do a little philosophy. The manager who makes numerous decisions each day at his desk may stand out under the stars at night and think philosophical thoughts about how small he is under the night sky. He may sit at his desk and ponder whether his son who is a marine and who has just shipped out for a combat zone will make it back, and if not, why not, and what all this means relative to decisions about capital spending and budget over-runs. He may ponder what to do about a long-time colleague, a steady solid performer, whose alcohol addiction or child custody battle has reduced work effectiveness below the minimum acceptable level. He may wonder fleetingly whether there is any connection between his long work weeks and frequent travel and his teenage daughter's experiments with drugs. He may be deciding how to deal with a troublesome whistle-blower, or a possible product defect. Now and then, we all do a little philosophy.

As long as we are going to do a little philosophy, it might be good to learn a little about philosophy. Some very insightful individuals have pondered these same questions, and others like them, and have produced answers that have been studied by others for hundreds or even thousands of years. Writings that survive that long, and are read and discussed by many generations of people with questions, might just be worth a look. The purpose of this book is not to produce philosophers or to provide definitive answers to life's toughest questions. It is to help managers to think about issues and reach ethical decisions in their work lives. By the end of the book, I hope it will be clear why philosophy, and especially that branch of philosophy known as ethics, is not really foreign to the objectives either of an MBA program or of a manager.

As with any field of knowledge, philosophy has limits to the topics or issues it considers. One key point that sets philosophy apart from the physical or social sciences is that philosophy deals with very general questions that underlie the foundations of the other sciences. For example, the branch of philosophy called metaphysics deals with basic questions of existence—what does it mean to say that something exists or does not exist? The branch known as epistemology deals with basic questions of what we know and how we know it. If you and I are talking face to face, there is not much question in the mind of either of us that the other exists and is speaking words that communicate meaning. Do sub-atomic particles, or the human soul, or justice exist, and if so, how do we know, and what can we know about them?

Issues of existence and knowledge are critical for each of the physical and social sciences as well as for applied disciplines such as business. To some extent, they are addressed by each science, but the issues raised and the tools used are really those of philosophy. The same is true for our uses of language. It is one thing to say that my love is like a red, red rose, but quite another to say that she is prickly and requires periodic applications of insecticide and fertilizer. Philosophy allows for and can explain the use of both poetry and scientific language. Without such distinctions, explanations of lightning as an expression of anger by the gods or as an electrical discharge would have to compete on equal terms. Since the recent financial crisis and recession, there has been a good deal of discussion of "the market." It is important to be clear on just who or what constitutes the market, and philosophical concepts can be critically important in addressing this issue.

The physical sciences, such as biology, physics and chemistry, rely on experiments as a way to establish and verify the truth of claims. To varying degrees, the social sciences, such as sociology, political science and organization theory, also rely on experiments. Philosophy, while it uses the findings of both the physical and the social sciences as input, does not rely on experiments to establish the truth of claims.

However, most philosophers accept the facts established through scientific experiments as grist for their theoretical mills.

Philosophy and Religion

Philosophy, like any discipline or field of study, has its rules and procedures. Some of these are accepted by almost all philosophers; others are the subject of considerable debate. Some philosophers have been deeply religious individuals (e.g., St. Thomas Aquinas) and others have been non-believers (e.g., Bertrand Russell). Philosophy deals with many questions that are also the subject of religion, but the two are not the same. One of the most commonly accepted rules or assumptions of philosophy is that religion or divine inspiration cannot be used to answer philosophical questions. This troubles many individuals, because their religion is central to their understanding of life and its most important issues. Because philosophy deals with a number of fundamental issues that are also the objects of religious consideration, it is important to be clear about the relationship of philosophy and religion.[2]

If one asks what is the right way for a human to live, or what are the principal goals of human life, or whether individual humans have a continued existence after their physical death, religion provides answers to these questions. Different religions provide different answers, but each religion accepts the fact that God says so, or God's inspired book (the Bible, Quran, Torah) says so, or God's designated spokesman says so, and this constitutes a valid reason for accepting an answer to these very basic and very important questions. Philosophy does not say that such answers are right or wrong; it simply says that when doing philosophy, they are inadmissible. Other sources must be found to justify or validate answers given by philosophy.

A religious person might well ask why, if religion provides clear and authoritative answers to life's most important questions, philosophy is needed at all. One practical answer is this. In the contemporary world, at least in Western countries, one deals with people who believe in a variety of different religions, and some who deny all religion. If people of varying religious beliefs and no religious belief are to hold serious conversations about how to live and act, some commonly accepted basis for discussion will have to be found.[3] Philosophy can provide such a common basis for discussion. A second important answer in terms of business practice is that most religions do not have a developed body of doctrine, in their sacred writings or in the works of their religious leaders and theologians, about business practices. The sacred books of most religions were written hundreds or thousands of years before the development of the large corporation or of modern business practices.[4] Thus these sacred books have very little to say directly about the morality of business practices. Even believers in the same religion might find themselves with very different answers to practical business issues based on the teachings of their religion.

Philosophy, then, provides a way for thoughtful people to discuss important issues of values and behavior with one another without reference to religion. It thus provides at least the possibility of common understanding and agreement on issues of business morality in a pluralistic society where individual religious beliefs (or lack of such beliefs) might otherwise preclude any hope of a common basis for discussion, much less of agreed-upon conclusions. Philosophy also provides a way to link specific issues of business practice with larger issues, such as what makes a good life, the role of business in society and ways to deal with conflicts of value in specific situations.

Clear Thinking and Proper Naming

One branch of philosophy, logic, deals specifically with rules for reasoning. In an important sense, logic underlies all of the other sciences. An example of the fundamental importance of logic in reasoning involves what Aristotle called the principle of non-contradiction. This principle states that a thing cannot be and not-be in the same way at the same time. We rarely think about such fundamental principles, but they underlie all of our reasoning. A thing cannot be both alive and dead at once. Either it is raining at a given location, or it is not. A chemical element has a certain atomic weight, but at the same time it cannot have a different atomic weight. In a criminal trial, an individual is found either guilty or not guilty of a given charge, but not both. In its pure, logical form, this principle seems innocuous enough. However, as we shall see later in the book, when a CEO or CFO is required to certify that a given financial statement gives a true picture of the firm's financial condition, the issue of true and not-true becomes a good bit more cloudy.

One basic premise on which philosophers generally agree is the importance of clear thinking. In order to think clearly and accurately about something, it is important to take care in naming things. If we are going to argue that something causes something else (a reduction in the capital gains tax will cause the economy to improve), we need to be clear about what is the cause, what is the effect, and whether we are in fact observing causation or correlation.

Clear thinking and proper naming of things are characteristic of philosophy. They are not unique to philosophy by any means, but they do distinguish philosophical analysis from more common kinds of talk and from a good deal of popular writing and journalism. As one reads the works of the great philosophers, it is striking to note that, even though they may take very different positions on the same issue, the care to name things correctly and to be clear and precise in thought processes is a common concern. The physical sciences share this concern for careful naming and step-by-step reasoning. The social sciences tend to be less precise in these areas. Terms like amoeba and velocity have very precise meanings in biology and physics; culture and emotion have less precise meanings in sociology and psychology.

Clear thinking and precise naming are also important in business disciplines. One of the most basic rules in accounting is that revenues should be matched with expenses. One of the most difficult problems in accounting is the same: what constitutes revenue or expense, and when should each be recognized in a given situation? Much of micro-economic theory revolves around the decisions of rational makers of goods and of the rational utility maximizers who purchase those goods. One of the more difficult problems in micro-economics concerns the degree to which either makers or buyers act rationally.[5] Marketing likewise has issues of clarity. If I sell you a car for $20,000 and immediately send you a rebate of $2,000, is this any different from selling you a car for $18,000 and not sending you a rebate?[6]

One particular topic on which philosophical analysis tends to be especially careful is that of causation. Anyone who has taken an introductory course in statistics knows that causation is not the same as correlation. There may be a snowstorm in New York City on the same day that a major company in Texas declares bankruptcy, but it does not take a detailed study to determine that the snowstorm did not cause the bankruptcy, nor did the bankruptcy cause the snowstorm. Much of science is dedicated to identifying and confirming causes. Philosophy also deals extensively with causation and uses the findings of science in explaining it. Thus philosophy as a discipline is not, as it is sometimes portrayed, highly abstract and far removed from the concerns of the real world.

Again, there are numerous parallels in the world of business. Do price reductions cause retail sales to increase in the week before Christmas or are last-minute shoppers driven by some other force? If I urge employees to put in a full day's work each day, and tomorrow they hear about impending layoffs, do they work harder because of my eloquence or their fear of losing their job? The famous Hawthorne studies of the 1930s concluded that productivity of a group of factory workers improved when lighting was increased and also when it was decreased. Ultimately, those doing the studies concluded that productivity improved because someone was paying attention to the workers![7]

Induction and Deduction: The Methods of Philosophy

If philosophy does not accept religion as a source of answers and does not rely on experiments, how does it reach any conclusions? There are two basic approaches that we take when we try to find answers, whether as philosophers, as scientists or as ordinary thinking humans. One is called induction, the other deduction. In its broadest sense, induction means that we reason from specific examples to a general rule. If I drop an object from a given height and measure the time it takes to fall a certain distance, I know one particular fact. If I drop other objects from different heights, carefully measure the time it takes each to fall a certain distance, and compare the results, I might conclude that there is a pattern or a rule about the rate at which some objects fall. As I further test the rule and find that additional examples also conform to the rule, I become more confident that the pattern or rule I have reached from my specific examples is valid or true. Note that I do not yet know why various objects fall at the rate they do. I can predict or affirm regularity without understanding causality.

The second basic approach to finding answers is called deduction. This approach starts with a general rule, applies that rule to a specific situation and argues that the results in the specific situation will be such-and-such because this is an example of the general rule, and that rule will apply to this particular occurrence. While we do not always realize that we are using deduction, this is a common method for making business decisions. If a CEO decides to aim for 15 percent growth in profits next year, he may be relying on an unspoken general rule that, in our industry, companies that attain 15 percent profit growth are favored and their stock goes up. He may also be relying on the fact that his company attained 12 percent profit growth last year, and the expectation of his directors and shareholders is that profit growth will increase by more than 12 percent next year. Note that the general rule is not questioned in deduction; the question at issue is whether this particular case is in fact an example of the general rule.

Philosophy by itself is a fairly abstract endeavor. It is concerned with general rules (either finding them or applying them). It is even more general than the physical and social sciences because it deals with questions and methods of reasoning that underlie all of these sciences. Yet, philosophy involves a good deal of practical knowledge of the real world in which scientists and managers operate. Induction as a method of reasoning tries to find general rules, but it relies on specific examples to attain these rules, and it then tries to confirm and extend these rules by testing other specific examples. Deduction starts with general rules, but its purpose is to explain specific examples as illustrations or examples of these general rules. In both cases, specific examples come from the practical world in which we live and conduct business. While philosophy is sometimes accused of being irrelevant to real-world concerns, the fact is that if we understand what philosophy is really about and what philosophers really deal with, its necessary links to the everyday world are evident.

The Branches of Philosophy

Some branches or divisions of philosophy are more abstract than others.[8] Earlier in this [reading], we noted that metaphysics is the branch of philosophy that concerns itself with questions of existence. This is perhaps the most abstract of all the branches of philosophy. Epistemology concerns itself with what we know and how we know it. Many philosophers have wrestled with the problem that our senses, which seem to be the primary sources for our knowledge, can deceive us. They then seek to show how we can know anything for certain. Another central question in epistemology is how we can know abstract things like numbers or dimensions. Plato, one of the greatest of the Greek philosophers, maintained that we know individual things in a shadowy way, but anything that we humans know is only a faint replica of the perfect thing that exists apart from us and our knowledge. While this might seem esoteric in the extreme, the practical implications of this question will arise [...] when we discuss such issues as rights and duties, and fairness and justice.

Logic, as mentioned above, is the branch of philosophy that deals with rules for analyzing and establishing truths, as well as for naming and classifying things. Some philosophers have maintained that logic is all of philosophy—that we cannot know or say anything meaningful except to talk about our own statements. While this rather extreme approach is hard to understand by those who struggle daily in the real world, this approach did occupy much of the attention of European and some American philosophers during most of the last century. Logic underlies mathematics, science and many of the practical tools we use in our daily lives. Computers would be impossible without the extensive application of logic in programming.

Rational psychology, or the philosophy of man, is the branch of philosophy that deals with what it means to be human. While this branch relies heavily on both biology and psychology, it addresses questions about such topics as reasoning and emotions from a more integrated perspective than any one of the physical sciences. The same Greeks who spent much of their lives discussing, arguing about and writing about philosophy were also great admirers of poetry and theater. Indeed, some of the greatest plays ever written were produced during the height of the philosophical period in Athens, and such key philosophers as Plato, Aristotle and Socrates regularly quoted from plays and from poetry. The philosophical attempts to understand what it is to be human drew widely and unapologetically from personal experience and from literature, as well as from science.

Aesthetics is the branch of philosophy that deals with beauty. What does it mean to say that a painting or a symphony or a sunset is beautiful? Why do standards of beauty change over time? Why do some people find beauty in rap music, while others find it in jazz or in classical symphonies? Are there any objective standards of beauty, or is it entirely a matter of personal preference? What should we teach our children in school about art or music? These and other such questions are the province of aesthetics. The answers over the centuries from philosophers have been many and varied, but the questions persist.

Political philosophy considers the nature of government and the relations of the individual and the state. Both Aristotle and Plato saw this as a part of ethics, or the branch of philosophy that deals with human interaction. This view no longer prevails. Philosophers have written extensively about the reasons why people form governments and what sort of government makes the most sense for humans. The limits of government and the relation between governmental laws and human liberty have been a topic of philosophy from the ancient philosophers to the present day.[9]

Finally, ethics is the branch of philosophy that deals with how humans should act in relations with one another. Ethics is about relationships. It can be defined as the study of social or interpersonal values and the rules for behavior that follow from these values.[10] If you were alone on a desert island, and no one needed you back, you could not really be ethical or unethical. Some philosophers maintain that an important part of ethics is an individual's relation to the environment, or at least to other living things. This area of concern is, for the most part, beyond the scope of this book. Ethics is also about actions as well as thoughts. [...] [W]e will see that one view of ethics defines good actions by their results and another view defines them by the intentions of the actor.

While the primary concern of this book is with ethics, and particularly with ethics as it applies to those people who are paid to manage the work of others, the above descriptions make it clear that the branches of philosophy intertwine. [...] [O]ne of the classic statements of the subject matter of ethics is Aristotle's question, "What is the good for humans?" Another way of asking this question is to inquire, "How should a human live?" In order even to begin to answer these questions, we must have some concept of what it is to be a human. Are humans free to choose among alternatives or are our actions pre-determined by genetics, upbringing or fate?[11] Does being human necessarily involve concern for other people, so that any guidance as to the good human life must include how we treat other humans? Is there a ranking of values that applies to all humans, so that when I try to decide what course of action to choose, I must value some actions or results more than others?

Philosophy and Business

These topics, and others like them, are quite different from the things that occupy managers in their day-to-day work life. In an MBA program, courses tend to be directed toward specific skills (finding new customers, calculating the cost and benefits of a proposed project, keeping the books correctly) or toward somewhat broader but still business-related themes (economics, strategy). Thinking about what makes a good life may be fine for people in church, or for poets, or maybe even for professors, but not for practical, down-to-earth, hard-headed executives and managers. Or perhaps there is more to this than meets the eye.

Business ethics is a topic of major concern, primarily because so much news about business in the recent past has highlighted some rather spectacular lapses in ethics leading up to the housing crisis and the recent recession. Previously, similar concerns about business ethics were raised in the early 2000s with the collapse of Enron and the revelation of major ethical lapses at companies like Tyco, HealthSouth and WorldCom. It was also a topic of concern in the late 1980s after the trials and convictions of people like Michael Milken, Ivan Boesky, Dennis Levine and others. About a century ago, some American CEOs became known as the "robber barons." Undoubtedly, we have not seen the last cycle of such behavior and subsequent concern for business ethics. However, many of my students who are managers do not really feel that they are criminals or robber barons, and they sometimes wonder why a program designed to teach mastery of business administration includes a segment on ethics.

Questions of ethics necessarily involve questions of metaphysics (existence and causation) and of epistemology (knowing). A number of years ago, managers at United Airlines chose to pay their workers more than managers at other airlines paid their workers. Presumably the managers at United thought that higher pay would result in some good (working faster, or smarter, or staying with the company longer, or not going out on strike) that could not be attained at a lower rate of pay. In other words, a higher pay scale would cause workers to do good things they would not otherwise do. Events proved the managers at United wrong. The company's costs (at least partly driven by higher labor costs) outran its revenues and it declared bankruptcy. How did they, or could they, know what results would be caused by their decision to pay higher wages and benefits? How were they mistaken in their conclusions? Did the managers at United do anything ethically wrong in managing the airline into bankruptcy, or were they just unlucky? In other words, should they have known what would and would not result from their decisions about wages and benefits? What about the executives at General Motors or at Chrysler? Both companies reduced wages in bankruptcy after agreeing over many years to a series of increases in wages and benefits that proved not to be sustainable.

Managers do not need to know a great deal about philosophy to do their jobs well, and there are many successful managers at various levels who have never studied philosophy at all. So why bother? The two purposes of this book are to make managers aware of the ethical implications of their actions and to provide them with tools for thinking through ethical problems that they face in the course of their work. The first of these goals, ethical awareness, does not require any knowledge of philosophy. However, the second goal does. [...] [W]e will see that various approaches to thinking about ethical dilemmas involve such notions as rights and duties, and fairness and justice. These are philosophical concepts, and to think clearly about them requires some basic understanding of philosophy.

For example, a manager might know intuitively or from reflecting on her experience that fairness is a desirable trait in management decisions and that it will promote better results than unfairness. But she still must ask whether fairness means treating everyone equally or assuring that, regardless of process, results are equal for everyone, or treating everyone in ways that are proportional to their skills and knowledge or their time on the job. Is it fair to pay all workers in a given job class the same wage, or to pay those who perform better a higher wage, or to pay those who have been on the job the longest the highest wage, or to pay those whose need is greatest the highest wage? Such questions cannot be answered thoughtfully without some analysis which is, at root, philosophical. Managers who make such decisions and do such analysis may not know that they are doing philosophy, but they are. One of the aims of this book is to help managers reflect on their decision-making processes in situations involving ethics and to improve the clarity with which they make such decisions.

Managers are not the only ones who might benefit from a bit of philosophy. Workers who do not have managerial responsibilities also make or have input into workplace decisions that have ethical implications. Professionals who advise management on compensation systems, administrative policies, legal or accounting matters, and mergers and acquisitions all have a role in decisions that have major ethical implications.[12] Other workers may not have input into such decisions but are affected by such managerial decisions and may be quite concerned about these decisions. Investors considering the purchase or sale of a company's stock or bonds have an interest in the accuracy and truthfulness of the company's financial reporting. Residents who live near a company's plant have concerns about emissions and pollution. Government officials concerned about terrorism have concerns about the sale of certain chemicals, computer systems or fighter planes. Journalists who criticize the actions of an individual company or of business in general might benefit from more perceptive analysis of the factors affecting management decisions.

Employees and voters also have impacts on how business is conducted and determine to some extent the range within which managers can make decisions. If employees, through their unions, demand compensation that is beyond the ability of management to deliver, constraints are put on the decisions of managers. If individual executives demand contracts guaranteeing them large amounts of severance pay, regardless of their performance, companies end up making payments that most rational people would, and do, question. If voters demand laws that extend paid vacations and leave to a significant portion of the working days available, as has happened in some Western European countries, and unions demand high wages and unproductive work rules, the ability of managers to price their products or services competitively can be seriously constrained.

While there are many individuals and groups that have some impact on the performance of organizations, in this book we will be mainly concerned with the decisions and actions of managers. Although they are often constrained, to a greater or less degree, by the actions and inactions of others, managers do still have the freedom to make choices in meaningful ways that affect and often determine the performance of the organizations for which they work. To some degree, organizations can and do influence the thoughts and actions of their stakeholders. Legislators are lobbied, unions are sometimes shown the financial details of a company's books, efforts are made to inform and persuade journalists. In the last analysis, managers must make specific decisions, and it is the use of ethical analysis in such decision-making that we will next consider.

Notes

1. It is a fascinating fact of history that Plato and Aristotle, generally recognized as "two of the greatest philosophers the world has seen" (Copleston, F. (1993). *A history of philosophy: Volume 1.* New York: Doubleday, p. 372) were respectively teacher and pupil. Plato founded his famous school, known as The Academy, in Athens in 388 B.C. Aristotle became his student at the Academy in 367 at the age of seventeen and remained there until Plato's death in 348 B.C.
2. Philosophers recognize Saint Thomas Aquinas as the greatest philosopher of the Middle Ages (roughly A.D. 500 to A.D. 1450). He is also recognized as one of the greatest theologians of the Catholic church. In his writings, he wrestled (not always successfully) with the distinction between philosophy and religion. Aristotle's work was lost to Western civilization for hundreds of years, but was preserved by Arab philosophers. For an account of Aquinas's role

in re-introducing Aristotle to Western thought, see Rubinstein, R. (2003). *Aristotle's children.* Orlando FL: Harcourt.

3. John Rawls, one of the most important philosophers of the twentieth century, deals with this issue at some length. His work is discussed in Chapter 6, on Fairness and Justice. Rawls states that one of the assumptions of his discussion of justice in national systems is that the people living in the sort of country he considers have different sources for their sense of values. Some of these sources are religious, but different people derive different values from their different religions. Other people in the sort of country he describes do not have any religion, and so do not derive their sense of values from this source. Somehow, he says, the basic laws and institutions must be agreed upon by all of these people, with their diverse sources of values. (Rawls, J. (2001). *Justice as fairness: A restatement.* Cambridge MA: The Belknap Press of Harvard University Press.) His discussion illustrates well the difference between religious sources of values and philosophical sources.
4. This issue is also true, to a large extent, of philosophy. Many of the great philosophers wrote their works before the first large business organizations arose in eighteenth-century England. Many of the major philosophers, including both Plato and Aristotle, thought and wrote extensively about the purposes and organization of government, but not about business organizations.
5. Behavioral economics is a relatively recent approach to micro-economics which tries to account for behavior that seems to contradict theories of utility maximization. This approach studies, through experiments, how people actually make choices in various settings and provides explanations that fit the facts revealed by these experiments. A quite readable presentation of behavioral economics is Dan Ariely's book *Predictably irrational, Revised and expanded edition* (New York: HarperCollins, 2009). A more recent review and discussion of the many studies that underlie this approach by a Nobel prize-winning psychologist can be found in Kahneman, D. (2011). *Thinking, fast and slow.* New York: Farrar, Straus and Giroux.
6. In accounting terms, there is a very real difference. If my company sells you a car for $20,000, it records that amount as revenue, even though it promptly mails you a rebate check for $2,000. If, on the other hand, my company sells you the car for $18,000, it records only that amount as revenue. In other words, we can sell the same number of cars for the same amount of money but increase our revenue by 10 percent (or more) simply by sending automatic rebates. Note that this is not true when mail-in rebates or other coupons are used because many customers do not take the necessary step to actually receive the rebate.
7. The Hawthorne experiments were begun in 1924 at the Hawthorne plant of Western Electric. As lighting conditions in an assembly room were first increased and then decreased, researchers were puzzled to find that productivity went up in both cases. Further experiments of various types followed. As researchers pondered the data they had gathered, they came to realize that social interactions as well as physical conditions have to be taken into account in order to explain the performance of workers, even in routine tasks. A discussion of the experiments and their results by one of the social scientists involved in the study, Fritz Roethlisberger, can be found in Shafritz, J. and Ott, J. (2001). *Classics of organization theory*, 5th edition. Orlando FL: Harcourt, pp. 158–166.
8. Readers interested in a more extensive discussion of the major branches of philosophy would do well to read sections of Volume 1 of Frederick Copleston's *History of philosophy* (New York: Doubleday, 1993). In this volume, Copleston provides discussions of both Plato's and Aristotle's views of the major divisions or branches of philosophy. His style is such that those without a background in philosophy can follow his discussion. In the 1993 paperback edition, the relevant sections on Plato are Chapter 19 (pp. 142–162) and Chapters 21–25 (pp. 207–262). Chapter 20 on The Doctrine of Forms is apt to prove too advanced for those without some background in philosophy. On Aristotle, see Chapters 29–33 (pp. 287–371). Also of interest is Chapter 34 (pp. 374–378), containing a comparison of Plato's and Aristotle's views.
9. One of the central issues in political philosophy relates to how much liberty individuals in a society can or should have, and what constraints society, through government and its agencies, should impose. As discussed in the next section of the chapter, ethics concerns itself with interpersonal values. It is not hard to see why Plato and Aristotle both saw political philosophy as an extension of ethics. It is a bit harder to see why this connection tends to be missed by more recent philosophers. Given the degree to which laws and regulations made by government both help and restrain business managers, as we will see throughout this book, the connection between political philosophy and ethics is important for our topic.
10. Isaiah Berlin said that:
    Ethical thought consists of the systematic examination of the relations of human beings to each other, the

conceptions, interests and ideals from which human ways of treating one another spring, and the systems of values on which such ends of life are based.
(Berlin, I. (2001). The pursuit of the ideal, in Hardy, H. and Hausher, R. (eds.), *The proper study of mankind: An anthology of essays*. New York: Farrar, Strauss and Giroux, p. 1)

11. Recent scientific advances in the study of genetics and of the structure and functioning of the brain have led some people to take a fresh look at issues of human freedom and determinism. For those interested in these issues, two books by well-respected scientists provide reasonably up-to-date information on what scientists now know and agree on in these areas and what topics remain to be explored. The books are: Wilson, E.O. (1998). *Consilience: The unity of knowledge*. New York: Alfred Knopf; and Pinker, S. (2002). *The blank slate*. New York: Penguin Books. As is often the case with such books by scientists, some basic issues, such as the degree to which humans are truly free to choose, receive much less attention than the factual issues that are the everyday concern of science. For instance, both books discuss at some length the influence of genes on human behavior and the way the brain processes signals from the outside world and forms memories. Neither book, in my opinion, gives a really satisfactory treatment of free choice by humans. However, these and similar books are worth reading because scientists have established many facts beyond reasonable doubt that uninformed people misjudge and, because of their misjudgments, make choices harmful to themselves and others.
12. Much has been written in recent years on the topic of CEO compensation. Many of the articles on this subject either assume or declare that CEO compensation is too high relative to that of other employees. At large U.S. corporations, the compensation committee of the board of directors recommends CEO compensation and typically the full board approves what this committee recommends. A small number of consulting firms provide information and recommendations to the compensation committees of many companies. Thus, the consultants at these firms have an important role in determining compensation at the CEO level, and their concern or lack of concern for fairness impacts American business. For an interesting commentary on charismatic CEOs and their compensation, see Khurana, R. (2002). *Searching for a corporate savior: The irrational quest for charismatic CEOs*. Princeton NJ: Princeton University Press.

Reading 3.5

Women, Gender and Feminism at Work

Allison Elias

Allison Elias, "Women, Gender and Feminism at Work," *Nevertheless, They Persisted: Feminisms and Continued Resistance in the U.S. Women's Movement*, ed. Jo Reger, pp. 204-220. Copyright © 2019 by Taylor & Francis Group. Reprinted with permission.

Throughout the 20th century, working women and their allies have used a variety of strategies to advocate for fair pay, safe working conditions and opportunities for promotion. Shifting economic, political, legal and social forces in the United States have shaped the nature of activists' efforts at different historical moments. Women of various identities (i.e., race, ethnicity, sexuality, age, class and citizenship status) have chosen to prioritize certain issues over others depending on distinct workplace experiences. As more women have entered the paid labor force in an increasingly broad range of occupations, momentum has shifted towards some issues and away from others. In general, contemporary feminist activism for workplace equality progresses along two tracks. Women who are educated as engineers, attorneys, physicians and bankers (i.e., professional careers) fight for opportunities to advance into positions of greater prestige and status. In this case, feminism and capitalism align as the most powerful companies bolster the ideals of sex equality, competing to recruit and retain the most talented women. Meanwhile, other women working as cashiers, home health aides, receptionists, housekeepers, and waitresses (i.e., blue collar careers) struggle to provide for themselves and their families. Their activist efforts focus on obtaining a decent wage, a more predictable schedule, as well as affordable health care and childcare. Despite the current divergence of these two paths of feminism, some issues such as sexual harassment have universal impact, bringing together women from an array of occupations and industries.

Indeed, gender as a category of analysis has played a crucial role in the construction of knowledge about work and activism (Scott 1986). How we actually conceptualize terms like work and activism reflects certain gendered values that have elevated paid labor over unpaid labor, industrial work over domestic work, and collective action over individual action. While men and women in agrarian societies both engaged in productive activities to maintain their families, the rise of a cash economy marginalized women's domestic tasks. Wage work moved outside of the home to a central site of production. The unpaid labor of wives, daughters and sisters became invisible in the formal economy. In the developing industrial economy, housework was recast a labor of love, demonstrative of familial devotion (Boydston 1990). The construction of public and private spheres, defined as the political and economic affairs of men in contrast to the reproductive care work of women, has resulted in the definition of work as wage-earning labor (Welter 1966).

In addition, the role of unpaid and forced labors of slave men and women in the Americas has remained tangential to narratives of industrialization. Arguing that slave labor was integral to the economic development of the United States, scholars have started to revisit the conventional view that slavery was an anti-capitalist enterprise (Cooke 2003). In his revisionist book, historian Edward Baptist presents a compelling argument about slavery as integral to U.S. industrialization (2014). The histories of white women and unfree laborers force us to approach current knowledge about work with a critical lens, asking whose experiences might be privileged or marginalized in modern understandings of the economy.

Because gendered definitions of work elevate the status of paid labor, the dominant stories of labor activism center on male manufacturing workers and trade unions. Scholars have focused on union activities despite the fact that at the high tide of unionism in the United States, still less than 35 percent of wage workers were members (Mayer 2004). In reality, men and women resisted their working conditions in many informal ways, some difficult to uncover given the limits of the historical record. Non-unionized women in New York City sweatshops formed friendships, sang songs, and discussed books to get through the tedious routine of manual, repetitive factory labor (Richardson 1990). Asserting control over their own bodies, Black domestic workers in early 20th-century Atlanta danced at jook joints long into the night, defying the moral expectations of their white employers (Hunter 1997). Utilizing the concept of "infrapolitics," historian Robin D. G. Kelley documented the agency of Black workers who engaged in everyday forms of resistance (i.e., foot-dragging, theft, or quitting) to confront the power of white employers (1994). Traditionally such action has been treated as supplementary to a grand narrative whereby labor history is the story of union history. Yet many women and men resisted the control of employers outside of union channels, and such seemingly inconsequential behaviors have influenced societal structures and institutions.

In this [reading], I first discuss women's appeals to unions for economic empowerment, and then I turn to the benefits and limits of legal remedies when advancing women's status at work. I focus on these two broad categories, unions and the law, because much of the scholarship situates women's workplace status as contingent upon inclusion in these two institutions. In their quest for economic empowerment and equal opportunity, women have gained greater access to the tools offered by unions and the remedies provided by the law. However, institutional logics continue to hinder women's advancement to a certain extent since unions and the law rely on gendered and racialized assumptions about work and the economy. While I make a clear distinction between utilization of union frameworks and appeals to the law, efforts to facilitate change often relied on several tools to undo gender-based injustices. Battles waged by feminists of the 1960s and 1970s, along with activists from the Civil Rights Movement, have normalized a collective belief in equality of opportunity. Women won fights to access workplace rights that are available to men.

Less successful have been feminist efforts to raise the economic status of care work by securing paid family leave or state-sponsored childcare. Thus, while contemporary feminists have remedies to correct for unequal treatment of men and women, subtle inequities arising from embedded gender norms and institutional structures are more difficult to dismantle.

Unions and Labor Organizing

Since the dawn of industrial capitalism in the United States, women have engaged in unions as members, educators, organizers, and leaders, defying the traditional narrative that women did not participate in collective workplace activism. Some of the first U.S. industrial workers, the Lowell Mill Girls, formed their own organization, the Female Labor Reform Association, in 1845 (Dublin 1981). In the South, laundresses working from their own homes in Atlanta formed The Washing Society in 1881, demanding higher pay and greater respect (Hunter 1997). And while men held the most senior leadership positions in the early 20th-century International Ladies' Garment Workers Union (ILGWU), female factory workers played an integral role in the development, maintenance and execution of union campaigns, as well as in efforts to develop educational programs for fellow shirt makers. When the ILGWU staged an eleven-week strike in 1909, Eastern European immigrant women built coalitions among a multi ethnic workforce. They even bridged class divides, enlisting upper-class white women as allies in sustaining the strike (Orleck 1995).

While some female labor activists challenged a separate spheres ideology, they also leveraged femininity to support male family members. During the Flint Sit Down Strike of 1936–37, women took shifts preparing, cooking, and serving food to their fathers, husbands and brothers while the United Auto Workers (UAW) strategically occupied the site of production. Just 75 women operated this kitchen for 24 hours a day, feeding several meals a day to more than 2,000 male protesters. Some women even served as human shields to protect their husbands from police brutality, cognizant that law enforcement would be reticent to inflict physical harm on women (Baugh-Helton 2017).

The Flint example notwithstanding, domestic ideology usually disadvantaged working women in their quest to achieve full economic citizenship. Most trade unions supported a family wage with men arguing that union pay should be substantial enough for them to provide for wives and children. Labor leaders, policymakers and social reformers viewed the family wage not as backwards but as a progressive means of wealth redistribution. Higher wages for men would shift a greater portion of capitalist wealth to the working class (Kessler-Harris 1982). Unions used the family wage reasoning to justify excluding women from their ranks, but also employers defended lower pay for women and job classification systems based on sex.

Even the economic disruption posed by World War II, which resulted in demand for women to further wartime production, did not dismantle pay inequity and occupational segregation. During World War II, women eagerly abandoned female-dominated work as department store clerks and restaurant employees to take traditionally male jobs and earn higher wages. White and black women built airplanes, made ammunition, and worked in shipyards although women of color held the lowest-paying jobs requiring exposure to toxic chemicals or physically arduous labor (May 1988). Although the federal government mandated that women war workers should receive equal pay for equal work, unions and employers reinvented sex-based distinctions to maintain men's advantages. They relabeled women's jobs as "light" and men's jobs as "heavy" to preserve pay differences. At the war's end, women begrudgingly relinquished their jobs (Milkman 1987), but they had gained newfound confidence that a woman could do the work of any man.

In the postwar era, as more white married women began to earn wages, journalist Betty Friedan published a best-selling book, The Feminine Mystique, encouraging college-educated, white suburban housewives to pursue careers as means of self-actualization. She wrote, "The only way for a woman, as for a man, to find herself, to know herself as a person, is by creative work of her own. There is no other way" (Friedan 1963: 472). Friedan, a liberal feminist, would become one of the founders of the National Organization for Women (NOW) in 1966. She believed in sex equality, which reinvigorated decades-old debates about how to best advance the status of working women. Throughout the first half of the 20th century, most advocates wanted economic justice, but they did not perceive fair treatment as calling for the same treatment of men and women. Historian Dorothy Sue Cobble has shown that from the 1930s until the 1980s, labor feminists "put the needs of working-class women at its core" (Cobble 2004: 3). Labor feminists wanted to remedy sex-based inequities by demanding that unions prioritize fair pay, paid maternity leave and childcare. As feminists like Friedan started to push for workplace equality in the 1960s, women like union leader Myra Wolfgang fought to preserve protective legislation for women. In her testimony to the United States Senate, Wolfgang spoke out against sex-based equality: "We are different, and different does not mean deficient" (Cobble 2004: 192). As arguments for equality gained steam in the 1960s and 1970s, and major unions issued statements in support of sex equality, adherence to the difference approach lost footing. By the 1980s, a paradigm had shifted, and sex equality became the standard for fair treatment.

During these decades of transition, the distinction between difference and equality, labor feminism and liberal feminism, rarely was clear. Union leaders such as Dorothy Haener of the UAW participated in the founding and development of NOW, perhaps the most significant feminist organization to promote sex equality under law. Furthermore, at the intersection of labor and liberal feminism stood the Coalition of Labor Union Women (CLUW). In 1974, more than 3,000 women—including both supporters and opponents of legal equality—came together to create a national organization to empower women in the labor movement. CLUW prioritized increasing women's membership and leadership in unions as well as moving concerns like pay equity and sexual harassment to the center of the labor agenda. Women of color shaped the agenda from CLUW's beginnings: about 25 percent of those at the founding convention were African American, Hispanic, Asian, and Native American women (Roth 2003).

Feminism of the 1960s and 1970s spurred greater organizing activity among pink-collar women as well. With one-third of working women holding low-paid, dead-end clerical positions, office activism arose across the nation during the feminist era. On December 16, 1977, eight women walked out of their jobs at Citizens National Bank in the small Minnesota town of Willmar. The Willmar 8 braved temperatures below zero to picket for higher pay and promotional opportunities. Even though the women went on strike to protest sex-based inequity, they did not consider themselves feminists. One woman stated that she did not know what feminism was, and another declared that feminists were immoral (Grant 1981). Even among those not considering themselves feminists, feminist ideology was changing expectations of what constituted fair treatment at work.

In addition to Willmar, other grassroots movements arose among clerical workers who wanted more rights (i.e., higher pay, promotional opportunities) and greater respect (i.e., acknowledgement of their contributions). Karen Nussbaum, a secretary at the Harvard Graduate School of Education, became inspired to form her own workplace consciousness-raising group, named 9to5, in 1972. 9to5 leaders wanted to convince others that their individual problems were part of a systemic pattern of sex-based workplace discrimination. By the 1980s, 9to5 was operating in more than 15 cities and had engaged thousands of women in newsletter distribution, public protests, lobbying efforts and professional workshops. To gain greater financial resources and bargaining power, in 1981 Nussbaum formed a sister union, District 925 of the Service Employees International Union (SEIU). A national clerical workers' division, District 925 held the possibility of extending membership to 16 million women. However, unionizing private-sector clericals proved difficult. Although SEIU District 925 won some fights on college campuses, it struggled to gain footing in private-sector banks and insurance firms (Elias forthcoming).

Unions turned their attention towards female-dominated, public-sector occupations, such as teaching, as well as towards certain gender-specific issues, such as pay equity. Labor feminists had prioritized pay equity decades earlier, but in 1979, the formation of the National Committee on Pay Equity brought together liberal feminist groups, professional women's organizations and trade unions as allies. Given that government employees had standardized job classifications and transparent salary ranges, public-sector unions, like the growing American Federation of State, County and Municipal Employees (AFSCME), could tackle pay equity issue more easily. Pay equity activists won some battles in union contracts with municipal and state governments. But private-sector compensation practices remained untouched. Pay equity never became codified into federal employment law as a tide of conservative politicians and judges successfully curtailed state intervention in business in the 1980s (Blum 1991).

Although women as a percentage of total union members has increased markedly in the last three decades, from 33.6 percent in 1984 to 45.5 percent in 2014, still 90 percent of women wage earners do not belong to a union (Institute for Women's Policy Research 2018). Labor activists are utilizing new strategies to empower low-wage women without requiring union membership. Attorney and activist Saru Jayaraman co-founded Restaurant Opportunity Centers United, helping workers to reform industry policies about pay and hours, as well as to prosecute illicit activity like wage theft. While women represent more than two-thirds of tipped restaurant workers, they constitute about 95 percent of domestic workers. Activist Aijen Poo founded the National Domestic Workers Alliance, which, by 2016, boasted a membership of 20,000 nannies, housekeepers and care givers, disparately women of color and immigrant women. The organization advocates for a Domestic Workers Bill of Rights, which has passed in several state legislatures. Labor leaders such as Jayaraman and Poo empower those who often lack a voice, seating wage-earning women on their boards and in other key leadership positions (Restaurant Opportunities Centers United 2018; National Domestic Worker's Alliance 2018).

The Power of the Law?

While activists have formed, supported and led labor organizations, others have turned to the law to improve the status of women, shifting strategies from embracing difference-based to equality-based rights.

While early 20th-century courts rejected protection legislation for men, relying on a liberty of contract found in the Fourteenth Amendment, those same judges upheld protections for working women because of their status as mothers or potential mothers. For women only, regulations regarding minimum wage, maximum hours, weightlifting limits, rest periods and occupational safety remained legal to preserve and prioritize women's reproductive capacity. The Supreme Court upheld an Oregon state law that limited female laundry employees to a 10-hour working day; in 1908 Justice Brewer wrote: "That woman's physical structure and the performance of maternal functions place her at a disadvantage in the struggle for subsistence is obvious" (*Muller v. Oregon*, 208 U.S. 412).

Most working women and their allies agreed with Brewer, supporting sex-specific protective legislation throughout much of the 20th century. However, some upper-class white women, forming the National Woman's Party, advocated for legal equality between the sexes. They drafted and lobbied for an Equal Rights Amendment (ERA) to the U.S. Constitution in 1923 (Cott 1989). Initially, most women did not support the ERA: not only was the idea of equality considered radical, but also sex-based legal distinctions were benefiting wage-earning women (Woloch 2015). In addition, the widespread belief that women and men had essential differences in mind and body actually gave professional women greater influence in the public sphere. During the Progressive Era and New Deal, most women who gained a voice in political and economic affairs did so because of conventional beliefs that white women had a more virtuous and moral nature that could temper the harsh realities of urban and industrial life. As white, college-educated women such as Jane Addams, Julia Lathrop and Florence Kelley confronted social problems, they moved concerns about women and children to the center of the government's agenda (Muncy 1991).

Another such reformer was Frances Perkins, who became the first female cabinet member when appointed Secretary of Labor in 1933. When crafting New Deal legislation, Perkins and other female policymakers aimed to preserve women's primary roles as wives and mothers. They saw this unpaid labor as valuable, not just to the family unit, but also as crucial to the health of the nation. Yet this elevation of women's maternal and domestic roles hindered women's economic independence and reinforced the family wage ideal. New Deal relief programs like the Works Progress Administration stipulated that only one member of a household could claim a publically-funded job, often traditionally men's work such as construction. In addition, women reformers designed, and then Congress enacted, Aid to Dependent Children (ADC) in 1935, which reinforced women's economic dependence since funding for poor mothers was contingent on not earning any wages (Gordon 1994). Lastly, a major legislative achievement, the Fair Labor Standards Act (FLSA) guaranteed a federal minimum wage and overtime to all full-time workers. However, part-time or seasonal work, often performed by women, was omitted. Southern legislators demanded that the bill pass exclude agricultural and household labor, too, which disparately impacted men and women of color (Kessler-Harris 2001). Exempting household labor from coverage meant that some of the most vulnerable women had no protection against low wages. They had to fight for FLSA inclusion, which live-out cleaners and other domestic workers finally achieved in 1974 although home care aides and personal attendants remained excluded (Boris and Klein 2012).

As more married white women entered into the workforce after World War II, the issues that immigrants and women of color had confronted for decades became topics of national discussion. Finding ways to reconcile women's roles as caretakers and wage earners moved to the White House's agenda. In

1961, President John F. Kennedy convened the President's Commission on the Status of Women to craft "recommendations for services which will enable women to continue their role as wives and mothers while making a maximum contribution to the world around them" (Executive Order 10980). The impetus for this Commission actually came from Esther Peterson, a labor leader who Kennedy appointed to direct the Labor Department's Women's Bureau. Peterson pushed to resurrect a 1947 proposal for a status of women commission. Even though Eleanor Roosevelt nominally headed the Commission, Peterson set the agenda and ran operations (Harrison 1988). While Peterson stacked the Commission with ERA opponents, some labor feminists—especially those working in sectors where women and men competed for the same jobs—began to embrace equal rights (Kessler-Harris 2001).

The convening of this Commission represented a critical moment of coalition for labor feminists and the rising tide of new, liberal feminists. Strategies of both equality and difference imbued the Commission's final report, American Women, which was widely read by the public. While by the turn of the 21st century the United States still had not enacted many Commission proposals (such as paid maternity leave, pay equity or publically funded childcare), the Commission did facilitate federal action on the issue of equal pay. Drafted by Peterson, the Equal Pay Act passed Congress in 1963 as an amendment to the FLSA. Initially it excluded most professional, administrative, and executive workers, and even after it was extended in the 1970s, many women remained outside of its protections (Palmer 1995). Because the law passed with language guaranteeing equal pay for equal work, it failed to provide remedy for many women who labored in female-dominated sectors. To correct all gender-based pay inequities, women would need state laws or union contracts guaranteeing pay equity, which seemed unlikely to materialize for most working women by the end of the 1980s (Blum 1991).

In addition to fighting for equal pay, working women and their allies pushed to include sex in a federal bill initially drafted to ban race discrimination. Title VII of the Civil Rights Act of 1964 became a most far-reaching federal policy of the 20th century to promote workplace inclusion for women and underrepresented minorities. Along with discrimination based on race, religion and ethnicity, sex-based discrimination became illegal in private workplaces that had more than 15 employees. Earlier scholarship once emphasized the addition of sex into Title VII as an attempt to defeat a bill that would advance the status of African Americans. Yet revisionist accounts demonstrate that feminist Congresswoman Martha Griffiths (D-MI) strategically permitted a Virginia segregationist to introduce the idea. Griffiths then argued that Title VII, without the inclusion of sex, placed white women at a disadvantage relative to African-American men (Mayeri 2011). With the support of segregationists and feminists alike, the Civil Rights Act became law on July 2, 1964 with language linking sex and race discrimination.

Title VII created the Equal Employment Opportunity Commission (EEOC), a government agency designed to investigate cases of employment discrimination and interpret the difference between cases of unlawful discrimination and legally-valid distinctions. Controversy arose over a provision called the bona fide occupational qualification (BFOQ) exception, which, when "reasonably necessary" for business operations, permitted distinctions based on sex, national origin, or religion. The media quickly capitalized on possible consequences of a narrow reading of the BFOQ. In 1965, the New York Times reported on the "bunny problem," alluding to the ridiculousness of permitting men to be Playboy bunnies (Kessler-Harris 2001). Many liberal feminists, however, wanted a narrow reading of the BFOQ to limit sex-based distinctions. Feminist legal scholars Pauli Murray and Mary Eastwood argued a close alignment of race and sex discrimination, contending that a broad BFOQ reading would significantly weaken Title VII's benefits for women (Mayeri 2011).

With a modest budget, the fledging EEOC, which lacked enforcement powers until 1972, initially chose to ignore questions surrounding the BFOQ exception and instead devoted scarce resources to combatting race discrimination. However, about one third of claims to the EEOC during its first year of operation concerned sex discrimination. Among those at the Commission's door were airline stewardesses backed by transport unions. The stewardesses claimed that airline restrictions based on age, height, weight and marital status were not reasonably related to performing their job duties. Attorneys for the airlines contended that customers preferred attractive, thin, young, single stewardesses, arguing that these restrictions should remain legal as a business necessity. After several years of hearings and investigations, the EEOC issued three rulings in 1968 holding that age and marriage policies were illegal under Title VII. Eventually the Supreme Court ruled against sex as a BFOQ for the job of flight attendant in 1972, allowing a man to enter the profession (Barry 2007).

The Supreme Court bolstered the momentum of liberal feminists by striking down state protective legislation. In 1967, NOW represented Lorena Weeks, who successfully won the opportunity to work a higher-paying job as a switchman, which required heavy lifting. Southern Bell previously had denied her the job because of a Georgia statute banning women from lifting anything above 30 pounds. In Illinois, Thelma Bowe won her case against Colgate-Palmolive, striking down another state law limiting the amount of weight women could lift at work. Given the legal and social tides shifting towards equality, many labor feminists began to temper their support for protective laws and embrace the benefits of Title VII. Major labor unions (the UAW in 1970 and then the American Federation of Labor-Congress of Industrial Organizations in 1973) abandoned their commitments to protective legislation and began to support both the ERA and full implementation of Title VII in the 1970s (Woloch 2015).

Just as women had to fight for inclusion into Title VII, they also had to lobby for coverage under the executive orders known as affirmative action. Designed to remedy past discrimination against African American men, these orders initially mandated that employers address racial bias only. But in the early 1970s, the Women's Equity Action League pressured government officials to add a provision for women, mandating that employers issue goals and timetables for sex as well as for race. Although affirmative action had limited reach for those facing low pay in pink-collar jobs, it played an important role in moving women into male-dominated occupations (Elias 2018). Rates of occupational segregation began to decline as women pursued careers in traditionally male occupations like dentistry, medicine, and law. The trades proved more difficult, however, as many blue-collar men guarded their territory, making women feel uncomfortable and even unsafe (MacLean 1999).

With feminist pressure, courts and legislatures expanded Title VII's reach to include older workers, mothers, and pregnant women. Unionized stewardesses joined forces with NOW leaders to lobby for the Age Discrimination in Employment Act in 1967 as an amendment to Title VII. Discrimination on the basis of sex plus another characteristic also became illegal so that employers could not discriminate against a subclass of women such as mothers (*Phillips v. Martin Marietta Corp.*, 400 U.S. 542, 1971). Labor unions, feminists and even religious conservatives lobbied for the Pregnancy Discrimination Act in 1978, adding pregnant women to Title VII's list of protected classes. Despite these victories, the structure of the law posed limitations. When seeking remedy under Title VII, women of color seemingly fell under two different protected classes: sex and race. Because employment law treated each as distinct categories, legal scholar Kimberle Crenshaw coined the term intersectionality (1989). Crenshaw was struck by a district court holding that black women did not constitute their own legal class. Title VII permitted charges of "race discrimination, sex discrimination, or alternatively either, but not combination of both" (*DeGraffenreid v. General Motors Assembly Div.*, 413 F.Supp. 142, 1976).

Eventually courts clarified that Title VII's sex clause included sexual harassment, but only after activists and scholars argued that such behavior should be illegal. The term sexual harassment emerged from several struggles at Cornell University in 1974. When Instructor Lin Farley addressed the topic of unwanted sexual attention in her Women and Work class, almost all of the female students had a story. Concurrently, office assistant Carmita Wood resigned from her position, having becoming physically ill after repeated, unwanted sexual attention from a male faculty member. The university denied her unemployment benefits, arguing that she had quit for personal reasons. Farley, along with Cornell colleagues and women from the Ithaca community, used the language of sexual harassment to describe Wood's experience. When the events at Cornell made headlines in a widely-reprinted *New York Times* article, the phrase "sexual harassment" entered the mainstream (Baker 2008).

As a grassroots movement took hold, legal scholar and activist Catharine MacKinnon deployed feminist theory to argue that harassment at work constituted an exercise of unjust male dominance. What appeared culturally to be an interpersonal interaction actually posed systemic disadvantages for women, limiting their economic mobility (MacKinnon 1979). In 1980 EEOC Commissioner Eleanor Holmes Norton added sexual harassment to its sex discrimination guidelines, defining it, as MacKinnon had, as characterized by either *quid pro quo* or a hostile work environment. The Supreme Court upheld the essence of the EEOC guidelines in *Meritor Savings Bank v. Vinson*. Mechelle Vinson was a bank employee whose supervisor intimidated her into having sex with him some fifty times over the course of three years. In 1986 the Court confirmed that harassment could be *quid pro quo*, whereby a supervisor uses his power to demand sexual acts; as well as hostile environment harassment, whereby supervisors or coworkers create an intimidating or offensive atmosphere. While the case validated the EEOC's definition of sexual harassment, it rejected another EEOC determination that employers should retain liability for the illegal actions of their employees. Instead, the Court held that Meritor Savings Bank did not have vicarious liability for the actions of Vinson's supervisor (Anderson 1987).

Public awareness of sexual harassment increased during the Anita Hill-Clarence Thomas hearings in 1991. When Judge Thomas, an African-American man, was nominated for a position on the Supreme Court, law professor Anita Hill, also African-American, spoke to the Senate Judiciary Committee during the vetting process. A decade earlier she had worked with Thomas at the Department of Education and at the EEOC. She maintained that he sexually harassed her while he responded that the entire hearing was a "high-tech lynching" (Berebitsky 2012: 272). After Thomas's confirmation, black feminists placed a full-page *New York Times* condemnation of the event. The group known as African-American Women in Defense of Ourselves berated Thomas for perpetuating the myth that African-American women have strong sexual urges and thus they cannot be physically violated (Berebitsky 2012).

Routinely popular discourse and legal opinions defined sexual harassment as men violating women, which marginalized those harmed by a person of the same sex. Lesbian, gay, bisexual, transgender and questioning (LGBTQ) employees and their allies challenged the heteronormative nature of anti-discrimination law. In 1998 the Supreme Court held that same-sex harassment could fall under hostile environment reasoning, nothing that "harassing conduct need not be motivated by sexual desire" to be considered sex-based discrimination (*Oncale v. Sundowner Offshore Services, Inc.*, 523 U.S. 75). Other LGBTQ issues had arisen decades earlier, including whether sexual orientation was an immutable identity, and thus protected under Title VII. LGBTQ activists argued that it should be considered a protected category like race or sex while employers and judges saw it as something that could be chosen or hidden (Turk 2013).

As of 2017, the status of LGBTQ rights under Title VII remains inconclusive although the EEOC and lower courts have ruled that sexual orientation and gender identity are protected categories. The Supreme Court's reasoning in *Price Waterhouse v. Hopkins* (490 U.S. 228, 1989), determining that Ann Hopkins had been denied partnership in large part because of stereotyping, set precedence that Title VII's prohibition of sex discrimination protected workers who did not conform to traditional gender norms (Herz 2014). In 2012, the EEOC supported protections for gender identity, and in 2015, the EEOC issued a decision that sexual orientation fell under Title VII's sex clause (*Macy v. Holder; Complainant v. Anthony Foxx*). Several district courts and the Seventh Circuity Court of Appeals have reached similar conclusions (*Hively v. Ivy Tech Community College*, 7th circuit, 2017). Despite these gains for LGBTQ individuals, Congress has not added a specific amendment to Title VII and the Supreme Court has not issued a ruling regarding LGBTQ protections.

Even with the support of Title VII, women or men who serve as primary care givers for their partners, parents or children face challenges regarding workplace equity and advancement. Feminist and labor organizations pushed for the gender-neutral Family and Medical Leave Act (FMLA), eventually passed in 1993. The length of leave mandated and the number of employees covered had decreased significantly after years of compromising with conservative opponents who fought regulations for small businesses. The FMLA provides 12 weeks of unpaid leave for employees who have been working at the same business for at least 12 months; have worked at least 1,250 hours over the past 12 months; and are working at a location with 50 or more employees within 75 miles. Only about 60 percent of private-sector employees are covered since those with several part-time jobs do not qualify. Among those not covered are many precarious workers who cannot afford to miss a paycheck. And although many professional men and women receive paid leave from their employers, they face pressures to prioritize work commitments amid family responsibilities (Williams 2000). Working women and their advocates continue to push for more assertive legal interventions, and by 2018, five states and the District of Columbia have passed provisions for paid leave. Feminists push to increase coverage on multiple fronts, arguing for expanding the definition of a family unit or for decreasing the number of employees required for coverage (Noguchi 2018).

Contemporary advocates also perceive greater pay transparency as a remedy to the gender pay gap since many women do not know they are receiving inequitable compensation. Lilly Ledbetter had worked as a floor manager at Goodyear Tire and Rubber Company in Alabama for more than a decade when she received an anonymous note informing her that she was earning thousands less per month relative to male colleagues. In 2007 the Supreme Court rejected Ledbetter's sex discrimination suit because she had filed her complaint more than 180 days after the initial discriminatory act of her first paycheck. Justice Ruth Bader Ginsburg wrote a stirring dissent, and activists from the National Women's Law Center and National Partnership for Women & Families publically condemned the decision. Upon assuming office, President Barack Obama signed the Lilly Ledbetter Fair Pay Act, which mandates that the statute of limitation starts following the last, rather than the first act of discrimination. It amended Title VII to clarify that a discriminatory compensation practice is unlawful each time compensation is paid (Boris 2011).

Conclusion

In the current political, social and economic climate, women with diverse identities who are working in an array of occupations and industries seem more different from one another than they are similar. While professional women prioritize upward mobility into managerial and executive roles, low-wage women care most about higher pay and affordable health insurance. Professional women push for progress in the name of a business case for diversity, arguing that greater numbers of female executives and board members will benefit the organization's bottom line. Covered by Title VII, they have moved beyond fighting for regulatory compliance. Now they are tackling important extralegal issues such as implicit bias. Disproportionately women of color and undocumented immigrants, working-class women continue to push for broader government protections. A rapidly changing global economy means that many low wage women turn towards the promise of collective action to address gaps in legal coverage.

Despite the divergent nature of feminist activism in the workplace, new movements have begun to unite diverse categories of women committed to change. First coined in 2006 by community organizer Tarana Burke, #MeToo spread across social media in 2017 as well-known Hollywood actors catapulted sexual assault and violence into mainstream discourse [...]. The #MeToo movement aims to expose the systemic disadvantages that vulnerable women and men face at work by encouraging survivors to break their silence. Dialogue has turned to women in other occupations, as 700,000 female farmworkers announced in *Time* magazine that they too experienced sexual harassment but lacked resources to report injustices. Cognizant of this uneven access to remedies, hundreds from the entertainment industry launched Time's Up in early 2018. This initiative between Hollywood activists and the National Women's Law Center establishes a defense fund to help working-class women to bring forward claims (Buckley 2018).

Despite criticism that the #MeToo movement excludes men, vilifies those accused or lacks appeal for older women, its momentum is undeniable. Millions of women and men of all ages are discussing sexual misconduct on social media, implying that #MeToo may unify diverse categories of women, strengthen feminist activism, and challenge traditional power relations in workplaces across the United States. Yet with the #MeToo movement in its infancy as of 2018, we are left wondering if certain issues such as sexual harassment will bring together women and men from various industries and occupations? Or will different work experiences and diverse demographic categories prevent strong alliances among women and men that are necessary to change cultural norms?

Workplace problems like sexual harassment force us to revisit our approaches to gender equity in a neoliberal political and economic climate. The mainstream belief in a business case for diversity promotes capitalism's meritocratic promise, contending that advancement of the most talented individuals will foster financial gains for the larger organization and collective benefits for the broader society. While capitalism has improved the physical wellbeing of millions, by advancing medical knowledge, improving maternal health and decreasing infant mortality, capitalism too can exploit women as reproducers and caretakers. In *The Guardian* in 2013, philosopher Nancy Fraser famously lamented that feminism had become "capitalism's handmaiden," warning against the neoliberal turn of "lean in" feminism. And indeed, not all women benefit to the same extent when feminism is folded into a capitalist framework. To what extent can new forms of collective organizing help to empower those who struggle in a rapidly-changing economy? How can the law become more effective in offering women not just equality of opportunity but also equality of outcome? And to what extent can employers' policies address systemic inequality, allowing all women and men to thrive? These are the questions of feminism in the 21st-century workplace, questions that remain to be answered.

References

Anderson, Katherine S. 1987. "Employer Liability Under Title VII for Sexual Harassment after Meritor Savings Bank v. Vinson." *Columbia Law Review* 87(6):1258–1279.

Baker, Carrie. 2008. *The Women's Movement Against Sexual Harassment.* New York: Cambridge University Press.

Barry, Kathleen. 2007. *Femininity in Flight: A History of Flight Attendants.* Durham, NC: Duke University Press.

Baptist, Edward E. 2014. *The Half That Has Never Been Told: Slavery and the Making of American Capitalism.* New York, NY: Basic Books.

Baugh-Helton, Tiffany A. 2017. "'We Didn't Know We Were Making History': The United Automobile Workers' Women's Auxiliaries in Great Depression and World War II Era Detroit." PhD dissertation, Department of History, Binghamton University–State University of New York.

Berebitsky, Julie. 2012. *Sex and the Office: A History of Gender, Power, and Desire.* New Haven, CT: Yale University Press.

Blum, Linda M. 1991. *Between Feminism and Labor: The Significance of the Comparable Worth Movement.* Berkeley: University of California Press.

Boris, Eileen. 2011. "Ledbetter's Continuum: Race, Gender, and Pay Discrimination." Pp. 240–256 in *Feminist Legal History: Essays on Women and the Law*, edited by Tracy A. Thomas and Tracey Jean Boisseau. New York: New York University Press.

Boris, Eileen and Jennifer Klein. 2012. *Caring for America: Home Health Workers in the Shadow of the Welfare State.* New York: Oxford University Press.

Boydston, Jeanne. 1990. *Home and Work: Housework, Wages, and the Ideology of Labor in the Early Republic.* New York: Oxford University Press.

Buckley, Cara. 2018. "Powerful Hollywood Women Unveil Anti-Harassment Action Plan." *New York Times.* Retrieved February 26, 2018. https://www.nytimes.com/2018/01/01/movies/times-up-hollywood-women-sexual-harassment.html.

Cobble, Dorothy Sue. 2004. *The Other Women's Movement: Workplace Justice and Social Rights in Modern America.* Princeton, NJ: Princeton University Press.

Cooke, Bill. 2003. "The Denial of Slavery in Management Studies." *Journal of Management Studies* 40(8):1895–1918.

Cott, Nancy. 1989. *The Grounding of Modern Feminism.* New Haven, CT: Yale University Press.

Complainant v. Anthony Foxx, EEOC DOC 0120133080, WL 4397641(1954).

Crenshaw, Kimberlé Williams. 1989. "Demarginalizing the Intersection of Race and Sex." *University of Chicago Legal Forum* 139:139–167.

DeGraffenreid v. General Motors Assembly Div., 413 F. Supp. 142(1976).

Dublin, Thomas. 1981. *Women at Work: The Transformation of Work and Community in Lowell, Massachusetts*, 1826–1860. New York: Columbia University Press.

Elias, Allison. Forthcoming. *Feminism at Work: Women, Gender, and Success in Corporate America.* New York: Columbia University Press.

Elias, Allison. 2018. "'Outside the Pyramid': Clerical Work, Corporate Affirmative Action, and Working Women's Barriers to Upward Mobility." *Journal of Policy History* 30(2):301–333.

Fraser, Nancy. 2013. "How Feminism Became Capitalism's Handmaiden—And How to Reclaim It." *The Guardian.* Retrieved May 1, 2018. https://www.theguardian.com/commentisfree/2013/oct/14/feminism-capitalist-handmaiden-neoliberal.

Friedan, Betty. 1963. *The Feminine Mystique.* New York: W. W. Norton.

Gordon, Linda. 1994. *Pitied but Not Entitled: Single Mothers and the History of Welfare*, 1890-1935 New York: The Free Press.

Grant, Lee. 1981. The Willmar 8. DVD. CA: California Newsreel. http://newsreel.org/transcripts/The-Willmar-8-transcript.pdf.

Harrison, Cynthia. 1988. *On Account of Sex: The Politics of Women's Issues*, 1945–1968. Berkeley: University of California Press.

Herz, Zachary. 2014. "Price's Progress: Sex Stereotyping and Its Potential for Anti-Discrimination Law." *Yale Law Journal* 124(2):396–446.
Hively v. Ivy Tech Community College. No. 15–1720 (7th Cir., April 4, 2017).
Hunter, Tera. 1997. To *'Joy My Freedom': Southern Black Women's Lives and Labors After the Civil War*. Cambridge: Harvard University Press.
Institute for Women's Policy Research. 2018. "Women in Unions." Accessed March 1, 2018. https://iwpr.org/issue/democracy-and-society/women-in-unions/.
Kelley, Robin. 1994. *Race Rebels: Culture, Politics, and the Black Working Class*. New York: Free Press.
Kennedy, John F. "Executive Order 10980." December 14, 1961. Retrieved March 1, 2018 (http://www.presidency.ucsb.edu/ws/?pid=58918).
Kessler-Harris, Alice. 1982. *Out to Work: A History of Wage-Earning Women in the United States*. New York: Oxford University Press.
Kessler-Harris, Alice. 2001. *In Pursuit of Equity: Women, Men, and the Quest for Economic Citizenship in Twentieth-Century America*. New York: Oxford University Press.
MacKinnon, Catharine. 1979. *Sexual Harassment of Working Women: A Case of Sex Discrimination*. New Haven, CT: Yale University Press.
MacLean, Nancy. 1999. "The Hidden History of Affirmative Action: Working Women's Struggles in the 1970s and the Gender of Class." *Feminist Studies* 25:43–78.
Macy v. Holder, 2012. EEOC DOC 0120120821, WL 1435995. April 20.
May, Elaine Tyler. 1988. *Homeward Bound: American Families in the Cold War Era*. New York: Basic Books.
Mayer, Gerald. 2004. "Union Member Trends in the United States." *Congressional Research Service*. Retrieved March 1, 2018. (https://digitalcommons.ilr.cornell.edu/key_workplace/174/).
Mayeri, Serena. 2011. *Reasoning from Race: Feminism, Law, and the Civil Rights Revolution*. Cambridge, MA: Harvard University Press.
Meritor Savings Bank v. Vinson, 477 U.S. 57(1986).
Milkman, Ruth. 1987. *Gender at Work: The Dynamics of Job Segregation by Sex during World War II*. Urbana, IL: University of Illinois Press.
Muncy, Robyn. 1991. *Creating a Female Dominion in American Reform*, 1890–1935. New York: Oxford University Press.
Muller v. Oregon, 208 U.S. 412(1908).
National Domestic Worker's Alliance. 2018. Accessed March 1, 2018. https://www.domesticworkers.org.
Noguchi, Yuki. 2017. "Proposals Aim to Combat Discrimination Based on Salary History." *NPR All Things Considered*. Retrieved March 1, 2018. https://www.npr.org/2017/05/30/528794176/proposals-aim-to-combat-discrimination-based-on-salary-history.
Noguchi, Yuki. 2018. "Lawmakers Agree on Paid Family Leave But Not the Details." *NPR All Things Considered*. Retrieved March 1, 2018 https://www.npr.org/2018/02/27/585133064/lawmakers-agree-on-paid-family-leave-but-not–the-details.
Oncale v. Sundowner Offshore Services, Inc., 523 U.S. 75(1998).
Orleck, Annelise. 1995. *Common Sense and a Little Fire: Women and Working-Class Politics in the United States*. Chapel Hill, NC: University of North Caroline Press.
Palmer, Phyllis. 1995. "Outside the Law: Agricultural and Domestic Workers Under the Fair Labor Standards Act." *Journal of Policy History* 7(4):416–440.
Phillips v. Martin Marietta Corp., 400 U.S. 542(1971).
Price Waterhouse v. Hopkins, 490 U.S. 228(1989).
Restaurant Opportunities Centers United. 2018. Retrieved March 1, 2018. http://rocunited.org.
Richardson, Dorothy. 1990. *The Long Day: The Story of a New York Working Girl, As Told by Herself*. Charlottesville, VA: University of Virginia Press.
Roth, Benita. 2003. *Separate Roads to Feminism: Black, Chicana, and White Feminist Movements in America's Second Wave*. New York: Cambridge University Press.
Scott, Joan W. 1986. "Gender: A Useful Category of Historical Analysis." *The American Historical Review* 91(5):1053–1075.
Turk, Katherine. 2013. "'Our Militancy is in Our Openness': Gay Employment Rights Activism in California and the Question of Sexual Orientation in Sex Equality Law." *Law and History Review* 31:423–469.
Welter, Barbara. 1966. "The Cult of True Womanhood: 1820–1860." *American Quarterly* 18(2):151–174.
Williams, Joan. 2000. *Unbending Gender: Why Family and Work Conflict and What to Do About It*. New York: Oxford University Press.
Woloch, Nancy. 2015. *A Class by Herself: Protective Laws for Women Workers, 1890–1990s*. Princeton, NJ: Princeton University Press.

Reading 3.6

Plato on Topos, Economy, and Transition

Janina Rosicka

Janina Rosicka, "Plato on Topos, Economy and Transition," *Economic Transition in Historical Perspective: Lessons from the Story of Economics*, ed. Charles Michael Andres Clark, pp. 1-26. Copyright © 2001 by Taylor & Francis Group. Reprinted with permission.

Introduction

Prior to the Enlightenment, most economic theorizing centred on abundance. The world of agrarian economies was described using terminology that suggested that the coexistence of wealth and poverty lead to an undesirable state of the economy; and that abundance, coupled with moderation, meant a desirable state of the economy. Within this view, economic man was seen mostly as a consumer. Although all agreed that everyone was dependent upon the gods or Fortune or Providence or Grace, as they determined the success or failure of the crops, man was still perceived as a 'joint' producer or creator of the state of economy. When man did not violate the eternal order he could reckon on the powers above. On the other hand, when he violated that order he could be sure of some sort of punishment. Thus economy and morality (in this case pleasing the gods) were closely interrelated. Generosity was connected with moderate consumption, and both of these features characterize good patterns of behaviour. Avarice was the central feature of bad behaviour. The recommended pattern of behaviour was that of those who lived in the country estates, whereas less than reputable behaviour was typified by those who lived in towns. Hence the common fears of commerce and town, and simultaneously, the praise of country and land. Myths, religion, theatre and *belles letters* all reinforced this manner of thinking.

Plato took part in this discussion, creating a theory which I would like to call the 'philosophy of economy space'. Living during a crisis of the Greek institution of the *polis,* Plato experienced first-hand the period of the transition, and an important part of his philosophy was dedicated to the transition. He combined cosmological, anthropological, historical, economical and psychological arguments in order to show regularities in the history of human race. These arguments were arranged by him to answer mainly two questions: 'what is the proper order of civilisation?' and 'what is disorder?' The proper order was described by him, in the *Republic* and the *Laws,* as the two models of the ideal state. Disorder was understood by Plato as the transition—a period full of chaos caused by commercial behaviours.

Based on the number pages Plato devotes to the problem of order in the *Republic* and the *Laws,* he clearly paid more attention to order than disorder. This part of Plato's thinking has been recognised as an important part of Plato's overall thought, and has been carefully examined by historians both of economic and political thought. In our century, because of the experience with fascism, Nazism, and Stalinism, Plato's social ideas are interpreted as totalitarian. In the history of economic thought Plato is presented as a philosopher who denied the importance of the economy; as a theorist who wanted to eliminate the influence of economic goals over people; and as an adherent of the total intervention of the state in the economy. In this way, the economic image of Plato was generally accepted as a philosopher who interpreted economic questions only in the context of moral discourse, and demonstrated his aristocratic distance from the economy, especially from trade. Because of this image, there has been a tendency to forget Plato's long-lasting impact on European economic ideas, and to neglect the fact that for more than two [thousand] years his instructions concerning economic behaviour have been accepted, analysed, and enriched by the Church writers, and then by the political thought of the old republicanism in the Baroque and the Enlightenment periods and later by German cameralism and the 'Hausevater-literatur'.[1]

My starting point is different. I am interested in Plato's understanding of transition, that is to say, the period between two different kinds of economic orders. So I am forced to put stress on Plato's understanding of disorder. This point of view provides an interesting, to my knowledge unknown, connection between Plato's cosmology expounded in the *Timaeus,* and the description of Atlantis and old Athens in the *Critias,* namely the connection between space and society. As understood by Plato, this connection involved a close relationship between the state of the human and social environment and that of the state of society, and in particular—in the economic dimension—the relationship between the economic efficiency of the human environment, and the stage of economic welfare of society. We can say, using modern economic terminology, that as Adam Smith created a modern economics connected market, division of labour and wealth, Plato created a theory of agrarian or traditional economy demonstrating a relationship between, on the one hand: both space and place, and on the other: wealth, division of labour and consumption.

Plato saw this relationship as a source of social disorder. This disorder was described by him as a growing discrepancy between the commercial goals of society and a way in which the space—the *topos* existed. He understood the transition as a period full of economic and social chaos, during which people's elementary practices—especially commercial behaviours and luxurious consumption—violated the physical, biological, and human spaces. We are accustomed to think about space and place in the economy as a market—this perfect flexible place. Plato thought about the *topos* of the economy as flexible, although not as flexible in comparison with man's growing needs.

From his theory of the transition, Plato appears as a very interesting economist. He differentiates his 'economics' on micro- and macro-levels; he employs four theoretical models: two of man's existence: social and in isolation, and two of the states; he considers the relation between population and the efficiency of the economy. We can find in his writings pre-Malthusian statements, a pre-Veblenian understanding of competition, and a pre-Hirschian idea of congestion.

Plato describes a cycle of the development of the human race from deluge to deluge and from surviving in mountains to a rise of civilisation in lowlands. Transition—according to Plato—is a period between two ways of human existence: in isolation and in community, the first takes place in the mountains, the second in lowlands. I will refer to these two different modes of existence further on as the Mountain and the Lowland. In fact there are two kinds of transition. First between the Mountain and the Lowland, after a deluge, during this period people try to overcome their isolation and establish a community; and the second between the end of welfare of the Lowlands civilisation, and the total disaster of this civilisation caused by a deluge. This deluge ended the second transition. The possibilities of the Lowland resources became exhausted and the people of Lowland were drowned. At that time only the Mountain people remained safe. Plato is not very interested in the first period of transition, however, the next period he studies very carefully. His goal is to describe the menaces of the Lowlands civilisation in order to admonish contemporary Athenians, and he wants to show activities that delayed or prevented this sinister transition. Plato's recipe is similar to recipes written by economists in the twentieth century, he wants to flatten a period of transition and to sustain as long as possible the period of true abundance.

Two notions: space and place; play a crucial part in the transition. The main human activities in the Lowland consist of bringing the Lowland space into cultivation. The economic space, according to Plato, appears only in the social space of the *polis*. People penetrate the whole space and their efforts result in a growth of the division of labour, which is accompanied by a growing population. These processes persist as long as the Lowland abundance can satisfy the needs of the growing population. However, once population has outgrown the abundance, that is all the space of the Lowland is filled, there will be not sufficient space for the growing population. This day of reckoning can be delayed by conquering new pieces of land, and thus wars become the main means of survival, but this is merely a delaying action.

According to Plato, the *topos* of the Lowlands are the source of abundance, and thus the transition emerges as a lack of possibilities for development. The result of economic growth is an overgrowth of economic and commercial space, provoking a shrinkage of human and physical spaces. The transition is a process of destruction, or corruption, of the true Man in man, and of the true *Topos* in *topos*. Plato elucidates why the transition came into being and what we can do in order to prevent the catastrophe.

To understand Plato's economic theory we should remember two things: first, he wants to find out the relationship between the general and the particular, and second, in his 'economics' there exists a basic relationship between space and economy. In the first part of this paper I intend to present Plato's main economic assumption, that the *topos* is a room for abundance (*Topos* and Abundance). Next I will try to reconstruct Plato's macroeconomic thinking about the social behaviour patterns in the Mountain (Mountain *Topos)* and in the Lowland (Lowland *Topos* and Transition). Then Plato's microeconomics will be described.

Here we see Plato's view that limited consumption is an economic virtue (Man and Economic Virtue). Afterwards I will bring forward Plato's arguments of the relationship between consumption, overabundance and the transition (Consumption and Transition; Plenty Supports Transition). In the final section of this [reading] Plato's general philosophy of economy, and the new economy will be presented together with his suggestion of how to prevent the transition (Philosophy of Economy Space; The New Economy a Contrivance of Transition).

Topos and Abundance

For Plato, a history of the macrocosm is a zigzag line leading from overabundance to harmony. At the beginning there were the absolute 'being and space and generation' (*Timaeus* 52d). Then, the Creator filled the space by means of the four elements: fire, water, land and air. There was chaos, and the elements were in overabundance. The wrestling of the elements in search of measure became a prelude to the emergence of the macrocosm. Each of the elements was supplied in abundance, 'all without reason and measure' however, the creator has written, by means of 'form and number', the macrocosm as perfect as possible: 'as far as possible the fairest and best, out of things which were not fair and good' (*Timaeus* 53b). The elements subjugated their local excess and the macrocosm found their global measure and balance. The state of global measure means that there is not a vacuum. The macrocosm rotates and this rotation 'compresses everything' within the macrocosm and 'will not allow any place to be left void', so every bit of space is occupied by things (*Timaeus* 58b).

All places within the macrocosm are filled by a form made from the elements. There are three kinds of beings: no born and not perishable ideas, being object of mind perception only; sensible things born, being always in motion, and perceived by sense; and the third kind (the most interesting for us), space—the *topos*.

> 'And there is a third nature, which is space and is eternal, and admits not of destruction and provides a home for all created things, and is apprehended, when all sense is absent, by a kind of spurious reason, and is hardly real—which we, beholding as in a dream, say of all existence that it must of necessity be in some place and occupy a space, but that what is neither in heaven nor in earth has no existence' (*Timaeus* 52b).

The *topos* is imperishable and it offers some space (a 'home' or a 'stay within itself' [Siwek's trans., Timajos, Kristias, 1986] to all beings that are born. The *topos* is invisible and we can perceive it only in an extra-sensory manner. It possesses no form itself, due to its role of giving a place to stay for all possible forms. The *topos* is the 'mother and receptacle of all created and visible and in any way sensible things is not to be termed earth or air or fire or water, or any of their compounds, or any of the elements from which these are derived, but is an invisible and formless being which receives all things and in some mysterious way partakes of the intelligible, and is most incomprehensible' (*Timaeus* 51ab).

Within the *topos* the elements are 'shaken by the receiving vessel, which, moving like a winnowing machine, scattered far away from one another the elements most unlike, and forced the most similar elements into close contact' (*Timaeus* 53a) and—in Siwek's translation—'they rendered blows to the *topos* which returned the blows with the same intensity'. The *topos* brings things into existence because everything has to be in its own place. The thing which has no place does not exist. The *topos* is a 'shelter' and 'seemingly a host' [Siwek's trans. Timajos, Kritias, 1986], 'the receptacle, and in a manner the nurse, of all generation' (*Timaeus* 49b), it gives a 'shelter'—the place of safety and it nourishes the born things.

So we can say that in its physical and biological dimension, the Earth embraces all the elements of the macrocosm, it has its own space in the macrocosm and it is able to offer places to others, especially to people. That means it provides shelter and is a host for people, and, like a mother, it offers its abundance to man. Man should worship his part of the Earth and revere her even more than his own mother. The Earth is a goddess and a sovereign of all mortals (*Laws* V 740a). Because of the Earth, man, in his turn, has received his place. The human *topos* is a seat of values which supply man's biological needs and gives him a sense of safety. Yet, not every place on the Earth is suitable for man. The Earth's area is marked by lowlands and mountains. The lowlands are fertile and there is space for life in community. The mountains are not fertile and cannot support communities, however it is possible for individuals to survive in such a place (*Critias* 110a). Only the lowlands part of the *topos,* which is a meeting spot of man and fertility, can create the possibility to establish a society. Thus, the external feature of the *topos* that makes it suitable for people is abundance.

This seemingly banal statement leads Plato to some unusual reflections concerning a good state of the Lowland's economic possibilities, and to his crucial question about the possible threats to these possibilities. He examines this question using two methods of analysis. In the first, he gives a historical and bucolic description of Old Athens and Atlantis, and contrasts it with his contemporary Athens (*Timaeus* 20e–26c, *Critias* 110a–121c). In the second, he develops generalisations based on two theoretical models, known as the 'City of Pigs' and the 'Luxurious City', and he again sets these models in contrast against each other (the Second book of the *Republic).*

Mountain Topos

Though the macrocosm has found its perfect measure, there is still the possibilities of local disasters, mainly deluges. Civilisation is created by the people living in the Lowlands and they, and their fortunes, are wiped out by the deluge. The story of the survivors of a deluge gave Plato the starting point for his economic and historical deliberations. Two similar versions of this story can be found in *Critias* and *Laws* (*Critias* 109e, 111ab; *Laws* III 677bc). Plato's circular view of human history supposes the rise and fall of cities and civilizations over the ages, frequently wiped out by a deluge (flood) or some other form of natural disaster.[2] Plato's starting point for explaining the origins of civil society is the period immediately after one of these events, when the cycle starts again. In the story the only people that survived the deluge are those who live in the Mountains. Though these people have a vague idea about the civilisation of the Lowland people, they are 'ignorant of the art of writing' (*Critias* 109d). Their efforts are concentrated mainly on the procurement of food and basic necessities, and they communicate with others in order to speak on this subject (*Critias* 110a). Man, faced with the limited biological possibilities of the Mountains, is forced to perpetual hard work. This coercion deprives man of freedom, which is understood by Plato as: time for seeking knowledge and for leisure. This lack of freedom prevents the Mountain people from developing intellectually, however they do not become corrupted (*Laws* III 678, 679).

The *topos* of the Mountain is described in a few sentences laid down in *Laws, Republic, Critias* and *Timaeus*. It is evident that Plato does not pay much attention to this case. The Mountain people are—in their physical and biological beings—doubly safe. They do not violate their *topos:* firstly, because they cannot do it; and secondly, because their environment's configuration counteracted its congestion. The Mountain people always remain primitive and due to this feature they will be spontaneously moral and enjoy a successfully life (*Laws* III 679abc). They do not have either good or bad knowledge. And only they, 'who are destitute of letters and education' (*Timaeus* 23a), will survive deluges. These people never endanger their place, and perhaps, that is the reason that they are practically imperishable. The *topos* of the mountains is the shelter of human race.[3]

Lowlands Topos and Transition

Plato's reflections on the Lowlands *topos,* and the transition, is based on the conviction that the present can only be understood by looking to the past. The Atlantis story forms one full circle of the human history circles; the Old Athens case, acts as an example of the transition in early stage, and Plato's analysis of his Athens demonstrates the last phase of the transition, a period just before a deluge.

In the beginning the narrative of the Lowland people was a happy story. In Old Athens people had preserved by maintaining an equal balance (measure) between overabundance and humiliating poverty. Athenian farmers and artisans create an autarkic society, abiding by the rules of simple reproduction. Generation after generation, the Athenians lived in houses with furnishings completely unchanged, living a simple life, and owning no silver or gold. The population was stabilised at a level of twenty thousand, with a balance between the number of men and women. Describing Athenian welfare, Plato emphasised the need to preserve autarky in spite of the land's overfertility. There were only two rules: to keep population and consumption stable. 'They aimed at the mean between splendour and meanness, dwelling in decent houses where they grew old, themselves and their children's children, each succeeding generation leaving them to another like itself' (*Critias* 112c). ... [T]he number of both sexes already qualified and still qualified to bear arms they were careful to keep, as nearly as possible, always the same, roughly some twenty thousand' (*Critias* 112d).

The civilisation of Atlantis enjoyed an even more fruitful economy; 'that sacred island, which then lay open to the sun, in marvellous beauty and inexhaustible profusion [abundance]' (*Critias* 115b). In his tale of Atlantis, Plato took pleasure in a numeral 'two' which was, together with twins, considered as a mythical symbol of fertility.[4] The beginning of the Atlantis tribe starts with Poseidon, who generated 'five pairs of twin male children' (*Critias* 113e). Two fountains of cold and hot water gave fertility, resulting in a double harvest (*Critias* 113b, 114b). Plato wrote about an 'abundance' of rare resources, such as 'orichalcum' (not identifed metal, probably brass), copper or zinc. Atlantis forests were well stocked with big game and deer, and even a 'great number' of elephants. Corn and pulse (a fertilizer) were found in an 'infinite abundance' and crops were perfect and various. There was enough water for swimming pools for people and cattle. Atlantis walls were coated with copper, zinc, and with *orichalch* ('which gleamed like fire' *Critias* 116c). The ruler's palace was golden and Poseidon's silver shrine was set with ivory. Two harbours were roofed with stone. Canals were set in the mountains in order to carry wood to the lowlands and return to the mountains with fruits from lowlands, and pool water was utilized to irrigate Poseidon grove. This all testifies to their expanded division of labour and advanced systems of transportation and communication. Atlantis houses were roomy and beautiful (*Critias* 115c–117e). Although the Atlantis economy was supported by subordinated provinces, Plato puts stress on its self-sufficient economy.

The discontinuous description of Atlantis in *Critias* is cut short after an episode showing growing turmoil (*Critias* 117e). It is the first symptom of Atlantis's corruption. The entire area 'was completely filled by a multitude of closely set houses, and the large harbor and canal were constantly crowded by merchant vessels and their passengers arriving from all quarters, whose vast numbers occasioned incessant shouting, clamour, and general uproar, day and night' (*Critias* 117e). Atlantis did not manage its fortune. 'But when the god's part in them began to wax faint by constant crossing with much mortality, and the human temper to predominate, then they could no longer carry their fortunes, but began to behave themselves unseemly. To the seeing eye they now began to seem foul, for they were losing the fairest bloom from their most precious treasure, but to such as could not see the happy life, to appear at last fair and blessed indeed, now that they were taking the infection of wicked coveting and pride of power' (*Critias* 121b).

In the Second Book of the *Republic* we are acquainted with the sequel to the Atlantis story—a description of the transition. The 'luxurious city' requires 'couches and tables and every other article of furniture, as well as viands, and fragrant oils, and perfumes, and courtesans, and confectionery; and all these in plentiful variety' (*Republic* II 373a). The town becomes richer and richer, ever more populated. These processes are accompanied by diminishing space.

> [Socrates] Then we shall also have to enlarge our city, for our first or healthy city will not now be of sufficient size, but requires to be increased in bulk, and filled out with a multitude of callings which do not exist in cities to satisfy any natural want; for example, the whole class of hunters, and all who practise imitative art, including many who use forms and colours, and many who use music, poets [...], rhapsodists, actors, dancers, contractors (*Republic* II 373b).

We see 'congestion', and decreased fertility, and there appeared a new, unknown formerly, state of poverty. There is no poverty in the Mountain, and in the period of abundance. The first is a period of heroic efforts, however there is no poverty because there are no differences among people. The abundance period introduces no social differences as well. It is in the period of overabundance when people start to experience social differences, and instead of the single state, in fact, there appears two states: the rich state and the poor state: 'a city must necessarily lose its unity and become two cities, one comprising the rich and the other the poor; who reside together on the same ground, and are always plotting against one another' (*Republic* VIII 551d).

Turmoil and congestion appear parallel with this 'bad understanding' of wealth. The Atlantis harbour becomes noisy and crowded with people (*Critias* 117e). The existing area of the state is not sufficient for the increasing number of habitants. As Atlantis was losing its divine element, and allowed itself to be possessed by turmoil, so this 'healthy town' became the 'luxurious town'. The town in the transition exists in a way which is truculent and prerequisite to conquest. The result is a war for land.

> [Socrates] The country too, I presume, which was formerly adequate to the support of its then habitants will be now too small, and adequate no longer. ... Then must we not cut ourselves a slice of our neighbour's territory, if we are to have land enough both for pasturage and tillage, while they will do the same to ours, if they, like us, permit themselves to overstep the limit of necessaries and plunge into the unbounded acquisition of wealth?
>
> Shall we say so?
>
> Certainly.
>
> It must inevitably be so, Socrates.
>
> Will our next step be to go to war, Glaucon, or how will it be? (*Republic* II 373de).

The state in transition steers all of its energy towards conquering space and resources, namely to things which it lost and which it will lose and lose again. In addition this process will be accelerated for two reasons: a growing population, especially of artisans, traders, and plebs (who are dangerous to the order of the town); and increasing expenditures on the continuously enlarging army (*Republic* II 374).

Plato uses the bare rock of the Acropolis contemporary to him, (*Critias* 111 abcd, 112b), to visualise this idea of a shrinking physical and biological space. Plato notes that the output of the Old Athens was more abundant than it is presently. Because of the soil erosion caused by the 'many formidable deluges in the course of the nine thousand years—that is the interval between the date we are speaking of and the present' the land has been made a 'skeleton of a body wasted by disease' (*Critias* 111c). Just as the overpopulation increased, the fertility of land and water—two main resources of an agrarian economy—were diminished, and the economy became a wasteful exploitation. Not utilised springs water flowing down into the sea; bare rock of Acropolis as 'human bones' instead forest hill; these show that Athens has already reached this stage of development. The Lowlands *topos* becomes overcrowded in relation to its fertility and physical space. This overpopulation resulted in a transgression of the natural barrier of the Lowland fertility. According to Plato, the *polis* should not go over this barrier. The *topos* is an eternal and not annihilated being (*Timaeus* 52b). This seemingly optimistic statement in fact means that people cannot create the *topos* by themselves; they can only adjust to its finite fertility.

The contraction of physical space generates congestion and lack of resources; and then subsequently it produces wars. The congestion results not exactly from the bare number of people, but from the covering of the Lowland human *topos,* by exploiting all of its resources. This congestion around resources negates the way which both fertility and human beings work. The friendly balanced relationship between people and their *topos* transforms into the chaos of congestion and in this way it starts to be corrupted. The economic activity cannot recognise its natural limits and it cannot stop by itself, because it cannot control itself. Economic processes, within the *polis,* are spontaneous and impetuous; their nature is elementally. They do not cement the state, contrary they split the state into two different spaces: the *topos* of wealth and the *topos* of poverty. The area of wealth has to defend itself against the area of poverty. As the area of poverty may want to change the internal order of the *polis,* the wealthy part of Lowland has to focus on its defence and on gaining more resources. Plato believes the earth is fully populated: 'The fact is that wherever the extremity of winter frost or of summer does not prevent, mankind exist, sometimes in greater, sometimes in lesser numbers' (*Timaeus* 22e). To gain the resources means the necessity to wage wars against ones neighbours. Plato emphasises that once initiated, social-economic movements can only intensify and provoke wars, and they will endure permanently till the global catastrophe—a deluge. Winning a war does not restore the old balance, because the enlarged area of the state will demand more people in the state economy and army. The wars can delay, for a time, the economic and ecological catastrophe. Only a deluge can restore the lost balance of the Lowlands societies and then people again go down the mountain, and take up once more their efforts. And it will last until people are taught how they should recognise the possibilities of their *topos,* and afterwards, to arrange a peaceful co-existence within the *topos.*

In the *Timaeus* Plato says the process of the stabilisation of the four elements has been accomplished within the macrocosm. He permits the possibility of local disasters caused by local imbalances. For him, such a disaster, specific for some parts of the Earth, namely the Lowlands, is the deluge. Economic activities lead people to a drastic violation of the Lowland *topos* and the way in which the *topos* demonstrates itself. The fertility ceases and the Lowland *topos* does not tolerate people, and for people's violence it answers by striking back, and using the coercion of a deluge, earthquake, or other cosmic disaster. Plato mentions mainly deluges, which he considered as historical turning points (in this way he describes the disappearance of Atlantis). For him the deluge is not a notion that perceived as an unfavourable aspect of the stars or gods, it is rather a way of the Lowland *topos* reaction to a thoughtless and wasteful economy. The macrocosm is perfect; its parts, as the Earth, are regionally not perfect; nevertheless everywhere are the *topos* and it operates in the same fashion, namely in relation to the Lowlands people, by means of fertility and deluge. From the history of Atlantis we know that those who wasted their chance for safe and healthy life given them by the *topos,* should be afraid of this sort of punishment. Only shepherds and peasants do not waste their chance and they remain in the Mountain (*Timaeus* 22de).

Plato's macroeconomic assumptions are derived from his cosmology. The Earth *topos* has a limited capacity for supporting people. It offers safety to the Mountain people, and a relative abundance to the Lowland people, though the latter have to pay the high price of annihilation of their civilisation due to their abuse of this *topos.* The amount of space is finite and will not increase, according to Plato, thus the macrocosm is shaped and people have to accept this fact. The limitations of the Earth *topos* force autarky; people must and can make a proper use of accessible means and they do not have not to cross their own Lowlands to renew resources. This last statement is very important. Plato understands the economic dimension of the Lowland *topos* as a space limited to the physical and biological possibilities of the Lowland. So the clue to macroeconomic practice is in adjusting to these limits. What is needed is to find the positive solution in two rules: economic autarky, understood as an adjustment to the Lowland physical possibilities; and consequently, as a limitation of the Lowland population by the product of the economic autarky. For Plato, the Mountains *topos* is a case study of the period when real scarcity existed.

The Lowlands *topos* is a case study of two periods: the abundance-welfare, and the overabundance or false scarcity (scarcity created by luxury). Both these examples show Plato's macroeconomic ideas.

Man and Economic Virtue

In *Critias,* Plato sets up a more picturesque description of the social and macroeconomic features of abundance–welfare. In the *Laws* and in the *Republic* he is more occupied by the microeconomic sphere and he tries to establish the limits of human needs. In his macroeconomic thinking he emphasises the importance of water and land resources, and the optimal number Lowland inhabitants. In his microeconomic thinking–analogous to these macroeconomic topics–he is interested in three main human needs, namely: drink; food; and propagation (*Laws* VI 782e). He investigates the issues of consumption, nature of wealth; and he investigates the relationship between wealth and poverty; and he tries to discover the most favourable human economic behaviours.

In the Second Book of the *Republic* Plato sets up a mental experiment where he builds up a state consisted of individuals immunised against economic passions (*Republic* II 369d–374e). The inhabitants of this hypothetical town possess houses, clothes and boots, though they use them only in winter. In the summer they work and sleep with no clothes on; sleep on willow brake, myrtle and bindweed, and eat wheat or barley cakes served on leaves, and 'not begetting children beyond their means'. They practise all these functions under their 'prudent fear of poverty and war' (*Republic* II 372bc). This not very refined consumption ensures that 'Living in peace and health, they will probably die in old age and hand on a lie life to their offspring' (*Republic* II 372d). An elder brother of Plato, Glaucon revolts against this diet, so Plato added extra figs, peas, broad beans, and acorns to this menu. Plato's generosity becomes a futile gesture and Glaucon names this town the 'City of Pigs'. The Platonic diet is similar to a description of the Orifice life (*Laws* VI 782c). In others fragments of the *Republic* Plato is not so rigorous, he wants to eliminate a mysterious 'Athenian confectionery' (*Republic* III 404e), or limiting himself to a comparison of a lack of modesty in eating to too big sails for ship (*Laws* III 691e). This diet, dated back to the period when humans were gatherers, becomes, next to both postulates from *Critias;* autarky, and effectively restrict population; hence the third condition of keeping the 'abundance-welfare' period.

Analysing consumption becomes Plato's starting point for defining true wealth. Lust for wealth corrupts man's spirit, causing of 'an incessant hunger gnawing at their souls' (*Laws* VIII 832a). This corruption manifests itself in aggression; Plato gives the example of an innkeeper who treats his clients as 'enemies' and wants a 'ransom' (*Laws* XI 919a). Man does not know what 'wealth' means, because he does not know himself. Non-reflective compliance with his passions, meaning a lust for wealth, kills the man in a man by focusing his attention on things not worth troubling with. In the *Gorgias* Plato named such a man a 'duck' which eats a lot and excretes a lot (*Gorgias* 494b). Wealth, and not the abundance-welfare, is followed by laziness, and supports the careless practising of professions and can even hinder work. We are able to 'put golden coronets' on the cultivator's head, however this stops him from working as a cultivator (*Republic* IV 420e). A newly rich potter becomes lazy and he too stops being a potter (*Republic* IV 421d). Poverty breeds unemployment, humiliation and crime. Poor man cannot afford to buy tools and they stop practising their profession. Both poverty and wealth promote subversive behaviours. In stating why wealth and poverty need to be kept out of the city, Socrates says: 'Wealth and poverty, said I, since the one brings luxury, idleness, and innovation, and the other illiberality and the evil of bad workmanship in addition to innovation' [in Grube's translation 'innovation' is translated as 'revolution' (Grube, 1992)] (Republic IV 422a). A rich man immorally conquers wealth, and his expenses are different from expenses of a moral man. By taking away wealth from others he creates a space of poverty. The nearness of poverty and wealth render envy and aggression and breeds insatiability and revolt.

This abnormal situation of man concentrating on his alimentary canal must be altered. Even in our body, the stomach (compared by Plato with a 'crib') is situated far away from our soul, in order to make 'as little noise and disturbance as possible, and permitting the best part to advice quietly for the good of the whole and the individual' (*Timaeus* 70e). Man should work to improve his life. He can do it even in the unfavourable conditions in Athens. In the First Book of the *Republic* Plato pays a 'wise and sensible' man from Piraeus, Cephalus, a visit. Cephalus' style of life is a compromising solution between the simplest life in the 'City of Pigs', and the luxurious life in the Glaucon's town. 'In the conduct of money' Cephalus stands 'midway' between his grandfather and his father, and he intends to leave to his sons 'not less but if anything rather more' (*Republic* I 330b). He makes good use of his property, so he knows his estate helped him to avoid temptations of 'deceit or falsehood', and supports him as an old-age insurance (*Republic* I 330e).

Plato expresses in many places (mainly the *Gorgias,* the *Republic,* and the *Laws)* his advice concerning a successful life. In his writings we can find a description of something like the 'four steps' way to the economic virtue, called by him 'to set his house in order' (*Republic* IV 443d) or in Witwicki's translation: the 'inward household' (Panstwo, 1958). He distinguishes four 'good' types of life: healthy, well considered, brave, and wise, and in contrast to these good lives, are four 'bad' lives: sick, foolish, cowardly, and licentious (*Laws* V 733e). In accordance with these styles of the good life, Plato formulates four rules: to exercise restraint in consumption (*Laws* IV 710a, V 729a); to keep in mind the importance of correspondence between individual and the external world (*Timaeus* 88c), to support harmony between quantity and quality (*Gorgias* 508a, *Republic* IV 441e, 443d); and the last, to compete in virtue (*Laws* V 731a). His counsels, concerning how to enjoy the healthy and well-considered life, and how to avoid the sick and foolish one, have a high economic content.

For him economic virtues are an important precondition for virtues of courage and the mind; and consequently, are a means to enjoy the most desired state of balance. The initial step consists in the subduing of an individual's temperament and passions. The next step is very important and it consists in the establishment of a harmony between the 'inward household' and the 'external household'. The external household embraces a whole social system understood as a place of man in his *polis.* After tidying himself up, man should be interested in state affairs. However, he is limited in the effect he can have on state affairs, so this task becomes a duty of politicians. With regard to a size of the Lowland supply of resources, the rulers have to establish the limits of the *polis* demand. They have insure the compliance with these limits and, if necessary, they should confiscate estate excess (*Laws* V 744de). These two steps: within man; and within society; in building the economic virtue mean a necessity of a perpetual adjustment to the Lowland possibilities and limits. The Lowland economy establishes the limits of both individual and social behaviours. The success of these stages relies upon a flexible control performed by both the individual on himself and by the politician on society. Wealth still remains a quantitative ('arithmetic') wealth, though it, due to the limitations and the laws, brings near the perfect state of the qualitative ('geometric') wealth. The third step consists in the subordination of the arithmetical wealth to the geometric one (*Laws* V 744c, VI 757a). For the economy, this is once more establishing a relationship between fertility and restraint in order to subdue quantity to quality. Economic activities must be ruled by the virtues; noble goals achieved by noble means, for example we should hunt for animals face to face, without snares, or nets (*Laws* VII 823–4). In fact, Plato's sentences lose their chivalrous context if we see them as ecological postulates for the elimination of wasteful economic activity. At last, the fourth step—the creation of community, which competes in virtue, and does not participate in the race for resources. Practising the virtue of restraint, man gradually builds his own virtue, in order to use his highest possible freedom, which allowed him to enjoy individual and social profits. His microcosm becomes reconciled with the macrocosm.

The economic virtues refers to the biological and physical sphere of life. Practising this virtue man can achieve a satisfaction of his biological and physical needs. The economic and biological balance of man characterises a symmetry: how much he wants, thus he gets in return. Moderate needs are satisfied by the Lowland nature. Plato shows man as an economic being depending on nature; however this dependence is not very burdensome. Two natural borders mark it: possibilities of the Lowland nature, and consumer possibilities of man.

Dominated by a lust for wealth, man remains in a nasty asymmetry. His wants are beyond measure, so he never attains fulfilment. Instead of emancipation he is troubled with his body diseases and he is tortured by insatiability. Man, being in the first stage of balance, lives a moderate life, not much troubled by economic things. His way of life will be honest because he does not contribute to the war or future catastrophe of deluge. Man, being in the total balance (a man of the geometric wealth), will be richer by the time, free from the lust for wealth, allowing him to practice wisdom and he will enjoy freedom for self-improvement.

We can clearly see Plato's idea of replacing the commercial understanding of scarcity and plenty with a fuller understanding of the ecological, political and economic consequences of man's economic practices. To live a beautiful (it means happy and fair) life, man's estate and his bodily needs must be subordinate to his soul. It is good that man wants scarce things, he has only to understand that virtue is the unique scarce thing. The majority of people do not know what true virtue is. The Athenian says in the *Laws* that 'not many of us who remain sober when we have the opportunity to grow wealthy' (*Laws* XI 918d). To practice the Platonic virtue is similar to going into a circle, the Ancient symbol of perfection. The nearer you are to the centre of the circle, the more you possess the virtues, and you are at a shorter distance from the centre and perfection. The centre is a point of both your perfection and your satiation. You have to seek and to conquer the moral good by means of exceptional efforts. Material goods possess quite opposite features. They are outside the circle, they have no limits, and by its elemental character they can without difficulty take control of man. Outside the circle there is no possibility, by means of the element and of the infinity, to reach freedom and wisdom. Both, the lack of chaos and finite, are understood as an approval of limitations, and are the proper means to realise the Man in man.

Plato proposes the way for the frill perfection of an elite only and he is well aware of the impossibility to create an entire community of men of virtue. His reflections on the economic and total balance, and about citizenship, and his models of ideal states, indicate that he preserves for the majority of the Lowland people the task of the first step—to make economic order within himself. It is significant that Plato starts the *Republic* with the description of a meeting with Cephalus, who is not only a positive example but something more. Plato teaches by Cephalus' example that the practice of virtue is not so difficult as it seems to most people. All can follow these steps along with the elite. The ruling elite has to provide the harmony between individuals and the Lowland fertility. They are given the higher consciousness of a choice—on the social level—between living in peace and war.

The scarcity of noble (virtuous) men caused both the need to control a society, and to proclaim laws. The control of society and the laws act as a substitute for the spontaneous reactions called for true virtue. The legislator has to fight on two fronts protecting his society from poverty and from wealth. The members of the wholesale trades are the most disturbing people in the Lowland. This is the part of society in need of the most moral tutelage, their attitudes are the most susceptible to corruption, and—in addition—their population increased the fastest dining the transition.

Consumption and Transition

The precondition for economic virtue, according to Plato, is the establishment of restrictions on individual consumption. Plato defines restraint by drawing an analogy to 'rhythm' and 'harmony' (*Timaeus* 47e). Rhythm and harmony should mark the limits of individual consumption, bringing order to our 'irregular and graceless ways'. Plato proposes a simple vegetarian diet due to its social and healthy good points (*Republic* II 372abcd). This is a universal diet, equally useful both during the period of abundance-welfare, and during the Mountain period or the first period after the deluge. This is the consumption of a man who is aware of the consequences resulting from different diets. The practice of a Platonic diet supports courage and wisdom in the individual. In the social dimension this diet does not demand too much of the state's land; does not subordinate citizens to foreigners; and does not provoke: aggression, congestion, turmoil, and noise. On the contrary, this diet allows for the autonomy of both the individual and the state. Man ceases being a 'duck' and can return to his uncorrupted nature. The limited consumption results in a limited, but autonomous, economy. In the pursuit of a growing economy the Lowlands may lose its autonomy. Plato wants to show harmony between man and his surrounding. Man's lust for abundance, health and fortune, is in fact, a wish full of harmony co-existence with the World. Experience of the abundance-welfare is a true man's acceptation of himself. Submission to the Lowland *topos* and acceptation of limitations mean liberation and emancipation of these limitations. These are the social rhythm of economic activities and the individual harmony of the good life. Even in Plato's Athens it is possible to enjoy such a life. The success of a such way of life is recounted by a wise man from Piraeus—Cephalus, who is an owner of a middle estate (*Republic* I 331ab).

Plato's general thesis is: the most desirable economic state of society is a balance between what nature has to offer and human needs, therefore we must come back to the macroeconomic level to investigate further the conditions for such a balance. The economy, in which individuals consume in a manner similar to the gather's diet, must be autarky resting on recognisable and renewable resources. Plato comes to a conclusion that there is a stable number of people who can live in the Lowlands without breaking this balance. Plato respects nature's capacities. We should not replace the fertility of nature with scarcity and congestion. Nature marks the borders to the division of labour and the specialisation of labour. The breaking of these borders creates an avalanche of the most unfavourable social phenomena. On the surface, in the transition, the welfare increases; there are more commodities, more wealth, and more satisfaction. However there is a growth in population as well. The new social phenomena's are: crowds and diseases. Starting with and concentrating in the wealthy, society falls into the trap of spiralling needs. A new need means anew profession, the new profession adds to society a new man, and this new man has to eat. Once stimulated, human needs grow and grow. This infinite chain of human needs may be satisfied only by war and the deluge.

Plato's point is that we should not forget the behaviour and lifestyle of the Mountain period in the Lowland period and enjoy, with restraint, things given by nature. Plato's argument is sophisticated; he takes differentiation of consumption into account. According to him, in the town there will be enough luxury goods, though there will be not enough food for the people who produced and deal in these luxury goods, and for the 'guardians'. The food and a lack of the main resources—land—are the main barriers of the demographic growth. So, the true wealth of the *polis* is land and water, and then people. The wealth of nations rests in a society having modest requirements and being content with its own resources.

Plenty Supports Transition

So far we have investigated the transition of the economy from abundance to scarcity. Plato does not stop at this point; he is more interested in the battle with plenty in itself. The main weapon, employed by him in this battle, becomes the measure. In Plato's dialogue *Symposium,* Socrates tells a story, told him by a priestess Diotima, about Abundance [Resource], the son of Restraint [Craft], Abundance took part in a banquet on the occasion of Aphrodite's birthday. He got drunk with the ambrosia and went to sleep. His lamentable situation was not wasted by begging Poverty [Need] and she, taking advantage of the situation, became pregnant with Eros [Love]. Being a son of such parents, Eros is an eternal 'poor fellow', tossed between a wise and rich father, and poor and uneconomical mother (*Symposium* 20 ID).[5] The moral of the story is clear: only the restraint—a measured life—provides the protection from poverty and excess which are close friends. Abundance should not get drunk with the ambrosia; it must be vigilant in order to avoid a transition to the overabundance. The overabundance breeds devastating insufficiency.

Plato thinks about the measure as a manager of virtue.[6] The task of philosophy is to investigate and to show a proper use of the measure. According to Plato, the measure is not only a norm, or logical criterion, or a sort of yardstick in order to define the states of plenty or scarcity. Platonic measure is in itself the true abundance, and everything beyond this measure is overabundance. First of all, he considers it as the border; outside of which there is a an area of danger. So, the economic part of the Platonic measure is not only a kind of an arithmetic mean between a number of people and quantity of products, in fact it is the safe area for human economic activities. Plato is not afraid of true scarcity and the period after the deluge. It is easy to deal with scarcity and it is easy to get some abundance, even if it takes generations. The Mountain period employs only the physical power of man, thus increasing output takes time. However, their efforts do not create any threats for their personality due to a lack of overabundance. What we have to be afraid of is the overabundance.

Written in this way, Plato expresses a fear of overabundance common in all agrarian cultures. This fear had prompted the Normans to bury their hoards of silver and gold, and customs of surfeit gorging and 'aggressive generosity' among the people of the Middle Ages. It would be visible even in mercantilist fear of surplus that does not find either a domestic or export market. The fear of plenty has organised a hierarchy of tribal and agrarian community values. The recommended activity was to give, not to take. Melville J. Herscovits named this economy the 'prestige economy'. This was a system in which gain comes through expenditure rather than through saving, and the highest position is reserved for those who most conspicuously spend the contributions of the less privileged [Guriewicz, 1976, pp. 220–44, Herscovits, 1955, p. 164].

Philosophy of Economic Space

Compared with the macrocosm, a human civilisation is situated in the initial stage. The chaos is produced by the clashing human passions taking devious paths between overabundance and scarcity. In general the macrocosm has overcome the general transition. However there are still possibilities for the local transitions. On Earth there is a particular place, namely the Lowland. The Lowland develops from disaster to disaster caused by deluges. Between disasters there are—according to Plato—three stages of economy marked by a supply of the *topos:* scarcity, abundance, and overabundance. From these three stages the most beneficial for man is the shorter period of the abundance. People in their history learned to use land fertility in order to overcome scarcity. Then they created a civilisation offering wealth, which was riot secure. Their wealth is a liability and they must pay a high price for it.

The price of this wealth depends on the place occupied by the people during the transition. Nearer the final catastrophe of the deluge the price is higher. However even in the very beginning of the transition, there is always the price of man's life. During the transition, man, seduced by verisimilitudes, lives a life of misery. As long as people do not learn how to avoid scarcity and overabundance, they can not enjoy abundance.

The macrocosm is a self-sufficient entity. Plato understands this self-sufficiency in a peculiar way. He writes in *Timaeus* that for the macrocosm to feed itself has to destroy itself; '... there was nothing which went from him or came into him, for there was nothing beside him. Of design he was created thus—his own waste providing his own food, and all that he did or suffered taking place in and by himself' (*Timaeus* 33cd). The macrocosm destroys one of its parts if within this particular part there appears a lack or an excess of the elements. In a similar way Plato thinks about the Lowland. The Lowland is self-sufficient when it is populated by the proper number of people in relation to its resources. Under [these] conditions people consume their natural part of the *topos,* and while there is no breaking other people's *topos,* there is no poverty. When the Lowlands borders becomes disturbed, the process of destruction begins. The Lowland starts to eat itself. In the very beginning there is not enough land and water. According to their physical and social possibilities, people take the *topos* away from others, or they are deprived of their *topos.* The area of poverty becomes wider and wider. The transition is the people's self-destruction.

Plato claims the human *topos* exists by its fertility. On the economic level the fertility is a class of resources. On the human value level the fertility is a class consisting of health and safety. So the human *topos* is a hotbed of human values, its space is marked by these values. Speaking Einstein's language, these values produce the *topos* space and bend it back. If some parts of the values are gone, the space of *topos* will lose some of its energy and it starts to diminish. The Lowland fertility supplies the pragmatic (biological and economic) part of the human *topos*. The economy in itself is not enough for the stability of the human *topos*. To prevent the self-destruction of the *topos* we have to try and establish a harmony between the *Topos* and people by filling the *topos* with human values. It means the reconciliation between the fertility of nature and human behaviour. History tought that people might replace the mythical order of things with the order of commercial values. This is due to the lack of serious reflection, and due to their society popularising bad patterns of behaviours by various means: myths, poetry, music, theatre. It is due too to the Lowland features: its soft limits, and flexibility. Plato states that there was about nine thousand years between the Atlantis deluge and his contemporary time. Nine was a magic Pythagorean number and plausibly Plato wants to suggest that the end of the circle is near and there is a possibility of a similar catastrophe in Athens, and we may read his theory as the writing on the wall to Athenians.

According to Plato, people as a society enjoy some freedom of manoeuvre both in time (these 9000 years!) and in the space. Plato understood human history in being non-linear; he stresses this feature when he considers different forms of government. The history of macrocosm teach us that the establishing of balance is possible, and the period of chaos is a period of the transition, which means it may come to an end. There are three positive solutions possible: 1) evolutionary, leave the overabundance and go towards the abundance; 2) once to establish and then to keep with the abundance; and 3) to try to stay between scarcity and abundance. In the *Republic* Plato chooses the last solution to propose to all of the population—the Mountain diet plus the Lowland's knowledge. In the *Laws* he considers the second variant as the holding of a balance between population and resources. Why he does not choose the easiest of these variants and even he does not discuss them? There is not a satisfactory answer. We can interprets the solution presented in the *Laws* as leading towards the *Republic* solution and say, follow Popper, that this was the totalitarian project. However we know from his letter (the *Letter* vii) Plato was an adviser to the Syracuse tyrant, and he recommended him to be a master of his passions. It seems he had tested this evolutionary solution and this test came off not very well for him. The tyrant used his authority for his own aims. Maybe this personal experiences could explain Plato's position.

Changes in the Lowland *topos* are elementally, meaning, in general, they do not repeat and are directed in different ways. The economy is wasteful and people competed aggressively for resources. Popper said that Plato first of all wanted to stop any change. However, it seems that Plato's goal is to give a new quality to change. He wants to guide social energy in order to reconcile the economic space with the mythical space. The new economic *topos* should be safe and create a base for the further self-improvement of man. So far, neither the Mountain nor the Lowland have created such a base. The Mountain people have no time to think about higher values. The Lowland people have no time too, because of their commercial activities left no time for other activities. On the one hand the Mountain isolation prevents the establishing of a society contrary to man's needs. Man has a lot of wants, and thus requires, in order to supply them, institutions of society, namely division of labour and specialisation (*Republic* II 369bc). On the other hand, society, which is so desirable to man's development, becomes a source of corruption, and then destruction. So Plato formulates his task as to not lose the *topos of* society and to preserve the safety of the

Mountain people. His society has to support the emancipation of man. Man's emancipation depends—first and foremost—on his independence from hitherto existing economic values and behaviours, which made commercial achievements a main goal of life. However, Plato does not want to impose restrictions on the economy and to limit it to a minimum. This area of human life has to become not exactly invisible, but it has to be deprived of ambiguity, which is created by commercialism. Man needs the society in which there is the division of labour. At a minimum he needs: rulers, guardians, peasants, and artisans. The people employed in this new economy cannot develop according to the 'World soul'. We know the main rules: autarchy given by the state and the good work of the individual. Plato specifies parts of the new economy and numbers: gathering, the 'noble' agriculture, handicraft, and other occupations which do not breed commercial temptations (*Laws* 743d). He wants the development of agriculture and the crafts, which adjusted to the *topos* resources, which will give support to the values of beauty, courage and wisdom. Building a new niche for people does not mean a negation of the economy; just the opposite, the new economy has to be a contrivance of the transition.

The New Economy: A Contrivance of Transition

In order to achieve the first stage of morality, Plato requires a healthy economy. The new economy should overcome difficulties resulting from the imbalances between the changing population, quantity of needed products and the stable Lowland fertility. In this connection he defines what is an economic success, and describes the transition in order to give a recipe to secure the economic Lowland *topos*.

Plato considers the growth of the economy caused by the division of labour and its specialisation which, in turn, causes a need to employ more people. This process develops spontaneously, and meets with no obstacles. In this way the continuously developing economy pulls up the growth of population. Because of the fact that the resources of land are stable, the growth in population means that the resources per capita diminishes. The state has to seek new resources. All of the Earth lowlands being populated, war remains as the only way to gain more land. War needs the army and the cost of holding the army becomes an additional burden, which increases the exhaustion of resources. Rarer and rarer resources, and competition (congestion) both create economic differences, and the society starts to split into rich and poor states. The transition means firstly—in a pragmatic order—wasteful economy, ruination of the *topos*, and destruction of man, and secondly—in the order of ideas—the unreasonable resistance of both man and society against the perfectibility of the macrocosm. God takes care of the human world during the Mountain period of scarcity and the first period of the true abundance. In the transition he leaves this world to its fate (*Statesman* 268c 274c). So far man and society do not learn to imitate their successful ancestors.

Economic success lies in the prevention of the transition, in other words, of reconstructing the previous state of the economy and environment. This is a closed economy limited by natural fertility. On the supply side nature (land and water) gives us the means of consumption, and on the demand side nature needs to have its natural fertility respected. The lack maintaining this balance brings on the transition, with all its problems.

In developing an anti-transition social programme, Plato draws a conclusion from the history of Athens and Atlantis. The population must be prudent, even in the easy period of the Mountain. Plato is leery of the favourable initial conditions of the fertility of the land (good configuration of the ground, plenty of water) and sees it as a mixed blessing. If the Lowland has too many advantages: fertile land, an easy access to the sea, plain lowland; the people will not develop good manners and social behaviours. Of the three initial conditions, Plato feels that only fertile land is necessarily good, however, even here he offers the stipulation that some parts of the land should be mountainous and unqualified for cultivation. These hindrances can result in a delay in the onset of the transition as they can give time for the people to reflect on the social goals to wish to achieve. Excesses of crops over needs, and nearness to the sea, created the danger of the development of wholesale trade and all that such trade initiates: the rise of commercial values, which as Athenian states (*Laws* IV 704d–705b) 'nothing is a more serious impediment to the development of noble and righteous character in society'.

Plato pays much more attention to the effect this has on man. In this regard he offers two propositions: it is impossible to establish the true welfare of society without the transformation of the human personality; and limiting the consumption of man is the best mechanism for preventing the transition. Plato's propositions have generated considerable reaction over the years. Is this a naive solution due to its unrealistic and utopian features? In our own time this might seem so. If one considers the vast sums of money spent on diets and weight lose products in the wealthy countries today we might conclude that limiting consumption is a utopian suggestion. However, considering the postulates formulated during other periods of the transition, especially in the Enlightenment period, it does not fall outside of the realm of possibility.

In an agrarian economy man is often seen as a consumer in a privileged position. In fact he has two privileges: first—he does not have to worry about food; and second—he receives this food almost for nothing. And it will be this way always, if only he shows restraint in digestion and in propagation. In addition to preserving this style of life, such a diet gives a promise of a long and healthy life. What more can man ask for? The only possible rational position is to accept this pattern of behaviour. In the cultures where feudal institutions persist longer, patterns of behaviours were dominated by this way of thinking.

Conclusions

After over two thousand years, it is clear that Plato's message still has relevance. From Plato's perspective, we are creating a society of small Tantaluses; we steal the ambrosia and the nectar of Gods and we deceive ourselves into believing that we can avoid punishment. We remain in our virtual world to try and touch the mirage of wealth but never to taste it. His analysis is based on two characters from Greek mythology: Tantalus and Sisyphus. Human history is seen as the history of endless learning and practices. With great effort people came together and helped in the period of scarcity. But, in conquering scarcity they created the bigger burden of insatiability, and eventually are killed by it in the future.

This interpretation of Plato's economic theory unexpectedly shows the importance of his economic thinking: firstly—for his philosophy and psychology; and secondly—for us, Plato appears as an Ancient Malthusian. Historians of economics have relegated Plato to secondary role in the history of economic thought. They have for the most part avoided his descriptions of Atlantis or Old Athens and instead only considered his conception of the ideal state in the *Republic* and the *Laws*. What the majority of commentators have taken for picturesque additions or non-important digressions, are in fact, a coherent entity. Plato takes the economy seriously and says that a lot depends on this sphere of human life. In the economic realm he starts his investigations, here also is situated the main cause of mankind's failures, and finally here he finds the confirmation of his recommendations. At last, in the majority of his statements on economy, especially in the *Republic,* the *Laws,* and the *Critias,* are based on an economic argument and perspective, which we can consider an economic theory. He creates his own economic nomenclature in which such the notions as: *topos;* fertility; abundance; over-abundance; scarcity; density; congestion; and environment; becomes the basic points of reference. Like all relevant economic theory, Plato's is shaped by its close relationship with his contemporary economic life. His economic theory is an economic and demographic warning to Athens.

Plato's economic thinking is sophisticated in its economic methodology as well as in its theory. In his methodology he is not a reductionist. His analysis of society are based on ideal models of the Mountain and Lowland (*Critias, Timaeus, Laws);* and two models of ideal states (*Republic, Laws);* and two models known as the 'City of Pigs' and the 'Luxurious City' (*Republic).* These models cover all the possible economic situations on macro and microeconomic levels. His theoretical arguments are verified or confirmed by means of the historical examples of Atlantis and Old Athens. In writing about the exhaustion of land and water resources, he is describing his contemporary environment. In his analysis of consumption he differentiates between the differing needs of particular social groups and professions.

His economics spread out between two macroeconomic poles: the Mountain, where there conditions of scarcity do not allowed for the establishment of society; and the Lowland, where eventually over-abundance brings about the society's downfall. We can overcome the state of scarcity, yet we are not capable of overcoming the state of surplus,—this is his main conclusion. It is interesting to note that Plato does not touch—by the traditional means—the subject of good crops or bad crops, in particular he refuses to explain the fertility of agriculture via disasters caused by the gods. The social context of the transition, and the resulting patterns of economic behaviours, are the culprit and not ill fortune. Neither nature nor man possesses automatic mechanisms that put limits and control the pursuit of wealth pursuit.

The general opinion that Plato is only interested in consumption is not quite adequate. He is interested in production. He analyses the Earth and land as the basic resources of production. In his economics, the Earth, written with a capital 'E', and land, written with a small 'l', gives space and produce goods. These conditions offered by the Mountain and the Lowlands give the *topos,* the main notion of Plato's economics. To establish the interrelation between space and economic practices is the great economic achievement of Plato. From this point of view we can compare Plato with Adam Smith. Smith showed the relationship between the division of labour and the quantity of production and the size of market. Smith's *topos* was expansive and limited just by the size of market. Plato shows the *topos* as a main aspect of the economy and he emphases its tendencies to bend and to limit the economic space. These tendencies resulted from the relation that connects the expansive *topos* of luxury goods with the limited space offered by agricultural products: the stable production of food. Therefore it is different from Smith's analysis of the division of labour, trade and handcraft. Plato worries that the results of the division of labour will lead to the increased consumption of food. In his opinion, in a developed Lowland civilisation, there is no danger of scarcity of luxury goods, however for this civilisation there is a limit on the production of food. Thus more luxury goods means more people which strains the lands capacity to produce food.

Although Plato is not read now by economists, the importance of Plato's economic ideas are testified by their vitality in the history of economic thought. The most obvious examples are the ideas of Malthus,[7] Veblen and Hirsch, the theory of economic crisis as well as economic ecology. His conclusion concerning the division of labour is Malthusian pessimistic; agriculture cannot cope with the elemental development of society. Apart from Malthus we may draw one more parallel, even closer to our times, between Plato's and both Veblen's and Hirsch's understandings of the economic competition and space—density and congestion.

During and at the turn of the nineteenth Century, Plato was seen as a great economic utopian (Gide and Rist, 1948, p. 213). The rigours of the ideal state, restrictions on propagation and consumption and experiences of fascism, Nazism, Stalinism, caused many in the 20th century to interpret Plato's ideas as an approval of totalitarism. Popper detected fascism and communism, Schumpeter wrote about fascism (Schumpeter, 1982, p. 55), and Galbraith mentioned Plato's 'partially inclination to communism' (Galbraith, 1987, p. 17), even a very influential philosophical commentator, Voeglin, was fascinated by Plato's vision of order. For all of them the starting point was Plato's thinking about the ideal state and the ideal social order. Popper was of the opinion that Plato has formulated a law of 'general degeneration' and therefore he considered that only a totalitarian state in which the main rule will be no change could be a good state. The economic analysis of the transition shows, according to Plato, only the state which can use its economic space intelligently can prevent the transition and to manage without corruption.

Looking for the rules of Plato's social order, a political philosopher, Eric Voeglin, finds the 'poleogonic construction', 'closely resembling the Hesiodan theogony' however its subject is the *polis,* not the gods (Voeglin, 1957, p. 96). This construction consisted of four different orders: 'the primitive *polis,* the luxurious *polis,* the purified *polis,* and the philosopher *polis'* (Ibid., pp. 97–8). According to him 'the transition from primitive to the luxurious *polis* was motivated by the human type in the person of Glaukon, whose endowments are [too] rich to find fulfilment in the simple life' (Ibid., p. 100). So he concluded that: 'The criteria of right order of human existence can be found nowhere but in the soul of the philosopher' (Ibid., p. 102). We can find the rules only in a philosopher soul, so we will not come across any other connection among these orders, for example between the *topos* and economic activities. Therefore, he explains, the meaning of the deluges in Plato's theory as a construction like 'deus ex machina'. He stated that Plato, in his examples of old Athens and Atlantis, was trying to put together the real political order and the mythical order: 'The myth of prehistoric aeon of Athens and Atlantis has the same relation to the problem of political order in history as the myth of the precosmic struggle between Nous and Ananke' (Ibid., p. 206). In my interpretation Plato thinks that human history works according to the cosmological rules described by him in the *Timaeus.* The peaceful coexistence between people and their *topos* results in the Lowlands welfare and a lack of poverty of the Mountain. The wars and the violation of balance of nature result in the deluge or other kind of catastrophe, which is the *topos* reaction on 'blows' (*Timaeus* 53a). Such is the nature of the *topos* that it 'returns the blows with the same intensity' (*Timaeus* 53a, Siwek's trans. Timajos, Kritias, 1986). We cannot improve our welfare by violating our environment because it is a violation of the cosmic rules. Thus Plato connects both the mythical and human order. Watching our environment we can find the instructions sent by the macrocosm. Our historical and empirical investigations can teach us to practice the economic virtue. Plato's virtue is not only inside the philosopher soul, it is also outside.

Historians of economic thought James Bonar, Henry William Spiegel and Eric Roll have defended Plato against these labels. Eric Roll has seen, in the *Laws* and the *Republic,* 'spiritual and romantic revolt' against commercialisation (Roll, 1987, p. 27), and he emphasised Plato's discovery of the connection between, on the one hand, the division of labour, and on the other—the city, commercialisation, and corruption (Roll, 1987, p. 27–31). I think Roll was right, it was a revolt against commercialisation, though it is legitimate to add to these adjectives another one: 'economic'. From the perspective of Plato's economics we can say that he gives a careful report of two different cultures: agrarian and commercial. His goal was to defend the values of the agrarian culture. However he did it not only by means of spiritual and romantic inspection but also used economic arguments. It is characteristic of Plato's writings that during his discussion about the ideal models or historical examples of Atlantis and Old Athens that he never relied on arguments based on high values. On the contrary his argumentation is very simple and strongly connected with everyday economic practice. He showed that the new commercial patterns of behaviour were doomed to unsatiated consumption, and this consumption became an economic and psychological source of individual, social, as well as environmental, disasters.

Was Plato's theory a true one? Did some of the Ancient civilisation decline because of the economic-ecological catastrophe? J. Donald Hughes states that the abuse of the environment was an important factor of the decline of Ancient civilisations (Hughes, 1975). In fact, there is much evidence to support this theory. The last archaeological investigations of Maya's culture provide evidence that an ecological catastrophe (namely the lack of land) was the causes of Maya's decline.[8]

When we [consider] Plato's theory of the agrarian economy, his description of the Lowland civilisation as a sinusoidal curve, in which short periods of order are interlaced with long periods of disorder, his proto-theory of crises, the first lecture on economic ecology as well as his pre-Malthusian relationship to man and nature, it seems we have to revise his place in the history of economics.

References

Baeck, L. (1992), 'Plato's Political Economy: Initiator of a Mediterranean Tradition', Research Papers in Economic Development, Katholiekie Universiteit Leuven.

Baeck, L. (1993), 'Greek Economic Thought: Initiators of a Mediterranean Tradition' in: Price, B., B., (ed.), *Ancient Economic Thought,* Routledge, London and New York, pp. 146–171.

Bonar, James (1967), *Philosophy and Political Economy.* George Allen-Unwin, London-New York.

Galbraith, John Kenneth (1987), *Economics in Perspective. A Critical History,* Houghton Mifflin Company, Boston.

Gide, Charles and Rist, Charles (1948), *A History of Economic Doctrines from the time of the physiocrats to the present day.* George G. Harap Company, London.

Guriewicz, A. (1976), *Kategorie kultury sredniowiecznej,* trans, by Dancygier, J., Panstwowy Instytut Wydawniczy: Warszawa.

Herskovits, Melville Jean (1955), *Cultural Anthropology,* Knoph, New York.

Hirsch, Fred (1995), *Social Limits to Growth,* rev.ed. Routledge, London.

Hollander, Samuel (1995), *The Economics of Thomas Robert Malthus,* University of Toronto Press, Toronto.

Hughes, Johnson D. (1975), *Ecology in Ancient Civilizations,* Albuquerque, NM, University of New Mexico Press.

MacIntyre, Alastair (1996), *Dziedzictwo cnoty. Studium z teorii moralnosci [After Virtue. A Study in Moral Theory],* Wydawnictwo Naukowe PWN, Warszawa.

Malthus, Thomas Robert (1960), *On Population,* ed. and introduction Himmelfarb, G., Random House, Inc., Modern Library, New York.

Landreth, Harry and Colander, David C. (1998), *Historia mysli ekonomicznej* [History of Economic Thought], Wydawnictwo Naukowe PWN, Warszawa.

Plato (1997), *Republic,* trans. by Davies, J. L., Vaughan, D. J., Wordsworth Classics of World Literature.
Plato (1992), *Republic,* translated by G. M. A. Grube, Hackett Publishing Company, Indianapolis.
Plato (1989), *The Collected Dialogues of Plato,* edited by Edith Hamilton and Huntington Cairns, Princeton University Press, Princeton.
Platon (1987), *Listy* [Letters], trans. by Maykowska, M., revis. by Pekcinska, M., Panstwowe Wydawnictwo Naukowe, Warszawa.
Platon (1986), *Timajos, Kritias,* trans. by Siwek, P., Panstwowe Wydawnictwo Naukowe, Warszawa.
Platon (1982), *Uczta* [Symposium]. Eutyfron. Obrona Sokratesa. Kriton. Fedon., trans. by Witwicki, W., Panstwowe Wydawnictwo Naukowe Warszawa.
Platon (1960), *Prawa* [Laws], trans. by Maykowska, M., Panstwowe Wydawnictwo Naukowe Warszawa.
Platon (1958), *Gorgiasz* [Gorgias], trans. by Witwicki, W., Panstwowe Wydawnictwo Naukowe Warszawa.
Platon (1958), *Panstwo* [Republic], trans. by Witwicki, W., Panstwowe Wydawnictwo Naukowe Warszawa.
Popper, Karl R. (1993), *Spoleczenstwo otwarte i jego wrogowie* [The Open Society and Its Enemies, vol. i, Urok Platona [The Spell of Plato], Wydawnictwo Naukowe PWN, Warszawa.
Roll, Eric (1987), *A History of Economic Thought,* Faber and Faber, London-Boston.
Schefold, B. (1997), 'Aristotle and Pre-Aristotelian Greek economic thought,' in: B. B. Price (ed.), *Ancient Economic Thought,* Routledge, London—New York.
Schumpeter, Joseph A. (1982), *History of Economic Analysis,* Allen-Unwin, London.
Skladankowa, M. (1989), *Mitologia Iranu* [Mythology of Iran], Wiedza Powszechna, Warszawa.
Smith, Adam (1899), *An Inquiry into the Nature and Causes of the Wealth of Nations,* George Bell and Sons, London.
Spiegel, Henry W. (1991), *The Growth of Economic Thought,* Duke University Press, Durham-London.
Veblen, Thorstein (1971), *Teoria klasy prozniaczej* [Theory of Leisure Class], Panstwowe Wydawnictwo Naukowe, Warszawa.
Voegelin, E. (1957), *Plato and Aristotle,* vol. viii of his *Order and History,* Louisiana State University Press, Baton Rouge.
Wolanski, N. (1999), *Zabijcza dieta—Majowie* [The killer diet—Majas, 'Wprost' August 15].

Notes

1. See L. Baeck's two articles: 'Plato's Political Economy. Initiator of a Mediterranean tradition' (1992) and 'The Mediterranean tradition in economic thought' (1993).
2. These deluges are often sent by the gods as punishment for living contrary to the dictates of the gods.
3. There is some possibility of a cosmic disaster even in the Mountains. Plato in the *Timaeus* describes it. *Critias* relates a story told by Solon: 'Now this has the form of myth, but really signifies a declination of the bodies moving in the heavens around the earth, and a great conflagration of things upon the earth, which recurs after long intervals; at such times those who live upon the mountains and in dry and lofty places are more liable to destruction than those who dwell by rivers or on the seashore' (Timaeus 22c). However this is only once when Plato mentions a possibility of such a disaster. In *Republic, Critias, Timaeus,* and *Laws* he writes—as Socrates—about the deluges, and these deluges becomes his object of interest, for two reasons: Athens was an example of the Lowland civilisations; and deluges—contrary to this cosmic-mountain disaster—happen more often.
4. See Skladankowa, M., Mitologia Iranu [Mythology of Iran], Warszawa 1989, pp. 73–109.
5. Bracketed terms are from *Plato The Collected Dialogues*.
6. In this way Alasdair MacIntyre has shown that 'measure' or its later equivalent 'restraint', as a manager of virtue, see his book *After Virtue. A Study in Moral Theory* (1981).
7. In Samuel Hollander's extensive book *The Economics of Thomas Robert Malthus* (University of Toronto Press 1997) there is no mention concerning Plato's inspiration. Contrary to the present, in Malthus' times Plato was widely read, and there is a possibility of such connection.
8. See Wolanski, N., Zabijcza dieta—Majowie [The killer diet—Mayas], 'Wprost' 15.08.1999.

Unit IV

Visual Arts and Business

> *"Art doesn't give rise to anything in us that isn't already there. It simply stirs our curious consciousness and sparks a fire that illuminates who we have always wanted to be."*
>
> —Kamand Kojouri

Images abound everywhere, at the touch of a screen, on billboards, and within workspaces. It follows that the astute businessperson develops competency in visual arts to gain an advantage in a competitive global environment. Visual arts frame a business with corporate logos, branding, and marketing, yet they contribute much more to the success of an organization. Arts influence structure, productivity, creativity, and problem-solving. Top companies, such as Target, Fidelity, and H&R Block, recognize the importance of the relationship between art and business.[1] In short, all organizations utilize the arts within their businesses.[2]

Aesthetics, the philosophical study of the arts and beauty, have been debated for centuries, from the time of Plato until the present.[3] Visual arts embrace the mundane, yet at the same time they provide escape from the everyday. Through aesthetic evaluation an ordinary object becomes extraordinary: An ancient water jug from the Byzantine period, for example, was functional while claiming beauty in its craftsmanship. Further, arts provide insight into cultures, the nature of work, and the business of life throughout history. Art demonstrates the realities and fantasies of life through painting, sculpture, textiles, photography, and the like. As a result, art fuels business as well as representing what influences business in an ever-changing economy.

Diverse populations, broadening consumer bases, and increased competition all support the call for aesthetic analysis in business and the ability to discern aesthetic quality.

The 21st century is an age of visualization via technology that provides unprecedented access to pictures, figures, and other visual representations of the world.[4] Technological accessibility creates a demand for aesthetically pleasing products, environments, recreation, and entertainment.[5] This trend has influenced the way that people do business. The old adage, "A picture is worth a thousand words," is highly relevant today. The importance of visual literacy via the arts in the business world is fourfold: The arts contribute to the identity of organizations; the arts contribute to organizational structure; the arts contribute to the success of organizations and the well-being of their employees; and the business of art itself has grown tremendously in the last few decades.

The most obvious application of the arts in a business world is found by looking within the walls of an organization. The choice of paint, the artwork on the walls, and the layout communicate the climate of an organization, its formality, and the transparency of the workplace, and correspond to the philosophy of the business itself. Art reinforces company values and beliefs through visual representations. A company's image needs to visually make a statement that sets it apart from its competitors.[6] The visual aspect of corporate media and material should be distinct in order to influence successful branding and marketing. Visual literacy shapes marketing strategies as well as product design, but it does not stop there. A consistency between product and environment is created through organizational visual arts.[7] Art tells the story of a business in many capacities.[8]

Art also provides a collective identity for employers and employees within an organization.[9] Studies have shown that the impact of visual arts in the workplace affects the well-being and mental health of employees. Lower levels of employee stress, a sense of belonging, feelings of ownership and commitment are impacted by visual images in businesses, at both conscious and subconscious levels.[10] Further, problem-solving skills developed through arts analysis contribute to achievement, social and emotional development, and equity in the workplace.[11] Art sparks dialogue between employees, thus creating a template for teamwork and cooperation. Competency in the arts leads to innovative thinking that can provide new directions for businesses.[12] An understanding of art unlocks creative potential within people.[13]

That potential is essential for business leaders. The ability to analyze art opens doors to other aspects of business success when the theory is applied to business models. Skills that are developed through arts analysis keep business leaders ahead of the competition while staying focused on target markets.[14] Participation with arts programs have helped business leaders shape new courses, discover unique markets, and design innovative programs that improve business at all levels by fostering the ability to draw ideas from a variety of sources, resulting in cohesion and correspondence in their creative work.[15] Arts analysis cultivates the ability to discern quality based on visual judgments.[16]

Successful artists are entrepreneurial role models for business leaders. They have earned their success in the face of intense competition, poor working conditions, and repeated rejection. Because they have worked deliberately toward success, it has eventually become theirs, beginning with ideas that need to be executed, pitched, and sold.[17] Leonardo DaVinci is an excellent example of business success—an artist, architect, musician, inventor, engineer, sculptor, mathematician, and painter who overcame tremendous obstacles before his contributions were recognized. He also continually broadened his knowledge base and abilities throughout his career.[18] Artists push ideas through complex systems to make them work.

In an era of government cutbacks, access to art and programs for artists often fall on the generosity of businesses. Corporate support of the arts provides a bridge between business and the community, and helps fill the gap between the arts and the public.[19] In addition, masterpieces of art provide portfolio diversification for investment.

Of course, business leaders do not need to become experts in art or art history; rather, they can draw from a general set of skills to analyze art, and create the mindset of an artist with some basic concepts. Art is about something in a space used for human purpose, in versions of ordinary objects or in the extraordinary. It is a channel that provides form to emotions and sensory stimulation. It is a process of perception that refreshes vision and expands our worldview. On a basic level, art can be understood as meaning through loose thematic association:[20]

1. **The sacred realm:** Our relationship to the sacred; used to honor, envision, and communicate sacred concepts.
2. **Politics and social order:** Social order and social structure; leadership; domination and oppression.
3. **Stories and histories:** Deeds of the human, animal, and superhuman.
4. **Looking outward:** Current social order of the everyday.
5. **Looking inward:** Shared human experiences.
6. **Invention and fantasy:** Imaginary worlds.
7. **The natural world:** The relationships of people with nature.
8. **Art as art:** Simply something to look at.

Themes provide a framework for artistic analysis and interpretation. This is not a random or arbitrary process. All aesthetics are activities in rational reflection; therefore, they draw evidence from a variety of sources for solid grounding, based on solid judgment. This research provides leverage for highly descriptive interpretation, focused on the artwork, not the interpreter.[21] It is a schematic process where one concept builds upon another. Responsible interpretation looks at the art in its best light, a skill that clearly transfers to employer/employee relations. The process of interpretation is highly personal and draws on other schools of humanity, such as history and philosophy. The background of the interpreter influences the Interpretation and subjects the artwork to diverse analyses. It is important to note that interpretation is not universal.

Some basic concepts are associated with arts analysis and interpretation:[22]

1. **Line:** A path traced by a moving path, used symbolically in art (directional, implied, and contour lines).
2. **Contours:** Boundaries we perceive of three-dimensional forms.
3. **Shape:** A two-dimensional form that occupies an *area* with identifiable boundaries. They may be

created by lines, a shift in texture, or a shift in color.

4. **Geometric shapes and masses:** Approximate the regular shapes and volumes of geography (e.g., square, pyramid, triangle).
5. **Organic shapes and masses:** Irregular and evoke the living forms of nature.
6. **A figure:** The shape we detach and focus on.
7. **The** ground: The surrounding visual information the figure stands out from, the background.
8. **Mass:** A three-dimensional form that occupies a *volume* of space (e.g., clay, architecture).
9. **Light and** shadow: Contain values of shades of dark and light.
10. **Color theory** (from Sir Isaac Newton): A ray of sunlight is broken up or refracted into different colors, which are arranged in order of the colors of the rainbow; color properties: hue (name of color), value (lightness or darkness of a color), and intensity (relative purity of color).
11. **Palette:** Range of pigments selected by artist.
12. **Warm colors**
13. **Cool colors**
14. **Monochromatic harmonies:** Variations on the same hue.
15. **Complementary harmonies:** Involve colors directly opposite each other on the color wheel.
16. **Analogous harmonies**: Combine colors adjacent to one another on the color wheel.
17. **Triadic harmonies:** Any three colors equidistant from each other on the color wheel.
18. **Simultaneous contrast**: Where complementary colors appear more intense as they appear side by side.
19. **Visual texture:** Eyes associate texture with artwork.
20. **Pattern:** Any decorative, repetitive motif or design.
21. **Vanishing point:** Parallel lines receding into distance that seem to converge until they meet at a point on the horizon where they disappear.
22. **Kinetic** art**:** Art that moves.
23. **Symmetrical balance:** The implied center of gravity is the vertical axis, an imaginary line drawn down the center of the composition.
24. **Asymmetrical balance:** Two sides that do not match.
25. **Mandela:** Circle in Sanskrit.

Authors in this unit address the practical application of arts in business as well as an overview of some basic art concepts. First of all, Fischer provides insight into what, exactly, constitutes art. Next, Taylor addresses the importance of the arts sector in global business. The next reading, by Kurt Mayer, transitions to the application of the arts from a management perspective.

Ibbotson and Dars demonstrate that business leaders facing complex challenges can learn creativity through constraints in the arts. Mayer demonstrates how management interaction with the arts can drive a learning environment and provide insight into innovative leadership.

Notes

1. Amenta, M. (2014, November). *The importance of art in business and communication.* https://prezi.com/lm0ggp2peioy/the-importance-of-art-in-business-and-communication/
2. Schiuma, G. (2011). *The value of arts for business.* Cambridge University Press.
3. Films for the Humanities & Sciences—Films Media Group. (2005). Aesthetics [Video]. Philosophy of the arts (Great ideas of philosophy). Films Media Group.
4. McCarthy, K. F., Ondaatje, E. H., Brooks, A., & Szanto, A. (2005). *A portrait of the visual arts: Meeting the challenges of a new era.* RAND Corporation.
5. McCarthy, K. F., Ondaatje, E. H., Brooks, A., & Szanto, A. (2005). *A portrait of the visual arts: Meeting the challenges of a new era.* RAND Corporation.
6. Anderson, M. (2005). The quality instinct: How an eye for art can save your business. *Journal of Business Strategy, 26*(5), 29–32.
7. Smith, R. (2016, October 18). Art in the workplace and how to choose it. *Work Design Magazine.*
8. Alfano, E. (2013, January 23). Does business need the arts to be innovative? Five executives weigh in. *The Huffington Post.*
9. Smith, R. (2016, October 18). Art in the workplace and how to choose it. *Work Design Magazine.*
10. Smith, R. (2016, October 18). Art in the workplace and how to choose it. *Work Design Magazine.*
11. Smith, F. (2009, January 28). *Why arts education is crucial and who's doing it best.* Edutopia. https://www.edutopia.org/arts-music curriculum-child-development
12. Anderson, M. (2005). The quality instinct: How an eye for art can save your business. *Journal of Business Strategy, 26*(5), 29–32.
13. Hendricks, D. (2015, January 12). *Can office artwork influence employee productivity?* Forbes. https://www.forbes.com/sites/drewhendricks/2015/01/12/can-office-artwork-influence-employee-productivity/#468618f01884
14. Amenta, M. (2014, November). *The importance of art in business and communication.* https://prezi.com/lm0ggp2peioy/the-importance-of-art-in-business-and-communication
15. Amenta, M. (2014, November). *The importance of art in business and communication.* https://prezi.com/lm0ggp2peioy/the-importance-of-art-in-business-and-communication
16. Anderson, M. (2005). The quality instinct: How an eye for art can save your business. *Journal of Business Strategy, 26*(5), 29–32.
17. Bacharach, S. (2015, August 7). *Why art is good for entrepreneurs.* Inc.com.
18. Rolling, J. H., Jr. (2016, July). Reinventing the STEAM engine for art + design. *The Journal of the National Art Education Association, 69*(4).
19. Alfano, E. (2013, January 23). Does business need the arts to be innovative? Five executives weigh in. *The Huffington Post.*
20. Getlein, M. (2008). *Living with art.* McGraw-Hill.
21. Barrett, *Principles for interpreting art.*
22. Getlein, M. (2008). *Living with art.* McGraw-Hill.

What Is Art? What Is an Artist? What Is Art History?

Julia C. Fischer

Part I: What is Art?

How would you define art? Who creates art? Why is art created? What purpose does art serve? What art forms and media are there? Take a moment now to think about these questions and come up with a definition of art.

Here's how the dictionary defines art: "The use of skill and imagination in the creation of aesthetic objects, environments, or experiences that can be shared with others." How closely does this match your own definition? Do you agree with this dictionary's definition of art? I see a couple of problems with this definition, the first of which is that art is "the creation of aesthetic objects." That is, art must be aesthetically pleasing. In other words, art must be beautiful. As we will see, however, art is not always beautiful. Furthermore, it is not a requirement for a work of art that it must be shared with others. Think of all the artists in the world who create works merely for their own pleasure and never show them to the world. Because other people do not see their work, does this consequently mean that they have not created works of art? Finally, do you think art necessarily involves skill? Think about the artworks you created in kindergarten and grade school. You may not have been highly skilled or talented, but I am sure your mother considered what you created to be art. Having said this, great art requires tremendous skill.

As you can already deduce, trying to define what art is can be a tricky business. Nevertheless, I think it is possible to come up with a definition that will serve us in this textbook. In its most simple form, art is a basic form of human expression. Art comes in a variety of forms, from music and poetry to dance and literature. In this textbook, we will, however, be focusing on the visual arts, which includes art forms like painting, sculpture, and architecture. What all these forms of art have in common is the fact that art is made by humans, and its purpose is to express or communicate something. From the beginning of humankind, we have wanted and needed to express ourselves in an artistic way. In fact, we could argue that the creation of art is what makes us human. Therefore, by creating and studying art, we can get a better sense of ourselves and the world around us. We have also come to realize that even though we live in the fast-paced, twenty-first century, we are still connected to the peoples of the past through their art and to humanity's constant desire to create.

As an aside, one thing that you should keep in mind is that up until about 150 years ago, no one would have even asked the question, "What is art?" In fact, until the late nineteenth century, art really didn't exist. That is, what we call art today actually served some pragmatic and utilitarian function. For example, we look at ancient Greek vases as very sophisticated works of art. However, in ancient Greek society, vases were not made for artistic reasons. Instead, they served pragmatic and utilitarian purposes like a storage of food and wine or, sometimes, even as a funerary vessel that was placed in a tomb or used as a grave marker in a cemetery placed in a tomb. As such, until the dawn of modern art in the late nineteenth century, works of art always served some kind of pragmatic function, from funerary to political to religious.

Returning to the question of what art is, we will now consider the following questions:

- Does a work of great art have to be by a great artist like Rembrandt or Michelangelo?
- Does it have to be beautiful?
- Must it be pleasurable to look at?
- Should it be made out of traditional materials like paint on canvas or a marble or bronze sculpture?
- Does a work of art have to be representational and naturalistic?
- Does it have to be in a museum?

First up is the question of whether a great work of art must be by one of the great artists. Think about some of the big names in art that everyone has heard of: Michelangelo, Vincent van Gogh, Pablo Picasso. It certainly must be said that it helps when a work of art is by one of these accepted great artists; it results in that work of art having a high status and prestige. A case in point is a small sculpture of Cupid that decorated the lobby of a Fifth Avenue mansion in New York City. For over 90 years, the residents of the mansion paid no attention to this marble statue of Venus' son. But then, in 1996, an art historian specializing in Italian Renaissance art and, specifically, Michelangelo, walked by this mansion and saw this sculpture through the window. Immediately, her jaw dropped for she recognized the sculpture as a lost masterpiece of the great Michelangelo. She immediately called upon other art historians to verify her claims. As the news of a possible Michelangelo spread, the Cupid sculpture was cordoned off, and people started to flock to the mansion to view what was now considered a great work of art. Nothing had inherently changed about this sculpture except that the name "Michelangelo" had been attached to it. Therefore, because it was by a great artist, it must be great, and it must be revered. In short, I am trying to say that it sure does help to have a great artist's name attached to a work of art, both in terms of its prestige and its worth.

Figure 4.1.1 *Student of Rembrandt, The Polish Rider*, 1655.

What if we have the opposite case? That is, what if there was a work of art that was always thought to be by a master but then was proven that it was actually not? This was the case with Rembrandt's *The Polish Rider* from the Frick Collection in New York City (Figure 4.1.1). For hundreds of years, scholars believed that the painting was by the great Dutch Baroque master. But in recent decades, the Rembrandt Research Project (RRP) has tried to determine how many works are actually by the great master himself. The project researchers carefully study Rembrandt's paintings, looking at the use of line and color, brushstrokes (which are like fingerprints or handwriting), and the way anatomical features are handled. After studying these factors in *The Polish Rider,* the RRP determined that the painting was not actually by Rembrandt himself. Instead, the work was mistakenly attributed to the Dutch master when, in fact, it was done by one of his students. As you can imagine, when the name Rembrandt was no longer associated with this painting, its value and merit in the art world diminished as did its status as a great work of art.

Another question about art that must be addressed at the outset is whether art needs to be beautiful. From earlier in the [reading], you already know the answer to this question. That is, art does not necessarily have to be aesthetically pleasing. To be frank, sometimes art is ugly. We might look at these works as failures and say to ourselves, "This artist has no talent and skill." But in actuality, the artist's goal may not have been the attainment of something beautiful in his or her art. Along the same lines, art also does not have to be pleasing to look at. While there are plenty examples of innocuous, lovely, and carefree scenes in art, there are also works that are harder to look at, including scenes of war, death, terror, and insanity.

Like beauty, art does not have to be representational, or naturalistic. In the West, we have traditionally had a preoccupation with art that mimics the natural world. If a work is abstract or non-representational, we might be tempted to say that the artist was not talented or skilled. But like beauty, an artist might not have representationalism as his or her goal. Perhaps the artist is exploring a new way of seeing the world. Or maybe the artist is concentrating more on an idea or a story and is not concerned with creating something illusionistic.

Art also does not have to be made of traditional materials like oil on canvas, fresco, marble sculpture, etc. [...]. This is especially the case for twentieth- and twenty-first-century artists who try to push the boundaries of art by using non-traditional materials like elephant dung, urinals, and dead animals.

Finally, a lot of the art that you will see is in various museums across the world. But by taking this course and reading this textbook, you will become attuned to the fact that art is pervasive. In other words, art is everywhere. From the walls of your dorm room or your parent's house to the downtown of your city to your college campus—art is ubiquitous.

Part II: What is an Artist?

The next question that needs to be addressed in this [reading] is: "What is an artist?" What roles have they served throughout history? First, however, the status of artists must be discussed. Throughout antiquity and the Middle Ages, artists were regarded as craftsmen or artisans, and they did not have a high status in society. (Of course, there are always exceptions to this rule. For example, Greek vase painters and sculptors enjoyed great prestige in ancient Athens.) It was not until the Renaissance that artists began to garner more prestige in society. This was due, in large part, to humanism, a philosophy that praises the accomplishments of individuals. During the fifteenth and sixteenth centuries, artists like Raphael and Albrecht Dürer began to promote the increased status of artists within their paintings. Following the Renaissance, artists continued to be highly regarded in society. We can all agree that artists enjoy this increased prestige today.

But what does an artist do? Take a look around you right now and you'll see the work of artists everywhere, from the chair you are sitting in to the computer you are working on. Artists design practically everything we use in our lives, from the buildings on campus to the pens with which we write. That was a huge definition of what an artist does, so let's break it down a little more in terms of what visual artists do with media like architecture, sculpture, and painting.

- Artists create places and buildings that are designed for human purposes. From the churches in which we worship and our homes to our college campus, throughout the millennia, artists have worked to create the places and buildings all around us.
- Artists also commemorate important events and record history. Flip through your world history book and you'll find paintings and sculptures illustrated inside that represent famous battles and

other historical events. Artists were the ones who commemorated and recorded these events.

- Artists give visual form to the unknown. How do we know what the Last Judgment looks like since this event takes place upon our death? We merely need to look at an artist's representation of this event, such as Michelangelo's famous fresco in the Sistine Chapel.
- Artists also give tangible form to feelings. If you yourself are an artist, you know that, many times, you use your paintbrush or your chisel in order to create something that will express your emotions in a potent way.
- Another thing that artists do is to make us see the world in a different way. They offer us an innovative view on life and its surroundings. Maybe we don't like what we see, which might be the case when you look at non-representational art, but art often requires us to think and go outside of our comfort zone.

Part III: What is Art History?

What is art history and what do art historians do? What is the point of studying works of art? In this course, we will treat works of art as historical documents: they are a reflection of their particular time and their particular place. An art historian tries to understand the meaning of a particular work of art by placing it within its historical and cultural context. Questions that the art historian asks include: Who was the artist? Who was the patron? Who was the audience, and how would it have responded to a work? What are its historical, cultural, political, or religious contexts? Basically, art historians are time travelers, trying to place themselves within a particular historical context, and they try to learn everything they can about a particular work of art.

This probably seems like a daunting task—the understanding of a work of art (and time travel). But there's actually a process that each art historian participates in. The first step in understanding what the work of art is all about is to examine its physical properties. What medium is the work? What technique is used? What is the size? Is there a frame? Ideally, we would only ever see works of art firsthand. Unfortunately, not all of us can hop on a plane to see Michelangelo's Sistine Chapel whenever we feel like it—so, often times, this initial information must be gleaned from books.

Next up, the art historian must perform a visual analysis of the work of art [...]. That is, how would you describe a particular painting, sculpture, mosaic, building, etc. Describe the composition: how are the figures arranged? What is the focal point? What kinds of objects are represented? Is the work symmetrical or asymmetrical? What is the artist's use of light? Describe the depiction of space. Is the artist concerned with replicated nature? What kinds of colors, lines, shapes, and textures are used?

With the initial investigation completed, the art historian then turns his or her attention to the content of the work of art. What is the story that is told? What symbols, or iconography, are utilized to tell this narrative?

Finally, the art historian integrates all of this information within the work of art's cultural context and Examine these historical, religious, societal, and political contexts to see how that informs his or her understanding. Finally, if you want an art historical cheat sheet, think:

SCSC: Subject, Composition, Style, Context.

What is the subject or narrative and how is it told? Describe the composition and how the figures are arranged. Then, discuss the style: is it naturalistic or abstract? Is the style typical for its period and culture? Finally, remember to integrate all of this into an examination of the context of this work of art.

Now, why is art history so fun? Well, art historians are constantly coming up with wacky and crazy theories about what famous works of art mean. Take, for example, Botticelli's *Venus and Mars* (Figure 4.1.2). This painting depicts the Venus, the goddess of love and beauty, and Mars, the god of war, surrounded by satyrs, half-man, half-goat creatures that are the followers of Bacchus, the god of wine. Mars is slumped over asleep while the satyrs mischievously play with his weapons.

After performing a detailed visual analysis, David Bellington recently offered a new interpretation of *Venus and Mars*. Bellingham focused on the satyr at the far right whose hand covers some kind of plant. Previous art historians summarily dismissed this plant as some kind of fruit. In contrast, Bellingham claimed that this plant was the key to understanding what was going on in Botticelli's painting. To that end, Bellingham enlisted the help of botanists, who identified the plant as datura stramonium, or poor man's acid. Basically, this plant is a drug, and the reason why Mars is slumped over is because he has passed out after taking the drug. What do you think of this new interpretation of Botticelli's famous painting?

Figure 4.1.2 Sandro Botticelli, Venus and Mars, 1483.

For Review (list of vocabulary and works)

- What is art?
- Does art have to be by a great artist?
- Does art have to be beautiful?

- Does art have to be pleasing to look at?
- Does art have to be made of traditional materials?
- Is all art in museums?
- What do artists do?
- How has the status of artists changed throughout the millennia?
- What is art history?
- *Student of Rembrandt, The Polish Rider*
- What is David Bellingham's new theory of Botticelli's *Venus and Mars*?
- Rembrandt Research Project (RRP)
- Representational
- Humanism
- Visual Analysis
- Content

Think About This

- What was your definition of art? Do you think that art must be created by humans? What about elephants using their tusks to spread paint around or cats using their paws?

Credits

Fig. 4.1.1: Source: http://commons.wikimedia.org/wiki/File:Rembrandt_-_The_Polish_Rider_-_WGA19251.jpg.
Fig. 4.1.2: Source: http://commons.wikimedia.org/wiki/File:Sandro_Botticelli_-_Venus_and_Mars_-_WGA2776.jpg.

Directing Creativity

The Art and Craft of Creative Leadership

Piers Ibbotson and Lotte Darsø

Piers Ibbotson and Lotte Dars, "Directing Creativity: The Art and Craft of Creative Leadership," *Journal of Management and Organization*, vol. 14, no. 5, pp. 548-551, 558-559.

Leadership, Creativity and the Arts

To state that the world has grown more complex is today self evident, but how to deal with this increased complexity seems less so, in spite of this being one of the major challenges for managers and organisations in the 21st century (Wheatley 1999; 2006; Palus & Horth 2002). Part of the difficulty is the change from industrial products towards more immaterial products such as services, experiences and transformations (Pine & Gilmore 1999). How exactly should managers and leaders lead and direct 'knowledge workers' (Drucker 1993), who have more knowledge about the specific topics than the managers themselves? And how exactly can they assure that knowledge workers are both productive and creative? Obviously, managers have systems and procedures in place for productivity, but how to address the increasing demand for creativity and innovation is still a major predicament.

The questions we want to explore and discuss in this article are thus: How can leaders live up to the demands of creativity and innovation? And more specifically, how can leaders direct creativity?

We will offer our response to the above questions by first examining some of the major leadership challenges today. This is followed by defining and discussing the concept of creativity as a boundary phenomenon and by outlining some of the obstacles and difficulties related to leading 'creatives'. We will then look at theatre directors and explore how they work out the balancing act between driving creativity and staying in control. The intention is to identify and discuss distinct qualities, skills and competencies that can inspire leaders in public and private organisations. In particular, we want to examine and discuss the concept of 'creative constraints' as an alternative to leading by setting targets. We conclude that perceiving creativity as a boundary phenomenon may help leaders understand, balance and direct creativity and our recommendation is for leaders to explore and learn to direct creativity by framing messages in original and inspirational ways and by communicating through attractive creative constraints (Ibbotson 2008). Thus on a more general level, by examining and discussing leadership approaches from the world of theatre essential aspects of creative leadership can be illuminated. The article is based on practical experience, qualitative interviews and literature.

For decades leadership has been one of the most popular topics of management literature (e.g. Micklethwait and Wooldridge 1997), and an analytical divide between leadership and management now seems generally accepted (Kotter 1990). Furthermore the managerial discourse has developed in such a way that leadership is generally seen as 'positive' whereas management is more 'negative', only surpassed by micro management, which is even worse. Nevertheless increasing global competition with changing world-economical balances, stock-holders' demands for economical gains, and threats of outsourcing whole departments is often dealt with traditionally by focusing on logistics, bottom-line and productivity, i.e. management by control. At the same time, however, there is a strong need for creativity and innovation in order to create new sources of income, in particular because 'old' products become obsolete at a much faster rate than earlier (Von Braun 1997). In a study examining how middle and senior managers talked about and understood leadership, Alvesson and Svenigsson (2003) found diverse as well as contradictory understandings of leadership. Contrary to the leaders' own understanding of leadership as visionary and strategic (in line with the general leadership discourse such as Collins and Porras 1994; Barrett 1998; Goleman 2000) they often found themselves occupied with administrative and operative issues, i.e. micro management. Alvesson and Svenigsson conclude that leadership, at least in the particular knowledge intensive organisation they were investigating, appeared much more fragmentary, contradictory and ambiguous than what is claimed in mainstream leadership literature. 'The 'ideological' discursive demands, reinforced and strengthened by corporate talk, collide with the 'practical' organizational demands also reinforced by corporate talk, creating anxiety and frustration' (Alvesson and Svenigsson 2003: 977).

How can leaders cope with such paradoxes? How can leaders tackle ambiguity? One of the new sources of inspiration for organisational change and development comes from the world of arts. On one hand this is, of course, not new at all, since the arts have inspired people for centuries. On the other hand some new trends are emerging leading to new approaches and possibilities of learning from artists and artistic methods (Barry 2008; Nissley 2007; 2002; Adler 2006; Kerr 2006; Darsø 2005; Buswick, Creamer and Pinard 2004; Austin and Devin 2003). A matrix framework of 'artful Creation' (Darsø 2004), based on empirical data from interviews with artists and business people, introduces four approaches for applying arts in business: 1. Artful capabilities and competencies, 2. conceptualising and prototyping, 3. CoLLabs (Collaborative Learning Labs) and practice spheres, and 4. social innovation and product innovation. As illustrated in Figure 4.2.1, the axes represent the degree of ambiguity (vertical axis) and the degree of involvement (horizontal axis). The first two approaches are based on art as a role model, whereas the other two involve artists in interaction with organisations and concerns art-based methods, practice and results.

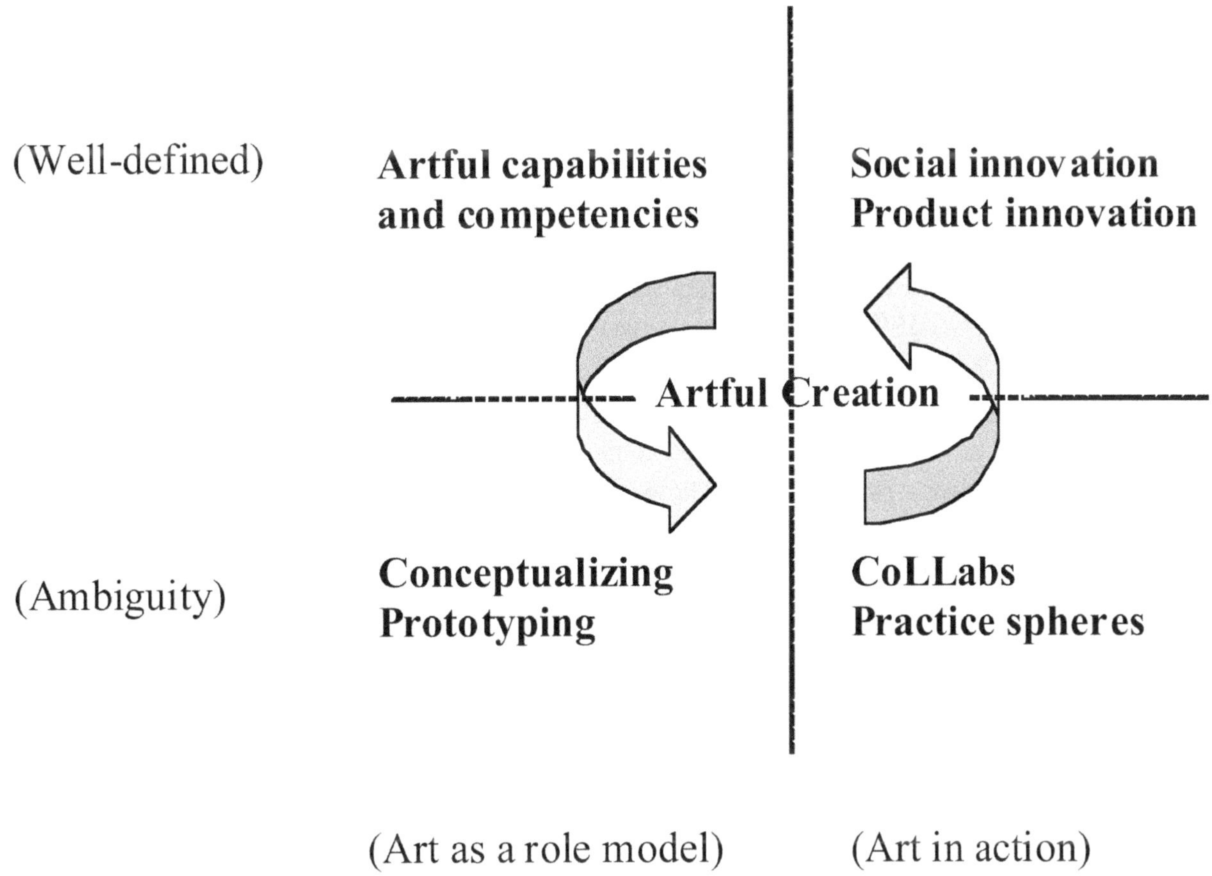

Figure 4.2.1 Matrix framework of 'artful Creation' (Darsø 2004).

Here we will mainly discuss the first two approaches, dealing with art in relation to developing new competencies and skills in leadership as well as art as metaphor and a 'motor' for conceptualizing, which involves focusing on perception, communication and mind-shifts. When regarding art as a metaphor, the most familiar example is probably improvisation. A special issue of *Organization Science* from 1998 portrays jazz improvisation, e.g. as a vehicle for organisational analysis (Weick 1998), as a metaphor for organizing in the 21st century by being flexible, adaptable and responsive to the environment (Hatch 1998), and as a technique for renewing strategy in organizations (Crossan 1998). On a similar note, John Kao wrote a best-seller on creativity, 'Jamming' (1996), involving a musical process metaphor. In the following we will examine the skills and competencies of theatre directors as a model for leadership.

Before we turn to the world of theatre we will briefly discuss and define creativity. Theories on creativity include studies on cognition (Zohar 1997; Simon 1986), on individual characteristics and capabilities (Maslow 1970; Chikszentmihalyi 1996), on the process of creativity (Edwards 1987) and on tools and techniques for creativity (e.g. de Bono 1994), among others. Here, however, we want to examine the creative process by suggesting that creativity be understood as a boundary phenomenon (Gell-Man 1994). The main idea is that in order to come up with something new individuals and groups need to enter a boundary zone where ordinary, habit-bound thinking and doing are stretched or compressed until novel and extraordinary ideas and solutions can emerge. Three questions are of particular interest and relevance here, in relation to theory and practice: 1) How can this space be understood and described? 2) How can you enter this space? 3) How can you direct people who are crossing through it, in order to emerge on the other side with a novel solution or idea?

Regarding the first question, as suggested by Ned Herrmann (1994), this space can be either psychological or physical—or both. The question of creative space has been illuminated and discussed from several different academic perspectives. In the 1990s, when chaos and complexity theories were first adapted to understand and analyse organisations, creativity was understood as an 'edge of chaos' phenomenon (e.g. Stacey 1996) in the space between stability and instability. In a study on the birth of innovation the dynamics between knowledge and ignorance were found to be central. In particular entering the field of uncertainty and ignorance seemed to trigger innovation (Darsø 2007; 2001). And in anthropology the term 'liminal' space has been coined to express that which is in-between, the fluidity of transcending experience (Turner 1982). These are all boundary phenomena. When the boundary is psychological the threshold consists of mental blocks, mental programming, schemata, or emotional obstacles, moods or idiosyncrasies. A creative boundary zone is generated when these phenomena are obliged to engage with speculative suggestions, e.g. 'what if? ...' questions. If the boundary is of a more physical kind it can be related to the size and dimensions of rooms or areas as well as to the aesthetical context, such as noise, light, smell, ugliness or beauty, etc. (Strati 2000). The psychological and physical boundaries are, of course, often interconnected and interdependent.

As for the second question regarding entering this creative space, several creative toolboxes and recommendations exist, a.o. by Edward de Bono (1994). Also artists have tried to describe what it takes to enter the 'zone' or the 'bubble' (Thwarp 2003). Most people would agree that you can't force people to be creative. Freedom to choose is an important ingredient for creativity to happen. Some people would therefore claim that the more freedom the higher the creativity. But, in our opinion, it is the contrary. Creativity, in fact, needs boundaries. But boundaries of a special kind. The terminology we want to introduce in the following, as an alternative answer to the second question, is that of creative constraints. We borrow this from the world of theatre where it is applied as a leadership tool by theatre directors for setting up attractive and motivational boundaries and for pressing and nudging actors into the space in which creative emergence may occur (the third question) (Ibbotson 2008).

Directing a play is a creative process: At one level it is an exercise in efficient project management; there is the deadline of opening night, sets to be built, actors to be rehearsed and the whole thing must come together on time, on budget and be successful, or you are ruined. However, to be successful the play must also innovate. Whatever it is, it must hit the audience as new, exciting, original and different, or people won't come. So theatre people particularly, have to innovate to stay in business. They also have to innovate within very tight constraints of timing and budget.

How do you get that balance between allowing for the creativity and innovation you need from all the people involved, (designers, actors, technicians, marketing), while at the same time making sure you open on time and on budget? ...

References

Adler NJ (2006) The Arts & Leadership: Now that we can do anything, what will we do? *Academy of Management Learning and Education* 5(4): 486–499.

Alvesson M and Svenigsson S (2003) Good Visions, Bad Micro-management and Ugly Ambiguity: Contradictions of (Non-)Leadership in a Knowledge-Intensive Organization, *Organization Studies* 24: 961–988.

Austin R and Devin L (2003) *Artful Making. What Managers Need to Know About How Artists Work*, FT Prentice Hall, Upper Saddle River, NJ.

Barry D (2008) 'The Art of ...', in Barry D and Hansen H (2008) (eds), *SAGE Handbook on New Approaches in Management and Organization*, SAGE Thousand Oaks CA.

Barrett R (1998) *Liberating the Corporate Soul. Building a Visionary Organization*, Butterworth Heinemann, Boston MA.

Buswick T, Creamer A and Pinard M (2004) (Re)Educating for Leadership: How the Arts Can Improve Business. Accessed at www.aandb.org.uk

Collins JB and Porras JI (1994) *Built to Last: Successful Habits of Visionary Companies*, Harper Collins, New York.

Crossan M (1998) Improvisation in Action, in Meyer A, Frost PJ and Weick KE (eds), Special Issue Jazz Improvisation and Organizing, *Organization Science* 9(5) September–October: 593–599.

Csikszentmihalyi M (1996) *Creativity. Flow and the Psychology of Discovery and Invention*, Harper Perennial, New York.

De Bono E (1994) *de Bono's Thinking Course* (Revised edn) Facts on File, Infobase, New York.

Darsø L (2001) *Innovation in the Making*, Samfundslitteratur, Copenhagen.

Darsø L (2004) *Artful Creation. Learning-Tales of Arts-in-Business,* Samfundslitteratur, Copenhagen.

Darsø L (2005) International Opportunities for Artful Learning, *Journal of Business Strategy* 26(5): 58–61.

Darsø L (2007) Is there a formula for innovation? in *Borsen Handbook of Leadership*. Translated 2007 from original Danish article (2003) *En formel for innovation*, Børsen Ledelseshåndbøger.

Drucker PF (1993) *Post-Capitalist Society*, Butterworth-Heinemann, Boston MA.

Edwards B (1986) *Drawing on the Artist Within*, Simon and Schuster, New York.

Gell-Mann M (1994) *The Quark and the Jaguar: Adventures in the Simple and the Complex*, WH Freeman & Co., New York.

Goleman D (2000) Leadership that Gets Results, *Harvard Business Review* March-April: 76–91.

Herrmann N (1994) *The creative brain*, The Ned Herrmann Group, Lake Lure NC.

Ibbotson P (2008) *The Illusion of Leadership. Directing Creativity in Business and the Arts*, Palgrave Macmillan, London UK.

Kao J (1996) *Jamming. The Art and Discipline of Business Creativity*, HarperBusiness, New York.

Kerr C (2006) The 'Learning Wave Trajectory Model': Exploring the nature and benefit of an 'artful' management education learning process. 20th ANZAM conference, Dec. 2006, Rockhampton QLD.

Kotter JP (1990) *A Force for Change. How Leadership Differs from Management*, Free Press, New York.

Maslow AH (1970) *Motivation and Personality* (2nd edn) Harper & Row, New York.

Micklethwait J and Wooldridge A (1997) *The Witch Doctors. What the Management Gurus are saying, why it matters and how to make sense of it*, Mandarin, Lo Angeles CA.

Nissley N (2007) Framing arts-based learning as an intersectional innovation in continuing management education: The intersection of arts and business and the innovation of arts-based learning'. In DeFillippi B and Wankel C (eds) *University and corporate innovations in lifetime learning*, Information Age, Greenwich CT.

Nissley N (2002) Art-based learning in management education. In DeFilippi B and Wankel C (eds) *Rethinking management education in the 21st century*, Information Age, Greenwich CT. pp. 27–61.

Palus CJ and Horth DM (2002) *The Leaders's Edge. Six Creative Competencies for Navigating Complex Challenges*, Jossey-Bass Business & Management Series, The Center for Creative Leadership, Jossey-Bass, San Francisco CA.

Pine II BJ and Gilmore JH (1999) *The Experience Economy. Work is Theatre & Every Business a Stage*, Harvard Business School Press, Boston MA.

Simon HA (1986) What we know about the Creative Process. In Kuhn RL (ed.) *Frontiers in creative and innovative management*, Ballinger, Cambridge MA.

Stacey RD (1996) *Complexity and Creativity in Organizations*, Berrett-Koehler, San Francisco CA.

Strati A (2000) The Aesthetic Approach in Organization Studies, in Linstead S and Höpfl H, *The Aesthetics of Organization*, SAGE London UK.

Turner V (1982) *From ritual to theatre: The human seriousness of play*, Performing Arts Journal Publications, New York.

Thwarp T (2003) *The Creative Habit. Learn it and use it for life*, Simon & Schuster, New York.

Von Braun C-F (1997) *The Innovation War. Industrial R&D ... the Arms Race of the 90's*, Prentice-Hall, Englewood Cliffs NJ.

Weick KE (1998) Improvisation as a Mindset for Organizational Analysis, in Meyer A, Frost PJ and Weick KE (Eds), Special Issue Jazz Improvisation and Organizing, *Organization Science* 9(5) September–October: 543–555.

Wheatley MJ (1999) *Leadership and the New Science. Discovering Order in a Chaotic World*, Berrett-Koehler, San Francisco CA.

Wheatley MJ and Frieze D (2006) Using Emergence to take Social Innovations to Scale. http://www. margaretwheatley.com/articles/emergence.html

Zohar D (1997) *Rewiring the Corporate Brain. Using the New Science to Rethink How We Structure and Lead Organizations*, Berrett-Koehler, San Francisco CA.

Reading 4.3

Art World, Art Business, Art Market

Jeffrey Taylor

Art as a Concept

Art as a concept is relatively new. All cultures have had a concept of treasure—essentially materials that are highly prized and have exchange value. Treasure, although it may have been constructed with great care and craftsmanship, still draws its value primarily from its input materials. Art, however, draws its value primarily from a knowledge of who made it, and, as a concept, has existed rarely in history. If we consider the Metropolitan Museum of Art in New York, the museum's entire first floor containing its massive Egyptian, Greek, Roman, African, Pre-Columbian, and Oceanic collections might be colloquially referred to as art (because of the building in which they are located), but virtually none of it was produced according to our modern notion of art. Most of it was produced to serve a religious function, and if not that, then as a form of state propaganda to glorify the ruling power. The makers of those objects were also not artists in the way we conceive of the profession now. They were not expected to express their own creative impulses, nor were they expected to innovate new methods of representation. They were crafting objects that would serve as repositories of divine power and lavished attention to detail in order that it should be worthy of that role.

The long transition from art's religious purpose to one that is purely secular took centuries to occur and only became widely accepted in the West in the nineteenth century and for much of the rest of the world only in the twentieth century. Even today art continues to borrow from the terminology of religion to express its value and describe the act of creation. In fact, the cult of Art is now frequently referred to as a sort of secular pseudo-religion that embodies all that is good and valuable in civilization, which gives meaning and purpose to people. The public spaces that are occupied by art have become so massive and widespread that we have coined a term to articulate its vast reach: the Art World. The term includes every activity and venue where art is present: museums, art galleries (both commercial and noncommercial), schools where art and art history are taught, and all the publications (books and journals) devoted to art, form just a short list of the full expansiveness of the term. It is often given to geographic or chronological designations to describe these categories in a more contained understanding: for example, the New York Art World, or the nineteenth century Paris Art World.

A less-broad term is the art business, which refers to all the activities surrounding the production, commerce, and exhibition of art. Furthermore, all the people who are somehow engaged professionally with art are involved in the art business. This term includes both commercial for-profit enterprises and also nonprofit entities who employ people and earn income through art. If money changes hands, whether to purchase objects or to purchase an entry ticket or an art publication: then it is part of the art business. An even more precise term, the art market, however, refers only to the commerce in art objects that involve changes in ownership. Only auction houses, commercial galleries, and other actors involved in the buying and selling of artworks can be described as part of the art market. The term art market may also be divided in to two distinctly different markets: the Primary Art Market and the Secondary Art Market. The Primary Art Market refers to artworks being sold for the first time, and essentially functions as a synonym for the contemporary art market. The Secondary Art Market refers to artworks sold for the second (or third or fourth) time, and is understood to mean the trade in older artworks. These three terms: Art World, art business, and art market essentially exist in concentric circles of an increasingly precise set of activities.

The Phenomenon of Collecting

Other species have been known to hoard, but humans are the only species known to collect. Although a convincing explanation to describe this tendency eludes us, it remains an undeniable phenomenon, and without this tendency to collect there would be nothing resembling art and no need to write this book. An aesthetic impulse among our ancestors can already be recognized in the Acheulian hand-axes that began to appear as early 150,000 bc, which lavish excessive care on the appearance of the tool beyond what is necessary to achieve its function. The inclination to hoard treasure can be found in nearly all ancient civilizations, but a systematic approach to collecting objects based on an understanding who made them (an emphasis on authorship) appears only twice in the ancient world. It first occurs in the Hellenistic kingdoms of the third and second centuries bc, carrying in to the Roman Empire. The other emergence of art collecting happens in China during the second Han Dynasty in the first and second centuries ad. What these two civilizations had in common was a historical perspective that led them to look upon their earlier periods as golden ages which spur a desire to collect the artworks that have survived from those lost eras.

Once a civilization has this historical perspective and an emphasis on the importance of who created an object, then the foundations for art and its market have been laid. Very quickly, then, this produces what Josef Alsop calls The Eight By-Products of Art (Alsop, 24):

1. Art collecting
2. Art market
3. Art history
4. Art museums
5. Antiques
6. Faking
7. Revaluation
8. Super-prices

The phenomenon of art collecting occurs when wealthy, powerful individuals begin to want to own objects based on an understanding of who made them. The art market then comes in to existence in order provide collectors with the objects they want, and will price the objects relative to supply and demand. Art history provides the historical perspective and a hierarchy of lesser masters and greater masters. Art museums, which become widespread in Roman times, help educate a wider public in a canon and its inherent hierarchy. Once fine (nonapplied) art forms are collected, soon all well-crafted applied art objects can be collected as well, producing a market for antiques. With like objects achieving vastly different market values due to their relative standing in the art historical hierarchy, the inclination to fake and forge artworks almost immediately presents itself. With values hanging so precariously on their attribution, values for an art object can plummet or rise suddenly with changes in attribution, producing the phenomenon of revaluation. With only a small group of canonical masters having widespread familiarity to the public, it follows that their works are dramatically more highly valued than those of most other artists who produced materially similar art works creating the existence of super-prices.

Once these eight by-products are in place, then a functioning Secondary Art Market has come in to existence. Despite its term, the Secondary Art Market usually precedes a contemporary or Primary Art Market. This is because living artists tend to still be treated like craftspeople, who are engaged to execute commissions. They do not produce art objects unless contracted to do so, and usually only if given an advance to cover expensive materials. More importantly, they do not produce with the approach of an artist trying to express themselves. They are trying to execute the instructions of the client who ordered the piece. Only when we see the presence of artists producing on speculation can we really consider there to be a functioning Primary Art Market.

Early Primary Art Markets

The earliest Primary Art Markets we can place at the Flemish market towns in the fifteenth century of what is today's Belgium. In Antwerp, around the church of our Lady of Pand, a market made up of itinerant merchants began selling pictures on a regular basis. Most of these pictures were prints, usually woodcuts, but their speculative production—where an artist produces without a clear notion of who will buy the art object—forms one of the core criteria for when a Primary Art Market comes in to existence. By the seventeenth century, slightly more north in what is today's Netherlands, a thriving three-agent model market began to take shape. The market can be described as three-agent because it involved an artist, a merchant, and a collector—rather than the old two-agent model of artist-commissioner or simply producer-consumer. The middle agent of the three-agent model, the merchant or dealer, often emerges from a class of failed artists, as well as framers and pigment, brush, and canvas suppliers who might accept paintings for re-sale or in barter for supplies. Artists who produce a painting without any clear idea of who might buy the work, essentially producing on speculation, will usually develop a signature theme or style: landscape, marine, interior genre, or still-lifes. These artists begin to try to predict what the market will want. They pay close attention to what styles and genres are selling well.

Paris as Center of the Art World

From the Renaissance period to the present, the art world has always had a center. The fifteenth century center was Florence, but would cede primacy to Rome in the sixteenth century. Rome would remain the undisputed art center until the middle of the nineteenth century. During the 1850s, the reorganization of Paris along Baron Haussmann's principles also saw it become the world center for the leisure economy. The Paris art market first grew up around the royal court and its Académie royale de peinture et de sculpture, which served as an alternate authority under which artists could work outside of the painters' guilds, the so-called Guilds of St. Luke. The Academy's teachers and students began to have yearly shows (intermittently) from 1648 in a room in the royal palace, the Louvre, known as the Salon Carré. By the middle of the nineteenth century, the yearly Salon was held inside the Grand Palais, and contained often up to 3,000 artworks. This business model of a state-run or statist-monopoly holding a once a year exhibition would be repeated across the Western world in the form of Art Unions [*Kunstverein* in German] in major and minor art centers. The organizations were usually civic based, but functioned virtually the same way as the Paris Salon, in that a large hall was procured, and a jury would select entrants to the exhibition.

During the mid-nineteenth century spending capacity among collectors remained anemic and therefore few collectors could buy full-scale oil on canvas paintings, and instead contented themselves with serial-printed lithographs. One of the attractions of the art union system was that its membership always received a lithograph of one of the exhibition's most esteemed works, and each member received a raffle ticket which might win them an original oil painting. The system also had a large number of rewards that could be distributed to artists, such as medals and cash prizes, or guaranteed purchase for the raffle (raffle winners could only redeem their winnings from a group of pre-selected works). By the 1870s most art unions were superseded by national art associations that functioned in an even closer imitation to the Paris Salon. All the disputes and disagreements about the composition of juries and the high rate of rejections point to a universal crisis of what we can call the Artist Proletariat. In the later nineteenth century schools of fine art were opening up in many major cities, sending ever more aspiring artists on to an already saturated market.

The result of the crisis of over-supply would come in the form of a series of ruptures that are often called Secessions. Paris had many, but perhaps its most famous would be the series of eight self-staged exhibitions held by the Impressionist group between 1874 and 1886. In Munich, the second most important art center after Paris, a group seceded from the main society in 1892 and became known as the Munich Secession. Vienna founded its own Secession in 1898, and Berlin followed in 1900. The Secessions themselves, however, proved just as unstable as the official salons they competed with. Secessions often followed secessions. The early twentieth century saw a bewildering array of self-staged exhibitions, group/movement shows, and other imaginative curatorial solutions. Overall, the ruptures produced one undeniable result, which was that the exhibition capacity of a given market was expanded and pluralized. Over the course of the twentieth century modernist artists began to migrate to private dealers who operated with far greater efficiency because they were petty despots in their own gallery and were not distracted by the disputes about the composition of juries that plagued all exhibition societies, whether salons or secessions.

During these same years, the Secondary Market (the market for older art works) and the antiques market also began to migrate from Holland to Paris and particularly to its primary auction house, Drouot. As a result of the French Revolution, however, much of the prime secondary market material began to be sold in London. During this period the two leading auction houses Christie's and Sotheby's came of age. It is also in London that the House of Duveen was founded as an antiques purveyor to the Royal Family.

The Shift to New York

Like other art centers on the European periphery New York witnessed its own secession, when a number of artists decided to compete with the dominant National Academy of Design (essentially the New York equivalent of the Salon) and hold an extraordinary exhibition involving vast amounts of European modernist art. Unlike other Secessions, New York's 1913 Armory Show happened only once, but it spawned a series of new artist organizations and, more importantly, served as a symbolic moment when the gravity of the Art World began to shift across the Atlantic. European dealers had been colonizing New York for many decades already, with Michael Knoedler taking control of a gallery established in 1846 to be a representative of the French lithographer, Goupil & Cie. In the 1880s, the dealer of the Impressionists, Paul Durand-Ruel, established a presence in New York, where his faltering business was rescued by American interest in the movement, which had been largely scorned in Europe. In the 1890s, the Duveen firm opened its New York branch, and it was there that young Joseph Duveen cultivated the taste for old master paintings among the new millionaire class. During the period between the two world wars, the migration intensified among dealers, artists, and collectors. Many leading figures of the European avant-garde—Marcel Duchamp, Max Ernst, Piet Mondrian, Andre Breton—would make New York their home.

New cultural institutions also began to proclaim an emboldened self-confidence. The Whitney Museum was founded to expressly promote American art. The Museum of Modern Art (MoMA) quickly became one of the dominant international taste-makers in determining the trajectory of canonical modern art. Both Solomon and Peggy Guggenheim (related—uncle and niece—but two very distinctly different people) played essential roles in the promotion of Abstract Art as New York's signature style. Solomon Guggenheim, under the influence of Hilla Rebay, founded the Museum of Non-Objective Art in 1939, which would ultimately become today's Guggenheim Museum. Peggy Guggenheim founded a short-lived institution called Art of This Century, which both served as a museum to European Abstract and Surrealist art, and also as a commercial gallery where it helped launch the careers Jackson Pollock and Mark Rothko. New dealers with strong commitments to the New York School, now called Abstract Expressionism, such as Betty Parsons and Sidney Janis began to fundamentally alter the way art was sold. Parsons introduced unframed canvases in a white, unadorned room. Janis relentlessly pushed up the prices of his leading artists, especially, as with Pollock, after they were dead.

From the late 1940s on, New York became the undisputed center of the Art World. It had already been the center of high-end Secondary Market dealing since the early twentieth century, but by the mid-century the Primary Market too had moved to New York. While the Secondary Market has remained fixed on the Upper East Side on Madison Avenue, the Primary Market made three major moves in the later twentieth century, migrating from 57th Street to Soho in the 1980s, and to Chelsea starting in the late 1990s. Now the Chelsea contemporary art district contains at least 300 galleries. In the 1980s the big auction houses, Christie's and Sotheby's entered the US market and increasingly began to shift the gravity of their most important sales from London to New York.

A Global Art World

Paris still plays a primary role in the antiques trade with the agglomeration of flea markets known as Marche aux Puces de Saint-Ouen continuing to serve as a leading wholesale center (especially for US antiques dealers) for furniture and a vast array of applied arts. London's role as secondary and antiques markets has declined precipitously in recent years as the city's ever rising real estate costs vastly exceed what can be earned in re-sale trades. None the less, London has found a new role for itself as a rival to New York in the area of contemporary art, and presents the first serious competitor to New York's pre-eminence in almost half a century. Other regional art centers continue to aspire to world-class stature, and many also now claim to be emerging rivals to New York: Los Angeles, Berlin, Shanghai, and Hong Kong. While these candidates may possess enormous buying power (Los Angeles) or a plethora of working artists (Berlin), none of them possesses the commensurate concentration of all sectors: Primary Market, Secondary Market, auction houses, antiques, museums, working artists in all media and associated professions such as academics, writers, art handlers, and appraisers ... nowhere does one find all these sectors in such concentrations as one finds them in New York.

Even though New York's primacy remains unchallenged, new centers of gravity have begun to emerge at a surprising pace across the United States and globally. All of the major American metropolises (Boston, Washington, D.C., Chicago, Los Angeles, San Francisco, and Miami) all boast significant self-confident art scenes. Western towns that make much of their income from skiing and outdoor recreation, such as Jackson, Santa Fe, Aspen, Telluride, and Crested Butte, also develop as art centers because of the concentration of both artists and collectors. One of the leading global trends is the practice of repurposing industrial structures for re-use as artists' studios, galleries, or exhibition spaces. This phenomenon is occurring all across the industrialized world, from the 798 district in Beijing to the Box Factory of this author's home town of St. Joseph, Michigan.

Overall, the art world is bigger than ever. The infrastructure and support for contemporary art across the globe continues to grow, but other sectors, especially antiques, have stagnated or gone in to decline. The Secondary Art Market complains that much of its business is being cannibalized by the auction houses. Furthermore, the art fair phenomenon, which has become a parallel market to the ones based around permanent venues, may have finally reached its peak saturation, with every major fair (Armory, Art Basel Miami) accompanied by nearly ten simultaneous satellite fairs. If one tendency is sure, it is that next year tens of thousands of new BFA and MFA graduates will throw themselves on the market in the hope of having a career as a working artist. As these artists struggle to get shown, they will be spurred to invent ever more creative exhibition conceptions and the art world will continue to evolve. …

Bibliography

Alsop, J. (1982) *The rare art traditions: the history of art collecting and its linked phenomena wherever these have appeared.* New York: Harper Collins.

Arts Meets Management

Kurt Mayer

Kurt Mayer, "Arts Meets Management," *Leadership Learning for the Future*, ed. Klaus Scala, Ralph Grossmann and Marlies Lenglachner, pp. 235-241, 247-248.

...

Arts and Management

Are arts incompatible with management on the whole? Or does management contain artistic elements and vice versa? What are the similarities and differences between management behavior and patterns on the one hand and artistic behavior and patterns on the other? In this section, we would like to delve into these issues and determine the basic values and patterns of the two areas of arts and management.

Arts....

The arena of arts is the arena of human creative will. The will to create is present in every human being and—individually different in extent and effect—is practised at work and in everyday life. Businessmen and businesswomen, politicians, educators, philosophers and even gardeners pursue their need for creation (Blanke 2002, p. 31). The phenomenon of playing children is not just an arbitrary action, but rather a form of creative activity. Art as a play developed to its highest level activates and expands the will to create. This concept of art is based on the perception of esthetics of a humanistic idea of man in the Age of Enlightenment.

> The human being only plays where he is human in the full sense of the word, and he is only a human being where he plays. This sentence, which seems to be paradox at first glance ... will, I promise you, carry the structure of esthetic art and the much more difficult art of life. (Schiller, 1795, as cited in Blanke, 2002, p. 31, translated from German by the author)

Furthermore, new studies in the field of the arts point out especially its irritating, disturbing and challenging effect:

> Therefore, rather than mollifying and comforting us, the artistic agenda exposes us to issues that disturb and challenge. ... We argue, that without this shock, the kinds of changes in consciousness and the social action necessary for creating a sustainable future will not occur. (Bathurst & Edwards 2009, p. 119)

This article also contains an interesting citation from a commentary in *The New York Times* in which she deals with the question of why works of art are often vandalized. In this regard, Roberta Smith argues that one widespread attitude is as follows:

> simple refusion to entertain paradox, to see art as a coalescence of grey areas, ambiguities and multiple interpretations. Art's job is to provoke thought in ways that are difficult to resolve and uncomfortable; it's a relatively neutral place to experience the unresolvable issues that dominate real life, to practice a kind of abstract flexibility that might move us toward resolution in real life. (Smith, 2004, as cited in Bathurst & Edwards 2009, p. 120)

Art has the power to question seeming unambiguousness and to expose ambiguity, grey areas, polysemy and different interpretations. Art is based on and fed by these ambiguities, by difficult and apparently insoluble questions, and is also able to unearth them. It is provocative and not always comfortable, though, to be confronted with these ambiguities and questions, but art allows us to handle these questions in a mature manner in our everyday life. Concerning this matter, Lotte Darso (2004) states:

> For the arts and artists ambiguity opens up for immense possibilities, different perspectives and new approaches. This concerns the artistic process as well as the finished artwork. One of the discerning features of art is indeed that it can inspire multiple interpretations. Ambiguity is an invitation to the freedom of changing perceptions and forms. (p. 40)

Moreover, Darso (2004) believes that ambiguity, as a key dimension in artistic processes and outputs of artistic creation, plays a decisive role in and is related to the condition of life in modern societies. Life in these societies is affected by ambiguities. This can cause confusion, but ambiguity as a value opens up new degrees of freedom, as well.

It is also important that the arts extend past the border of pure intellectual dedication, "enabling us to feel at a deeper level the issues that a work might provoke" (Dean, Ottensmeyer, & Ramirez, 1997,

p. 422), which demands an emotional answer and in turn makes this answer possible. Bathurst and Edwards (2009, p. 119) also point out an emotional root of the effect of arts and describe this "heightened emotional response" as a basis for enabling transformation processes on the organizational and societal level ("provides the motivation for radical change").

So, at first glance we can summarize the area of arts is based on the elements of creative will, inspiration and irritation, as well as grey areas, ambiguity and emotions. And what about management? Does management action contain artistic elements? If it does, what are these elements? Where are their borders?

... and Management

Henry Mintzberg (2004, 2009) alludes to the fact that management is not what it is often considered: namely an aggregation of special business functions, such as marketing, finance, and so forth. In contrast to this view, he conceives management—and he does not make any difference between leadership and management, because in his perspective one requires the other—as a trio of capabilities: (1) practically acquired technical skills, (2) a dash of artistic capability and (3) a solid analytic body.

There are similar arguments by Fredmund Malik, management consultant from St. Gallen who associates management with art, science and common sense (Malik, 2006). Also, Schumpeter saw the action of his central economic player, the "dynamic entrepreneur," in the context of arts:

> He adds something to the data. He forms and pulls them together in a new way, like great artists do. ... He does not act because of immediately expected demand. He imposes his products on the market. Neither any new machine, nor any new brand would be created under the pressure of demand. (as cited in Blanke, 2002, p. 63)

In line with Mintzberg, Malik, and Schumpeter, Blanke points out the similar initial situation of arts and management. Both fields have similarities where materials, a physical structure and an idea are combined in a creative process. In this context, he quotes Erich Colsman, a businessman, who explains the connection between arts and management.

> For me art is an attempt to peel something out of a raw material or a situation to exaggerate and to bring it to an impact. This is my manner of management: To create a symbiosis out of a given market situation and organizational structure, which is more than the very construction of it. In this respect every organizational process is an artistic process, because I need to arrange the process in a way that every single person can use his/her potential, otherwise he/she will not stay or rather do what he/she would be able to. (Erich Colsman, Barthells-Feldhoff GmbH & Co. KG, as cited in Blanke, 2002, p. 62)

This analogy is impressive, as management processes are creative acts which are able to activate and develop the will of creation, as described above concerning the field of action of arts. Blanke interprets this picture of artists and managers as twins, who stand back-to-back and transmute everything they lay their hands on to expedite the work together.

However, such an idealistic and smoothed picture which is based on the common will to create disregards other important dimensions which characterize the field of arts, but are not existent in today's management structures: ambiguity, disturbance, irritation and emotion. Lotte Darso (2004) concludes:

> For business, however, ambiguity and uncertainty is uncomfortable and in most cases something that must be reduced or controlled. Business people prefer to work with specific goals, detailed plans and accurate measurements. (p. 40)

This rational approach of management is based on a fixation on tools and techniques, such as competition analysis, business games, scholastic mathematized market models and case studies in particular, without considering the context in which these tools are utilized (Mintzberg, 2004). The students of business schools mainly learn how to elaborately interpret facts, further actions are based on their results. Management is primarily understood as a science. In this restricted perspective, decisions are based on logical analysis models, which are not irritated by simple human issues and problems. The hegemonic reflection of management at universities and the specialized media creates a heroic picture of management, where managers stand above the company and make decisions and develop strategies on their own based on analysis, management ratios and controlling instruments.

Darso (2004) points out that the implementation of Taylorism in the second industrial revolution led to a fragmentation and collapse of the platonic "Big Three: the Beautiful, the Good and the True." From then on, only the True was appreciated, and pure objective reasoning has become the main instrument of perception, whereas the Good and the Beautiful have been neglected (p. 27). From the perspective of organizations, the machine metaphor dominated in the 20th century (Simon, 2009, p. 41, Purg in this volume). Organizations, as well as their structures and processes, were considered rational entities. Emotions were a disturbing factor which management had to eliminate or at least control.

After these initial reflections on the values, logics and patterns of the two areas of arts and management, we can draw some preliminary conclusions. On the one hand, there are obvious similarities, since a process of creation and creative will is at the core of action in both areas. On the other hand, the area of management additionally and simultaneously exhibits principles of action which fundamentally differ from the area of arts. The rational approach of management refers to management as a science and focuses primarily on control and tools. This is a far reach from irritation, the imponderables of life and complexity. This is management far away from the arts.

Arts Interventions and Their Potential Added Value for Management and Organizations

> It is hardly possible to overrate the value ... of placing human beings in contact with persons dissimilar to themselves, and with modes of thought and action unlike those with which they are familiar. ... Such communication has always been, and is peculiarly in the present age, one of the primary sources of progress. (John Stuart Mill in 1848)

Based on these preliminary considerations, we would like to focus on interaction between art and economy. If the rationales of arts and management are similar and different at the same time:

Why should and how can arts interventions be apt to changing the behavior of companies and their organizational strategies in a way that they can not only survive better, but also make organizational behavior and strategies long lasting? To approach this question, we will differentiate between learning processes on (a) an individual level, focusing on personal and team development, and (b) an organizational level, focusing on organization-wide change and transformation.

The Build-Up of Competence in Art and Skills on an Individual Level

In the early 21st century, we are facing an increasingly complex, chaotic and confusing environment for organizations. The progressively unpredictable market and nonmarket conditions, volatile and ever-changing economic landscape, a complex brew of rapidly advancing technologies and ecological challenges are pushing more and more organizations into unchartered waters. One of the amazing effects in connection with the complex, chaotic and innovative economy is the tendency to develop new competences and skills to deal with our professional—as well as our private and public—life. Especially leaders and executives are increasingly recognizing their need to develop competencies mainly rooted in emotional and social intelligence. Reflection, creativity, a sense of responsibility, entrepreneurship, the ability to work in a team and conflict management are just a few of the soft skills that are valuable for employees and managers alike (Mayer, Neugebauer et al., 2010; Grossmann, [...]). These challenges call for abilities which are deeply rooted in our personality, and acquiring them requires complex learning processes. Art and arts intervention can play a major role in the development and refinement of these new skills and competences on an individual level.

Danica Purg [...] refers to leadership development programs that use arts as a source of inspiration for new leadership:

> Arts help us to see the symptoms of forthcoming change, to understand them, and to respond to them. We discovered that leaders can learn from a violinist, from a conductor, a painter or an actor. It brings leaders from purely rational thinking to using intuition and imagination, very important attributes in increasingly complex environment.

The growing number of creative subjects that are neglected in favor of scientific subjects at schools results in employees and managers lacking artistic and creative abilities. Arts interventions are able to enhance psychosocial competences and to compensate these shortfalls. On the one hand, they stimulate the creative and artistic potential, while on the other hand scrutinizing our habitual perception and behavior (Blanke, 2002, pp. 22–23). Maier [...] gives us a very vivid example of a low-threshold arts intervention with bankers. He asked 30 bank employees to share their account of the latest crisis in the form of a fairytale. Just by inviting them to recount their experience in the form of a fairytale, the common expert talk was avoided and hence they looked at the story in a different perspective.

Artists are paving the way and taking on the role of an agitator, becoming an activating and interpreting force. The key role of artists could be to support us in broadening our perspectives to see more and to get in touch "with both internal and external forces that we might otherwise not notice" (Schein, 2001, p. 81). Artists' specialized way of perception, combined with the expressive realization of their perceptions via their personal instruments, creates new perspectives, hones one's own perception and helps to differentiate between inner and outer forces in everyday situations.

As mentioned above, art has the power to irritate, disturb, and challenge us. This means that you are taken away from the security of everyday life and confronted with uncomfortable situations that you would normally try to evade. Existing subtle drawbacks are discussed and an examination is encouraged. The reaction to this challenge is demonstrated in the "Live and Direct" arts intervention of the multinational company Unilever. Actors supervised the process for months and eventually put their experiences into a theatre performance to display the problems and relevant emotions for employees and managers. In this way, it was possible to show drawbacks the management had not previously been aware of (Boyle & Ottensmeyer, 2005, pp. 16–17).

Lakoff and Wehling (2012) point out that the "Deep Seated Frames" that structure our understanding of the world and form our value-based common sense are completely resistant to learning by standard communication because contradictory factors are just faded out. Arts intervention utilized to "disturb, provoke, shock, and inspire" (Schein, 2001, p. 81) could mean the difference and create a new way of learning.

Summarizing this section, we could say that arts interventions and artists "can stimulate us to broaden our skills, our behavioral repertory and our flexibility of response" (Schein, 2001. p. 81). Important in this context is the capability of arts interventions to stimulate and strengthen the "art of improvisation." As Stark and Dell [...] point out, improvisation is the ability

> not only to cope with unknown potentials and uncertain processes, but also to redesign patterns and minimal structures (Cunha & Cunha 2008), out of which implicit knowing in organizations is constructed, in a creative way.

Exercises in improvisation can cause subconscious emotions to surface. Spontaneity and intuition, both dimensions of improvisation (Darso, 2004, p. 47), include hidden emotions in the emotional repertoire and broaden and improve human behavior. If managers are challenged with the task of reacting to conflicts, this will require a certain ability regarding improvisational skills. It is not about satisfying one's own needs, but those of each and every team member. Hence, improvisation requires creativity. And creativity "is important for leadership because it is the component whereby one generates the ideas that others will follow" (Sternberg, 2003, as cited in Styhre & Eriksson, 2008, p. 4). Successful arts interventions will put us in touch with our creative self. In the end, it is nothing less than our own creativity that enables us to perceive the environment from a different angle, to realize new ways of work and to support our self-fulfillment. ...

References

Blanke, T. (2002). *Unternehmen nutzen Kunst, Neue Potentiale für die Unternehmens-und Personalentwicklung* [Corporations using Arts, New Potential for Corporate Development]. Stuttgart: Klett-Cotta.

Boyle, M. E., & Ottensmeyer E. (2005). Solving business problems through the creative power of the arts: Catalyzing change at Unilever. *Journal of Business Strategy, 26*(5), 14–21. Retrieved from http://www.emeraldinsight.com/Insight/viewPDF.jsp?contentType=Article&Filename=html/Output/Published/EmeraldFullTextArticle/Pdf/2880260503.pdf

Darso, L. (2004). *Artful creation: Learning-tales of arts-in-business.* Frederiksberg, Copenhagen: Samfundslitteratur.

Dean, J. W., Ottensmeyer, E., & Ramirez, R. (1997). An aesthetic perspective on organizations. In C. L. Cooper, & S. E. Jackson (Eds.), *Creating tomorrow's organizations: A handbook for future research in organizational behavior* (pp. 420–437). New York, NY: John Wiley & Sons.

Lakoff, G., & Wehling, E. (2012). *The Little Blue Book: The essential guide to thinking and talking democratic.* New York, NY: Simon and Schuster.

Malik, F. (2006). *Führen, Leisten, Leben. Wirksames Management für eine neue Zeit* [Managing performing living: Effective management for a new era]. Frankfurt/New York: Campus.

Mayer, K., Neugebauer, Ch., Lesjak, B., & Timel, R. (2010). Learning for the Future in Management and Organizations. IFF-Working Paper, unpublished.

Mintzberg, H. (2004). *Managers not MBAs: A hard look at the soft practice of managing and management development.* San Franisco, CA: Berrett-Koehler.

Mintzberg, H. (2009), *Managing.* San Francisco, CA: Barret-Koehler.

Schein. E. H. (2001). The role of art and the artist: Society for organizational learning & Massachusetts Institute of Technology. *Reflections, 2,* 81–83. from http://osr-nw.org/downloads/2010-conf-schein_role_of_art_and_artist.pdf

Simon, F. B. (2009). Wurzeln der systemtheoretischen Organisationstheorie [The roots of systemic organizational theory]. In R. Wimmer, J. O. Meissner, & P. Wolf (Eds.), *Praktische Organisationswissenschaft. Lehrbuch für Studium und Beruf [Practical organizational: Textbook for students and professionals]* (pp. 40–52). Heidelberg, Germany: Carl-Auer Verlag.

Styhre, A., & Eriksson, M. (2008). Bring in the arts and get the creativity for free: A study of the artists in residence project. *Creativity and Innovation Management, 17*(1), 47–57.

Unit V

Sociology, Anthropology, and Business

"The deviant and the conformist ... are creatures of the same culture, inventions of the same imagination."

—Kai Erikson

Sociology

People behave differently from place to place depending on a number of factors, including levels of comfort and familiarity, purpose, and position. We don't act in isolation; instead, our conduct is influenced by surrounding groups and environments. We act and react to accommodate or resist the behaviors of people with whom we associate, according to societal standards and the social construction of groups. Sociology is the study of social structures and institutions, how they came to be, and how society functions, particularly in relation to social stratification, social change, and problems.[1] Business sociology is concerned with the behavior of groups and how that influences individual performance, productivity, retention, and other factors that contribute to the bottom line.

Sociological analysis is a schematic process. As such, concepts are building blocks that continually build upon each other with theoretical evolution to create a more holistic picture of segments of society. The sociology of work, employment, and industrial relations are complex.[2] Business sociologists are interested in questions of power, authority, values, beliefs, social control, and ideologies.[3] A workplace issue or question provides the starting point for sociological research then to pinpoint associated problems to manage the study.

Schools of sociological thought tackle the entirety of the human experience, issue by issue. The breadth of topics researched by sociologists is wide, from aging to criminology, to social stratification and organization and much more.[4] Most of these issues apply to business in varying settings, as business and work are integral to the mundane. However, it is beyond the scope of this book to address each subject. Instead we will look at sociological schools of thought, key terminology, and their applications to business sociology.[5]

- **Structural function theory:** Assumes that society is a unified whole as a result of the contributions of separate structures; deviance clarifies moral boundaries and promotes cohesion of group.
- **Conflict theory:** Assumes social conflict is the basis of society; values and norms of a dominant society represent the most powerful groups in society to the disadvantage of others; definitions of deviance are applied unequally based on power relationships within society.
- **Symbolic interactionism:** Assumes that interaction and meaning are key to society and that meanings are created through interaction; values and norms are social constructions that may vary over time and by context; deviance is relative.
- **Postmodernism:** Assumes that social reality is diverse and constantly changing.

Corporate philosophies influence the strategy used by sociologists, largely based on social interests related to productivity. The studies may take place within the organization or related to stakeholders outside of the business; thus, context and social climate influence t he r esults o f a nalysis. Traditional sociology dealt with classic issues such as the family, home, and work. Issues that have more recently come to the forefront of business sociology are related to globalization.[6] In addition, the overlap and interplay of different issues in the workplace influence sociological research today.[7]

Business schools have incorporated some sociological research in management courses since the 1960s, but with today's diverse and interactive world, research on the motivations of groups and the ability to analyze social factors are essential to business students as they enter the business world.[8] Studying sociology helps to develop your analytical thinking and capabilities. Sociologists analyze qualitative and quantitative data to determine the effects of phenomena on a population. This analytical method of thinking helps those in business with the ability to research market data and eventually draw conclusions from that data.[9] Business requires an understanding of people—large populations in particular. After all, no business relationship is possible without personal bonds.[10] Sociology provides the educational background needed for managers to understand their employees and customers. The sociological knowledge base established in business schools transfers readily to real-life business settings.

Business leaders who understand sociology are able to anticipate stakeholder needs, isolate problems, and develop effective solutions for pressing issues in the workplace, such as handling employees, market research, and public relations.[11] Even old-school sociology has relevance in today's business world. Managers who utilize sociology in the workplace as part of their analytical toolbox have insight into the background of organizational bureaucracy and structural problems within organizations, yet this is a relatively untapped field among managers.[12]

At its most basic level, power in organizations, or the ability to get people to do something (in agreement or not), is best analyzed through a sociological lens. Sociologists develop correlative factors in various relationships shaped by both official/formal power and inherent power. The role of knowledge and the distribution of organizational knowledge contribute to power by position. Power structures in business are typically hierarchical and relationships are shaped by rank and status.[13] Organizational charts provide visual representations of power relations within organizations. Innovative management models are mechanical or organic, and that influences the distribution of power within companies. Mechanistic businesses are organized by clear-cut hierarchy, with vertical interaction between managers and workers. On the other hand, organic organizations are more fluid, with lateral communication rather than top-down instruction, and they are characterized by the contributive nature of knowledge achieved by specialization throughout the ranks. Sociologists also analyze deviance and sites of resistance within organizations.[14]

Traditional sociology theory remains relevant today. For legal as well as moral reasons, the stakes are high for corporate compliance, and classic sociological theory addresses issues of compliance that are played out every day in the workplace. In the 1960s, Amitai Etzioni introduced three categories of compliance that are still applicable now: coercive compliance, remunerative compliance, and normative compliance. Managers and workers behave in accordance with government mandates as well as along official and unofficial organizational lines of authority.[15] Further, the focus in business research has shifted from an emphasis on bureaucratic organizations to market structures, demonstrating the significance of Émile Durkheim's earlier work on self-interest and the stability of society. Ethics in business are a big part of that conversation, connecting classic sociological analysis to our contemporary world.[16]

Sociologists use the scientific method in research. They pose a question and research issues surrounding that question. Next, they develop a hypothesis based on their research. The hypothesis is then set to task with rigorous testing and experimentation. The sociologists then develop a theory based on their research and test findings.

Sociological analysis includes the collection of both quantitative and qualitative data. Some sociologists argue that the use of quantitative data is objective and that qualitative data skews the research because of the subjectivity of the researcher. Other sociologists argue that qualitative research provides an authenticity that gets at the "why" of actions in ways that statistical data cannot.[17] The following key terms apply to both types of analysis:[18]

- **Sociology:** Scientific analysis of society and social behavior.
- **Group:** A collection of people who share attribute(s).
- **Society:** A group of people with collective and patterned behavior that distinguishes their group from others.
- **Structure:** A stable social institution that meets the needs of society by serving specific purposes to maintain social order.
- **Qualitative analysis:** Research using non-numerical data; subjectivity is inevitable.
- **Ideologies:** Systems of beliefs in a society, often used to justify the status quo.
- **Correlation:** A relationship between variables in which they change together, directly or indirectly related.

- **Causation:** A relationship between variables in which change in one triggers a change in the other.
- **Focus group:** A group interview process for research centered on specified topic(s) that allows interaction among group members.
- **Group cohesion:** Sense of solidarity or team spirit among members of a group.
- **Groupthink:** Conformity among members of a group.
- **Deviance:** Belief and/or actions that violate a social norm.
- **Stigma:** A trait or attribute that devalues a person or group's identity.
- **Social mores:** Norms with moral significance related to core values of a society.
- **Taboo:** Counter-normative behavior or action that stirs up extreme negative feelings or shock.
- **Social control:** Mechanisms used to promote conformity to normative standards in society.
- **Subculture:** A group within a society that is differentiated from dominant culture by distinguishing values and behaviors.
- **Counterculture:** A group within a society that openly rejects the values and norms of the mainstream society.
- **Power:** The ability to control others in their actions.
- **Coercive power:** Power that is reinforced by force or enticements.
- **Authority:** The valid right to hold and/or use power.
- **Social stratification:** Hierarchical division of groups within a society.
- **Social inequality:** Unequal distribution of resources and status among members within a society.
- **Social mobility:** The movement of individuals or groups within social classes of a society.

This list is also useful for anthropology.

The following list provides key concepts that are applicable to both sociological and anthropological methodology:[19]

- Participant observation: The research takes place in the natural setting of the study. It offers a front row seat to the lives of those studied. The researcher is able to both observe and participate in activities of the culture to varying extents when this strategy is used. They are able to process information through records, analysis, interviews, and other data onsite. There are certain factors that need to be considered with participant observation that affect a study:
    - Trust is essential for validity.
    - Research is time consuming.
    - The observer cannot always be present.
    - There are questions of authenticity: The observer can affect participants' behavior.
- Self-reflexivity: The researcher needs to maintain an awareness of personal focus, bias, preconceptions, and so forth throughout the analysis. By doing so, these factors are considered in the analysis and can be dealt with accordingly (reword) researcher recognizes their subjectivity by being conscious of self and reflecting on that in analysis.
- Building rapport: Researchers need to develop trust and relationships of mutual respect.

- Contextual understanding: Researchers develop an in-depth understanding of the conditions in which something exists or occurs.
- Identifying key informants: Researchers establish relationships with people on the inside who provide detailed information on circumstances and the context of the study; often known as experts.
- Listening for diverse local voices and points of view: Researchers see as much representation as possible from different people in varying circumstances in the study, beyond the key informants.
- Ethnography: The central research method used in cultural anthropology. Here are the necessary elements of ethnography:
    - the written text used to report research results
    - based on field notes
    - a record of the researcher's evolving understanding of the local context
    - cultural mapping
    - historical timelines (cultural and economical)
    - calendars of events
    - life stories
    - fieldnotes that reveal rather than attempt to conceal the partiality of the researcher's experience

The readings in this unit demonstrate the utility and necessity of business sociology. Watson first demonstrates how to understand organizations, the nature of work, authority relations, and management in the 21st century. Then, Joseph addresses classical sociological theory and its relevance to today's world. He draws from multiple researchers in forming a case for business sociology in business leadership, organizational analysis, power relations, and operations.

Anthropology

"It is always of interest to know what strikes another human being as remarkable."

—Graham Greene

Anthropology and sociology are cousins in the social sciences; however, there are distinctions between the two. Anthropology is the study of human beings, both past and present, in terms of physical character, environmental and social relations and culture. It can also be known as the scientific and humanistic study of human species and their various diversities; whereas sociology is the study of the development, structure, interaction and behavior of organized groups of human beings.[20]

Social systems are value systems with a collective of the individual beliefs of members of a society concerning relationships of economic, political, social, and religious institutions, practices, and actions. Business is a social institution in which conflict and cooperation are played out on a daily basis.[21] In business, anthropological analysis provides insight into the interaction between people and their environments, motivations to act in a particular way, and the impact that past actions have had on present conditions. Anthropologists seek to advance the knowledge of what makes us human through different aspects of the entire human experience, from past to present.[22]

Humans have the capacity and instinct to adapt and perpetuate values, behaviors, and beliefs in their lives. Anthropologists study the ways that these factors influence and shape institutions and the impact that institutions have on people, both directly and indirectly.[23] Culture is not genetically hardwired – we do not inherit it biologically. We learn it from our parents and other people who are around us as we grow up. What sets our species apart from most, if not all, others is our heavy reliance and even dependence on culture for survival.

Although anthropology has long since moved beyond the understanding of culture as collective values and beliefs, organizational culture interplays with authority and dynamics such as inclusion and alienation. In business anthropologists need to expand the definition of culture to include the components of modern business structures and contemporary ideologies.[24] Business as a social institution is a social system with social actors who can make or break an organization. Anthropology provides qualitative analysis to find out what drives people.

Philosophy, history, and other schools of humanities influence anthropology. Like philosophers, anthropologists are driven by what they consider to be the universal human trait, curiosity. That provides a basis for questions relevant to both historical situations and contemporary cultural practices. These questions include

- how, when, and where human life arose
- why cultures have evolved
- how languages evolved
- how distinctions of rank came into being
- anything else that seeks to understand the whole of human existence

To get at these issues, anthropologists apply the scientific method to their research, similar to sociologists. However, anthropological knowledge is based on the researcher's interpretation of events without the development of quantitative research. The methodology is subjective, so the credibility of the researcher is vital to the success of a study. Anthropologists do research onsite as well as virtually.[25] As with the other schools of humanities, this type of knowledge is built on existing knowledge, which will be expanded by future research. There are five methods of anthropological inquiry, which may or may not be used together:[26]

- Comparative method: This approach addresses the co-evolution of cultural elements uses cross-cultural comparisons in attempts to explain similarities and differences among people; correlate two or more elements across cultures.
- Biological/evolutionary anthropology: This approach depicts *Homo sapiens* as a genus and species, and is concerned with the biology, evolution, and genetic diversity of people, from fossils and human skeletons to human genetics

- Archeology: The application of archeology to business focuses on the interpretation of artifacts to make sense of ways of life. (Note that there is a distinct movement among archeologists to classify archeology apart from anthropology.)
- Linguistic anthropology: This method addresses the relationship of language and culture; how language shapes and perpetuates culture through socialization, ritual, and discourse.
- Cultural anthropology: This method asks how we, as humans, are shaped by cultural practice.

Business anthropologists provide insight into organizational phenomena as an alternative to more formal methods of inquiry.[27] They study business fields, including management, operations, marketing, consumer behavior, organizational culture, human resources management, and international management.[28] They help identify real problems in everyday business. Here are some issues that business anthropologists analyze:[29]

- corporate cultures
- knowledge management
- cultural audits
- organizational change
- product design and development
- marketing and consumer research
- globalization and cross-cultural issues

The anthropology readings in this unit each present a strong case for the use of anthropology in business. Guang Tian makes the distinction that applied anthropology improves business through doing, thinking, and writing from a global vantage point. Ervin follows with an analysis of the role of applied anthropology in determining the need for change in business. Finally, Ferraro and Briody address the integration of applied anthropology cross-culturally. They argue that the issues that anthropologists uncover cannot be ignored by successful businesses.

Notes

1. OMICS International. (n.d.). Sociology – research articles. https://www.omicsonline.org/sociology/research-articles.php
2. Parker, M. (2015). Between sociology and the business school: Critical studies of work, employment and organization in the UK. *Sociological Review*, *63*(1), 162–180.
3. Joseph, M. (1989). *Sociology for business: A practical approach*. Polity.
4. Michie, J. (Ed.). (2011). *The handbook of globalisation*. Edward Elgar Publishing.
5. Michie, J. (Ed.). (2011). *The handbook of globalisation*. Edward Elgar Publishing.
6. Burrell, G. (2017). Virtual special issue on 'sociology and business ethics'. *Journal of Business Ethics*, *144*(1), 1–4.
7. Hill-Collins, P. (2013). Pushing the boundaries or business as usual? Race, class, and gender studies and sociological inquiry. In Calhoun, C. (Ed.), *Sociology in America: A History* (pt. 17).
8. Parker, M. (2015). Between sociology and the business school: Critical studies of work, employment and

organization in the UK. *The Sociological Review, 63*(1), 162–180.

9. Marquis, A. (n.d.). *Importance of studying sociology in business.* Small Business—Chron.com. http://smallbusiness.chron.com/importance-studying-sociology-business-23995.html
10. Mandják, T., & Szántó, Z. (2010). How can economic sociology help business relationship management? *Journal of Business & Industrial Marketing, 25*(3), 202–208. https://doi.org/10.1108/08858621011027795
11. Mandják, T., & Szántó, Z. (2010). How can economic sociology help business relationship management? *Journal of Business & Industrial Marketing, 25*(3), 202–208. https://doi.org/10.1108/08858621011027795
12. Burrell, G. (2017). Virtual special issue on 'sociology and business ethics'. *Journal of Business Ethics, 144*(1), 1–4.
13. Joseph, M. (1989). *Sociology for business: A practical approach.* Polity.
14. Brinkmann, J. (2019). The potential use of sociological perspectives for business ethics teaching. *Journal of Business Ethics,* 156, 273–287. https://doi.org/10.1007/s10551-017-3636-x
15. Joseph, M. (1989). *Sociology for business: A practical approach.* Polity.
16. Hendry, J. (2001). After Durkheim: An agenda for the sociology of business ethics. *Journal of Business Ethics, 34*(3/4), 209–218.
17. Hill-Collins, P. (2013). Pushing the boundaries or business as usual? Race, class, and gender studies and sociological inquiry. In Calhoun, C. (Ed.), *Sociology in America: A History* (pt. 17).
18. Ferris, K., & Stein, Jill. (2018). *The real world: An introduction to sociology* (6th ed.).
19. Denes, A., (2012, July). Intangible cultural heritage and museums learning resources. Princess Maha Chakri Sirindhorn Anthropology Centre.
20. Evans-Pritchard, E. E. (2013). *Social anthropology.* Routledge.
21. *Business, Society and Environment* (2013) 103–11.
22. Miller, B. D., Van Esterik, J., & Van Esterik, P. (2007). *Cultural anthropology.* Pearson/Allyn and Bacon.
    Belshaw, C. S. (1959). The identification of values in anthropology. *American Journal of Sociology 64*(6), 555–562.
    Mace, R., Pagel, M., Bowen, J. R., Gupta, B. K. D., Otterbein, K. F., Ridley, M., ... and Voland, E. (1994). The comparative method in anthropology [and comments and reply]. *Current Anthropology, 35*(5), 549–564.
    Stanford, C., Allen, J. S., & Antón, S. C. (2011). *Biological anthropology: The natural history of humankind.* Pearson Education.
    Nichols, D. L., Joyce, R. A., & Gillespie, S. D. (2003). Is archaeology anthropology? *Archeological Papers of the American Anthropological Association, 13*(1), 3–13.
    Duranti, A. (Ed.). (2009). *Linguistic anthropology: A reader* (Vol. 1). John Wiley & Sons.
23. Science Daily. (n.d.). Anthropology. Reference terms. https://www.sciencedaily.com/terms/anthropology.htm
24. Caulkins, D. (2013). Changing rhetoric of corporate culture. In *Companion to Organizational Anthropology* (pp. 56–73).
25. Albu, O. B., Larsen, F., Sigurdarson, H., Andersen, K., & Hansen, L. L. G. (2013). What is business anthropology? An ethnographic study of an explorative workshop. *Journal of Business Anthropology,* CS5.
26. https://www.americananthro.org.
27. Ybema, S., Yanow, D., Wels, H., & Kamsteeg, F. H. (2009). *Organizational ethnography. Studying the complexities of everyday life.* SAGE.
28. Guang, T. (2013). *Why is business anthropology important?*
29. Walle, A. H. (2013). *Rethinking business anthropology: Cultural strategies in marketing and management.* Greenleaf Pub.

Reading 5.1

Studying Work, Society and Organisation

Tony Watson

Tony Watson, "Studying Work, Society and Organisation," *Sociology, Work and Organisation: Seventh Edition*, pp. 3-11, 411-464.

Key Issues

- What is work?
- What is 'thinking sociologically'?
- How can we most helpfully think about 'social organisation', 'society' and 'societies'?
- What role has sociology played historically in understanding a changing world and what role might it play in understanding contemporary issues and transitions?
- In what ways can sociology be understood to be a science?
- In what ways do sociologists use theories, adopt various research methods and work within differing philosophical (or 'methodological') assumptions?

People, Work and Society

Sociology is a resource which people can use to understand better how the social world 'works', so that they can act more effectively in the various social spheres in which they lead their lives. One of those spheres is work. Yes, but already in the opening words of this book, we have used the word 'work' in two rather different ways. When we say, for example, 'I want to understand better how modern banking works', and when we state that 'my father used to work in a bank', we are not speaking of the same thing. 'Work' is one of those words that is used in many different ways. It is also used very frequently. It is the eighty-seventh most common word in English, occurring 3 million times in the *Oxford English Dictionary* (Hargraves 2014).

If we are going to study human work activities and how they are organised and experienced, we need to decide how we are going to use the term 'work'. This is not a matter of producing a final and absolute definition of work. Sociology, like all scientific and other forms of systematic study, proceeds by deciding what is likely to be the most useful way of characterising the topics being studied. Certain types of economic inquiry in a modern industrialised society might best be conducted by defining work in terms of task-based activities for which people are paid by an employer, client or customer. However, this would exclude all those tasks that we refer to as 'housework' for example. This would be a serious omission given that, in Brown's (1997) words, 'without the enormous volume and unremitting cycle of domestic labour the formal economy of jobs and pay packets would cease to function'. Pettinger *et al.* (2006) build on this insight in their suggestions for a 'new sociology of work', one which pays close attention to the 'blurry line between work and not-work'. Glucksmann (2006) suggests that such a sociology of work might look at such activities as the cooking and preparing of meals, recognising the fusion of work, non-work and skill acquisitions which such activities entail. But we have to careful here. If we include in the scope of the sociology of work all task-oriented activity in which effort is expended, then we risk extending our study to such activities as walking across a room to switch on a television set or packing a bag to take for a day on the beach. We need a compromise that gives sufficient focus to our studies without limiting them to activities with a formal economic outcome.

There are two main aspects of work that a sociological concept of work needs to recognise. The first is the task-related aspect of work and the second is the part played by work in the way people 'make a living'.

Work

The carrying out of tasks which enable people to *make a living* within the social and economic context in which they are located.

Thinking about work in this way associates it with the expenditure of effort to carry out tasks, but it limits it to something that has an economic element—in the very broad sense of dealing with problems of survival in a world of scarce resources. But the notion of 'making a living' implies much more than just producing enough material goods to ensure physical survival. People do not simply extract a living from the environment. Work transforms environments in many ways and, in the process, creates for many people a level of living far in excess of basic subsistence. But it does more than this. It also relates intimately to how people shape their very lives and identities. And people's lives are significantly shaped by the circumstances in which they have to work. The work people do becomes closely bound up with their conception of self. In looking at how people 'make a living', we are looking at how they deal with both the economic and the social or cultural aspects of their lives.

Work is a social, economic and cultural phenomenon. It is not simply a matter of behaviour. Work occurs in societies, and as with work, we have to conceptualise 'society' before we can systematically examine the role of work in human societies.

Society

The broad pattern of social, economic, cultural and political relationships within which people lead their lives, typically but not exclusively in the modern world as members of the same nation state.

Social Organisation, Work Organisations and Thinking About Work Sociologically

Sociology provides us with a range of insights, concepts, theories and research findings which help us understand the wide range of work and work-related activities that occur in the context of the broader social and cultural arrangements.

Sociology

The study of the relationships which develop between human beings as they organise themselves and are organised by others in societies and how these patterns influence and are influenced by the actions and interactions of people and how they make sense of their lives and identities.

This definition of sociology incorporates the basic insight which is shared by all the social science disciplines: that human life does not happen randomly or by individuals and small groups following their instincts in order to survive. Social life is organised. If there were no organised patterns in social life, there would be no predictability to our lives, no sense of order and nothing to stop people killing and robbing from each other as they pursued selfish interests. For this reason, we can identify various patterns of *social organisation* existing throughout human history. Hunter gatherer lives were socially organised as was life in the Roman Empire or in African nomadic tribes. However, a characteristic and dominant institution in contemporary industrial-capitalist societies is that of the bureaucratised work organisation. Thus, in the societies in which we currently live, there is general *social organisation* (a pattern of social structures, cultures, institutions and so on). Within this there is a set of *work organisations* that operate—sometimes in co-operation with each other, sometimes in competition with each other—to produce and provide goods and services and administer social, political and economic aspects of life.

Whether we are dealing with activities at the level of the individual, the group or the work organisation, the essential characteristic of the sociological perspective is that it *ultimately relates whatever it studies back to the way society as a whole is organised.* Sociology works on the assumption that no social action, at however mundane a level, takes place in a social vacuum. It is always linked back to the wider culture, social structure and processes of the society in which it takes place. These structures, processes, norms and values, with all their related inequalities, ideologies and power distributions, are the source of both constraints and opportunities which people meet in conducting their lives. The better and more widely these cultures, structures and processes are understood and the better the connections between specific actions or arrangements and these basic patterns are appreciated, then the greater is the opportunity for the human control over work, industry and every other kind of social institution.

Let us illustrate this argument by trying to make sense of a simple piece of 'everyday' work-related human behaviour. One might interpret this, first, as if one were simply a casual observer and, second, as if one were a sociologist.

If we were viewing this scene as strangers to this work organisation, whether or not we were formally trained as sociologists, we would be thinking about both the personal and the work relationship between these people: were they a married couple, lovers or simply people sharing a lift to work? We would wonder how this aspect of their relationship related to the authority relationship between them: presumably one of them was 'the boss', was the more highly paid, the more highly trained, and had the right to give instructions to the other. If we were more consciously sociological in our speculations, however, we would draw on our knowledge of 'sociological' matters such as social class, educational and career opportunity structures, bureaucratic authority structures, culturally normal patterns of workplace layout and the patterns of behaviour, rules, assumptions and expectations associated with work activities in this particular society and culture at this particular time in history.

Snapshot 5.1.1

A man and a woman arrive at work

A man and a woman get out of a car and walk into an office block. One of them goes into a large private office and closes the door. The other sits at a desk outside that office alongside several other people. The person in the private space telephones the one in the outer office, and a few minutes later, the latter individual takes a cup of coffee and a biscuit into the person in the inner office.

If it were the man that entered the private office, we might note that standard 'norms' were being followed with regard to gender relationships. But if it were the woman who 'played the role' of the senior person—the presumably higher paid, more qualified individual with greater authority—we might begin to reflect on how this individual has come to challenge established patterns. How had she come to break established norms? What opportunity structures had she used, what barriers had she overcome? To what extent were her actions and her relatively unusual position in the workplace part of a broader pattern of social change?

In analysing this simple piece of mundane activity in this way, we are thinking sociologically. In asking these questions, we are asking sociological questions. And, in doing so, we are engaging with issues of power and life chances in a way that both enhances our 'academic' understanding of relationships at work and, at the same time, offers understandings of possibilities and practices which have the potential to inform human choices that might further—or, for that matter, resist—social change.

Choices, Constraints and Opportunities in Work and Society

Sociology's potential as a resource for informing human choice is something to which we will return shortly. First, however, we need to reinforce the point about working arrangements and social patterns being both the outcomes of human actions and factors helping shape those actions. Sociology has been defined here as something that looks at how human beings organise both themselves and each other. In looking at how people think and behave, it looks for cultural patterns and 'structures' in social life. These patterns are seen as both the outcome of the activities of individuals and as things that in turn, influence, encourage and constrain the individual. If, for example, it was the man in Snapshot 5.1.1 who was the more senior of our two social actors, he might tell us in an interview that his current role as the organisation's head of information technology was the outcome of a series of *choices* that he personally made in his life. The woman, to whom he gives a daily lift in his company car, might talk to us about how she chose to train and work as an office secretary.

As sociological observers, we would not want to discount these claims to choice or 'agency' in these individuals' career patterns. Nor would we say that there were no individual choices behind the pattern whereby the great majority of the important 'decision-makers' in this organisation are currently men and most of the secretarial and 'personal assistant' workers are women. Choices have clearly been made. Nobody forced these people into these jobs. Each human individual is an agent, with wants, aspirations and a sense of identity which they bring to any decision to speak or act. But, at the same time, we are likely to be aware that the pattern we have observed is, in some sense, an outcome of the way the 'society' in which these people grew up channelled male and female children into different spheres of activity. There were clearly pressures on each child from the world around them: from role examples observed as they grew up to the opportunities made available to boys and girls in both education and initial employment.

It is easily possible to see two mutually exclusive alternative types of explanation emerging here: agency and choice on the one hand, and structural 'channelling' on the other. Sometimes sociologists talk of making a choice between *voluntarist* and *structural* frames of reference and modern sociological thought is characterised, as Swingewood (2000) observes, 'by a continual tension between ... a voluntarist model which emphasises the creative and active role of agents, and a structural model which focuses on institutions and processes which constrain and determine the course of action'.

To use terms which have been around as long as there has been social thought, we can speak of explanations which emphasise free will and explanations which stress determinism. This is something that sociologists try to go beyond. To develop an explanation of the patterns observed, we need an analysis which considers the way these individuals came to shape their career interests and 'choose' their aspirations in the light of their previous experiences in life and what they have learned from the cultural and parental influences upon them to be the appropriate and possible types of work for them to enter. There is an interweaving of individual and social factors, of free choice and of constraint. We might simplify this, as Figure 5.1.1 does, by saying that individuals make society and society makes individuals.

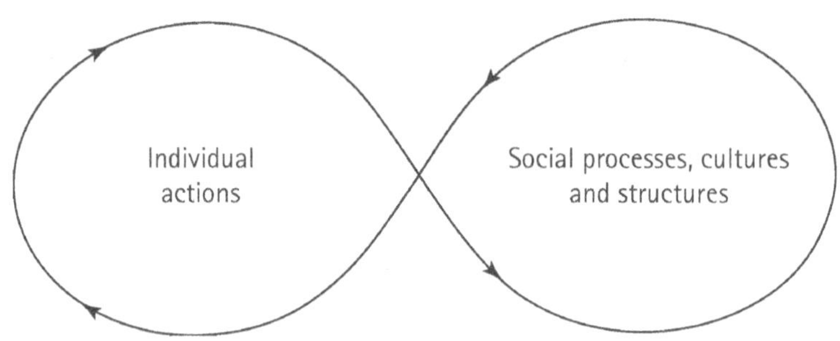

Figure 5.1.1 Individuals make society and society makes individuals

The analytical distinction between individual actions, on the one hand, and 'the social' on the other does not fully parallel the free will and determinism distinction, however, because it is possible to talk of an individual's actions being severely constrained, if not determined, by factors such as their individual genetic make-up. Equally, it is possible to see social structures as providing opportunities for individuals to realise their individual interests ('climbing the ladder' of the class structure, say), as well as seeing people constrained by such structures (being excluded from an activity because of one's gender or race, for example). Human beings are makers of social patterns and are also made by them. These patterns both constrain us and enable us to achieve our purposes. But these patterns or 'structures' are not objectively existing entities outside of human patterns of interaction, even though it may at times feel as if they have this kind of forceful presence.

Sociology is not simply the study of 'the social', of societies, of social structures. Neither, of course, is it a study of individuals' activities, aggregated in some way to give us a view of societies as little more than the sum of their parts. It is, rather, a study of the interrelationships between the individual and the social whose greatest potential lies in examining the processes whereby human initiatives and choices shape and are shaped by patterns of human interaction and power.

Work and the Sociological Imagination

In one of the most influential reflections on what sociology can contribute to human life, Mills (1970) identified the *sociological imagination* as a way of switching 'upwards' from an initial focus on the private problems of individuals. Such problems arise in the case of Mathieu and Valerie, who face losing their jobs, in Snapshot 5.1.2. It would be helpful if one were, first, to identify what some of the personal troubles of this couple might be in these circumstances. Second, one can go on to consider how their personal predicament might relate to broader 'public issues'.

Snapshot 5.1.2

The personal troubles of Mathieu and Valerie

Mathieu and Valerie are a couple in their thirties who have three young children: two at primary school and one at nursery school. For the past dozen or so years, they have both done assembly work at a car factory which, under a variety of owners, has been part of the industrial city in which they live for many years. The current owners have decided to move all the work to a newly built factory in Eastern Europe—arguing that the 'cost patterns' and the 'potential for innovation' in that setting make it imperative for them to cease operating in the city in which Valerie was born and into which Mathieu moved when he and Valerie first set up home together.

The first 'personal trouble' which is likely to confront the couple is that of a large drop in their family income. Neither of them is likely to know of alternative jobs in the city. They are likely to be distressed at the prospect of losing their heavily mortgaged home and to worry that, even if they choose to sell the house, they will have serious difficulties because many other redundant workers are likely to be putting their properties on the market at the same time. Also, if they are able to move, whether within the city or beyond it, they will worry about the children's education. They are likely to have struggled to get the children into the schools in which they are currently very happy. They are likely to hate to take their children away from these schools and from the various friends and relatives that are such an important part of the lives of the whole family.

Although, as human beings, we are likely to be very concerned for Valerie, Mathieu and for all the other families affected by this big business decision, our distinctively sociological interests move us to a further level of concern. The sociological perspective places human predicaments such as these in their broader context. Mills (1970) characterised this broader context as raising 'public issues' and this language immediately suggests to us a range of matters such as the levels of employment and unemployment in the city, the quality of educational provision for young children in this society and the nature of housing markets. These issues would require us to draw on other social sciences in addition to sociology—economics in particular. We would look at issues ranging from the state of the international market for manufactured goods and managerial, governmental and trade union policies, to patterns of technological change and patterns of business ownership. And within the analysis which we would undertake there is considerable potential for distinctly sociological matters such as patterns of urban change, gender differences in careers and child-rearing, class and power in business decision-making, the relationship between work and personal identities, the impact of globalising trends on different nation-states and so on.

Sociology, then, shifts the level of focus from that of the close-up on individuals and their working life to that of the 'big picture' of the society in which they live. Sociology is not simply 'painting a picture', however broad that might be, however. It goes beyond this to look for regularities, patterns, structures and processes. The events in Valerie and Mathieu's city will be set in their historical context and the overall structure of the several societies involved—the industrial bases, the political-economic systems of both eastern and western Europe and the ways in which these fit into patterns of global change. In analysing these structures and processes, the sociologist would try to show how they potentially both constrain people as well as enable people to further their personal wishes, whether these people be corporate managers, politicians and trade union officers or 'ordinary' employees like Mathieu and Valerie.

This distinctly sociological way of thinking means stepping outside our normal 'everyday' common sense way of thinking about our working lives and adopting what is perhaps the most basic sociological insight of all: that there is more than one way and one way only for men and women to organise their lives. In other words, the way society *is* is not necessarily the way society *has to be*. In the realm of work this means that the way we currently organise production and distribution does not possess some immutable inevitability. It is only one of a range of possibilities. Baumann and May (2001) refer to sociology's ability to help us appreciate its 'anti-fixating' power. We are reminded, they say, that what we might think of as the 'natural, inevitable, eternal aspects of our lives' have come into being as a result of the exercise of 'human power and human resources'. This, in turn, suggests that social patterns are not 'immune and impenetrable to human action—our own action included'. A world that might have seemed 'oppressive in its apparent fixity' is shown to be a world that could be 'different from what it is now'. We are thus encouraged not to surrender to what might, at first, seem to be irresistible pressures and circumstances.

The original sociologists were thinkers striving to make sense of the dislocations of their age, as we shall shortly observe. The attempts by the classical sociological thinkers to make sense of their time are invaluable to us because, in an historical location more marginal than our own, they were better able to look at the industrial capitalist world in the light of conceptions of alternatives (Watson 2009b). This is the humanistic significance and the continuing relevance to us today of people like Marx, Weber and Durkheim. They were perhaps more aware of alternatives on a societal level than we are because they were better placed historically to contrast the modern and the industrial with the traditional, the urban with the rural, and so on. ...

Bibliography

Baumann, Z. and May, T. (2001) *Thinking Sociologically*, Oxford: Blackwell.

Brown, R. K. (1997) 'The changing practices of work', in R.K. Brown (ed), *The Changing Shape of Work*, London, Macmillan: 20–53.

Hargraves, O. (2014) *It's Been Said Before: A Guide to the Use and Abuse of Clichés*, Oxford: Oxford University Press.

Mills, C.W. (1970) *The Sociological Imagination*, Harmondsworth: Penguin.

Pettinger, L., Parry, J., Taylor, R. and Glucksmann, M. (eds) (2006) *A New Sociology of Work?* Oxford: Blackwell/Sociological Review.

Swingewood, A. (2000) *A Short History of Sociological Thought*, Basingstoke: Macmillan.

Watson, T. J. (2009b) 'Work and the sociological imagination: the need for continuity and change in the study of continuity and change', *Sociology*, 43(5): 861–877.

Sociology for Business

Martin Joseph

[...]

Why Do Sociologists Study Organizations? Why Do They Theorize about Them?

Much of the literature on organizations comes from sociologists, though psychologists and management theorists make their contribution too. If you understand why sociologists study organizations, you'll be able to see how their studies can help managers and business people in dealing with organizations and their problems. Here then are a few possible 'answers' to the questions that head this section.

1. As mentioned, sociologists are interested in questions of power, authority, values, beliefs, social control and ideologies. Why do people believe in ideologies? Why do they obey rulers or overseers; how do those in authority maintain control? These concepts and questions, difficult to isolate for sociological analysis in society as a whole, are present with greater clarity within organizations.
2. Organizational problems such as apathy can occur over a wide range of organizations such as the commercial firm, the hospital, the army, trade unions, etc. A sociological analysis of organizations assists our understanding of such problems; for example, apathy has been shown to be frequently linked to over-zealous

control.

3. The organizational 'rule books'—the official management instructions—are of great interest for sociological study. Instead of seeing the rules as just rules, the sociologist might ask, 'what do these rules really mean?' What are the underlying assumptions made by managers and managed? Who gains by the rules and do these rules reflect an ideology? Who loses?' This sort of enquiry can sometimes make sociologists unpopular with management, but it is a vital part of the process of understanding what actually goes on.
4. Theories are attempts to get closer to the truth. They are always approximations (sociologists recognize that people have individual characteristics and responses), but they help to illuminate our understanding of situations. Through debate between sociological researchers and others theories are refined or discarded and replaced.
5. The management approach to organizational theory tends to stress how members ought to behave, or could be encouraged to behave, in order, for example, to increase the efficiency of the organization [...]. By contrast the sociologist studies people as they actually are in their natural settings, at home with the family, at work with the colleagues, at college with their fellow students and so on. This is one of the ways in which sociologists try to be objective and 'value-free' in their research.

So far it has been shown that there is a variety of reasons for the sociologist's interest in organizations, especially the fact that power, authority and ideologies may be more clearly analysed in discrete organizations. But, as just mentioned, organizations are not separate from the rest of society. Organizations could be seen as reproductions of society—reproducing also the social class divisions of society. Thus some have argued that members of the upper social classes can influence the recruitment of members of their own class to high positions in important organizations[1] (and 'self-recruitment' can apply at all levels in the organization). Nowadays the traditional claims of property and inheritance have to be supplemented with relevant education and technical expertise. The success of the higher class in obtaining high positions depends partly on wealth, which buys education, for example, and partly on 'correct' social background, and this ensures that high office holders are usually endowed with 'correct' attitudes, values and ideologies.[2] Not only do managers and directors share similar values; they often own a considerable proportion of their firms.

The value-free approach

Value freedom in sociology means that researchers should not be influenced by the beliefs they are studying. Instead, they should study these beliefs in a 'scientific' and 'objective' way, producing just the facts. They should not make their own judgements about these beliefs, nor advocate particular beliefs, values and ideologies. Many critics of sociology say it cannot be scientific because one cannot measure beliefs and concepts, with which it often deals. It is very hard to attain a value-free sociology because our own values keep intruding. For example, a sociologist researching low-paid workers may sympathize with their feelings, but should not allow this sympathy to influence his findings. Although it is hard, sociologists should either strive to avoid influencing their work with their own values, or make their own values clear in their writing.

A Management Approach to the Theory of Organizations

The theories of organization quoted so far are to a large extent sociological. It would be interesting to examine some management theories on organizations in order to see more clearly any hidden assumptions that are being made. It would be impossible to examine the whole range of management theory;[3] it should also be unnecessary. If readers can sociologically analyse theories for themselves, then there is no need to 'learn' the author's views. Instead it will be useful to tackle what are perhaps the two central problems of most organizations, ones that feature in most management theories of organization, communications and decision-making, and see what the management theorists have to say about them.

Good Communications in Organizations

Good communication is an essential element in decision-making in an organization. It is also essential for the participation of employees, or at least for genuine consultation. Ideally there should be smooth *two-way* consultation; that is, both up and down the organization hierarchy. What impedes communication downwards? What impedes communication upwards?

One of the impediments to downward communication is the excessive secrecy of leaders and supervisors referred to earlier. British government departments are notorious for excessive secrecy, but many business organizations are guilty of this too. Why is this? One possible explanation, mentioned before, is the link between information and power. It can be argued that control over information is critically important in mobilizing the power needed to put decisions into effect; in one study of a prison where all reports had to pass through a custodial hierarchy, that hierarchy was able to distort the goals of a prisoners' rehabilitation programme being run from outside that prison. A member of an organization who controls the flow of information is known as a gatekeeper. Often gate keepers are in a position of power (such as a head warder in a prison), and often they distort the information they pass on (or do not pass it on at all).[4] It seems from this that handing over information can involve handing over power, keeping knowledge to oneself makes others who rely on the use of the knowledge dependent on oneself; hence secrecy bolsters the position of management. How many times have staff who have been made redundant complained that they were not warned? If they had been warned, they might have come up with an alternative proposal to solve the problem, which management wanted to solve by redundancy. Sometimes there may be a feeling that lower level employees cannot be trusted with information, or that they may misinterpret it. Better not to say anything than to risk causing misunderstandings!

There are other barriers to downward communication, built into the structure of most organizations. One is that communication *takes time;* most managers have large workloads and have not been taught to put communication at the top of their list of priorities (because the effects of communication can rarely be precisely measured in terms of output). Another problem, related to this, is that managers have little training in communication skills.

Turning to impediments to upward communication; often it is lower-level employees who know first that something is amiss. Usually they are not the people who can make a decision about solving the problem. For example, the manual worker on the shop floor may be one of the first to spot faults in the product; the ordinary salesperson may be the one most likely to know why a product is not selling; the private secretary will be aware of the defects of office procedures; the clerk in an outpatients' clinic knows many of the defects in the administration of the system, though they may go unnoticed by the consultant. Why does this information often fail to reach the decisionmaker? Managers, administrators and workers may act as gatekeepers for information, for example in preventing undesirable information from reaching the decision-makers. They may not wish to be the harbingers of bad news, especially if it may reflect on their running of their department, or machine.

A further difficulty is that managers and non-managers often have quite different viewpoints. There may be a cultural divide. Communication can be much easier within the workforce itself than between superiors and workers. Often subordinates avoid consulting supervisors for fear of making a mistake.[5] They do not want to be judged. Of course it should be mentioned that there are cliques and conflicts of interest within management itself that also work against horizontal flow of information.

What can management do to improve communications? Management theories argue that as far as possible managers should aim at the free flow of information, up and down, horizontally and diagonally. Having clearly stated goals helps towards clear communication because:

- it lessens misunderstandings;
- it is an aid in discovering where conflict is (which is the first step towards resolving it);
- the setting of goals for the future is an aid in anticipating where the future setbacks might occur.[6]

One way of achieving clear goals in business organization is through 'management by objectives', in which management's aims are translated into particular goals for each person in the organization.[7]

What is the purpose of company meetings? A management view

"In practice, even the most apparently futile of meetings usually serves some wider corporate purpose as well as preserving the mental health of those who attend: it builds and maintains the communication network, it gives a feeling of security, it helps to sort out status and quasiterritory, and it reaffirms identity and the sense of belonging. No corporation could survive or be described as a corporation if every member travelled in from his private house by his private car to his private office, met no one during the day, and travelled back in the evening. Any Corporation Man or Women who found himself or herself in that position for a few weeks would start to wonder how long it would be before he or she got the sack. A certain amount of factory work is in fact very like this, since the noise or the demands of the operation make each person into an island: it is hardly surprising that if the corporation does not bring its members together for regular meetings, they seek assembly and association through the unions. But at the higher and more comfortable levels, most corporations have found ways of channelling this need for association into useful and productive purposes, and in fact the more visibly effective and valuable the meeting the more it fulfils all the social and therapeutic needs as well."[8]

Another method of improving communication might be through setting up joint committees of managers and non-managers in order to decide upon problems of mutual interest. An example of this was the Joint Productivity Councils set up in Britain during the Second World War. It might be objected that such committees blur the fact that decisions have to be taken, and responsibility has to be taken for these decisions. In this respect too many committees could weaken the organization. A committee may be useful as a response to temporary problems such as a move, or a disciplinary matter, or a disagreement on a specific matter, but after the item has been dealt with the committee should perhaps be dissolved. On the other hand, joint committees may be useful for handling long-term issues and planning. It is important to point out that the efficacy of these cooperative committees depends on management's perception of them: do they regard them as *legitimate* mechanisms in the firm? It also depends on whether the workers respect their 'representatives' and feel that their interests are being properly looked after.

Improving communications may be achieved by improving the communication skills of individuals—especially managers. Examples of this would be training in report-writing, faster reading and 'management', plus advice and counselling, and so on. Against this it might be said that people learn best on the job, and such classes might be resented by older adults (not least by well-educated managers). However, communications skills should certainly be taught to business and management *students*.

A Sociological Assessment of 'Bad Communications'

A sociologist might make some objections to the sort of 'solutions' to the problems of communication considered here. It seems a truism that in many organizations people tend to keep to their own groups and not speak to out-groupers. Often there are separate canteens, car parks and toilet facilities for managers and non-managers. Make the test for yourself in your own organization. Thus, if you are a student, look around your college refectory. Do the lecturers have their own separate dining-room? Within the student refectory itself students may look alike and appear to be mixing freely. However, if you look a little closer you will probably see that these students are in their own groups; business studies students talk to business studies students; accountancy students talk to their fellow accountancy students, and so on.

Thus in an organization people are quite likely to keep to their own sub-groups, e.g. an occupational group or, say, their own office or work-group. Secretaries may form one group, computer programmers another. The rule seems to be 'birds of a feather flock together'.

It is not surprising therefore that managers do not mix and communicate much with other organizational members. There is, moreover, a cultural divide that has already been referred to. So too has class difference. [...] [M]anagers (and professionals) have *careers;* most other employees have *jobs*. Careers confer greater knowledge, information and power on managers, and this is reflected in the organization's communication system. Further a career implies:

- a logical lifelong progression to higher positions through promotion—and competition for these higher positions;
- devotion to the task;
- devotion to the employing organization.

While this may apply also to some other employees, a job normally implies that money is the main consideration. There seems to be a social divide between those who have jobs and those who have careers. Overall the problem with the management theories is that they *ignore* real conflict; they assume that if only management could communicate well to staff, staff would be happy with management's decisions. Yet in reality the involvement of staff is often alienative [...].

Another reason for this lack of contact and communication between managers and others is lack of trust. The two groups sometimes do not trust each other. Some managers may feel that the workforce has to be watched all the time, and only basic information is communicated to them.

Really good communications and good decision-making are vitally linked. You cannot have one without the other. Bad decisions, no matter how 'well' they are communicated, will not lead to harmony or efficiency in the firm.

Decision-Making in Organizations

Basically the problems an organization faces in its decision-making are: which goals to pursue; what means can be used; what technology is available; what personnel is available. The various strategies are set out below.[9]

		Preferences regarding possible outcomes	
Beliefs about cause/ effect relations	Certain	*Certainty* Computation	*Uncertainty* Compromise
	Uncertain	Judgement	Inspiration

Good decision-making means trying to reduce the uncertainties involved, making it as routine as possible, as in computation. To achieve this the following suggestions are made.

- Maintain good communications, as discussed in this [reading].
- Do not make false assumptions (easier said than done). Quite often bad decision-making is the result of false assumptions, especially in personnel management and industrial relations. The next section indicates the nature of these false assumptions.
- The theme of this section has been that the better the communication the less the likelihood of false assumptions and therefore bad decision-making. Probably the real barrier is that the different parties tend to have different values and this leads to a biased view of what is really going on (that is to say the parties see only what they want to see). The parties do not see or hear or understand each other because unconsciously they do not wish to—it would be threatening to do so. One example of this is Ian McGregor's book on the miners' strike in 1984/5, when he was Chairman of the National Coal Board. The book's title is *The Enemies Within.*[10] Is this the sort of language that encourages good communication?
- Maybe the emphasis should be less on making right decisions and more on *making decisions come right*. This implies adaptability and listening to others (stop commanding and start co-operating). Section 10 tries to show why this is easier said than done. Perhaps also managers over-emphasize the need for decisions. If there were more genuine consultations and involvement at work—more autonomy and less control—there would be much less need for management decision-making.

Question

What are the obstacles to less control and more autonomy at work?

How Rational are Organizations? A Sociological View

Organizations and the individuals within them are the products of society's institutions and of the prevailing values in society. Just as individuals and societies have beliefs, values and ideologies, so too do organizations. These ideologies cannot be described in purely rational terms; they are based on beliefs, hopes and fears. Nevertheless, they influence organizational decision-making, which is usually intended to be rational. Obviously it is important to understand the nature of these ideologies in order to understand decision-making in organizations. Most ideologies are beliefs that favour the powerful in society—in this case higher management. [...]

Although the values and goals of organizations vary, there are some common organizational ideologies. The management ideology of 'scientific management', [...], is one—and one that includes several elements. The common elements of organizational ideologies to have been called: structuralism; psychologism; consensualism; welfareism; legalism. These will be considered and explained in turn.[11]

Structuralism

Structuralism, assumes that the way the organization is structured is not a matter of choice; that the structure of the organization is neutral in terms of conflict between groups and is based on the application of rational scientific principles. Structuralism stems from the deeper assumption that the principles of management generally are neutral, rational and scientific. This is the basis of a phrase often heard among managers—'there is no alternative'. The members of the organization are thought to be allocated to their positions in it according to rational criteria. People at the top are there because of their expertise. This 'expertise' tends to become mystified, having its own 'special language' which excludes junior members of the organization.

Structuralism includes an ideology of achievement. Hierarchy and the use of power is seen as inevitable and natural; the opposite is seen as anarchy and chaos. Those in the low-status positions in the organization are there through their own failure or lack of ability. All this is seen as inevitable rather than capable of change.

Psychologism

Progress through the organization is seen in terms of the member's ability and attitude. As with structuralism, the structure of the organization is seen as given; therefore if change is desirable it is the individual who must change, not the organization. Thus, *when things go wrong it is natural for managers to think that the fault lies in the employees* rather than in the structure of the organization or bad decision-making by managers. Personnel are seen as objects and resources amenable to rational measurement, utilization and change. Hence managers and management departments in colleges prefer the term 'behavioural *science*' rather than psychology or sociology, because it implies that behaviour can be measured and modified.

In training, members are encouraged to see themselves as the good 'company' person, to feel more involved in the organization, and to see their future in terms of the company's future. The achievement of this coincidence is the objective of *in-service* training courses, and company conferences.

Consensualism

Consensualism assumes that all members of the organization have the same goal. Where a breakdown occurs in the organization this is due to some fault in the individual or to a failure of communications. To some degree, the members of an organization do have the same basic goals: the survival of the organization; but the stress on consensualism may hide the fact that there is more than one way to achieve a desired end.

Thus consensualism assumes that all members of the organization agree with its goals. In reality the individual member is powerless and cannot influence decisions.

Welfareism

Welfareism is the attempt by management to engage subordinates' commitment through the apparent delegation of authority, through job enrichment and through apparent participation generally. This appears to be reasonable enough except that such actions could be ploys to maintain effective managerial control. Even where a democratic leadership style is adopted it is evaluated in terms of, say, productivity rather than the true welfare of the members, and in any case managerial control is ultimately retained.

Legalism

Legalism is based on the idea that there is a free contract between management and the employee, by which the employees contract to sell their labour and commitment to the organization. This also assumes management's right to manage on behalf of the owners, and the employees' obligation to obey instructions.

The objections to these assumptions are firstly that the contract is not free and equal. The employer is more powerful (in terms of rights over employees), and the employee's need of the money is usually strong. Secondly, employees, despite the legal assumptions, do not *freely* agree to obey instructions, but will often combine to try to achieve some control over their pay and working conditions. So when employees strike they may be deemed, by management, to have broken their contract (and this is supported in certain circumstances by the Industrial Relations Act 1983). On the other hand, changes required by management in working practices are assumed to be part of management's right to manage. Resistance to this change in the 'contract' by workers is not seen in the same light as workers' attempts to change things.

Question

Taking as an example an organization with which you are familiar, such as your college, firm, etc., or an organization in the news, give examples of structuralism, psychologism, consensualism, welfareism, and legalism. If you cannot find actual examples of all these, suggest hypothetical ones.

Here are some final general observations. The hierarchical structure of organizations is a reflection of the class-based values of our society. The hierarchical nature of organizations is a result of unquestioned assumptions rather than any necessary relationship.

We must also always question what we mean by efficiency. Efficiency for whom or for what? Thus it may appear efficient to close uneconomic pits in terms of profit for mine owners, but it is not efficient in terms of unemployment, loss of 'social capital', such as derelict houses, schools, roads, etc., and ill health (which imposes costs on the health service). It is efficient for an individual accountant whose firm charges others for her time *not* to keep records of how her time is spent; she can get more 'work' if she spends no time on record-keeping. But for her firm this is very inefficient. Conflicts of this kind arise all the time.

Question

Give examples illustrating the different meanings of efficiency—efficiency for whom?

Suggestion: You could for example examine a firm which is closing down, or laying off some staff, or one that is expanding very rapidly. What does efficiency mean for the firm's directors, for the staff, for the community?

...

Notes

1. J. Scott, *Corporations, Classes and Capitalism* (Hutchinson, London, 1985), pp. 266–8.
2. G. Salaman, *Class and the Corporation* (Fontana, London, 1981).
3. For an overview of other organizational theories, see D. S. Pugh et al. (eds), *Writers on Organizations* (Penguin, Harmondsworth, 1983).
4. M. Pettigrew, *The Politics of Organisational Decision-Making* (Tavistock, London, 1973), p. 28.
5. P. M. Blau, *The Dynamics of Bureaucracy* (University of Chicago Press, Chicago, 1963), pp. 126–7.
6. J. O'Shaughnessy, *Patterns of Business* (Allen and Unwin, London, 1966).
7. J. W. Humble, Improving Business Results (McGraw Hill, Maidenhead, 1966).
8. A. Jay, *The Corporation Man* (Jonathan Cape, London, 1972), pp. 201–2).
9. Adapted from J. D. Thompson, *Organization in Action* (McGraw-Hill, London, 1967), p. 134.
10. I. McGregor with R. Tyler, *The Enemies Within* (London, Fontana/Collins, 1986).
11. Most of this section is based on G. Salaman, Work Organisations: Resistance and Control (Longman, London, 1979).

Business Anthropology: An Overview

Robert Guang Tian

Robert Guang Tian, "Business Anthropology: An Overview," *Rethinking Business Anthropology: Cultural Strategies in Marketing and Management*, ed. Alf H. Walle, pp. 197-201, 210-213.

Introduction

The roles and functions of business anthropologists are widely recognized (Jordan 2010), especially ethnographic investigations involving consumer research (Malefyt 2009). In addition, business anthropologists help organizations cope with demographic variations involving ethnic and cultural distinctiveness (Schwartz 1991). In some cases, business anthropologists interface between management and the workforce (Reice 1993).

Business anthropologists serve in many roles (Jordan 2010; Marrewijk 2010; Morais and Malefyt 2010); representative assignments include product design, organizational structure, improving the efficiency of daily operations, and so forth. No matter what the mission, however, business anthropologists tend to rely upon similar methodologies and analytic techniques including participant observation, interviewing, focus groups, survey methods, and network analysis (Aguilera 1996; Corbett 2008). Relevant substantive topics include beliefs, values, social structures, and gender-related behaviour, and so forth (Marrewijk, 2010, Ybema *et al.* 2009).

Although business anthropology can be viewed as a subset of applied anthropology (Gwynne 2003; Jordan 2003), Gwynne reminds us that business anthropology tends to serve private sector organizations pursuing the profit motive. Because much business research is of a propriety nature, furthermore, questions related to professional ethics can emerge if researchers and the organizations that hire them are not candid regarding their findings (Gwynne 2003).

Due to time constraints and the cost-conscious nature of practitioner-oriented research, investigations are usually of a much shorter duration and use fewer informants than academic or scholarly studies (Hafner 1999). In any event, the anthropological approach invariably asks questions such as "Why do people do what they do?" and "What are the full implications of doing so?"

In her recent article on the importance of business anthropology, Jordan (2010) suggests that business anthropology can be effectively divided into three fields: (1) *organizational anthropology* (the study of organizations, including their "cultures," work processes, directives for change, and so forth), (2) *the anthropology of marketing and consumer behavior,* and (3) *design anthropology* (product and services design). Agreeing with Jordan, I believe the field is destined to expand in additional directions including (4) the *anthropology of competitive intelligence and knowledge management* (Tian 2009) and (5) *the anthropology of international and cross-cultural business* (Ferraro 2006; Lillis and Tian 2009). These last two roles, not discussed here at length, can be viewed as a wave of the future and, to a degree, are addressed in Walle's text (above).

In this overview, a range of methods and tools of business anthropology are discussed with reference to the current development of the field and the way it is evolving to serve decision makers in the practitioner world. Long ignored or reduced to intellectual second class citizenship by those who favor scientific and quantitative methods, business anthropology is increasingly recognized as possessing a different but equally legitimate methodology and mission.

In order to demonstrate the contributions the field is poised to make, a number of research initiatives within business anthropology are discussed including:

1. Exploring corporate cultures
2. Tacit knowledge management
3. Cultural audits
4. Addressing organizational change
5. Product design and development
6. Marketing and consumer research, and
7. Addressing globalization and cross-cultural issues.

It is hoped that these non-exhaustive discussions regarding the role of business anthropology are useful.

Corporate Cultures

The days of allowing business organizations to be led by those who lack cultural competence are fading. Grant McCracken (2009), for example, argues that organizations need a chief cultural officer that can foster proactive adaptation instead of merely reacting to circumstances.

A business, like a society or subculture, exists within a cultural, legal, and social context and is made up of individuals that may possess idiosyncratic differences. Participants may be of both genders, span a wide range of ages, possess different educational backgrounds, and varying levels of ability. Business anthropologists have a crucial role in developing a systematic understanding of specific organizational cultures (Kotter 1991; Reeves-Ellington 1999).

From an anthropological point of view, organizations are groups of people who operate within a social system that tends to evolve over time and, to a greater or lesser extent, exhibit (internal as well as external) stress and change. Business anthropology can help generate a better understanding of corporate cultures by documenting and analyzing both formal and informal knowledge that exists within them (Garza 1991).

Unfortunately, explaining to managers that examining these questions will contribute to organizational success can be difficult. Thus, on many occasions decision makers fail to recognize the importance of the field (Aguilera 1996).

Gwynne (2003) observes that business anthropologists have a wide number of tools to employ including Lévi-Strauss' structuralism, Malinowski's functionalism, Geertz's symbolic approach, and so forth. [...] Each paradigm investigates people, culture, and social institutions in a distinctive manner; this variety provides a broad menu of qualitative tools.

No matter what approach is adopted, business anthropologists tend to view an organization as a "community" of people that is studied, analyzed, and understood as a social or cultural group (Gwynne 2003). Working to implement organizational changes can smooth the way for change by identifying cultural contexts. Thus, Judith Benson observes: "I worked closely with individuals whom I recognized as potential roadblocks ... I spent time with these major stakeholders to understand their points of view. At the same time, I worked with team members so that they could develop the process ... in a way that blended with rather than confronted the existing cultural context" (Benson 2000).

Today, decision makers recognize that organizations develop a milieu that is analogous to a "culture." Once this intellectual leap is made, business anthropologists have a vital role in helping decision makers choose alternatives that are appropriate for the corporate culture of the organization.

The Management of Tacit Knowledge

Patricia Burke suggests that observing how employees actually behave, think, and function is a vital contribution that business anthropologists are uniquely qualified to provide. Tacit knowledge consists of habits and thinking that is unstated, implicit, intuitive, and could easily be overlooked. In the discipline of knowledge management, the concept of tacit knowledge refers to areas of information and understanding that are difficult to communicate to others (Burke 1988).

The process of transforming tacit knowledge to explicit understanding is known as "articulation" or "codification." A factory worker, for example, may possess an "informal mental map" of the way raw materials actually flow through a production facility. This tacit knowledge may be more accurate than formal descriptions of the procedure developed by management. By studying tacit knowledge, business anthropologists may be able to document useful options and understandings that would otherwise remain elusive (Gwynne 2003). Tacit knowledge can provide valuable insights (Baba 1998) even though those who possess it may not recognize its value. As Michael Polanyi once observed, we know more than we can tell (1966).

Business executives who adequately document their employees' tacit knowledge can improve the efficiency of the organization. Doing so can be envisioned as "tacit knowledge management." The insights and grassroots techniques informally developed by long-term employees, for example, can sometimes be "captured" and taught to others (Baba 1986) via lectures, written guidelines, or simply by encouraging seasoned employees to provide informal advice (Laabs 1992).

Tacit knowledge can be envisioned as unwritten folklore or grassroots knowledge.[1] Anthropological methods are particularly useful when gathering this sort of informal knowledge and action. Business anthropology, therefore, has a vital role to play in tactical knowledge management.

Cultural Audits

Cultural values and preferences affect how the stakeholders of an organization respond. A strategy or initiative that is successful in one social, cultural, or organizational situation may not work effectively under other conditions. Cultural audits examine current practices, programs, and processes in order to identify their cultural appropriateness or inappropriateness. The results of a cultural audit are often kept confidential because organizations seldom air their problems in public (Gwynne 2003).

The cultural audit examines the organization's cultural and social characteristics, such as its assumptions, norms, philosophy, values, and relationships among employees. Ideally, the culture of the organization supports its vision and mission (Strathern 2000). Gwynne (2003) suggests that business anthropologists involved in cultural audits might be interested both in (1) employees' positive and negative opinions and (2) their suggestions for improvement. The audit can also identify values, feelings, attitudes, and expectations about the organization.

Sometimes business anthropologists who function as cultural auditors interview members of the organization's board of directors or even its stockholders. The information collected from a wide variety of sources is synthesized in a report typically containing specific recommendations.

A cultural audit undertaken at General Motors (GM) provides a good example. The managers observed that some former expatriates experienced morale problems upon returning home (Briody and Baba 1993). Many returnees felt their overseas work was not appreciated and that their status in the company suffered because of overseas service.

A series of interviews determined that some of GM's domestic operations were administratively linked, or "coupled," with overseas operations, while others were not. The domestic employees of "de-coupled" operations developed chauvinistic attitudes (Garza 1991) and possessed little understanding or appreciation for, the importance of their expatriate counterparts. As a result, employees returning home after an overseas assignment often had less promising future opportunities.

Based on this cultural audit, recommendations were made regarding how GM could improve returning employees' productivity and job satisfaction through the establishment of an exchange program in which American and foreign workers traded places for a few years in ways that prevented their careers from becoming side-tracked (Garza 1991; Gwynne 2003).

References

Aguilera, F. (1996) "Is Anthropology Good for the Company?," *American Anthropologist* 98. 4: 735–42.
Baba, M. (1986) *Business and Industrial Anthropology: An Overview* NAPA Bulletin No. 2 (Washington, DC: NAPA).
Baba, M. (1998) "Anthropologists in Corporate America: 'Knowledge Management' and Ethical Angst" *Chronicle of Higher Education* May 8: B4–B5.
Benson, J. (2000) "Challenging a Paradigm in Two Directions: Anthropologists in Business and the Business of Practicing Anthropology," in P.L.W. Sabloff (ed.) *Careers in Anthropology: Profiles of Practitioner Anthropologists,* NAPA Bulletin 20: 23–7 (Washington, DC: American Anthropological Association).
Briody, E. and M. Baba (1993) "Explaining Differences in Repatriation Experiences: The Discovery of Coupled and Decoupled Systems," *American Anthropologist* 93. 2: 322–44.
Burke, P. (1998) "Anthropological Approach," *Inside Knowledge* 2. 1: 3–12.
Cohen, M. and E. Sarphatie (2007) *Gezocht: Antropoloog m/v* (Amsterdam: Aksant).
Corbett, S. (2008) "Can the Cellphone Help End Global Poverty?," *New York Times Magazine* April 13, 2008.
Hafner, K. (1999) "Coming of Age in Palo Alto," *New York Times* June 10, 1999: G1–G8.
Jordan, A. (2010) "The Importance of Business Anthropology: Its Unique Contributions," *International Journal of Business Anthropology* 1. 1: 3–14.
Jordan, A. (2003) *Business Anthropology* (Prospect Heights, IL: Waveland Press).
Garza, C. (1991) "Studying the Natives on the Shop Floor," *Business Week* September 30: 74–8.
Gwynne, M. (2003) *Applied Anthropology: A Career-Oriented Approach* (Boston, MA: Allyn & Bacon).
Kotter, J. (1991) *Corporate Culture and Performance* (New York: Free Press).
Laabs, J. (1992) "Corporate Anthropologists," *Personnel Journal 7.* 1: 81–7.
Lillis, M. and R. Tian (2009) "Cross-Cultural Communication and Emotional Intelligence," *Marketing Intelligence & Planning* 27. 3: 428–38.
McCracken G. (2009) *Chief Culture Officer: How to Create a Living Breathing Corporation* (New York: Basic Books).
Malefyt, T. de Waal (2009) "Understanding the Rise of Consumer Ethnography: Branding Technomethodologies in the New Economy," *American Anthropologists* 111. 2: 201–10.
Morais, R. J. and T. de Waal Malefyt (2010) "How Anthropologists Can Succeed in Business: Mediating Multiple Worlds of Inquiry," *International Journal of Business Anthropology* 1. 1: 37–48.
Polanyi, M. (1966) *The Tacit Dimension* (Gloucester, MA: Peter Smith, repr. 1983).
Reeves-Ellington, R. (1999) "From Command to Demand Economies: Bulgarian Organizational Value Orientations," *Practicing Anthropology* 21. 4: 5–13.
Reice, H. (1993) *Occupational Subcultures in the Workplace* (Ithaca, NY: ILR Press).
Schwartz, R. (1991) *Art of the Long View* (New York: Doubleday Currency).
Strathern, M. (ed.) (2000) *Audit Cultures: Anthropological Studies in Accountability, Ethics, and the Academy* (London: Routledge).
Tian, R. (2009) "Competitive Intelligence, Knowledge Management, and Anthropology," 2009 International Conference on Human Resource, Organizational Behavior and Leadership Science Proceedings, Beijing, China.
van Marrewijk, A. (2010) "European Developments in Business Anthropology," *International Journal of Business Anthropology* 1. 1: 18–36.
Ybema, S. D. Yanow, H. Weis and F. Kamsteeg (2009) *Organizational Ethnography. Studying the Complexities of Everyday Life* (London: Sage).
Yticel, R. H. Elibol and O. Dağdelen (2009) "Globalization and International Marketing Ethics Problems," *International Research Journal of Finance and Economics* 26: 93–104.

Notes

1. Alf H. Walle, personal communication.

Reading 5.4

Applied Anthropology and Change

Alexander M. Ervin

Alexander M. Ervin, "Applied Anthropology and Change," *Cultural Transformations and Globalization: Theory, Development, and Social Change*, pp. 241-244, 261-282.

[...]

Some Realities About Applied Anthropology and Theory

The realms of anthropological nonacademic practice are highly diversified. It is hard to define the subdisciplinary boundaries of applied anthropology, other than that it attempts to put anthropological knowledge to work in the solving of a huge variety of human problems. The locations of practice are many—government departments, international government and nongovernment development agencies, tribal governments, multicultural and ethnic organizations, schools, inner-city community development centers, corporations, advocacy groups, social movements, local not-for-profit organizations, and more. The problem domains rapidly increased since the 1960s—medicine and physical and mental health, education, technology transfers, industry, organizational culture and structure, social justice, poverty reduction, environmental sustainability, economic development, community development, cultural resource management, Indigenous affairs, immigrants, refugees, and multiculturalism, business, and others.

The roles vary—researcher, administrator, broker, advocate, policy analyst, trainer, community developer, policy maker, evaluator, assessor, technical writer, social marketer, and program deliverer. When research is involved, it can include ethnography, social survey techniques, sophisticated statistical analysis, social indicators, participant observation, public records, and established applied methodologies, such as needs assessment, program evaluation, social impact assessment, rapid assessment, and participatory-action research.

Theories and conceptual frameworks may be implicitly drawn from mainstream anthropology but they may also and are indeed just as frequently drawn from other disciplines. The phenomena under study rarely can be compassed by existing theory coming out of the core academic discipline. Academic anthropology, itself, has and continues to borrow from other disciplines, as they do in turn from anthropology.

Pragmatism is called for in the choice of method and theory for application and that almost always extends to minimizing or the complete exclusion of theoretical discussion in our technical reports. Those who commission our works are almost never interested in anthropological theory and its advancement. Much of the literature in applied anthropology remains isolated in technical reports intended for those who commissioned the study (van Willigen 1991). Those engaged in full-time practice may find little of value when they scan the latest academic journals that generate theoretical discussions straying from the problems demanded of practice, such as researching ways to minimize damage from substance abuse through an inner-city program, to design an effective low-income housing project, or to come up with [an] effective crisis and resettlement program for an impoverished population facing a natural disaster.

There are applied anthropologists in two broad contexts—academic and nonacademic, nontraditional practice settings. Collectively both sets have gained some basis of academic training—theory, method, institutional domains (health, economy, etc.), and areal studies during their time at university. Practitioners, working full-time outside of academic settings, can then improvise upon this training for more practical concerns. In more recent years, many have received additional specialized training directly in the applied practice of anthropology at over three dozen, nontraditional, specialized programs in the United States.

Having written a text (Ervin 2005) on the nature of applied anthropology, I can speculate on what characteristics unify applied anthropology and what ties it to general anthropology. Culture, with all its controversies and variations on meaning, still has a significant hold on mainstream anthropology and likewise provides a meaningful entry point for applied anthropology, especially when there are major cultural differences between intended beneficiaries and program designers. Related for applied anthropologists is the domain of policy, which is akin to culture in that it is ideological, behavioral, institutional, formal, informal, and subject to negotiation, thus operating in many ways like culture. The applied anthropologist needs to know the policy context of her subject area—such as in health care, refugee relocation, or education.

Holistic and comparative analyses can be hallmarks of both academic and applied domains. Anthropologists are always looking at how many institutional and behavioral domains may stream into or impinge upon each other—spiritual beliefs, control of resources, status, and so forth upon health and health care, for instance. Anthropologists have often been called into development or policy contexts because of the puzzles of unintended consequences. Comparative analyses have long been part of general anthropology. Likewise they can be quite useful in the policy domain as exemplified by the kinds of understandings that have been generated through impact assessment—relevant, for example, in the large-scale development projects.

Accurate, on-the-ground, detailed, community or institutional studies are the hallmark of both academic and applied domains. Ethnography and participant observation are essential components of both academic and applied practices. However, applied anthropology may contain more borrowed or multidisciplinary techniques in methodology, especially quantitative ones. Time constraints may impose themselves in applied projects, so there is more attention to rapid assessment techniques than in academic research but there may also be more direct expectations of standards of validity and reliability.

When it comes to theory, though, there may be much less pattern matching than with the discussed dimensions. The dilemma is illustrated through the title of a book (Hill and Baba 2000), *The Unity of Theory and Practice in Anthropology: Rebuilding a Fractured Synthesis*. The expected seamless link between theory and practice, suggested by Malinowski earlier in this [reading], has not occurred. Although one might point to sociologist Everett Rogers (2003) and his multidisciplinary colleagues as an exception, in their long-term collaboration in testing, critiquing, and refining the details in the transmission of innovations. Research and debate about the details of development, as discussed in this [reading], might be considered as another possibility.

Occasional theoretical examples akin to discovering phenomena "clinically" in the context of ongoing practice are possible, and such constructs may then be discovered to have wider implications in other circumstances. One outstanding example of this is Merrill Singer's (2009) work as a practitioner dealing with the ravages of drug use in impoverished U.S. communities. He developed the concept of "syndemic." Here contexts of social injustice, inequality, socially driven structural violence, poor housing and nutrition, and chronic underemployment converge to simultaneously result in health problems of hunger, malnutrition, drug-related illness and infectious diseases (e.g., HIV/AIDS and tuberculosis), extreme mental stress, and violent crime. The underlying social etiology is common and needs to be addressed.

Another approach might be to stitch together a new theoretical framework from interdisciplinary threads to deal with practical issues. One example concerns development in agriculture whereby, for instance, an issue might be assessing the suitability of introducing new crop species or varieties along with their associated practices and technologies. An interdisciplinary approach called farming systems analysis arose combining biological knowledge of soils, waters, flora, fauna, pests, weather, and so forth, along with social and cultural variables of divisions of labor, land tenure, systems of exchange, primary and secondary units of production and exchange, and other variables. This was done to assess current needs and to systemically discover where otherwise unanticipated consequences of introduced dimensions of agronomy might occur (DeWalt 1985; Shaner and Schmehl 1982). Another example, discussed earlier, would be interdisciplinary theories advanced in the realm of social impact assessment.

Yet another approach labeled "praxis" is taken by Wayne Warry (1992) but different than the way Bourdieu (1977) used it, along with a very parallel associated with Merrill Singer (1994): "community-centered praxis." They place the emphasis in developing theory through applied practice. The real difference, however, is in developing new theory along with lay people to generate locally meaningful policy and practice. Here professionals engage in ongoing dialogue to refine collaborative reflection and action toward the changes necessary to improve circumstances. New theory emerges in discussion of solutions and guiding principles that are of coherence to both the practitioners and the community members. It is not a reflection of textbook theory but is revised and tested through the actions of jointly conceived programs. Singer illustrates through a community action program for needle exchange involving blacks and Hispanics in Hartford, Connecticut. Warry exemplifies with a collaborative project of research and action with a First Nations government and its communities in the transfer of the control of health services from the Canadian federal government to First Nations jurisdiction. ...

References

Bourdieu, Pierre
1977 Outline of a Theory of Practice. Cambridge UK: Cambridge University Press.
DeWalt, Billie R.
1985 Anthropology, Sociology and Farming Systems Research. Human Organization 44(2): 106–114.
Ervin, Alexander M.
2005 Applied Anthropology: Tools and Perspectives for Contemporary Practice. 2nd Edition. Boston: Allyn and Bacon.
Hill, Carole, and Marietta Baba
2000 The Unity of Theory and Practice in Anthropology: Rebuilding a Fractured Synthesis. NAPA Bulletin No. 18, Washington, DC: National Association for the Practice of Anthropology.
Rogers, Everett M.
2003 Diffusion of Innovations. 5th edition. New York, NY: Free Press.
Shaner, W.W., and W.R. Schmehl, eds.
1982 Farming Systems Research and Development: Guidelines for Developing Countries. Boulder, CO: Westview Press.
Singer, Merrill
1994 Community-Centered Praxis: Toward an Alternative Non-dominative Applied Anthropology. Human Organization 53: 336–345.
2009 Introduction to Syndemics: A Critical Systems Approach to Public Health. San Francisco, CA: Jossey-Bass.
van Willigen, John
1991 Anthropology in Use: A Source Book on Anthropological Practice. Boulder, CO: Westview Press.
Warry, Wayne
1992 The Eleventh Thesis: Applied Anthropology as Praxis. Human Organization 51: 97–106.

Cultural Anthropology and Global Business

Gary P. Ferraro and Elizabeth K. Briody

Gary P. Ferraro and Elizabeth K. Briody, "Cultural Anthropology and Global Business," *The Cultural Dimension of Global Business*, pp. 1-10, 23-27, 302-318.

Introduction: Global Connections

In little more than two decades, the world has become increasingly more interrelated. To illustrate, computer parts manufactured in six different countries are assembled in Malaysia before being transported by a Dutch freighter and sold to a Russian entrepreneur. Since joining the World Trade Organization in 2001, China has become one of the largest (and certainly one of the most rapidly expanding) economies in the world, and its present day economic challenges pose a real threat to other world economies. Clothing for children's dolls, sewn on Korean-made machines by Taiwanese workers, are assembled on dolls by Mexican workers according to U.S. specifications and then sold to parents in London and Chicago in time for Christmas. The American-based computer giant IBM has more than 430,000 employees working in some 40 different countries. Recently, a North Carolina man traveled to Bangkok, Thailand, to receive 22 dental crowns (and other dental work) by a Western-trained oral surgeon for less than one-third of what it would have cost back home. A German becomes the president of a Swedish kitchenware company, while an Indian university professor purchases (online) shares from a Swiss-based mutual fund for his retirement portfolio. The examples of the world becoming inextricably interconnected are simply too numerous to count.

To remain competitive in this rapidly globalizing world, most businesses, both here and abroad, have needed to enter into international/cross-cultural alliances. The overall consequences of this trend have been that more and more companies have engaged in activities such as joint ventures, licensing agreements, turnkey projects, and foreign capital investments. Since the end of the Cold War in the late 1980s, world economies have experienced dramatic changes; collectively these changes have been subsumed under the term globalization. This term has become one of the most overused and poorly understood words in the English language.

To be certain, countries and cultures have been interdependent for centuries, but when the Berlin Wall came down in 1989, the world began to change in some dramatic ways. Forces were unleashed that have had, and will continue to have, profound effects on all cultures and nations of the world. They include a new integration of world markets, technology, and information that is oblivious to both national and cultural borders. This post-Cold War globalization is driven by free-market capitalism and the questionable idea that the more a country opens up its markets to free trade, the healthier its economy will become. The economics of globalization involve lowering tariff barriers while privatizing and deregulating national economies. The North American Free Trade Agreement (NAFTA) and the European Union (EU) are two examples of the globalization of markets. The result of the globalization of markets is that goods, services, and ideas from all over the world are making their way into other cultures.

Box 5.5.1 A flatter world

What follows are just a few illustrations of how extensively the lives of all of the world's peoples are interconnected:

- The percentage of the U.S. population that is foreign-born has grown from 4.7 percent in 1970 to 8 percent in 1990 and to 14 percent in 2016.
- Coca-Cola sells more of its product in Japan (population: 127 million) than it sells in the United States (population: 319 million).
- Internet users worldwide increased approximately 832 percent between 2000 and 2015.
- Direct foreign investments in the United States have increased from $50 billion in 1990 to $148 billion in 2013, an increase of 294 percent. And, in the opposite direction, U.S. direct investment abroad has grown from $46 billion in 1990 to $365 billion in 2013, an increase of 790 percent (Jackson 2013: 2).
- The nationality of many globally branded products is often difficult to pin down. For example, Stolichnaya vodka, originally made from grains grown in Russia, uses Latvian spring water, is filtered, blended, and bottled in Riga, the capital of Latvia, is sold throughout the world in bottles made in Poland and Estonia, and is sealed with caps made in Italy.
- Many high-skilled jobs formerly performed in the developed world are now being

performed abroad, such as a CPA in Bangalore, India, filling out auditing forms for a company in Copenhagen; a mathematician in Mumbai, India, tutoring a high school student in London via email; or a Western-trained Thai surgeon in Bangkok performing a heart valve operation in Thailand (which costs over $200,000 in the United States) on a New Yorker for $10,500.

- More than half of U.S. franchise operators (e.g., Dunkin' Donuts or KFC) are in markets outside the United States.
- Owing to a shortage of priests in North America, local Catholic parishes are sending mass intentions (requests for masses said for a sick or deceased relative) to India. Catholic priests in India (who have more time than North American priests and need the money) are now conducting the masses in Hindi on behalf of North American Catholics after receiving the requests via email. Americans are outsourcing not only manufacturing jobs, but also their religious rituals to India.
- Artistic styles and traditions also are being globalized. In recent years we have witnessed recording artist Paul Simon collaborating musically with Ladysmith Black Mambazo, a singing group from South Africa; Sting recording fusion music with Cheb Mami from Algeria; and Jaz Coleman, lead singer with a British rock group, collaborating with Maori singer and poet Hinewehi Mohi.

At the same time that world trade barriers are falling, a concomitant revolution is going on in the world of information technology (IT). In the mid-1980s, only a handful of people in the world could operate a computer. Today, computers are as common in the home as the radio was in the 1940s. Moreover, the development of digitization, fiber optics, satellite communication, and the Internet now enables people to communicate with one another instantaneously. With the advent of e-commerce, anyone with a good product, a computer, a telephone, access to the Internet, a website, and a FedEx account can become a potential entrepreneur. Globalization has encouraged the participation of large numbers of new players in the world market. It is now *possible* to enter the global economy virtually overnight, with very little capital outlay, and become a global competitor by the next afternoon.

Indeed, the nation-state of the twenty-first century sometimes plays second fiddle to the powerful forces of the highly integrated global economy. During the early summer of 2002, India and Pakistan, both with nuclear capabilities, were on the brink of war over the issue of Kashmir. The two countries were rattling their sabers, as the leaders of the United States and Western Europe tried to bring the two parties back from the brink. In the end, the de-escalation of hostilities between India and Pakistan was brought about by pressure exerted by the IT industry—not the U.S. government (which has more military firepower than the next 15 most powerful nations).

Since the early 1990s, the global revolution in IT has had an enormous impact on the Indian economy, accounting for 40 percent of India's gross domestic product. Drawing upon the large tech-savvy Indian population, many of the world's largest companies (including American Express, Motorola Solutions,

Siemens, Shell, Nike, Sony, and General Electric) have their back rooms and research facilities in India. If you lose your luggage anywhere in the world, it will likely be tracked down by an Indian techie in Bangalore (India's Silicon Valley). Accounting, inventory control, payroll, billing, credit card approval, and customer service, among other functions, for many of the world's largest corporations are electronically managed by highly skilled engineers, computer scientists, and information technicians in India. With India so intimately involved in the IT lifeblood of so many large corporations, the possibility of India going to war could seriously disrupt the world's economy. In the final analysis, it was the powerful international corporations that convinced the Indian government to disengage with the Pakistanis under the threat of taking their IT business elsewhere. Thus, in the words of Thomas Friedman (2002: 13), "in the crunch, it was the influence of General Electric, not General [Colin] Powell, that did the trick."

The Perspective of Cultural Anthropology

Cultural anthropology seeks to understand how and why contemporary peoples of the world differ in their customs and practices and how and why they share certain similarities. It is, in short, the *comparative* study of cultural differences and similarities found throughout the world. But learning about the wide range of cultural variations serves as a check on those who might generalize about "human nature" solely on observations from their own society. It is not at all unusual for people to assume that their own ways of thinking and acting are unquestionably rational, "natural," or "human."

Consider, for example, the nonverbal gesture of negation, shaking the head from side to side, found in certain parts of the world. In parts of India, people use this very same gesture to communicate not negation but affirmation. In fact, there are any number of ways of nonverbally communicating the idea of negation, all of which are no more or no less rational than shaking the head from side to side. The study of cultural anthropology provides a look at the enormous variations in thinking and acting found in the world today and how many different solutions have been generated for solving the same set of human problems. Moreover, the cross-cultural study of the workplace and consumers by anthropologists can help global corporations craft solutions to problems of working together as efficiently as possible.

Anthropology does more than simply document the enormous variation in human cultures. As a social science, anthropology works to identify, describe, and explain the commonalities. For example, for any society to continue to exist over the long run, it must solve the basic problem of how to pass on its total cultural heritage—all the ideas, values, attitudes, behavior patterns, and so on—to succeeding generations. Should that complexity of cultural traditions not be passed on to future generations, that society will very likely not survive. Saudis have solved this problem by developing Koranic schools, which pass on the cultural traditions to the younger generations; in parts of West Africa, "bush schools" train young adolescents to become adults; in our own society, we rely on a formal system of compulsory education, complete with books, desks, and teachers. Although the details of these educational systems vary enormously, all societies in the world—today or in the past—have worked out a system for ensuring that new generations will learn their culture. Thus, the science of anthropology attempts to document the great variations in cultural forms while looking for the common strands that are found in all cultures.

In addition to being comparative, the anthropological perspective has several other distinctive features. First, to a greater extent than other social scientist, anthropologists analyze cultural differences and similarities *firsthand*. Rather than relying on secondary information gleaned (often by other people) from questionnaires, interviews, and census reports, cultural anthropologists use participant observation as a major method for collecting culturally comparative information. When cultural anthropologists use participant observation, they share in the everyday activities of the local people while making systematic observations of people eating, working, playing, conversing, dancing, exchanging goods, fighting, or any other activity that might illuminate their cultural patterns.

A second distinguishing feature of anthropology is holism in that it is concerned with (1) all peoples throughout the world and (2) many different aspects of human experience, including family structure, marital regulations, house construction, methods of conflict resolution, means of livelihood, religious beliefs, language, space usage, and art among many others. And finally cultural anthropology, unlike other social science disciplines, emphasizes viewing another culture from the perspective of an insider. For decades, anthropologists have made the distinction between the emic (insider) approach (describing another culture in terms of the categories, concepts, and perceptions of the people being studied) and the etic (outsider) approach (in which anthropologists use their own categories and concepts to describe the culture under analysis). For the last half century, there has been an ongoing debate among anthropologists as to which approach is more valuable for the scientific study of comparative cultures.

Thus, cultural anthropologists are trained to analyze the sociocultural organizations of various types of societies. In the early twentieth century, cultural anthropologists devoted their energies to the analysis of small-scale, technologically simple, and usually non-Western peoples. Over the last half century, however, cultural anthropologists have become more involved in the study of complex societies. Yet whether dealing with simple or complex societies, the focus of cultural anthropologists has been the comparative study of sociocultural organizations wherever, or in whatever form, they may be found.

Figure 5.5.1 Cultural anthropologist Ed Tronick conducts participant observation fieldwork among the Efe people of Zaire, now the Democratic Republic of Congo.

Source: EdTronick/Anthro-Photo.

When hearing the phrase *cultural anthropologist*, the average American often imagines a drab, eccentric, elderly, bookish professor wearing sensible shoes and natural fiber clothing, and having little or nothing to do with anything outside the classroom. Anthropology, however, is neither dangerous (like the movie version of Indiana Jones) nor irrelevant. To counter this popular view that cultural anthropology is of little use in helping to understand the world around us, an increasing number of cultural anthropologists have applied their theories, findings, and methods to a wide range of professional areas, including economic development, business, health services, education, and urban administration. In fact, business and organizational anthropologists work inside some of the leading manufacturing and service companies in the world. These firms understand that anthropology brings a unique perspective on sociocultural issues to their organizations, both at home and abroad. Anthropologists not only help companies design products, but also develop culturally sensitive marketing strategies and organizational processes that incorporate an understanding of consumers, employees, and external communities.

This book rests on the fundamental assumption that to operate effectively in today's global business arena one must master the cultural environment by means of purposeful preparation as well as by becoming a lifelong student of culture. Now, as in the past, most globetrotting businesspeople acquire their cross-cultural expertise while on the job, and they consider hands-on factors such as business travel and overseas assignments to be the most important experiences. While not minimizing the value of experiential learning, this book argues that, *in addition to* on-the-job learning (and in most cases, before entering the global marketplace), successful international businesspeople must prepare themselves in a very deliberate manner to operate within a new, and frequently very different, cultural environment.

Cultural Anthropology and Business

Anthropologists have been working in business and industry since the early 1930s; useful historical and contemporary overviews of the field are those by Marietta Baba (1986, 2006, 2009) and Ann Jordan (1994, 2010, 2013). The human relations school of organizational research emerged from the Hawthorne Project and produced a number of ethnographies (i.e., descriptive and systematic accounts of culture) showing how informal cultural patterns could influence managerial goals (Mayo 1933; Roethlisberger and Dickson 1939; Gardner 1945; Warner and Low 1947; Richardson and Walker 1948). Also during this early period, some anthropologists turned their attention to consumer behavior (Warner and Lunt 1941; Gardner and Levy 1955), and later, a focus on occupations (Van Maanen 1978; Gamst 1980; Applebaum 1981; Coy 1989).

Since the last two decades of the twentieth century, the field of business anthropology has evolved into two prominent streams of research and practice. One research stream has focused on organizational cultures, both domestic and global, along with global teams and partnerships (Gregory 1983; Serrie 1986; Suchman 1987; Dubinskas 1988; Sachs 1989; Hamada 1991; Hamada and Sibley 1994; Orr 1996; Gluesing and Gibson 2004; Briody and Trotter 2008; Cefkin 2009; Meerwarth *et al.* 2008b; Briody *et al.* 2010; Krause-Jensen 2010; Van Marrewijk 2010; Caulkins and Jordan 2012; A. Jordan 2013; B. Jordan 2013; Garsten and Nyqvist 2013; Nakamaki *et al.* 2016). For example, Frank Dubinskas' edited volume examines how time is understood in such places as high-energy physics laboratories, start-up biotechnology firms, hospital radiology departments, and an engineering company. Dubinskas writes, "Managers appear as short-term and biologists as long-term planners. ... What managers see as 'immaturity'—not coming to completion—the scientists see as necessary, ongoing development" (Dubinskas, 1988: 26–27). [...]

Figure 5.5.2 Consumer anthropologist Timothy de Waal Malefyt conducts a videotaped interview with a female consumer in her home.

Courtesy of Timothy de Waal Malefyt.

A second stream consists of a critical mass of business anthropologists in consumer research, product design, and advertising (Miller 1994; Sherry 1995; Moeran 1996; Squires and Byrne 2002; Blomberg *et al.* 2003; Malefyt and Moeran 2003; Arnould and Thompson 2005; Sunderland and Denny 2007; Diamond *et al.* 2009; McCracken 2009; Wasson and Squires 2012; Griffiths 2013; Oliveira 2013; Denny and Sunderland 2014; Moeran 2014). Ken Erickson is one such consumer anthropologist. He has learned many times over that marketing and sales manager models do not match reality on the ground. A personal printer manufacturer hired him to figure out why Brazilian consumers, many of whom bought personal printers, were not buying the company's ink cartridges. Erickson discovered that lower middle class households were printing at the LAN House, the term for a neighborhood Internet café; it was much more cost effective for them. Some of the company's Brazilian managers saw no such places where they lived and thus did not believe that LAN Houses were important. Eventually Erickson's team of Brazilian ethnographers prevailed. The printer manufacturer responded by carving out a new niche with LAN Houses and marketing affordable bulk ink printers and bulk ink refill bottles to them. We feature numerous examples of product design and marketing throughout the book.

A third stream is design anthropology in which anthropologists are actively involved in the design of products and services, often in collaboration with experts from fields such as design, engineering, and computer science. (Squires and Byrne 2002; Blomberg *et al.* 2003; Metcalf and Harboe 2006; Gunn and Donovan 2012; Sanders and Stappers 2012; Wasson and Squires 2012; Gunn *et al.* 2013; Ingold 2013; Smith *et al.* 2016). Bill Beeman (2015b) is involved in a project to help make "smart systems" smarter. He and his colleagues are working with a medical equipment design firm to make the design process better. To do that requires integrating the qualitative human factors data identified by design anthropologists with quantitative data produced by mechanical engineers and computer scientists. It also entails figuring out how to weight the product design decisions, which today are based largely on intuition and judgment. Fundamental to design anthropology is that consumers do not know or cannot articulate fully what they want in a product. Beeman (2015b) states, "This creates an informational vacuum where more sophisticated aspects of competitive viability are unknown, and where the elements that create 'consumer delight' are also unknown." This specialty within business anthropology is a significant growth area.

The anthropological perspective can be useful in the study of purely domestic business organizations, which are frequently composed of many social components that come from different backgrounds, hold contrasting values and attitudes, and have conflicting loyalties. For instance, the company vice president will not likely have much in common with the assembly-line worker, the union representative, the president of the local Sierra Club, the government inspector, the janitor, or many members of that diverse group called the "buying public." And yet, if the organization is to function effectively, that corporate manager needs to know about the values, attitudes, expectations, concerns, and behavioral patterns of all these people, and others as well. In short, domestic business organizations can be viewed as minicultures (composed of different people with different roles, statuses, and value systems) that operate within the wider national cultural context.

The number of MA and PhD anthropologists working in the private sector for corporations and consulting firms has increased dramatically in the past four decades. Many high-tech multinational firms such as Microsoft, Google, and IBM have anthropologists on their staff working in the areas of research, marketing, management, human resources, and new product development. What is it that well-trained cultural anthropologists bring to the private sector? They are valuable because of their cross-cultural perspective, their capacity to study very specific behavior in its proper cultural context, and their primary research technique of participant observation, which reveals what people *actually do* in contrast to what *they say they do.*

Today, research and design firms, which develop new products, are actively recruiting anthropologists to help them gain deeper insights about their customers through participant observation research. One such anthropologist, Susan Squires, who has worked in new product development for many years, conducted participant observation research on U.S. families during breakfast time (Squires 2002: 108–114). While hanging around the breakfast tables in middle-class homes, Squires found that, with both parents working, getting children ready for school was hectic at best, and often children ate "on the run" rather than having a traditional sit-down breakfast. She also observed that both parents and children frequently ate bananas on the way to office and school respectively, because they are nutritious, portable, disposable, and fun to eat. If a new breakfast product were to be developed, it would have to meet the needs of a number of family members. For example, it would need to be nutritious, banana-like, portable, disposable, versatile, and fun to eat. Based on her anthropological observations of actual behavior, Squires developed a new breakfast product designed for the children of a two-parent working family on-the-go called "Go-Gurt." The first yogurt served in a tube, Go-Gurt is a healthy, high-protein food that had sales of over $37 million during its first year on the market.

Failure to consider the cultural context in the domestic organization can lead, and has led, to misunderstandings, miscommunication, costly marketing blunders, lawsuits, and generally an undermining of organizational goals. When moving into the area of international business, however, the need to be aware of cultural environments becomes even more critical. Here the magnitude of the cultural differences is vastly greater; consequently, breakdown of communication usually increases geometrically.

One of the most common factors contributing to failure in global business is the erroneous assumption that if a person is successful in the home environment, he or she will be equally successful in applying technical expertise in a different culture. Yet, research has shown that failures in the global business setting—including partnerships and joint ventures—most frequently result from an inability to understand and adapt to foreign ways of thinking and acting rather than from technical or professional incompetence (Black *et al.* 1992; Adler 2002; Thomas 2002; Maurer and Li 2006). At home, U.S. businesspeople equip themselves with vast amounts of knowledge of their employees, customers, and business partners. Market research provides detailed information on values, attitudes, and buying preferences of U.S. consumers. Middle- and upper-level managers are well versed in the intricacies of their organization's culture. Labor negotiators must be highly sensitive to what motivates those on the other side of the table. Yet when Americans turn to the global arena, they frequently deal with customers, employees, and fellow workers with a dearth of information that at home would be unimaginable.

The literature is filled with examples of business miscues when U.S. corporations attempted to operate in a global context. Some are mildly amusing; others are downright embarrassing. All of them, to one degree or another, have been costly in terms of money, reputation, or both. For example, when firms try to market their products abroad, they often assume that if a marketing strategy or slogan is effective in, say, Cleveland, Ohio, in the United States, it will be equally effective in other parts of the world. But problems can arise when changing cultural contexts. To illustrate, an airline offering service to Brazil advertised that it had comfortable "rendezvous lounges" in its business class section, without realizing that the word *rendezvous* in Portuguese refers to a room for illicit sexual encounters. Chicken entrepreneur Frank Perdue decided to translate one of his very successful advertising slogans into Spanish, but the translated slogan didn't produce the desired results. The slogan "It takes a tough man to make a tender chicken" was translated into Spanish as "It takes a virile man to make a chicken affectionate." And the American Dairy Association's wildly successful ad campaign "Got Milk?" had the unfortunate translation "Are you lactating?" when used in Mexico. Although all these cross-cultural advertising blunders cause us to chuckle, they can result in a loss of revenue and even product credibility.

These are only a few of the examples of the price paid for miscalculating—or simply ignoring—the cultural dimension of global business. The most cursory review of the global business literature will reveal many other similarly costly mistakes. If American businesspeople are to meet the challenges of an increasingly interdependent world, they will need to develop a better understanding of how cultural variables influence global business enterprises. A healthy dialogue between cultural anthropologists and members of the global business community—which this book seeks to foster—is an important step in achieving that needed understanding. …

… Corporations Also Are Cultures

Just as societies, tribes, religious communities, and neighborhoods all are cultures, so too are corporations. Shared values, behavior patterns, and communication styles all help the employees of a firm, from a clerk to the CEO, both feel and express a common identity. A corporate culture, in other words, helps ensure that people at all levels of the organization are pulling together in the same direction. Successful corporate cultures manage to integrate *symbols* (such as a corporate logo), *legends* (stories about past successes and failures), *heroes* (influential managers from the past), *communication patterns* (language and nonverbal cues), *shared values* (what the organization stands for and believes in), *patterns of social interaction* (expected forms of behavior between those of different statuses and roles), *rules* to follow (including work processes and procedures), and *shared experiences* (such as working together on successful projects). The process of developing and maintaining a healthy corporate culture involves a number of distinct activities including:

- establishing trust and respect as a foundation for workplace interaction and collaboration;
- identifying and building on a common work ethic among employees in pursuit of organizational goals;
- setting clear expectations, soliciting input, gaining consensus, and resolving conflict;
- documenting the essential organizational features, including "lessons learned," and integrating them into everyday practice;
- making the culture visible to employees on a regular basis so that behavior and expectations are aligned (i.e., "walking the talk");
- orienting new employees to their work tasks, colleagues, and the corporate culture generally.

Having a well-defined and explicit corporate culture not only increases efficiency but it also contributes to overall competitiveness (Barney 1986). When a formerly domestic corporation decides to globalize its operations, it needs to pay attention to globalizing its culture as well. A corporate culture that works well for employees in Sydney, Australia, may need to be at least partially redefined in Jakarta, Indonesia, where a new office has been opened. This certainly does not mean that a corporation should jettison its corporate culture when operating abroad. Rather, it means that hitherto domestic companies need to modify their cultures to accommodate local cultural realities. It is, in other words, not possible for a corporation to export its culture wholesale to Indonesia and expect local workers to check their own cultures at the door each morning.

Successful multinational corporations (MNCs), as they have expanded their overseas operations, have developed somewhat localized versions of their original corporate cultures. As McCune (1999) illustrates, when Wal-Mart, the largest retailer in the United States at the time, opened its first discount store in

Germany, it found that some features of its corporate culture (first developed in Bentonville, Arkansas) were not warmly embraced by their German employees. Workers had no difficulty with company cheers such as "Who's Number One? The Customer!" However, they balked at applying Wal-Mart's "10-foot rule," which required all employees to greet any customer within a 10-foot radius. This rule is not enforced among Wal-Mart employees in Germany because both employees and customers place a high value on their privacy when they are shopping. Thus, Wal-Mart had the good sense to realize that it would be counterproductive to allow its corporate culture to supersede the local German culture. Instead, Wal-Mart permitted a local variation of the corporate culture that was more compatible with local German culture. What is important to realize is that neither version of the corporate culture sacrifices the overarching cultural principle that the "customer is number one!"

Box 5.5.2 How do you define the culture of a start-up?

All corporations—whether large or small, well-established or start-ups—are cultural entities. Yet, there are a number of questions that corporate leaders need to ask themselves such as: Has our corporate culture been planned and structured in a purposeful, deliberate way, or did it just emerge by default? How aware are our employees about the nature of our corporate culture? Is our corporate culture helping us meet our goals and objectives, and if so, to what extent? Or, since we are a start-up company, how do we define and structure our start-up culture in such a way as to support our work better, improve our efficiency, make valuable contributions to our industry, and enable our workforce to maximize their personal satisfaction? According to Corey McAveeney (2013):

> Each company has a unique way of instilling company values. For example, Boundless, a Boston-based provider of free digital textbooks, had a strong sense of their values from day one. The way Ariel Diaz, co-founder and CEO at Boundless saw it, was that the values should be something attainable for everyone on the team. He and Aaron White, a co-founder at Boundless, created a succinct way to communicate the values and make it fun. At team meetings Diaz presents a "Cultural Achievement Award" to employees who have exemplified one of the four company values, represented by: The Beast (the hardest worker), The Architect (the best strategist), Indiana Jones/Lara Croft (the dedicated adventurer looking for results), and The Most Interesting Person In the World (a well-rounded, funny, charismatic individual). Even as the team at Boundless expands, there is a clear understanding of the expectations and purpose.

Philippe d'Iribarne (2002) provides two detailed case studies (one of a combined Italian-French microelectronic company headquartered in Geneva and the other a French food company located in Mexico) showing how Western corporate cultures can promote supportive communities of highly motivated workers by building upon deep-seated local cultural values. In Morocco, Islamic norms and values were combined with Total Quality Management values to transform SGS-Thomson's factory culture, whereas in Mexico, norms and values regarding family and the pursuit of a higher moral purpose were combined with the traditional corporate model of Danone of France. In both cases, it was not the imposition of a foreign corporate culture over local cultural values. Rather, organizational excellence was achieved by integrating local cultural values and behavior patterns into the Western corporate culture. These two case studies demonstrate the fact that cultural differences are not de facto obstacles to creating efficient production facilities. In both situations the company managers (1) took the time and energy to understand local cultural realities, and (2) were willing to adapt their management practices and corporate cultures to the local cultural context in Morocco and Mexico.

Cultural Differences in Business: Challenges and Opportunities

This book is written with the primary objective of integrating the insights and findings of cultural anthropology with the practice of global business. When focusing on the nature of cultural differences, we cannot avoid pointing out the many pitfalls awaiting the naïve (culturally uninformed) businessperson ready to engage the global marketplace. In fact, at times, the reader might be overwhelmed with the daunting number of cultural differences that can result in needless misunderstandings (and a lack of success) when marketing, negotiating, or managing abroad. The purpose of focusing on cultural differences is not to discourage the reader from entering the realm of global business, but rather to educate the reader to (1) understand the cultural features different from one's own, (2) use that knowledge to alter one's own behaviors so as to meet one's professional objectives more effectively, and (3) assist organizations and individuals in developing solutions to the cultural problems they encounter.

Thus, the more knowledge we have about our culturally different business partners, the more likely we will avoid cross-cultural misunderstanding. We are not suggesting that we eliminate, or even reduce, the number of the cultural differences by having you either (1) give up your own culture, or (2) force your own culture upon others. Rather, it is important to recognize cultural differences, learn about them, and also understand that cultural differences provide opportunities for *individual* and *organizational synergy*. When people from two different cultures work cooperatively in an atmosphere of mutual understanding and respect, the outcome can be more productive than either group working independently.

For example, a manufacturer of cell phones may want to expand its markets into Africa. One effective strategy for obtaining a larger market share of cell phones is for the firm to create an ongoing dialogue between its international marketing department, its new product development department, and the local African sales representatives in cities such as Lagos, Nigeria, Nairobi, Kenya, and Dakar, Senegal. The local sales force knows the local needs, which professions can be served best by cell phones, which features are most important, and what people would be able to afford. These local salespeople would know that local fishermen would profit handsomely by having the capacity to contact various restaurants and fish markets via cell phone while they head back with their day's catch. These fishermen would not need all of the "bells and whistles" found on many cell phones, but rather an inexpensive way to communicate to their customers while they are several miles out at sea. Once the local fishing industry has been identified as a potential new market, the R&D people can develop an inexpensive phone that would meet the needs of the fishermen. Thus by pooling their different areas of expertise, the company and the local African sales representatives can develop new products more effectively to expand the cell phone market.

It is also important to understand that cultural differences can be used as assets rather than liabilities when MNCs form task-oriented teams based on cultural diversity. It has long been known that culturally diverse groups (provided that all members understand and respect the cultural perspectives of one another) perform tasks better than culturally homogeneous groups. For example, in experiments conducted by Warren E. Watson and his colleagues (1993), socially and culturally diverse work groups outperformed more homogeneous ones when the tasks were open-ended and the goal was to generate as many creative solutions as possible. Thus, if managed successfully, cultural diversity within an organization can be an asset rather than a potential liability, that is, something that must be eliminated from the corporate structure as quickly as possible.

Cross-cultural Scenarios

Read the following cross-cultural scenarios. In each mini-case study, a basic cultural conflict occurs among the actors involved. Try to identify the source of the conflict and suggest how it could have been avoided or minimized. Then see how well your analyses compare to the explanations in Appendix A.

1–1 Bernice Caplan, purchaser for women's apparel for a major New York department store, had just taken over the overseas accounts. Excited and anxious to make a good impression on her European counterparts, Bernice worked long, hard hours to provide information needed to close purchasing contracts in a timely manner. Stefan, one of her Dutch associates in Amsterdam, sent an urgent message on May 1 requiring information before the close of day on 6/5. Although Bernice thought it odd for the message to be marked URGENT for information needed over a month away, she squeezed the request into her already busy schedule. She was pleased when she had whipped together the information and was able to send it by May 10, three full weeks before the deadline. She then placed a telephone call to Stefan to make sure that he had received the fax and was met with an angry, hostile response. The department store not only lost the order at the agreed-upon cost, but the Dutch office also asked that Bernice be removed from their account.

Where did Bernice go wrong?

1–2 In what was considered a "hostile takeover," a U.S. corporation purchased a regional wine-producing vineyard in Limoges, France, in a strategic maneuver to enter the European market. Frank Joseph, a human resource specialist, was sent to Limoges to smooth the ruffled feathers of the vineyard's workers. Along with videos and propaganda on the merits of working for a Fortune 500 corporation, Frank also brought to Limoges a number of company logo items. In what was intended as a goodwill gesture, he presented the workers with T-shirts, ball caps, ink pens, and coffee cups to take home to their families. Over the next several weeks, Frank never saw any of the company's logo items being worn or used by the workers. Instead, the workers were uncommunicative toward him and at times even hostile.

Why was Frank treated in this manner?

1–3 A fertilizer manufacturer headquartered in Brussels decided to venture into the vast potential of third-world markets. The company sent a team of agricultural researchers into Rwanda to test soils, weather conditions, and topographical conditions to develop locally effective fertilizers. Once the research and manufacturing of these fertilizer products had been completed, one of the initial marketing strategies was to distribute, free of charge, 100-pound bags of the fertilizer to selected rural areas. It was believed that those using the free fertilizer would be so impressed with the dramatic increase in crop productivity that they would spread the word to their friends, relatives, and neighbors. Teams of salespeople went from hut to hut in those designated areas, offering each male head of household a free bag of fertilizer along with an explanation of its capacity to increase crop output. Although the men were very polite, they all turned down the offer of free fertilizer. The marketing staff concluded that these local people were either uninterested in helping themselves grow more food and eat better, or so ignorant that they couldn't understand the benefits of the new product.

What was ethnocentric about this conclusion?

References

Bibliographic resources

Adler, Nancy J. 2002. *From Boston to Beijing: Managing with a world view.* Cincinnati, OH: South-western.

Applebaum, Herbert A. 1981. *The culture of construction workers.* New York, NY: Holt, Rinehart and Winston.

Arnould, Eric J. and Craig J. Thompson. 2005. Consumer culture theory. *Journal of Consumer Research* 31(4): 868–882, March.

Baba, Marietta L. 1986. *Business and industrial anthropology: An overview.* NAPA Bulletin No. 2. Washington, DC: American Anthropological Association.

Baba, Marietta L. 2006. Anthropology and business. In *Encyclopedia of anthropology*, edited by H. James Birx, 83–117. Thousand Oaks, CA: Sage Publications.

Baba, Marietta L. 2009. W. Lloyd Warner and the anthropology of institutions: An approach to the study of work in late capitalism. *Anthropology of Work Review* 30(2): 29–48.

Beeman, William O. 2015b. Ethnography for smart service systems in product design, EPIC Perspectives, April 21, www.epicpeople.org/ethnography-for-smart-service-systems-in-product-design/?utm_source=EPIC+Past+Attendees+%26+Community&utm_campaign=ab2aae29ec-EPIC_news_articles4_14_2015&utm_medium=email&utm_term=0_9d6d93b52d-ab2aae29ec-196977877, accessed February 29, 2016.

Black, J. Stewart, Hal B. Gregersen, and Mark E. Mendenhall. 1992. *Global assignments: Successful expatriating and repatriating international managers.* San Francisco, CA: Jossey-Bass.

Blomberg, Jeanette, Mark Burrell, and Greg Guest. 2003. An ethnographic approach to design. In *Human-computer interaction handbook: Fundamentals, evolving technologies, and emerging applications*, edited by Julie A. Jacko and Andrew Sears, 964–989. Mahwah, NJ: Lawrence Erlbaum Associates.

Briody, Elizabeth K. and Robert T. Trotter, II, eds. 2008. *Partnering for organizational performance: Collaboration and culture in the global workplace.* Lanham, MD: Rowman and Littlefield.

Briody, Elizabeth K., Robert T. Trotter, II, and Tracy L. Meerwarth. 2010. *Transforming culture: Creating and sustaining a better manufacturing organization.* New York, NY: Palgrave Macmillan.

Caulkins, D. Douglas and Ann T. Jordan, eds. 2012. *A companion to organizational anthropology.* Malden, MA: Wiley-Blackwell.

Cefkin, Melissa, ed. 2009. *Ethnography and the corporate encounter: Reflections on research in and of corporations.* New York, NY: Berghahn Books.

Coy, Michael W., ed. 1989. *Apprenticeship: From theory to method and back again.* Albany, NY: State University of New York Press.

Denny, Rita and Patricia Sunderland, eds. 2014. *Handbook of anthropology in business.* Walnut Creek, CA: Left Coast Press.

Diamond, Nina, John F. Sherry Jr., Albert M. Muniz Jr., Mary Ann McGrath, Robert V. Kozinets, and Stefania Borghini. 2009. American girl and the brand gestalt: Closing the loop on sociocultural branding research. *Journal of Marketing* 73: 118–134, May.

Dubinskas, Frank A., ed. 1988. *Making time: Ethnographies of high-technology organizations.* Philadelphia, PA: Temple University Press.

Friedman, Thomas L. 2002. India, Pakistan, and G.E. *New York Times*, August 8, p. 13.

Gamst, Frederick C. 1980. *The hoghead: An industrial ethnology of the locomotive engineer.* New York, NY: Holt, Rinehart and Winston.

Gardner, Burleigh B. and Sidney J. Levy. 1955. The product and the brand. *Harvard Business Review* 33(2): 33–39, March–April.

Garsten, Christina and Anette Nyqvist, eds. 2013. *Organisational anthropology: Doing ethnography in and among complex organisations.* London, UK: Pluto Press.

Gluesing, Julia C. and Cristina Gibson. 2004. Designing and forming global teams. In *Handbook of global management: A guide to managing complexity*, edited by Henry W. Lane, Martha L. Maznevski, Mark E. Mendenhall, and Jeanne McNett, 199–226. Oxford, UK: Blackwell.

Gregory, Kathleen L. 1983. Native-view paradigms: Multiple cultures and culture conflicts in organizations. *Administrative Science Quarterly* 28: 359–376.

Griffiths, Michael B. 2013. *Consumers and individuals in China: Standing out, fitting in.* London, UK: Taylor & Francis.

Gunn, Wendy and Jared Donovan, eds. 2012. *Design and anthropology.* London, UK: Taylor & Francis.

Gunn, Wendy, Ton Otto, and Rachel Charlotte Smith, eds. 2013. *Design anthropology: Theory and practice.* London, UK: Bloomsbury Academic.

Hamada, Tomoko. 1991. *American enterprise in Japan.* Albany, NY: State University of New York Press.

Hamada, Tomoko and Willis E. Sibley, eds. 1994. *Anthropological perspectives on organizational culture.* Lanham, MD: University Press of America.

Ingold, Tim. 2013. *Making: Anthropology, archaeology, art and architecture.* Abingdon, UK: Taylor & Francis.

Jackson, James, K. 2013. U.S. direct investment abroad: Trends and current issues, Congressional Research Service, December 11, p. 2.

Jordan, Ann T. 1994. *Practicing anthropology in corporate America: Consulting on organizational culture.* NAPA Bulletin No. 14. Arlington, VA: American Anthropological Association.

Jordan, Ann T. 2010. The importance of business anthropology: Its unique contributions. *International Journal of Business Anthropology* 1(1): 15–25.

Jordan, Ann T. 2013. *Business anthropology*, 2nd ed. Long Grove, IL: Waveland Press.

Jordan, Brigitte, ed. 2013. *Advancing ethnography in corporate environments: Challenges and emerging opportunities.* Walnut Creek, CA: Left Coast Press.

Krause-Jensen, Jakob. 2010. *Flexible firm: The design of culture at Bang & Olufsen.* New York, NY: Berghahn Books.

Malefyt, Timothy deWaal and Brian Moeran, eds. 2003. *Advertising cultures.* Oxford, UK: Berg.

Maurer, Steven D. and Shaomin Li. 2006. Understanding expatriate manager performance: Effects of governance environments on work relationships in relation-based economies. *Human Resource Management Review* 16(1): 29–46.

Mayo, Elton. 1933. *The human problems of an industrial civilization.* New York, NY: Macmillan Company.

McCracken, Grant C. 2009. *Chief culture officer: How to create a living, breathing corporation.* New York, NY: Basic Books.

Meerwarth, Tracy L., Robert T. Trotter, II, and Elizabeth K. Briody. 2008b. The knowledge organization: Cultural priorities and workspace design. *Space and Culture* 11(4): 437–454.

Metcalf, Crysta J. and Gunnar Harboe. 2006. Sunday is family day. *Ethnographic Praxis in Industry Conference Proceedings*, September 1, pp. 49–59.

Miller, Daniel. 1994. *Modernity, an ethnographic approach: Dualism and mass consumption in Trinidad.* Oxford, UK: Berg.

Moeran, Brian. 1996. *A Japanese advertising agency: An anthropology of media and markets.* Honolulu, HI: University of Hawai'i Press.

Moeran, Brian. 2014. *The business of creativity: Toward an anthropology of worth.* Walnut Creek, CA: Left Coast Press.

Nakamaki, Hirochika, Koichiro Hioki, Izumi Mitsui, and Yoshiyuki Takeuchi, eds. 2016. *Enterprise as an instrument of civilization: An anthropological approach to business administration.* Tokyo, Japan: Springer Japan.

Oliveira, Pedro. 2013. *People-centered innovation: Becoming a practitioner in innovation research.* Columbus, OH: Biblio Publishing.

Orr, Julian E. 1996. Talking about machines: An ethnography of a modern job. Ithaca, NY: Cornell University Press.

Sachs, Patricia, ed. 1989. Special issue: Anthropological approaches to organizational culture. *Anthropology of Work Review*, Editorial 10(3): 1, Fall.

Sanders, Elizabeth B.-N. and Pieter Jan Stappers. 2012. *Convivial toolbox: Generative research for the front end of design.* Amsterdam, the Netherlands: BIS Publishers.

Serrie, Hendrick, ed. 1986. *Anthropology and International Business.* Studies in Third World Societies, No. 28. Williamsburg, VA: College of William and Mary.

Sherry, John F., Jr., ed. 1995. *Contemporary marketing and consumer behavior: An anthropological sourcebook.* Thousand Oaks, CA: Sage Publications, Inc.

Smith, Rachel Charlotte, Kasper Tang Vangkilde, Mette Gislev Kjaersgaard, Ton Otto, Joachim Halse, and Thomas Binder, eds. 2016. *Design anthropological futures.* London, UK: Bloomsbury Academic.

Squires, Susan. 2002. Doing the work: Customer research in the product development and design industry. In *Creating breakthrough ideas: The collaboration of anthropologists and designers in the product development industry*, edited by Susan Squires and Bryan Bryne, 103–124. Westport, CT: Bergin and Garvey.

Squires, Susan and Bryan Byrne, eds. 2002. *Creating breakthrough ideas: The collaboration of anthropologists and designers in the product development industry.* Westport, CT: Bergin and Garvey.

Suchman, Lucy A. 1987. Plans and situated actions: *The problem of human-machine communication*. Cambridge, UK: Cambridge University Press.

Sunderland, Patricia L. and Rita M. Denny. 2007. *Doing anthropology in consumer research*. Walnut Creek, CA: Left Coast Press.

Thomas, David C. 2002. *Essentials of international management: A cross-cultural perspective*. Thousand Oaks, CA: Sage Publications.

Van Maanen, John. 1978. *Policing: A view from the street*. New York, NY: Random House.

Van Marrewijk, Alfons. 2010. European developments in business anthropology. *International Journal of Business Anthropology* 1(1): 26–44.

Warner, W. Lloyd and Paul S. Lunt. 1941. *The social life of a modern community*. New Haven, CT: Yale University Press.

Wasson, Christina and Susan Squires. 2012. Localizing the global in the field of technology design. *In Applying anthropology in the global village*, edited by Christina Wasson, Mary Odell Butler, and Jacqueline Copeland-Carson, 251–284. Walnut Creek, CA: Left Coast Press.

Unit VI

Globalization and the Application of Humanities in Business

"We cannot hope to create a sustainable culture with any but sustainable souls."

—Derrick Jensen

Cultural Competence

Cultural competence is crucial for business leaders in terms of interpersonal dynamics, organization, structure, and progress. The diversity of core beliefs, entrenched views, languages, and cultural behavior point to the continually changing landscape of today's global world.[1] The benefits of cultural competency far outweigh the costs of ignorance rooted in culture conflict in business settings. It is not an easy process, but it pays off, as outdated organizational structures and beliefs are confronted with the intent to broaden, strengthen, and sustain a growth trajectory. Successful leaders recognize the importance of a culturally competent organization built by culturally competent employees, who work continually to increase their capacities for understanding worldviews that lie beyond their own experiences.[2]

> Leaders today are well aware that their organization's culture is an asset that must be managed with purpose and care. The trouble is, there isn't a playbook that makes it obvious how to do this. Sometimes, even the most well-meaning CEOs don't

> fully connect with the real issues that motivate people. This critical gap—between leaders' perceptions of what people care about and the actual realities of the culture—can prevent a company from achieving its desired results.
>
> Fortunately, it's possible to close this gap. Armed with a deeper understanding of their company's culture and the day-to-day behaviors that shape it, leaders can find new opportunities to achieve their business goals—and new allies to help drive the effort.[3]

Businesses, together with governments and NGOs, must work together to advance our global society, informed by stakeholders.[4] Some issues are widespread, such as education and school attainment,[5] while others are context-specific. The ultimate goal is to create sustainable progress for people, the environment, and business.

Sustainability

The world population is growing at a staggering rate. The United Nations' Department of Economic and Social Affairs projects the world population to reach nearly 10 billion by the year 2050, based on astonishing statistical analysis. Between the years 2000 and 2012, there was an increase of 1 billion people living on earth.[6] Three years later, in 2015, the world population reached 7.3 billion, with a growth rate of 1.8% per year. These statistics indicate that fifteen years from now, the year 2030, the world population will reach over 8.5 billion.[7]

The concept of sustainability is a hot topic in today's corporate world; in fact, research identifies it as a "megatrend."[8] However, it is not a new issue. Proponents of corporate social responsibility (CSR) have incorporated sustainability into their vision for decades. This movement started as early as 1953.[9] The role of business in society continued to be an issue throughout the 1960s, 70s, 80s, and into the 90s.[10] With the upsurge of globalization, CSR movements became widespread. In particular, the ability of a corporation to become sustainable is in high demand. Sustainability is a broad category that is subject to wide interpretation. In fact, labeling a system as sustainable is multi-dimensional and cannot be neatly defined.[11] Accordingly, an integrative approach to classification is required in order to capture the essence of what sustainability looks like. There are, however, some generalizations that can be used in consideration of sustainability. The World Commission on Environment and Development defined sustainability as "the development that meets the needs of the present without compromising the availability of future generations to meet their own needs."[12] In short, a corporation's vision of sustainability implies a corporate commitment to long-term projections and practices that are intellectually and financially consistent with the efficient use of resources, the promotion of good health, safety, and sound leadership.[13]

Corporate sustainability is a multi-faceted and evolutionary process within various contexts.[14] However, there is a recognized bottom line that includes three factors: environmental issues, societal issues, and business arenas.[15] The inherent assumption within those categories is a core objective that producers and consumers alike are doing their part to save the planet.[16] The means by which they strive to accomplish this goal are as varied as the corporations that participate, as are the range of issues that fit underneath the sustainability umbrella, ranging from conservation of resources to human rights advocacy.

The divergent nature of sustainability avoids solid definition, so at this point, corporate sustainability is not regulated. As a result, conflicting procedures, criteria, practices, and so forth abound in the field. In many contexts, the lack of opacity in the process is yet another problem associated with a lack of uniform standards for sustainability. Trade-offs in practice are not always visible. There is a call among researchers for the need to establish sustainability standards so that the adopters understand and actually live up to the principles of corporate sustainability without uncertainty and ambiguity.[17]

Although a set criteria or set of standards has not been accepted on a worldwide level, divisions of governments, advocacy groups, and corporations have set forth standards which often overlap or complement each other. For example, in the United States, the Department of Agriculture has established five guidelines that provide a general framework from which to draw research on sustainability.[18] In the UK, the UK Sustainable Development Commission has produced a description of characteristics for sustainable food supply chains.[19] Meanwhile, advocacy groups, such as the Pacific Institute, a global water think tank that uses scientific leadership to influence international efforts in sustainable water qualities, has developed a sustainable ideal by which corporations can measure their sustainability efficacy. The Pacific Institute and others envision a world in which private sector businesses utilize natural resources sustainably with full management of their global footprint. Corporations would, in this ideal, respond to the needs of all stakeholders to act responsibly.[20] The angles of sustainability are complex, so for the purpose of this study, we analyze one portion of the sustainability equation, that of sustainable farming.[21]

First of all, from a business angle, sustainability does not fit neatly into a traditional cost/benefit analysis.[22] Because the concepts of sustainability are measured in terms of economic, natural, and social capital, the success of sustainability programs is not necessarily quantifiable, tangible, or measurable in a short-term assessment.[23] Further, the business case does not capture the success of sustainability programs because the sustainability concept does not stand alone. Corporate sustainability is supported by sustainable development, corporate social responsibility, stakeholder theory, and accountability. Disciplines such as ethics, philosophy, social justice, ecology, and business law combine issues of strategic management and economics in analyses of sustainability.[24] A corporate sustainability model must necessarily take these schools of thought into consideration through the examination of input, processes, outputs, and outcomes in assessing the success of a sustainability strategy.[25]

Corporate sustainability is described in large part in terms of aspirations, goals, and achievements. Aspirations and goals would ideally place corporations in the position of role models for corporate citizenship on social and environmental issues.[26] Translating aspirations into reality is a challenge.[27] Sometimes the aspirations are achieved or even exceeded, but they often fall short of the mark. Responsible corporations admit to their shortcomings and learn from their mistakes as they establish new parameters for new aspirations. Throughout this intricate process, ethical considerations are a must. Social and environmental aspirations and the means to carry them out require transparency through systems of accountability and audits in order to ensure that corporate actions actually do reflect the rhetoric of their sustainability programs. Partnerships and watchdog advocacy groups play important roles in the scrutiny of sustainability initiatives. In addition, the development of successful sustainability requires sharing knowledge and collaboration among competitors.

Organizations such as The Sustainability Consortium bring corporations, NGOs, and other leaders in the movement together to achieve socially responsible goals in terms of sustainability on a global level. They value scientifically based knowledge and informed stakeholders, and focus on impact.[28] Such collaborative approaches to business initiatives demonstrate yet another divergence from the traditional business case. In fact, sustainability initiatives require a drastic paradigm shift with consideration of numerous context-dependent factors.

The readings on multinational issues begin with Velo, who presents a history of globalization as well as predictions of the immediate future, targeting business leaders who will face this unprecedented period of rapid change. She analyzes the consequences of decisions and change in a global world. Next, Asargy, Frutos-Bencze, and Samii link community, social well-being, CSR with profit maximization. Then, Lozano, Albareda, Ysa, Roscher, and Marcuccio explain the role of government in CSR public policy creation and the implications of legally mandated and/or voluntary CSR for business. The final reading brings us full circle with our initial conversation. Brands and Gavin examine the new world order following the COVID-19 pandemic. They show connections between economics, health, safety, diplomacy, security, ethics, technology, and more as they create a bold vision for the future, in a world where the human connection propels success.

Notes

1. Lewis, R. D. *The cultural imperative: Global trends of the 21st century.*
2. Taggart, A. (2007). Beyond diversity: Becoming a culturally competent organization. *Ivey Business Journal, 71*(7), 1.
3. Aguirre, D., Davidson, V., & Oelschlegel, C. (2018, December 6). Closing the culture gap: Linking rhetoric and reality in business transformation. https://www.strategy-business.com/article/Closing-the-Culture-Gap
4. Buhmann, K. (2013). It's our business. In *Corporate social and human rights and responsibilities* (pp. 145–164).
5. Hanushek, E. A. (2013). Economic growth in developing countries: The role of human capital. *Economics of Education Review, 37*, 204–212.
6. The United Nations Department of Economic and Social Affairs (2013, June 13). World population projected to reach 9.6 billion by 2050.
7. The United Nations Department of Economic and Social Affairs Population Division. (2015). *World population prospects: The 2015 revision.*
8. Forster, A. (2013). Sustainability: Best practices in the food industry. *UW-L Journal of Undergraduate Research, XVI*, 1.
9. Wilson, M. (2003, March/April). Corporate sustainability: What is it and where does it come from? *Ivey Business Journal.*
10. Salzman, O., et.al. The Business Case for Corporate Sustainability: Literature Review and Research Options. *European Management Journal, 23*(1), 27.
    D'Amato, A., et. al. *Corporate social responsibility and sustainable business: A guide to leadership tasks and functions.* Center for Creative Leadership. See p. 4.
11. Amini, M., & Bienstock, C. C. (2014, August). Corporate sustainability: An integrative definition and framework to evaluate corporate practice and guide academic research. *Journal of Cleaner Production, 76*, 12.
12. Forster, A. (2013). Sustainability: Best practices in the food industry. *UW-L Journal of Undergraduate Research, XVI*, 1.
13. Smith, J. (2014, January 22). The world's most sustainable companies of 2014. *Forbes.*
14. Wilson, M. (2003, March/April). Corporate sustainability: What is it and where does it come from? *Ivey Business*

Journal.

15. D'Amato, A., et.al. *Corporate social responsibility and sustainable business: A guide to leadership tasks and functions*. Center for Creative Leadership. See p. 1.
16. Forster, A. (2013). Sustainability: Best practices in the food industry. *UW-L Journal of Undergraduate Research*, *XVI*, 1.
17. Wijen, F. (2015, April 14). Trade-offs in the adoption of sustainability standards. *Alliance for Research on Corporate Sustainability*.
18. Subchapter I: Findings, Purposes, and Definitions, US Code, Title 7, Chapter 64-Agricultural Research, Extension and Teaching.
19. Smith, B. G. (2008, February 27). Developing sustainable food chains. *Philosophical Transition B of the Royal Society Publishing*.
20. The Pacific Institute: https://pacinst.org
21. Gibby-Wachter, K. (2016). *Sustainable farming: Corporate rhetoric or reality?* Unpublished case study.
22. Winston, A. The fundamentals of a corporate sustainability program. www.greenbiz.com
23. Dyllick, T., & Hockerts, K. Beyond the business case for corporate sustainability.
24. Wilson, M. (2003, March/April). Corporate sustainability: What is it and where does it come from? *Ivey Business Journal*.
25. Epstein, M. (2008). *Making sustainability work: Best practices in managing and measuring corporate social, environmental, and economic impacts*. Berrett-Koehler.
26. Smith, B. G. (2008, February 27). Developing sustainable food chains. *Philosophical Transition B of the Royal Society Publishing*. See p. 36.
27. D'Amato, A., et.al. *Corporate social responsibility and sustainable business: A guide to leadership tasks and functions*. See p. 2.
28. https://sustainabilityconsortium.com

Culture and Globalization

Veronica Velo

The aim of this [reading] is to review the history of globalization and predict the consequences of its immediate future development in order for executives to reflect on the potential consequences in a world that has been changing faster than ever before and will continue to do so geometrically in the years to come.

Contextualizing Background Information

The definition of the term "*globalization*" has evolved through the years, sometimes including a few notions in it that would afterwards be excluded and vice versa. In spite of all the variations in the construction of the concept, there are at least two common factors that have remained constant across the changing attempts to qualify the phenomenon, namely its origins as a natural step in history, and its unavoidability.

Indeed, researchers agree that worldwide situational characteristics such as relative global peace, the international flow of information, the reduction of trade barriers, the international spread of technology, and the evolution of global market segments have contributed to a complete change in the way trade takes place and this has impacted societies and intersociety links as well. In a nutshell, it is generally agreed that globalization is about a new way of trading without borders that originated out of the conjunction of different historical events and that cannot be stopped.

As an example, Toyne and Walters have defined globalization in 1989 as follows: "the process of focusing an organization's resources on the selection and exploitation of global market opportunities consistent with and supportive of its short and long-term strategic objectives and goals." Prior to that, Levin had already defined it in 1983 as the "convergence of the markets of the world," and Ohmae had already described the process as an "integrated way of production."

> Below are several definitions of the cultural phenomenon.
>
> Tom G. Palmer of the Cato Institute defines globalization as "the diminution or elimination of state-enforced restrictions on exchanges across borders and the increasingly integrated and complex global system of production and exchange that has emerged as a result."
>
> Thomas L. Friedman has examined the impact of the "flattening" of the world, and argues that globalized trade, outsourcing, supply-chaining, and political forces have changed the world permanently, for both better and worse. He also argues that the pace of globalization is quickening and will continue to have a growing impact on business organization and practice.

It would be difficult to establish a precise date for the birth of the globalization phenomenon. Some authors would argue that in fact it had originated with trade itself, but as a matter of convenience, and to concentrate on the most influential portions of its historical evolution, we will only describe the main phases having shaped progress in international trade operations from the Second World War onwards.[1] In fact, since then, a series of stages have followed and it could be generally agreed that we still find ourselves in the midst of the events. In order to simplify the study of the evolution of globalization and its impact on culture, we will divide the history of the process into phases.

The first phase we consider is called "**Home**" because the basic trend at that point (immediately after the Second World War) consisted in simply exporting the excess production with no alterations or with just very simple ones. The main idea was to liquidate stocks or to accept orders of an existing product from abroad, but this product would be entirely designed and conceived for the local market. For example, a producer of chairs would manufacture them using local labor, and following specifications that would correspond to the demands of the local public. In case there was an excess of production, it would be sold abroad, but without taking into consideration any adaptations to the foreign public. Producers just "let" foreigners buy their product.

By the 1950s, inspired businesspeople realized that their expertise could be transformed into business opportunities abroad, and therefore they proceeded to the development of units in different locations, which functioned more or less independently, but that were designed to deserve each local market in which they operated. Because each unit would act domestically, but in different locations, this phase in the globalization process is called "**Multilocal**." The added advantage of this method was that it allowed the expansion of operations in cases where the local market was saturated or to take advantage of opportunities elsewhere. To continue with the previous example, in this case, chairs would be produced in different places using local labor, designing them to satisfy the needs and tastes of the local markets and to be sold to the local people through the practice of local techniques and aiming at pleasing the local clients and customers.

In the 1960s, developments in travel and telecommunications technology enabled the first stages of global production, the outsourcing of processes and the importing of inputs from economically viable locations. This new way of production allowed progress into the standardization of goods, at a significantly lower price. Applied to the example of the chairs, in this stage a Swedish manufacturer would buy the wood from Finland, the design from Canada, do the assembly in Mexico, and then distribute the standardized product across the world. Due to the diversity and number of countries involved in the process, this phase is called "**International**."

By the 1980s, the need for a differentiating factor became key to those wanting to compete on the cost battlefront. Those able to marry quality and low cost managed to gain competitive advantage and were therefore able to position themselves strategically. The main idea consisted in taking the multinational phase one step further by customizing the product or service to particular markets at the last step of their production. This way would ensure that cost conditions were met and that at the same time the offer would match the requirements of the local demand. In the case of chair production, the main processes would be universal (design and production procedures), but at the last points, slight alterations (size, color, distribution systems, etc.) would be made in order to adapt to specific preferences. Because of its intended capacity to meet the needs and wants of every segment, without sacrificing cost-saving standardization, this phase is called "**World**."

By the year 2000, economic blocks had relatively stabilized in terms of free circulation of goods and workforce, which accelerated the division of tasks into high versus low added value producing. Post-industrialized nations initiated a process of relocation of their manufacturing activities abroad, keeping the core competency at home, mainly concentrating on "brainwork" and replacing factories in foreign locations. Ecological issues start to gain importance in the minds of citizens and this increased sensitivity promoted the evolution and acceleration of the same dynamics. As creativity is considered as a key success factor in this phase, cross-cultural thinking is promoted and developed nations start to compete in the attraction and retention of the brightest minds across the globe. To continue with the same example, in this case the chair would be designed in Sweden by the best designers from everywhere in the world, produced in China and distributed using an American company. This phase is called "**Decentralized**."

The most recent developments in trade have allowed the development of networks of thought, which, distributed across the globe, act as the concentrators of know-how and creativity, which will then be applied in the production and marketing of goods wherever manufacturing takes place. Because the way of working implied in this new phase is much decentralized and operates through networks, it has been named "**Networked**." In this sense, thought occurs wherever the brains are located, which act as "centers of knowledge," operating in very small and reactive structures all over the world, which concentrate and dissolve as soon as the tasks and projects are accomplished.

The table below synthesizes the evolution of globalization since the Second World War providing main characteristics of each phase:

Phase	Description
Home (immediately following the Second World War)	• Producing for locals, exporting the rest, • Less product variety, • No interest in satisfying foreign needs, • It is up to the client to perform his/her own "customization," • Foreigners buy a product that is foreign to them.
Multilocal phase (1950–1960)	• Tackling opportunities abroad by producing and selling abroad for foreign consumption, • Adaptation to each one of the local cultures in which the company is present, • From product orientation to market orientation, • Each subsidiary acts as a local company abroad, • Locals are sometimes unaware that the capital is foreign, • Customized products for local clients in each location.
International phase (1960s)	• Price becomes the key differentiating factor, because many companies produce almost the same, • Low cost becomes a priority over cultural preferences, • The cheaper, the better, • Economies of scale.
World phase (1980s)	• Top quality AND low cost becomes the baseline. • Competitive advantage comes from strategic thinking, mass customization, and outlearning competitors. • Mass production with small adaptation to local markets at the end of the value chain allows keeping cost down while pleasing local markets at global scale. • The concept of "glocalization" (think global, act local), is born.
Decentralized phase (2000)	• Stabilization and enhancement of large production blocks. • Definition of pre-industrialized/industrialized and post-industrialized countries. • Sensitivity to ecological matters. • Cross-cultural thinking in design as a productivity enhancer.
Networked phase (2020)	• Knowledge-based society meets production needs. • Project-based operations led by networks of SMEs. • Quick reactions, first move players, creativity, and innovation. • Research-focused approach. • Knowledge-based networks.

The different stages in the globalization process have affected cross-cultural management differently and different cultures have faced this phenomenon in very different ways, according to their own characteristics and socially developed tools to face the issues relating to changes in ways of working and the evolution of international trade.

As an example of the previous statements, we can quote another Wikipedia entry, which also quotes an interesting point of view relating to globalization.

> Finally, Takis Fotopoulos argues that globalization is the result of systemic trends manifesting the market economy's grow-or-die dynamic, following the rapid expansion of transnational corporations. Because these trends have not been offset effectively by counter-tendencies that could have emanated from trade-union action and other forms of political activity, the outcome has been globalization. This is a multi-faceted and irreversible phenomenon within the system of the market economy and it is expressed as: economic globalization, namely, the opening and deregulation of commodity, capital and labor markets which led to the present form of neoliberal globalization; political globalization, i.e., the emergence of a transnational elite and the phasing out of the all of the statist period; cultural globalization, i.e., the worldwide homogenization of culture; ideological globalization; technological globalization; social globalization.

The different phases in the globalization process have impacted cultures involved in the process in many ways. Whereas in the domestic phase, dealing internationally consisted basically in speaking a common language at least basically or communicating through translators on very specific and objective matters (i.e., prices, delivery options, conditions, contract clauses), other phases have required the enhancement of a more evolved communication arena.

For instance, in the multilocal phase, some companies decided to delegate responsibility for the operations to local managers (this was the preferred American style), and these agents also operated as the interface between headquarters and the subsidiaries, absorbing most of the cross-cultural biases and disruptions. Other companies (in general this was the preferred French style) sent expatriates to deal with local uses and operational standards, bearing in mind that the general practice designed at headquarters was the one to be put into practice at local level. In any case, each subsidiary would very much act local and also think local and headquarters would not mind very much about specifications or ways of doing things abroad, as long as the financial objectives were met. The impact of globalization on society up to this stage was not very important, as it implied little work mobility and no change in production processes or management procedures.

It was probably during the multinational phase that globalization produced the strongest impact on societies, as the production patterns were applied universally, but designed from headquarters. Companies started producing gains that allowed them to expand without borders and enhance their overall power and governmental lobby capacity as never seen before. Many consumer products were standardized and consumed in similar manners across the globe and labor was hired where it was cheaper, not always considering the impact of this choice on local welfare or even sometimes human rights (i.e., child labor was employed, health and safety conditions of employees were often not respected, etc.).

During the global phase, quality became an issue, imposing new regulations on international producers. Even if the international consumers felt tempted by the cheaper products during the first stages of globalization, soon they became disappointed by the poor quality of what they bought and this reality gave a new kick to local small manufacturers. Once the globalization process was perfected, numerous SMEs across the globe disappeared, remaining unable to compete with the giants, causing unemployment.

The problems that arose with globalization during the first phases, in particular during the multinational phase mostly concerned underdeveloped and developing nations. The most recent stages, nevertheless, mainly affect the most developed countries. The decentralized and the networked phases of globalization brought with them the need to exploit the brainpower of nations to their maximum in order to generate and support the knowledge based society. In this sense, as the manual operations are executed in specific locations, leaving the high added value activities to concentrate in headquarters (postindustrialized countries), there was a two-way flow of population: unqualified workers received incentives to move to destinations where the factories were, and at the same time, qualified brains were welcomed by postindustrialized nations, who wanted to attract those able to perform high added-value tasks.

The networked phase, though, because of its location independent characteristics, does not call for the physical presence of the workers where they perform their professional tasks, and therefore should reduce the amount of migration through different methods. Strategically positioned networks concentrate brainpower in locations worldwide and these units interact on short-term projects worldwide. Even if the networked phase mostly concerns qualified workers, this arrangement will probably equally concern the less-qualified portion of the population, as developments in technology will progressively allow the replacement of routine jobs currently done by men, by machines.

The new landscape beyond 2010 will probably be designed by networks, which as predicted will act beyond national borders and the ruling class will probably be the most qualified and powerful, or at least the one that would have accessed knowledge and know-how to the point of becoming indispensable for the networks.

Many have wondered whether globalization would destroy multiculturalism and the answer to that question cannot easily be found. Some authors like Geert Hofstede may state that globalization can only affect practices (the way we do things), but not values and therefore the inception of new products and techniques would only have a limited impact on culture. On the other side, mobility will be enhanced and networks will be established, which would indicate that probably culture would be more affected by the fact that one belongs to a network or not, rather than by nationality.

Multicultural regions like the EU are trying very hard to find a common denominator in order to develop a common sense of belonging across member states with varied levels of success. On one side, the Christian tradition was intended to be a strong linking factor, but the incorporation of Turkey within the block would strongly challenge this fact. Perhaps it is the idea of a common future together that would link countries, or the facilitated internal mobility could at some point generate a powerful sense of unity. Whether this unity will ever mean the loss of identity is arguable.

Pressure groups have wanted to limit the extension of the impact of globalization, but the phenomenon is just unavoidable: for as long as technology is put in hand to disseminate ways and uses, globalization will continue to expand. In any case, nations have been subject to the invasion of other cultures for centuries and they are in fact the result of the conjunction between the old and the new—whether the "new" is imposed or just voluntarily acquired. Just as an example (amongst thousands of others), no matter how unified, unique and ethnically homogeneous a nation like France could seem, it is just the result of the conjunction of a huge number of cultures that have occupied its current territory through the centuries: Romans, Celtics, Germanics, Vikings, Gauls, Normans, and so on have contributed to change and to stability and to what we know today as France.

Perhaps what is essentially different since the big impact of globalization has started to take place is the way in which change is absorbed. Until now, the incorporation of new uses and costumes was confined to the specific geographic territory in which it took place (i.e., the Romans invade Gaul and then the Gaul discovers pizza), but the new practices did not go beyond each geographic confinement individually. Contrary to that, nowadays incoming factors (inventions, technology, Facebook, iPads, etc.) affect the globe in its entirety at once, on the spot and at the same time and in the same way and therefore evolution tends in many ways towards the same uses and customs, or at least to the same practices across the world, at the same time, as if a huge force was invading the planet as a whole.

This very particular aspect of the way in which change in cultures takes place due to technological progress (which recognizes no land borders) has led and continues to lead to two very specific and very particular characteristics of current times: (1) culture will increasingly develop in terms of subcultures and less in terms of national cultures and (2) the big social and economic differences will not be geographical, but knowledge-based.

The first effects of these changes are visible already: for instance, changes in education start to occur. Traditionally in most countries primary school education was in many ways a preparation for war: from the study of national anthems and other battlefield songs to the presentation of the glory of the nation through the victories of its heroes, children from almost every country were taught that they were part of a group to which they owed loyalty in exchange for protection. Most of us have been brought up that way. A more creativity-enhancing, free-thinking, culturally friendly, nonracist education is being generated in order to respond to the new needs of the world, which tends towards an innovation-led paradigm as opposed to a field-owning regime which might at some stage and with little anticipation call for the blood of youngsters to defend the common property.

In the old days in which immigration only took place gradually, it was easier to recognize foreigners: in many cases they looked different. It was easy to create stereotypes, to judge and to set areas of the population apart. As the world develops towards innovation and the knowledge based society, the differences that used to be visible become unreliable: nations are multiracial and in order to attract the best brains from wherever they come from, the way a person looks will less and less be considered as a reliable indicator of his/her position in society, his/her wealth, or his/her background.

For years and years, the notion of "security" has been strongly linked to that of "nationality" or "inhabiting a land." Most basic rights are acquired through a nationality. Our nation's reason to exist is that it provides safety and security, plus a sense of belonging to those constituting it. This is part of the social contract that we have been socialized upon. Within the new circumstances, with networks assuming the role of job providers and status warrantors, the fact is not so certain any longer. Some nations (the UK for instance), start publishing brochures in which they mention a new concept "one needs to **deserve** to be a citizen" ... this implies a huge change in the collective mental programming. People do not just "obtain" a nationality, they need to actually be worthy of it.

Terrorism has somehow contributed to change in mental programming. The "enemy" might be within us. At first, terrorism was linked to Muslim extremists, radicalists, or specific groups outside civilized society. Until recently, criminal acts were countered by nationalism, which would correspond to the traditional reaction of land versus enemy (i.e., the United States versus Bin Laden). But since terrorism is now becoming the action of individuals **within** society (i.e., Anders Behring Breivik's mass murder in Norway), the old ways of patriotically aligning against the common foreign enemy seem to have lost their efficacy. And other forms of security impose themselves (socially accepted technological espionage being one of them).

When living in conditions in which change is happening faster than we can realize, where parameters are evolving at such a rate that we cannot follow, and at times where everything we had always considered as true, may simply be not so any longer, societies need to adapt and mentalities need to change.

Nations will probably not define us and protect us for much longer to the same extent as they used to. Having lived on a piece of land for many generations may no longer guarantee safety, security, or even identity. Identities may need to be self-constructed to a higher extent and it might become necessary to work to deserve to be part of a group that provides for some of our needs.

So, how will humanity satisfy its own need for identification, social belonging, and interaction with peers? For years, the main socialization factor was belonging to a culture, a country, a region, and so forth, and identity was made visible through symbols and external materialization of them. Globalization has an important influence in turning most of these symbols into anecdotal picturesque objects that remind us more of the history of a place than of the history of people themselves.

We find ourselves at present in the midst of a transition from a situation in which nation states provide safety and security, identity, and status; to a new one in which all these assets are to be merited and the networks to which one is linked to determine each one's position in society (which is borderless) and grant the sense of belonging. Safety and security does not come from solidarity towards those who share the same nationality, but from the fact that our lives become visible to everyone through the information we volunteer through our computer at every moment.

The transition is harsh to go through, as it leaves us frozen in front of a new framework of mind to adapt to and to operate from.

In this sense, collective cultures may need to alter their criteria of connections in order to adapt them to the networks that will determine the new social ruling; masculine societies will have to recognize that in order to support the new ways of production gender can no longer be a barrier if we are to maximize the use of the brainpower that exists in each block; internal locus of control cultures will need to depart from their need to adapt to the unknown, rather than mastering it; synchronic cultures will need to focus on the future, rather than on the past; status will be more achieved than ascribed; power distance will be shorter and emotionals will need to control how they express themselves, as information that is put online will remain on record forever.

Using This Information

To reflect and get ready for the years to come!

Discussion Point

Now review the following statements and comment on them. What do they mean? Who could have said them?

- "Think global, act local"
- "The doctrine of free trade, if applied globally, will be a disaster"
- "Economies should not be self-serving structures, but directed at promoting the stability and contentment of the societies within which they operate"
- "Europe faces a future of unemployment, poverty and social instability"
- "Britain will become the Mexico of Europe"
- "A reason for this is our quasi-religious belief in free trade. A moral dogma which was born when Britain was the manufacturing centre of the world"
- "A world of fence-off regions with economies that reflect local conditions, cultures and needs"

Get Into Globalens.com

Go to the www.globalens.com web page and access the following cases:

- Detroit Motors and General Auto: A Case Study in Globalization, Outsourcing and Automation
- Western Union: A Case for Global Expansion
- Globalization Comes to Nakamura Lacquer Company
- Jim Thompson Thai Silk Company
- NAFTA Arrives at Maxwell Tomato Farms
- Vostok Watches

Now compare the previously listed cases of companies entering the globalization process and determine in which aspects they were successful and in which they were not. What are common issues that appear in all cases? What are particular/industry specific matters?

Prepare a comparative table like the one below and then elaborate in writing.

Issue	Detroit	Western Union	Nakamura	Maxwell	Vostok	Another company of your choice
Adaptation to new tastes						

Problems with employees						
Different demands from different markets						
Etc.						
Etc.						
Etc.						

Reference

Adler, N. J., & Gundersen, A. (2007). *International dimensions of organizational behavior* (5th Revised ed.). Cincinnati, OH: South Western College.

Notes

1. Adler and Gundersen (2007).

Sustainability, Social Enterprise, and Impact Investment

Nader H. Asgary, Dina Frutos-Bencze, and Massood V. Samii

Nader H. Asgary, Dina Frutos-Bencze and Massood V. Samii, "Sustainability, Social Enterprise, and Impact Investment," *Global Business: An Economic, Social, and Environmental Perspective*, pp. 285-301.

Learning Objectives

- Describe the history and the concept of **sustainable development**
- Understand the advantages and challenges of **sustainability assessment frameworks**
- Identify common **sustainability assessment indices**
- Define **Social Enterprise** and **Impact Investing**

Opening Case

Divine Chocolate: Cocoa Fair Trade

Divine Chocolate Limited is a unique chocolate producer. The company is an international social enterprise that is 44% owned by farmer cooperatives in Kuapa Kokoo, Ghana. Kuapa Kokoo stands for "good cocoa growers" and its mission is to empower farmers in their work, increase women's participation in all the activities of the cooperatives, and develop environmentally friendly and sustainable processes for the cultivation of cocoa. Beyond passing 44% of its profits to the cooperatives' members, the organization pays the Fairtrade premium of $2,000 per ton of cocoa. Farmers then democratically decide how to spend the Fairtrade premiums. The proceeds have been previously used for skills and training initiatives, community improvements including water wells, schools, and clinics, as well as bonuses for farmers.

Figure 6.2.1 Divine Easter Eggs.

https://www.flickr.com/photos/wheatfields/2310153414/in/photolist-5bXnzq-XPryAJ-4w998h-7b2zeF

The first ever Divine Chocolate bar was sold in United Kingdom's confectionary market in 1998. In 2007, a sister company was set up in the United States. Today, customers can purchase delicious Divine Chocolate online. For its continued growth and impact, Divine Chocolate won several awards including the Guardian's Sustainable Business Award for Social Impact Innovation in 2015.

For more information, visit the company's website: http://www.divinechocolate.com/us/about-us

Based on

https://www.theguardian.com/sustainable-business/2015/apr/30/cocoa-farmers-spread-the-taste-for-divine-chocolate; http://www.divinechocolate.com/us/

https://www.britishcouncil.org/society/social-enterprise/news-events/news-international-social-enterprise-champions

1. *What characteristics make Divine Chocolate a social enterprise?*

2. *Investigate and describe the requirements to obtain a "Fair Trade" designation.*

Introduction

The demand for businesses to conduct their operations in a sustainable manner is continuously increasing. Nowadays companies are expected to support and advance the interests of their stakeholders. This trend has resulted in the development of concepts such as business ethics, corporate social responsibility (CSR), discussed earlier, and also concepts such as sustainability and social enterprise. The opening case of the [reading] showcases a company with a mission to empower farmers, and develop environmentally-friendly means for the cultivation of cocoa. In the era of global transparency consumers are informed and reward companies that are sustainable, ethical and socially responsible.

This [reading] discusses sustainable development, the Global Reporting Initiative (GRI) framework, social enterprise, Social Return on Investment (SROI), and impact investing concepts and their influence on businesses.

Corporations deal with a wide variety of sustainability issues in their operations, directly or indirectly. Advances in technology have allowed for more efficient equipment, machines, buildings, and other devices which need less energy to keep running. Technology has also allowed for safer processing of industrial waste that can be toxic to the environment.

Sustainable Development

Similarly, to the concept of corporate social responsibility, the concept of sustainable development is present in discussions about economic development and the environment. That, however, has not always been the case. In 1972, Donella Meadows, Dennis Meadows, Jørgen Randers, and William Behrens III (1972) published their well-known book titled *Limits to Growth* in which they demonstrated that population and economic growth increase exponentially but are limited by the resources available. When this concept was presented, the idea of sustainable development was unknown. However, in retrospect, what the authors described in their book was the early alarm that initiated the drive for sustainable development (Meadows, Meadows, Randers, & Behrens III, 1972; Meadows, Randers, & Meadows, 2004).

It was only after the 1972 United Nations Conference on the Human Environment in Stockholm, when the terms **environmentally sound development** or **eco-development** began to be used more frequently and sustainability gained popularity. Although back in the 70s these concepts were not accurately defined, it was obvious that the type of development implied by the term **eco-development** and sustainable development were different from the type of development discussed until then (Daly, 1997).

In the early 1980s, the first major breakthrough in conceptual insight came from the formulation of the *World Conservation Strategy* by the International Union for Conservation of Nature (IUCN),[1] the World Wildlife Fund (WWF), and the United Nations Environment Program.[2]

The debate provided a platform that allowed for the addition of a range of issues such as efficiency, distribution of equity, conservation, resource management and inter-generational responsibility that had not been included before.

In the late 1980s the term "sustainable development" began to gain wide acceptance after its appearance in a document called *Our Common Future*, also known as the *Brundtland Report* published in 1987 by the Brundtland Commission (or the World Commission on Environment and Development, WCED). This report is considered to be the milestone that started the process of re-thinking the established ways of living and governing by introducing the idea that sustainable development can be achieved through governance and society's involvement (Sachs, 2006; Stiglitz, 2006). In addition, some economic, social, and political prerequisites for sustainable development were identified. The report also provided the most commonly accepted definition of **sustainable development**—"development that meets the needs of the present without compromising the ability of future generations to meet their own needs" (Brundtland, 1987; Trzyna, 1995).

The strength of the sustainable development concept is that it reflects a change in the vision of how the economic activities of human beings relate to a finite environment. A condition of sustainable development is that the regeneration of raw materials and the absorption of waste are kept at ecologically sustainable levels. In other words, the regeneration and waste absorption of resources should be in equilibrium. This shift of thought involves the replacement of the standard economic quantitative measures of expansion such as economic growth with qualitative societal and environmental norms as the way to move forward. However, this shift is resisted by most economic and political institutions which are founded on traditional quantitative growth (Brundtland, 1987; Moran, Wackernagel, Kitzes, Goldfinger, & Boutaud, 2008; Trzyna, 1995).

At the macro level, sustainable development commonly relates to the concept of the **triple bottom line** (TBL) (Pope, Annandale, & Morrison-Saunders, 2004):

1. Economic growth (Profit)
2. Social equity (People)
3. Protection of the Environment (Planet)

The basis of the **economic component** is the principle that the well-being of a society has to be maximized and poverty has to be eradicated through the efficient use of natural resources (Redclift, 1987). The **social component** deals with the relationship of the society with the economy and the environment. Such relationship is very broad and includes issues such as the welfare of people, the access to basic health and education services, minimum standards of security, and respect for human rights. It also refers to the development of various cultures, diversity, and pluralism. The issue of equitable distribution of benefits and access to resources is an essential component of both the economic and social dimensions of sustainable development.

It is better to tackle the economic and social sustainability components separately. The definition and main characteristics of each sustainability dimension are contrasted in the summary presented in Table 6.2.1. There is some overlap between the two dimensions.

Table 6.2.3 Comparison of Social and Economic Sustainability

Social Sustainability	Economic Sustainability
Definition	
Achieved by systematic community participation and strong civil society.	Achieved by maintenance of capital.
Characteristics	
Social cohesion, cultural identity, diversity, etc. constitute a part of social capital. This human capital requires maintenance and replenishment. Investments in the education, health and nutrition of individuals are now accepted as part of economic development.	Seeks the maintenance of capital. Economists prefer to value things in monetary terms, therefore valuing correctly natural capital, intangible, intergenerational, and common-access resources such as air is crucial in order to measure economic sustainability.

The concept of sustainable development has also shifted the perspective of how governments should make policies. Governments have the complex task of finding the appropriate balance between the competing demands on natural and social resources, without slowing down economic progress. Since the economic, social and environmental aspects of any actions are interconnected, they must be considered in an integral manner. It is especially important not to consider only one of these dimensions at a time to avoid errors in judgment and unsustainable outcomes. For example, the focus on profit margins only has historically led to social and environmental damages that in the long-term end up costing society. Similarly, taking care of the environment and the ability to provide social services depends a great deal on economic resources. The interconnected and interdependent nature of sustainable development also requires thinking beyond geographical and institutional borders in order to coordinate strategies and make good decisions (Strange & Bayley, 2008).

Sustainability Assessment

Sustainability assessment is often described as the process in which the implications of an initiative on sustainability are evaluated (Spangenberg, Omann, & Hinterberger, 2002). This generic definition includes a broad range of different processes.

Sustainability assessment is increasingly viewed as an important tool to aid evaluation of progress toward sustainability. However, this is a new and evolving concept and there are few examples of effective sustainability assessment processes implemented so far.

Many of the existing assessment frameworks are examples of integrated assessments directly derived from the **Strategic Environmental Assessment** (SEA), the **Sustainability Impact Assessment** (SIA), and the **Environmental Impact Assessment** (EIA) frameworks that incorporate economic, environmental, and social considerations. This approach is also known as a “Triple Bottom Line” (TBL) approach to sustainability that we discussed above. These integrated assessment processes usually either try to find ways to minimize unsustainability, or attempt to achieve TBL objectives (Gasparatos et al., 2007; Jansen, 2003; Pope, Annandale, & Morrison-Saunders, 2004).

There is an ongoing debate about sustainability assessments. The major conclusions regarding sustainability assessment frameworks can be summarized as follows:

1. Sustainability assessment must assess the sustainability of an initiative in addition to assessing the final outcome.
2. Societal goals should be conceptually clear.

However, according to some scholars, the consensus about sustainability assessments is that any sound assessment should include the following (Gasparatos, El-Haram, & Horner, 2007, 2009):

- Integrate economic, environmental, social, and institutional issues as well as their interconnections.
- Consider the consequences of current actions far into the future.
- Recognize the uncertainty regarding the results of current actions.
- Engage the public.
- Incorporate intra- and inter-generational considerations.

The challenge of making sustainable development operational is the ability to evaluate and manage at a macro level the complex interrelationships among economic, social, and environmental objectives. At the United Nations Conference on Environment and Development in 1992, documents that outlined a plan and the principles to achieve sustainable development were put forward. These documents are known as the Agenda and the **Rio Declaration**. The Agenda and the Declaration had a wide range of initiatives that brought the sustainability concept closer to be an operational guide for assessing sustainability (Agenda 21, 1993; Dernbach, 1998).

In order to measure the progress toward sustainable development, it is necessary to identify operational indicators that provide manageable and accurate information on economic, environmental, and social conditions. Since the early 90s many indicators have been developed. The **Compendium of Sustainable Development Indicators** lists more than 500 sustainable indicators (Parris & Kates, 2003).

Sustainable Development Indices

Böhringer and Jochem (2007) reviewed eleven sustainable development indices and studied their consistency and meaningfulness. They concluded that the indicators listed in Table 6.2.2 are concise and transparent, but that they do not appropriately use fundamental scientific requirements such as the technical aggregation method, the normalization of variables and their weighting, as well as the commensurability of input variables (Böhringer & Jochem, 2007).

Table 6.2.2 Sustainable Development Indices

Acronym	Sustainable Development Indicator	Website/Source
EF	Ecological Footprint	https://www.footprintnetwork.org/our-work/ecological-footprint/
HDI	Human Development Index	http://hdr.undp.org/en/content/human-development-index-hdi
ESI	Environmental Sustainability Index	http://sedac.ciesin.columbia.edu/data/collection/esi/
EPI	Environmental Performance Index	https://epi.envirocenter.yale.edu/
EVI	Environmental Vulnerability Index	http://www.vulnerabilityindex.net/
EDP	Environmental Adjusted Domestic Product	https://unstats.un.org/unsd/environmentgl/gesform.asp?getitem=467
LPI	Living Planet Index	http://www.livingplanetindex.org/home/index

The general conclusion is that sustainability indicators and indices can be powerful tools, but only if they are used appropriately. Even though the methods used for assessing the consistency and transparency of these indicators is relatively objective, a certain subjective **bias** is bound to exist. Composite indicators may give ambiguous and unreliable information if they are poorly constructed or misinterpreted. The lack of a clear understanding of how the indicators are developed and what information they convey is critical for policy-making decisions using such indicators. The incorrect interpretation of indexes and indicators may result in flawed policy decisions that could lead to the increase of economic disparities, promote environmental damage, and even decrease the possibilities for long-term sustainability (Golusin & Munitlak Ivanovic, 2009; Mayer, 2008; Siche, Agostinho, Ortega, & Romeiro, 2008; Singh, Murty, Gupta, & Dikshit, 2009).

> **Exercise.** *Should indexes be used when assessing sustainable development of a country? Explain and illustrate with an example.*

Sustainable Development Goals

The **2030 Agenda for Sustainable Development,**[3] adopted by all United Nations Member States in 2015, established **17 Sustainable Development Goals** (SDGs). The common aim of these goals is to improve health and education, reduce inequality, and spur economic growth, all while tackling climate change and working to preserve our oceans and forests. Member States recognized that this is an urgent call for action and that to achieve the goals a global partnership is necessary. The Sustainable Development Goals are:

1. No Poverty.

2. Zero Hunger.
3. Good Health and Well-Being.
4. Quality Education.
5. Gender Equality.
6. Clean Water and Sanitation.
7. Affordable and Clean Energy.
8. Decent Work and Economic Growth.
9. Industry, Innovation and Infrastructure.
10. Reduced Inequality.
11. Sustainable Cities and Communities.
12. Responsible Consumption/Production.
13. Climate Action.
14. Life Below Water.
15. Life on Land.
16. Peace and Justice Strong Institutions.
17. Partnerships to Achieve the Goal.

Social Enterprise

The recognition that businesses have responsibilities beyond making profit and providing goods and services has resulted in the development of the social enterprise concept. **Social enterprises** can be defined as "organizations that address a basic unmet need or solve a social problem through a market-driven approach" (Social Enterprise Alliance, 2019).[4] Social enterprises can be both non-profit and for-profit, if the actions of the organization significantly contribute to addressing a social issue.

The **Social Enterprise Alliance** recognizes three models of social enterprises. Some social enterprises are opportunity employers; those are organizations that provide jobs for people who face significant barriers to mainstream employment. Other social enterprises contribute to social change by providing transformative products and services. Finally, donate back social enterprises donate a portion of their profits to social projects or nonprofits that address social issues. Table 6.2.3 highlights companies with each social enterprise model.

Table 6.2.3 Social Enterprise Examples

Opportunity Employer	Transformative Product or Service	Donate Back
Akola Jewelry	Benetech/Kiva	Everly

Table 6.2.3 Social Enterprise Examples

Akola Jewelry is a jewelry company that provides jobs to women in Uganda who work with raw materials for jewelry, as well as women with criminal records in Dallas, TX, who assemble it and work in distribution centers.	Based in Palo Alto, Benetech develops technology that improves lives of people around the world. The company tackles problems such as education, human rights, environment, and poverty.	Everly is a contemporary clothing company that partnered with Global Hope Network International to help a village in Myanmar. Through the program, villagers are empowered to find solutions to issues in several key areas including wellness education, and family income generation.
	Kiva, a non-profit organization uses a blend of technology, systems, and culture "to connect people through lending to alleviate poverty."	
https://akolaproject.org/	https://benetech.org/ https://www.kiva.org/	http://everlyclothing.com/

Impact Investing

The trend towards social conscientiousness has influenced investing approaches, as well as business missions and operations; the field of impact/sustainable investing has been growing rapidly. **Impact investments** can be defined as the following: "investments made into companies, organizations, and funds with the intention to generate social and environmental alongside financial return" (Global Impact Investing Network).[5]

In a way, impact investing is an equivalent of social entrepreneurship in the world of finance (Asgary & McNulty, 2017). Just like social entrepreneurs, impact investors look for more than simply economic return. The growth of impact investing provides major opportunities for financing social projects. Various innovative ways of mobilizing funds for social issues have been developed in the field. Some examples include Social Impact Bonds (SIBs), ethical funds, and public-private partnerships.

Measuring Impact

The rise of **social entrepreneurship** affects investing and incentivizes corporate social responsibility and sustainability centered business models. In turn, this has created a need for frameworks and tools to measure the social impact of businesses (Asgary and Maccari, 2019).

The **Global Reporting Initiative** (GRI)[6] is a network-based organization that pioneered the world's most widely used sustainability reporting framework (GRI, 2014). The core goal of the Global Reporting

Initiative framework is that the disclosure of a company's economic, environmental and social performance becomes a widely accepted standard practice.

The GRI provides a reporting framework that outlines the principles and performance indicators that organizations should use to measure and report their economic, environmental, and social performance. A **sustainability report** based on the GRI framework is expected to provide a relatively accurate picture of the sustainability performance of the reporting organization. In addition, the report is supposed to be somewhat balanced because it includes both the positive and the negative contributions of the organization.

The sustainability reports created based on this framework are required to disclose the outcomes and results that occur within the reporting period. Usually that reporting period is a year. Since different companies and organizations follow the same framework and the reports cover a particular period, these reports can be very useful in benchmarking and assessing the sustainability performance with respect to voluntary initiatives, performance standards, norms, codes, and laws. In addition, the organization's performance can be tracked over time as well as compared with other organizations and companies in a similar category.

One of the advantages of the GRI reporting framework is that it applies to any size company and it is independent of the location and the sector of the company. In other words, small companies can use the framework, as well as companies with geographically dispersed operations.

GRI Reporting Framework Dimensions

Economic Dimension. The economic dimension of the framework accounts for a company's impact on the economic systems at local, national, and global levels, as well as the impact on economic conditions of its stakeholders. Some of the economic indicators in this dimension include the flow of capital. Financial performance is crucial to understand the sustainability contribution of an organization to the larger economic system.

Environmental Dimension. The environmental sustainability of a firm is determined by the firm's impacts on the natural systems where the company operates. These include living and non-living ecosystems. Environmental indicators used in the framework are related to the performance of the inputs relative to the outputs. In addition, it includes measures that indicate the level of environmental compliance with laws and regulations of the company, as well as indictors that measure the impacts of the company's products and services on biodiversity.

Social Dimension. The indicators used to determine the company's sustainability performance in the social dimension measure aspects related to labor practices, education, product responsibility, and human rights.

To encourage the use of the GRI framework to address environmental sustainability concerns, we need to create a positive loop that connects a firm's environmental sustainability to the performance of the firm. If this positive relationship is developed, the firm will improve its performance and practice an environmentally friendly behavior at the same time. One way to develop this positive relationship is to encourage buyers to consider the environmental aspect of the firm as criteria to choose a product.

Another tool used to measure impact of organizations is the **Social Return on Investment** (SROI); it similarly considers social, economic, and environmental impact of the organization. It can also be applied to evaluate or plan individual projects of a given organization. The major challenge associated with the tool is that there is no standard way to conduct the SROI analysis and there is no single organization that is responsible for conducting it. The approach, however, is growing in popularity, which illustrates the need for its continuous improvement.

Conclusion

Increasingly small, medium, large and multinational are interested in incorporating sustainable practices into their value chain and business model. While this trend may mean that the maximization of profit is not the main goal, businesses are comfortable investing in practices that in the long run will have a positive impact on the environment and society at large. A main driver of this behavior are the Millennials and Generation Z who according to research are generations more concerned about the negative impact a business may have on the environment. Subsequently, multinationals are incorporating sustainable growth and social issues in their strategies.

TBL Connection The Millennial Marketplace and Propagating the Triple Bottom Line

Millennials now represent the world's most important consumer category. It is forecasted that about 70% of millennials are willing to spend more on brands that embrace sustainability, social responsibility, or a cause they care about.

A bottom line that focuses on more than just profit allows a company to make smart long-term decisions rather than dedicate every resource to increasing a number. Because of this, the triple bottom line can provide businesses with a certain amount of sustainability. As more businesses choose to pursue goals beyond maximizing profit, the Benefit Corporation, or "B Corp," has arisen to standardize the process of incorporating a triple bottom line and tracking social and environmental impact. Becoming a certified B Corp involves assessments, the completion of a disclosure questionnaire and background checks, as well as the possibility of an annual site review to confirm the accuracy of certain responses.

B Lab is a nonprofit that certifies potential B Corps after ensuring they meet the standards. Since B Lab was formed in 2006, more than 2,000 businesses, including clothing giant Patagonia, have been B Corp certified.

While millennials and Generation Z seem to be spearheading the movement, the triple bottom line is more than just a generational fad. Acknowledging that there's more to business than profit allows a company to accept social and environmental responsibility for its actions and puts it on track to creating a more sustainable future for everyone. For more information, visit https://bcorporation.net/about-b-lab.

Based on: https://www.forbes.com/sites/deeppatel/2017/07/28/the-millennial-marketplace-and-the-propagation-of-the-triple-bottom-line/#1580d098d04a

1. *If a business is turning a healthy profit, provide examples of ways the business can consider incorporating a TBL. Illustrate with examples.*
2. *What is the process of becoming a B Corp certified company?*

[Reading] Review

Key Terms

- Eco-Development
- Brundtland Report
- Sustainable Development
- Sustainability Assessment
- Sustainability Indices
- Social Enterprise
- Impact Investment
- Global Reporting Initiative

Questions & Assignments

Questions

1. Analyze social enterprise effectiveness. Explain and illustrate with an example.
2. Briefly describe the concept of economic sustainability. What challenges and opportunities are created for MNEs by the growing trend of supporting economic sustainability?

Assignments

1. Work with a partner and develop an idea for a social enterprise. Which model does your social enterprise follow? Is it a for-profit or a non-profit? Pitch your idea to the class.
2. Suppose a consumer product corporation works with a credit card company to allow 5% of the

price of its products, if charged by the credit card, to go to a non-profit foundation that helps low income families in the region where purchases were made. Analyze the impact of such a policy on all stakeholders.

Suggested Reading

GRI Standards. Downloadable versions are available with registration. Registration is free https://www.globalreporting.org/standards/gri-standards-download-center

UN Sustainable Development Goals https://www.un.org/sustainabledevelopment/sustainable-development-goals/

The Coca Cola Company Sustainability Report 2017/2018 https://www.coca-colacompany.com/content/dam/journey/us/en/private/fileassets/pdf/2018/2017-Sustainability-Report-The-Coca-Cola-Company.pdf

Sachs, J. (2015). *The age of sustainable development.* New York, NY: Columbia University Press.

Yunus, M., & Jolis, A. (1998). *Banker to the poor: The autobiography of Muhammad Yunus, founder of the Grameen Bank.* London, England: Aurum Press.

https://socialenterprise.us/about/social-enterprise/

https://thegiin.org/impact-investing/

References

Asgary Nader and Maccari Emerson (2019). Entrepreneurship and Innovation: Opportunities and Challenges, Routledge.

Agenda 21, E. (1993). *The United Nations Programme of Action from Rio de Janeiro.* New York, NY: UN Department of Public Information.

Asgary, N. H., & McNulty, R. E. (2017). Contributions and challenges in the struggle to end poverty: the case of Kiva. *Information Technology for Development, 23*(2), 367–387.

Böhringer, C., & Jochem, P. E. P. (2007). Measuring the immeasurable—A survey of sustainability indices. *Ecological Economics, 63*(1), 1–8. doi:10.1016/j.ecolecon.2007.03.008

Brundtland, G. (1987). Our common future: Report of the 1987 World Commission on Environment and Development: Oxford: Oxford University Press.

Daly, H. (1997). *Beyond growth: the economics of sustainable development*: Beacon Pr.

Dernbach, J. (1998). Sustainable Development as a Framework for National Governance. *Case Western Reserve Law Review, 49*(1), 1.

Gasparatos, A., El-Haram, M., & Horner, M. (2007). A critical review of reductionist approaches for assessing the progress towards sustainability. *Environmental Impact Assessment Review, 28*(4–5), 286–311. doi:10.1016/j.eiar.2007.09.002

Gasparatos, A., El-Haram, M., & Horner, M. (2009). The argument against a reductionist approach for measuring sustainable development performance and the need for methodological pluralism. *Accounting Forum, 33*(3), 245–256. doi:10.1016/j.accfor.2008.07.006

Golusin, M., & Munitlak Ivanovic, O. (2009). Definition, characteristics and state of the indicators of sustainable development in countries of Southeastern Europe. *Agriculture, Ecosystems & Environment, 130*(1–2), 67–74. doi:10.1016/j.agee.2008.11.018

Goodland, R., & Daly, H. (1996). Environmental Sustainability: Universal and Non-Negotiable. *Ecological Applications, 6*(4), 1002–1017.

Jansen, L. (2003). The challenge of sustainable development. *Journal of Cleaner Production, 11*(3), 231–245.

Mayer, A. L. (2008). Strengths and weaknesses of common sustainability indices for multidimensional systems. *Environment International, 34*(2), 277–291. doi:10.1016/j.envint.2007.09.004

Meadows, D. H., Meadows, D. L., Randers, J., & Behrens III, W. W. (1972). *The Limits to Growth: A Report for the Club of Rome's Project on the Predicament of Mankind.* New York, NY: Universe Books.

Meadows, D. H., Randers, J., & Meadows, D. L. (2004). *The limits to growth: the 30-year update*: Chelsea Green.

Moran, D. D., Wackernagel, M., Kitzes, J. A., Goldfinger, S. H., & Boutaud, A. (2008). Measuring sustainable development—Nation by nation. *Ecological Economics, 64*(3), 470–474. doi:10.1016/j.ecolecon.2007.08.017

Parris, T. M., & Kates, R. W. (2003). Characterizing and Measuring Sustainable Development. *Annual Review of Environment and Resources, 28*, 559–586.

Pope, J., Annandale, D., & Morrison-Saunders, A. (2004). Conceptualising sustainability assessment. *Environmental Impact Assessment Review, 24*(6), 595–616.

Redclift, M. (1987). *Sustainable development: Exploring the contradictions*: Routledge.

Sachs, J. (2006). *The end of poverty: Economic possibilities for our time.* New York, NY: Penguin Press.

Siche, J. R., Agostinho, F., Ortega, E., & Romeiro, A. (2008). Sustainability of nations by indices: Comparative study between environmental sustainability index, ecological footprint and the emergy performance indices. *Ecological Economics, 66*(4), 628–637. doi:10.1016/j.ecolecon.2007.10.023

Singh, R. K., Murty, H. R., Gupta, S. K., & Dikshit, A. K. (2009). An overview of sustainability assessment methodologies. *Ecological Indicators, 9*(2), 189–212. doi:10.1016/j.ecolind.2008.05.011

Spangenberg, J. H., Omann, I., & Hinterberger, F. (2002). Sustainable growth criteria Minimum benchmarks and scenarios for employment and the environment. *Ecological Economics, 42*(3), 429–443.

Stiglitz, J. E. (2006). *Making globalization work.* New York, NY: WW Norton & Company.

Strange, T., & Bayley, A. (2008). *Sustainable development: linking economy, society, environment OECD Insights*

Trzyna, T. (1995). *A sustainable world: defining and measuring sustainable development*: International Center for the Environment and Public Policy for the World Conservation Union (IUCN).

Notes

1. IUCN. (1980). World Conservation Strategy: Living Resource Conservation for Sustainable Development. Retrieved from https://portals.iucn.org/library/efiles/html/WCS-004/cover.html
2. UNEP. (1992). Rio Declaration–Rio Declaration on Environment and Development–United Nations Environment Programme (UNEP).
3. https://sustainabledevelopment.un.org/post2015/transformingourworld
4. https://socialenterprise.us/
5. https://www.globalreporting.org/Pages/default.aspx
6. GRI–https://www.globalreporting.org/Pages/default.aspx

Reading 6.3

Introduction

Governments and Corporate Social Responsibility

Josep M. Lozano, Laura Albareda, Tamyko Ysa, Heike Roscher, and Manila Marcuccio

Corporate social responsibility (CSR). In the last seven years, this phrase has made an impressive entrance on the economic and business scene and also the political and social scene. Just listing the terms that have been laid on the table during that time, and clarifying them, would be enough to fill a book: social action, socially responsible investment, management by values, corporate citizenship, business ethics, the triple bottom line, reputation, and so on. But it is not merely a question of terminology: the diversity of names is only the visible part of the existence of a multitude of initiatives, proposals and experiences that neither share the same quality nor respond to the same type of options. It is precisely this issue of quality and options that we still need to address.

So, we propose to clarify what we understand by CSR and how we can tackle the broad topic that has arisen under its auspices. In this regard, we believe that when we talk of CSR we should make a distinction between three aspects:

1. Agenda: the variety of practices, measures and proposals that come under the term CSR.
2. Understanding: what we understand by CSR—and the various terms associated with it—and, therefore, what business model is proposed and what role enterprise is

considered to play in society.

3. Vision: what project for society CSR conforms to.

In recent times, as a result of haste, pressure, and the interests of the various actors involved, we have run the risk of becoming engulfed in the multiple issues that make up the agenda. This might lead us to forget that, ultimately, the development of CSR cannot be seriously tackled unless it is linked to a corporate vision and a vision for society. Obviously, this does not mean that specific measures should not be undertaken—because we need a great many of them—but the only way to avoid CSR becoming just another fad or a new consultancy product is to be constantly aware that it offers a great opportunity to redraft a corporate vision and a vision for the nation, and therefore also an opportunity to ask ourselves what we want to do in the future and what it means for us to do it. Otherwise, there is the danger that CSR will become a pure speculative bubble; a piece of rhetorical, ideological and—needless to say—advertising speculation.

The presence of CSR has grown exponentially in all sorts of organizations: some companies have incorporated it into their corporate agenda, assigning management responsibilities to it in their organisation chart, and asking themselves what they were doing and what they ought to be doing; some social organizations have identified it as a new strategic area for action, and in some cases have set themselves up rather as guardians of the cause; some political organizations have seen it as a new opportunity for political initiative, legislative or otherwise; academic institutions have demonstrated the incorporation of CSR into their curricula; advisers and consultants of all sorts have created services linked to it; countless associations, foundations and forums have been set up with a view to fostering it, either in general or concentrating on certain aspects of it. Each of them has seen, and legitimately so, that CSR also provides an opportunity for differentiation and awareness, among other reasons because information related to this sphere has mushroomed in the media.

Once we have proved that we know how to do something, it is probably time to ask ourselves how we are doing it and from what perspective, above all because CSR only has any meaning as an internalised long-term commitment. CSR is at the same time a road and a direction, and not something that is immobile or fixed; and precisely for this reason, we should resist the temptation to present it to public opinion as a race to see who manages to project the best image in this respect.

Ultimately, CSR should be managed and manageable; however, it cannot be reduced to a new technique or area of management, nor to the urgency to do something, nor to the demand that others do something. On the contrary, it is a matter of turning CSR into a corporate identity and corporate project. Sometimes this makes for a poor fit with the concerted pressure exerted by the various actors: this is an issue that—if it requires anything—requires trust and credibility. Hence the need to bear constantly in mind that no discourse on CSR is possible without it first being placed in a reference framework.

Defining a Possible CSR Reference Framework

In the European context, the Green Paper 'Promoting a European framework for Corporate Social Responsibility' (2001) and the subsequent 'Communication concerning corporate social responsibility: A business contribution to sustainable development' (2002) published by the European Commission have undoubtedly become the yardstick for approaching this issue. Nevertheless, when these documents are mentioned, it is often forgotten that the European Union's ambitious strategic objective was formulated prior to this, in the Final Declaration of the Lisbon European Council (March 2000): by 2010, 'to become the most competitive and dynamic knowledge-based economy in the world, capable of sustainable economic growth with more and better jobs and greater social cohesion'. The crux of the matter lies in this desire to combine competitiveness, economic growth, sustainability and social cohesion. One can understand more fully the framework of CSR, since from this perspective it is not limited to a reactive response to new demands and pressures exerted by society on enterprise but rather can be seen as a response by enterprise, on a business level, to a series of collective challenges that are at the same time economic and social.

The European Commission (2001a) defines CSR as 'a concept whereby companies integrate social and environmental concerns in their business operations and in their interaction with stakeholders on a voluntary basis.' The way the Commission tackles this issue underlines two aspects: the 'what' and the 'how'. As far as the 'what' is concerned, it emphasises the fact that companies should make social and environmental commitments in their actions; and as for the 'how', it stresses the voluntary nature of those commitments. At present the controversy is focused on the latter point, voluntariness, which some on occasions reduce to a ridiculous mixture of good deeds and good will. Several social actors have located at the centre of the debate—and of their pressure—the issue of the extent to which this integration should be merely voluntary. In this way, we find ourselves at a dead end: the business world tends to consider the voluntary nature of CSR as unrenounceable, while many social (and political) agents understand that mere voluntariness should be the first thing to go.

The work we present here stands precisely at this crossroads. We could say that, rather than an answer, it is intended to find a way out. In this respect, it is stressed that the fundamental issue is to initiate a deliberation that will enable us to build a joint perspective, the basis for a shared reference framework from which not only will we be able to answer the questions we ask ourselves, but even understand better and formulate more accurately the right questions. Consequently, our approach starts from the supposition that *the right question is not about CSR regulation, but what policy governments should adopt towards CSR*. We should ask ourselves *what public policy we need in order to develop CSR;* only in this context is there any meaning to the question about regulation, which after all is no more than a tool—and not the only one—of that policy.

In short, we believe that the two dominant debates about CSR (the 'what' and the 'how') are unsolvable, and that we will waste a great deal of energy unless we explore the 'why', which can only be expressed through the business model and the social model that provide the framework for the CSR debate. This is why we insist that we must put an end to the fiction that the CSR debate is limited to the issue of whether it is accepted or not, and begin to realise that there may be—indeed there are—several visions of the nature and the scope of CSR.

CSR: Where Do We Stand?

Increasingly, the CSR debate highlights the fact that, in a globalized world, it is not just products and services that compete but also business models, management models (an aspect that is often neglected) and governance national models. In this context, when we talk of CSR we have to bear in mind the existence of non-coincident approximations, even if we focus on Europe and the United States and allow ourselves to forget the rest of the world. In the USA, the main issues regarding CSR revolve for the most part around management in relation to the stakeholders (especially those with most power to lobby or pressure), the establishment of relations with the community, and business action aimed at society, which are frequently described as CSR because they are carried out by companies, rather than because they affect the company's business core. On the other hand, in Europe CSR tends to be linked increasingly to an overall vision of the company, with more attention to all the processes in which it is involved and greater sensitivity towards the political and social context in which it operates. In this regard, our work highlights a very important issue: *we have noted a symptomatic similarity between the models of public policies on CSR that we have identified and the various welfare state models.* However, we also think that this correspondence is more than just a phenomenon to take note of; it poses a political and entrepreneurial challenge: it shows us that in the debates on CSR sometimes more questions converge than we are willing to accept. We hold that it would be a case of short-sighted pragmatism to reduce CSR, from the political arena, to just another instrumental tool available to governments to shore up the crisis of the welfare state. It would be tantamount to giving answers to the future by answering questions from the past. Rather, it would appear to be a matter of coming to terms with the fact that social governance in our interdependent world demands at the same time a new vision of the contribution companies make to society, a new relationship between the political and business actors, and the ability to develop a shared diagnosis and a shared perspective about the nature of the main challenges facing our societies in order to enable us to contextualise that vision and that relationship.

Roome (2005) notes that, in the approach taken to CSR in each country, several elements converge:

- The political and institutional structure
- The political style and processes
- The social structure
- The intensity of the attitude to voluntariness, as opposed to the acceptance of regulation and state control
- How the role of businesses is described locally and nationally
- The role and the positions of NGOs and citizens' associations in society
- The characteristics of the educational system and the values conveyed by it
- What is expected of leaders
- Historical traditions

Therefore, in the CSR discourse that is built in each nation it is important to take into consideration the following sequence (Figure 7.2.1).

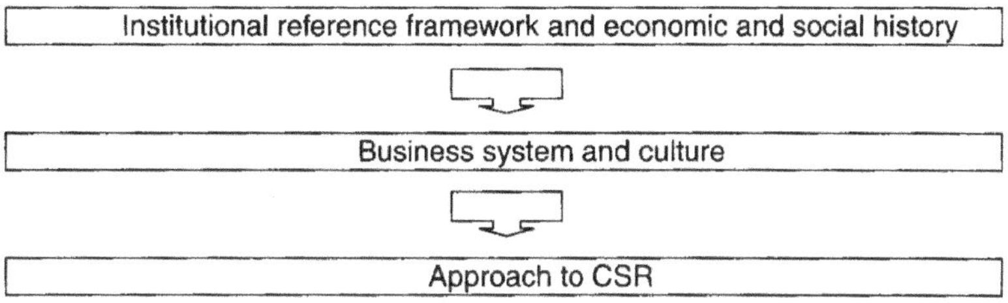

Figure 6.3.1 CSR background on a national framework.

Adapted from Roome (2005)

All the above makes it increasingly necessary for companies and countries to be fully aware of the need to fashion their own approach to CSR. We consider that the most innovative notions regarding CSR are those that link it to the revision of globalisation processes. The most stimulating ideas on this topic come from those companies, public institutions and research or academic institutions that place CSR within the debate generated by the intersection between the action (positive and negative alike) of transnational corporations, the emergence of a global civil society and public opinion, and the reconstruction of the role of states and their interrelationships. As a result, CSR no longer refers simply to the relations between business and society, but crystallises as a way of rethinking the role of business in society, incorporating as a core feature a perspective of governance and sustainability. For this reason, we believe that in talking of CSR at the same time we must also ask ourselves about our corporate vision and our vision for the country.

In order to tackle this issue we need leadership, commitment and conviction, above all in the field of business (obviously), but also in the political and social spheres. We need to create a public space where it is possible to share, spread and recognise significant experiences. We need to strengthen a business culture that is open to dialogue and partnership. We need the CSR agenda to take shape in strictly business terms, and not to be induced or conditioned from outside the business world.

CSR brings us, then, to ask ourselves whether our nation is capable of taking form also as an economic and social space, because CSR is also about how companies and countries differentiate themselves in an interdependent world. Perhaps in the real future, in a globalized world, 'made in X' will become a label associated not just with the quality of that country's products and services but also with the responsibility, credibility and sustainability of its companies.

Building the Nation Also as an Economic and Social Space

Without a shared vision, public—and indeed corporate—reflection on CSR boils down to no more than the pragmatic result of the correlation of forces and the play of interests, the occasional effervescence of rhetoric and persuasion, or the scenario of a (not always bloodless) conflict of convictions.

The time has come to expound openly that CSR constitutes one of the great opportunities for innovation, differentiation and legitimation available to businesses today. Only with a project and a vision can specific CSR agendas—agendas tailored to each company—become what they really are: a learning opportunity.

To put it plainly, there can be no successful companies in failed countries, but neither can there be successful countries with failed companies (the so-called business successes in failed countries are simply an obscenity). In a globalized world, linked to the emergence of the knowledge society, interdependence is a structural fact. No one can hope to build and consolidate their future without taking interdependencies into account. Economic life and social life may not coincide, but there is no way that they can be conceived and developed separately. Economic development is linked to the fabric of social and cultural relationships in which economic activity is carried on, and in which these relationships are mutually reinforced. There is no such thing as a really viable business that is not linked to some extent to the region in which it operates. Today, due to the growing predominance of networks, this mutual involvement in the region and with the region has to be deliberately built, because it no longer comes automatically through the inertia of a more or less stable and comfortably established society.

These ideas have led to discussion on the competitive advantage of nations (Porter, 1990). The discussion does not stop there, though, but goes on to consider the ethical wealth of nations (Donaldson, 2001). Basically, this wealth does not consist of the number of preachers they have or the level of their specialised intellectual production, but above all the quality of their professionals' actions, the coherence and consistency of their institutional framework, the reference values that make up their social relations and the life of their organizations, and so on. In this light, fostering the development of CSR in a nation constitutes, in our opinion, one of the touchstones for the articulation of its competitive advantage and its ethical wealth, because it explicitly gives structure to a corporate vision and a vision for the nation in the context of a globalized world. In other words, *grasping the nettle of CSR brings us to set forth a way of understanding the role of business in society and at the same time contributes to shape a nation as a space in which the relationship between the economy and society is not schizophrenic* (Figure 7.2.2).

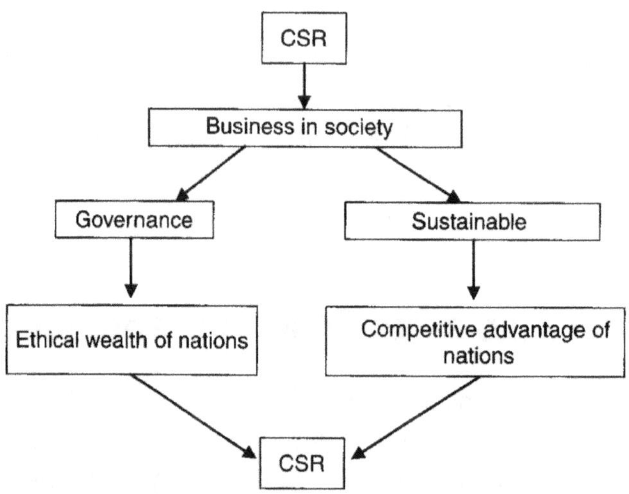

Figure 6.3.2 CSR, governance and sustainability

Source:Lozano, ESADE

Incorporating CSR into the public—i.e., economic, political and social—agenda reminds us that neither companies nor nations are possible without a shared vision: a shared corporate vision and a shared vision for the nation, each in its own differentiated register, because the CSR debate is always a debate about the society we wish to build and how companies contribute to the building process. Furthermore, it is a debate about what sort of enterprise we want and need, and about what we require socially and culturally in order to achieve it. In short, it is a debate that deals with where we want to direct our efforts, what common ground lies between our commitments and what we want to become collectively.

In our opinion, this makes it necessary to create and have access to areas where issues like the ones below can be publicly formed and aired. Incidentally, these issues will also have to undergo systematic public deliberation if we are to avoid their become pieces in a jigsaw puzzle that everyone fits in at their whim.

- *CSR: actors involved.* How to develop companies' relationships with their social environment(s). This means identifying and becoming better acquainted with the various actors that affect business activities or that may be affected by them. This interrelation should not be seen as management of potential risks but as an opportunity to build relationships. At this point it is essential to stress one aspect that is often forgotten: CSR should not be conceived as the sort of activity that is tacked on to what we would call the core of the business. On the contrary, although it might seem obvious, CSR corresponds to the business, and it only means anything if it is undertaken from the business activity itself and integrated into its strategy, not as a series of peripheral measures, however interesting and useful they might be.
- *CSR and partnership relations.* We can infer from this the need to explore in depth a possibility that is quite highly developed in some countries: the creation of new forms of cooperation between businesses, public administrations and social organizations. The creation of these areas of comfortable partnership presupposes two aspects: first, that there is a dialogue enabling the construction of a common vision and goals; and second, that each actor strictly plays its own part, because fostering CSR does not mean that businesses stop being businesses and start performing duties that do not belong to them, nor that they should be subordinated to the demands of public administrations or social organizations. CSR only means that businesses should be businesses, but at the same time asks what sort of businesses they should be.
- *CSR and creation of social capital.* As a result of the above, the possibility arises of increasing the consolidation and development of social capital, inasmuch as the spread of CSR—and also of partnership culture—has a strong impact on the consolidation of the network of economic and social relations. However, this also imposes the need to promote an institutional network making the importance of CSR possible and visible.
- *CSR and business discourse.* Consequently, the development of CSR locates the economic and social dialogue in a new perspective: CSR is inseparable from the consolidation of a new business discourse that is capable of locating business legitimacy on a set of coordinates that includes CSR. However, it would be fatal to fall into another error: to think that what we are saying only implies business changes. CSR only makes sense if all organizations (public, social, etc.) pull their weight and assume their own social responsibilities, and if they do so as a result of a reflection on what role they should play in the emerging society. In this respect, coherently facing the challenge of CSR also constitutes an opportunity for the leadership of the business world that

should not be wasted or overlooked.

- *CSR: innovation and coherence.* CSR can become one of the cores of business innovation and cohesion. It is impossible to develop it if it is not linked to the corporate identity, the way of doing things that is particular to each organisation, and its culture. CSR is not addressed by just drafting a document stating how important it is. There is a great deal to be done in connection with this issue, but CSR does not end with these activities; it should end up actually affecting the organisation's genetic code. This requires steady coherent work and commitment, not the generation of pseudoevents to satisfy the onlookers or certain members of top management. Precisely because CSR is a question of organisational DNA, it is pointless to try and reduce it to a matter of local sensitivity for globalized corporations, as if the fact of being rooted in a region were a sort of servitude from which the company has yet to free itself. On the contrary, in a globalized world we can never forget that this vision always takes shape in social contexts that are determined locally.
- *CSR: from rhetoric to good practices.* This means that we also need to know and spread the most innovative and coherent initiatives and measures being taken in CSR. This emphasis on good practices requires us to refute four clichés that together constitute the heaviest burden the development of CSR has to overcome. First, rhetoric on CSR should not (only) serve to state that there is still a long way to go and to criticise irresponsible behaviour; rather, it should provide an opportunity to differentiate and highlight socially responsible action (given that CSR is one of the great opportunities for business differentiation). Second, we must avoid the impression that companies develop CSR out of nothing; they do it working from the basis of their own track record: CSR is a vision that allows us to innovate, but also to strengthen, consolidate, reinforce and indeed expound ways of operating that have come to form part of business practice. Third, not all companies talk, live and manage CSR in the same way; each does so from its own profile and sector. In other words, CSR is not the exclusive property of large corporations, even if the predominant specific approaches and tools seem to have been designed for companies that are stock market listed and highly exposed to consumer markets. If it is true that there is no CSR without a corporate vision and a vision for the nation, non-listed companies, family firms and SMEs have something to say on the subject. And fourth, CSR is not only about philanthropy (making donations), particularly in a European context, nor should it systematically give rise to any additional cost. ...

References

Donaldson, T. 2001. The Ethical Wealth of Nations. *Journal of Business Ethics,* vol. 31 pp. 25–36.

European Commission. 2001a. *Green Paper—Promoting a European Framework for Corporate Social Responsibility.* COM (2001) 366-final. Brussels.

———. 2002a. *Communication: Corporate Social Responsibility: A Business Contribution to Sustainable Development.* COM (2002) 347-final. Brussels.

Lozano, J. M. and C. Folguera. 2003. *Danone en Ultzama.* ESADE.

Porter, M. 1990. *The Competitive Advantage of Nations.* New York: The Free Press.

Roome, N. 2005. The Implications of National Agendas for CSR. In Habisch, A., J. Jonker, M. Wegner and R. Schmidpeter (eds) *Corporate Social Responsibility across Europe.* Berlin: Springer.

COVID-19 and World Order

Hal Brands and Francis J. Gavin

Hal Brands and Francis J. Gavin, "COVID-19 and World Order," *COVID-19 and World Order: The Future of Conflict, Competition, and Cooperation*, pp. 1-20. Copyright © 2020 by Johns Hopkins University Press. Reprinted with permission.

The coronavirus crisis was a shock, but should not have been a surprise. Public health experts had been warning about the dangers of viral pandemics for years. SARS, H1N1, Ebola, and MERS had highlighted the risks of diseases that raced across borders and the need for effective national and global responses. Not long before the first reported cases of COVID-19 in Wuhan, China, both the Johns Hopkins Center for Health Security and the Kissinger Center for Global Affairs Senior Fellow Dr. Kathleen Hicks had organized separate exercises that highlighted how profoundly a fast-moving virus could endanger the international system and US national security.[1]

Yet these warnings went largely unheeded and the world was not prepared to react effectively when the crisis began. COVID-19 overwhelmed national and international efforts to contain the pandemic while exposing deep flaws in the global public health infrastructure. The institutions most responsible for public health—the World Health Organization (WHO) for the world, the Centers for Disease Control and Prevention (CDC) for the United States—have not performed well. As we write, the world has seen more than 18 million confirmed cases of COVID-19 and rising. The United States has been especially hard hit, with over 5 million confirmed cases and the spread still not under control.[2] The science and epidemiological knowledge surrounding the virus is evolving, new therapies are being developed, and intensive efforts to create an effective vaccine all provide some hope. Until then, COVID-19 will dominate the international landscape.

Even after the virus is contained, the consequences will be with us for some time. This is because the pandemic arrived at an especially troubling moment for the world. In the past few years, many have commented on the fraying of international arrangements to provide for a stable, peaceful, and prosperous world order.[3] What had been feared for some time was now seen as a stark reality: many of the norms, institutions, and practices that upheld the liberal international order and marked American leadership since the end of the Cold War and, in some cases, the end of the Second World War, were under enormous stress. The causes are many and interconnected: the reemergence of great-power political rivalry, marked by the worsening and increasingly toxic relationship between the two largest powers, the United States and China; the increase in populism and nationalism, as well as a seeming loss of faith in democracy as authoritarianism increases its grip on many parts of the world; the dizzying and disorienting effects of new technology; and numerous other causes. These challenges have manifested as a polarized United States grows increasingly uncertain about its role in the world, as many around the world lose faith in the benefits of globalization and interdependence, and as a raft of new transnational concerns, ranging from climate change to disinformation, reveal the shortcomings of existing international institutions.

The crisis does provide an opportunity, however. This volume is a multidisciplinary effort to assess the current state of world order, analyze the effects of the COVID crisis, and offer insights and ideas for the future. The crisis has made clear that much work needs to be done to improve our national and global public health capabilities and institutions and to elevate the threat of disease and pandemic to a higher priority in our national and international security frameworks. This book, however, is premised on something more: the idea that the crisis highlights a number of other pressing national and global challenges, in areas ranging from climate change to relations with China. We believe this crisis is potentially a crucial pivot point, providing an opportunity to rethink—and perhaps revitalize—our current international system. This book begins a much-needed conversation about how to shape international relations in a post-COVID world.

World Orders, Old and New

Historically, efforts to construct effective international arrangements emerge after periods of war, crisis, and turmoil.[4] The Peace of Westphalia ended the vicious wars of religion that had plagued Europe and constructed a comparatively stable system based on the balance of power among nation-states. The 1814–1815 Congress of Vienna was marked by the masterful diplomacy of Count Metternich of Austria and Lord Castlereagh of Great Britain, who worked with other European leaders to tame the wars and ideological fervor unleashed by the French Revolution.[5] These efforts arguably kept the peace in Europe until the Crimean War and prevented any one European power from dominating the continent until the start of the 20th century.

What was left of the Concert system collapsed with World War I, leading to a series of efforts over the succeeding decades to rebuild world order. The Versailles conference after the First World War was inspired by American President Woodrow Wilson's desire to build a peace based on national self-determination, open diplomacy, the ends of arms races, and collective security through a League of Nations—the cures, he believed, to the pathologies of imperialism, militarism, and cutthroat diplomacy that had brought on the conflict. This vision failed as the United States retreated from the system Wilson proposed while lingering and unresolved grievances from the war poisoned the international climate. A global depression, the rise of violent, revolutionary regimes, and the onset of the Second World War destroyed the system created at Versailles and revealed the desperate need for effective mechanisms to generate world order.[6]

Learning from this failure, American planners worked with their allies to start constructing the postwar order before the war even ended. Conferences between the three major players—the United States, the Soviet Union, and Great Britain—at Tehran, Yalta, and Potsdam mixed plans to win the war with efforts to coordinate the postwar peace. International meetings at Bretton Woods and Dumbarton Oaks designed global institutions such as the International Monetary Fund, the World Bank, and the United Nations.[7] American officials hoped for a seamless, integrated world order that would bring the leading nations together in avoiding war and maintaining a secure, prosperous peace.[8]

Yet the Cold War spoiled this vision of "One World," and what emerged in the years and decades that followed was not one order but several. In the economic realm, the so-called Bretton Woods order, which was focused on the capitalist world, created a system that encouraged revitalized global trade but prioritized domestic reconstruction, regional integration, and stability. This system frayed in the 1960s and 1970s, and after a time marked by some disorder, was replaced by the more open, globalized system we have now, based on flexible and market-determined currencies, large-scale global investment and trade, and the dominance of dollar-denominated banking and finance.[9] International security evolved in unexpected directions as well. The United Nations system, premised on state sovereignty and universal principles, was overshadowed by a bipolar system that saw intense ideological and geopolitical rivalry between two rival superpower blocs led by the Soviet Union and the United States.[10] The United States ended up leading a secure, prosperous international order—but one that was limited to the "free world" rather than the entire world.

The superpowers nonetheless cooperated to create a third order: a very successful nuclear order, based upon their shared interest in limiting the dangers posed by the "absolute weapon." This order was built around a series of bilateral and global arms control treaties—including the 1963 Partial Test Ban Treaty, the 1968 Nuclear Nonproliferation Treaty, and the 1972 Antiballistic Missile and Strategic Arms Limitation Treaties—as well as less formalized norms and practices, from tolerance of satellite overflights by the enemy (necessary to reduce the danger of surprise attack) and an implicit understanding, which evolved over time, that nuclear weapons were not merely powerful bombs but were in a category all their own.[11] Though it came under constant pressure, this element of order—rivals working to manage and limit the dangers of new technologies—was more successful than anyone expected and perhaps provides a model for con temporary challenges.

The unexpected end of the Cold War and the rapid demise of the Soviet Union highlighted both the success of these postwar arrangements and the need to rethink world order for a new era. It was also a time of great intellectual creativity, as scholars such as John Mearsheimer, Francis Fukuyama, John Ikenberry, Charles Krauthammer, and Samuel Huntington offered innovative conceptual frames to understand a rapidly changing world.[12] Events moved quickly. Germany was peacefully reunified and the European Union project flourished; democracies emerged around the world, and some long-simmering conflicts and civil wars were resolved peacefully.[13] The United States, working through the United Nations, built an impressive coalition to enforce collective security and expel Iraq from Kuwait. To the surprise of many, some elements of the postwar era, such as the North Atlantic Treaty Organization, were not only maintained but expanded. Other institutions, such as the International Monetary Fund, were re imagined. Over time, still other institutions, such as the World Trade Organization (WTO) and Group of Twenty (G20) were inaugurated. The post–Cold War era was marked by a combination of multilateralism and American ideals and power, as the United States found itself in a commanding position in world affairs. To the extent that there was a single world order, it was largely an expansion and modification of the liberal system that had taken root in the non-communist world after World War II.[14] As this system took on increasingly global dimensions, it was a time of hope and promise.

That period of optimism now seems like a distant memory. The 9/11 attacks on the United States, followed by difficult, controversial wars in Iraq and Afghanistan, exposed new sources of insecurity. The war in Iraq, in particular, drained US energies and shook international support for American power. The 2007–9 financial crisis pummeled the global economy and undermined faith in the market. Populism rose and the movement toward democracy weakened.[15] As China's economy boomed, that country did not, as many had hoped, embrace liberal principles, but instead challenged both regional and global norms and institutions while descending deeper into authoritarianism. Information technology, once seen as a liberating force, showed its darker side through cyberattacks and disinformation campaigns; climate change loomed as a potentially existential challenge. Both the vote of the United Kingdom to leave the European Union (Brexit) and the unexpected election of Donald J. Trump as US president on a campaign of "America First" made 2016 the year when it was clear the existing world order was imperiled. The principles and values that many believed were the cornerstone of this order—openness and innovation, democratic practice and tolerance, interdependence and globalization—were viewed with suspicion by large swaths of America and the world.

[...] COVID-19 highlighted and exacerbated many of the strains that were already testing the post–Cold War system. The pandemic was so disruptive because it exploded in a world that was already increasingly disordered. The question of how to reconstruct world order after COVID involves dealing with not just the disease but also the under lying problems it revealed. How should we diagnose and understand these challenges to world order, and what principles and policies should shape our efforts moving forward?[16] [...]

World Order after COVID

[The volume this reading is originally from] is an undertaking of the Henry A. Kissinger Center for Global Affairs at Johns Hopkins University School of Advanced International Studies (SAIS). Inspired by its namesake, the renowned diplomat and scholar Henry Kissinger, the Center is dedicated to better understanding and applying the lessons of history in order to make sense of an increasingly complex world. Since its inception in 2016, the Center and its scholars have engaged deeply with questions of world order. The COVID-19 crisis has offered an opportunity to convene global experts from Johns Hopkins University and other leading institutions to understand a landmark crisis and plot a course for the future.

This volume draws upon that expertise to address issues ranging from global public health and climate change to international institutions and great-power rivalry. The particular challenge of our moment is that it is impossible to grapple with questions of world order without considering "hard" and "soft" security issues, novel transnational challenges and timeless geopolitical contests, and politics within states as well as politics between them. As always, addressing any of these subjects requires a historical perspective as well as an eye to the future.

Part I of this book thus focuses on *Applied History and Future Scenarios*. It includes essays that use the past to highlight overlooked or misunderstood dynamics of the current crisis and that push us to think imaginatively about the future. These intellectual tasks are particularly important in times of radical uncertainty: in these moments, grounding ourselves in history, or systematically assessing the different paths the future might take, yields the greatest payoff.

Jeremy A. Greene and Dora Vargha employ a historical mindset to address the most basic question we confront today: When will we move from a "world of COVID" to a "world after COVID"? The answer they offer is that we are unlikely to see any single moment that marks the end of the pandemic. Rather, there will be a gradual recession of danger that never fully goes away and that probably will not match the easing of restrictions put in place to deal with that danger. Margaret MacMillan asks why we are so often surprised by catastrophes that might have been predicted, why some leaders and societies cope better than others, and how we can deal with the lasting consequences of great shocks—issues we can better understand by revisiting the trajectory of major upheavals in the past. Using history as a guide, Philip Bobbitt considers why many faddish predictions about the post-COVID world may be wrong and offers his own future scenario—that of a deepening crisis of constitutional order in major nation-states—as a way of pushing us to prepare for an uncertain future.

Part II deals with *Global Public Health and Mitigation Strategies*. These issues are now of incontestable importance to world order because of the horrific human toll pandemics can take and the way that epidemiological catastrophes can trigger economic and geopolitical ones. There is no guarantee, after all, that the end of COVID will bring a respite from aggressive global disease. It might mark the beginning of a new era of even more catastrophic outbreaks.

In response to this danger, Tom Inglesby offers a detailed program for making pandemics lose their power, and in doing so reminds us that the dichotomy between unilateral and multilateral responses is a false one. Lainie Rutkow argues that policy makers must not, in the aftermath of the crisis, lose the sense of urgency that a pandemic creates. Rather, they must raise the profile of public health measures that are often invisible until a crisis breaks, while cultivating new collaborations and networks within and between nations. Finally, Jeffrey P. Kahn, Anna C. Mastroianni, and Sridhar Venkatapuram consider the ethics of global health in a post-COVID world. In their view, the crisis reveals the limitations of bioethics as a field and underscores the need for a more holistic conception of what makes a global health system morally just. Without such a shift, we will be ill-equipped to address global health challenges that can wreak havoc on the entire world.

Part III moves to *Transnational Issues: Technology, Climate, and Food*. In each of these areas, purely national solutions to accelerating challenges are unworkable. And in each of these areas, COVID-19 has highlighted the urgency of action.

For Johannes Urpelainen, a pandemic is a terrible thing to waste. He contends that the crisis, by temporarily suppressing global emissions, has created an opportunity to invest heavily in green technologies and perhaps head off the worst impacts of climate change. Jessica Fanzo reminds us that COVID will dramatically worsen food insecurity around the world—a development likely to heighten political instability, geopolitical conflict, and other forms of strife. "Without food security," she tells us, "there is no world order." Finally, Christine Fox and Thayer Scott point out that COVID has intensified the technological rivalry between the United States and China and that Washington must deepen its collaboration with other democracies if it is to manage the consequences of a technological revolution that creates as many risks as opportunities.

Part IV covers *The Future of the Global Economy.* In hindsight, we are likely to remember COVID-19 as an economic crisis as much as an epidemiological one. For it not only brought the global economy to a standstill—triggering the most rapid, if perhaps temporary, de-globalization the world has ever seen—but also revealed the weaknesses of existing international institutions for managing the global economy and the dangerous dependencies globalization had created.

Benn Steil argues that the pre-COVID economic order is probably not coming back. But instead of reverting to isolationism or persisting in the search for a single, integrated global economic order, the United States should consider the "two worlds" approach it took during the Cold War. This means limiting reliance on the authoritarian world while deepening American integration with other democracies. John Lipsky examines why institutions, such as the G20, worked relatively well in dealing with the fallout from the global financial crisis but have performed so poorly in handling the economic dimensions of the pandemic and what this tells us about the future of global economic governance.

Lipsky's essay serves as a bridge to part V, which covers *Global Politics and Governance.* For those who believe in the virtues of the liberal international order, the most shocking aspect of the COVID crisis is surely the degree to which many of the order's key institutions—from the WHO to the G7—underperformed or proved incapable of constructive action. Failures of governance at the domestic level were accompanied by failures of governance at the global level. Any post-COVID effort at world order will have to begin with an understanding of what went wrong.

Anne Applebaum points to a variety of factors—the abdication of American leadership, the determined Chinese effort to capture international institutions, and the fact that bodies created in the 20th century may lack the speed and agility the current moment requires. Fixing the system may require fundamentally rethinking what role we expect deeply entrenched, bureaucratic entities to play in global politics. Henry Farrell and Hahrie Han believe that the liberal institutional order was collapsing even before the crisis began because of a growing deficit of democratic accountability. They, too, argue for a fundamental reimagining that reconnects the international system with the publics it is meant to serve. Janice Gross Stein asserts that the world is becoming more contested and competitive after COVID and that consensus-based institutions are unlikely to perform well in such a world. If international governance is to work, it will have to go "off-site," into informal networks and plurilateral coalitions working outside of existing bodies. Finally, James B. Steinberg argues that the best way of salvaging some order from potential chaos is by rebuilding a system that emphasizes arrangements for addressing shared challenges, sets rules and norms for emerging technologies, engages public and civil society, and safely manages a competitive US–China relationship.

Part VI is also about high politics, focusing on *Grand Strategy and American Statecraft*. World orders are, to a great extent, a reflection of the policies and values of the most powerful global actors. And if COVID has revealed significant weaknesses in the post–Cold War order, it has also raised profound questions about what grand strategy the United States should pursue in the future—or whether it even wishes to lead that order.

Interestingly, the authors in this section mostly offer glass-half-full interpretations, while contending that American grand strategy should adapt but not change fundamentally. Hal Brands, Peter Feaver, and William Inboden argue that the pandemic need not make the world far more menacing for the United States. It could, rather, create opportunities to pursue a smarter, more geopolitically savvy globalization, to reinvest in partnerships with liberal democracies, and to forge a stronger counterbalancing coalition against a neo-totalitarian China. That will, of course, require more enlightened American leadership than is currently in evidence; it will also require that the United States address dangers from pandemics and other "soft" security threats without hollowing out its capability to meet "hard" security challenges. Similarly, Thomas Wright calls for the United States to resist the understandable urge to fundamentally reorient its grand strategy toward transnational issues. The better option would be a "free world" strategy focused on improving the resilience and solidarity of the world's democracies against great-power revisionism and resurgent authoritarianism.

Kori Schake also offers a moderately optimistic take, arguing that the pandemic could ultimately result in a renaissance of American global engagement, the strengthening of the domestic foundations of US power, and stronger efforts by free societies to deal with China's rise. Finally, Kathleen H. Hicks sees the crisis as an opportunity to revisit core elements of American grand strategy and improve the mix of tools the United States uses to protect and pursue its interests in the world. Hicks is also relatively bullish on the long-term strength of democracies, seeing the protests for racial justice as a sign that political will and even consensus is emerging for much-needed change.

Looming over so many of these issues is the topic covered in part VII: *Sino-American Rivalry*. If before the crisis China and America already seemed headed for a deep and prolonged competition—a new Cold War, as some have termed it—that trajectory seems all the more pronounced since the pandemic struck.[17] Positions have hardened on both sides of the Pacific; the hostility has become palpable, even as the reality of interdependence has never been clearer.

Elizabeth Economy offers a stark assessment of the challenge that Xi Jinping's China poses to the existing world order. She argues that while the United States has increasingly embraced a strategy of competing with, and even containing, Beijing, that strategy is unlikely to succeed unless Washington also reinvests in a broader concept of a world order centered on democratic values and solidarity among the liberal democracies. Graham Allison calls instead for America to seek a "rivalry partnership" with Beijing, in which the two competitors seek to make a world "safe for diversity" and find common ground in areas where their interests overlap. Eric Schmidt contends that technology has become the central axis of great-power rivalry and outlines an agenda meant to allow the United States to win this new "great game" without forgoing all the advantages of interchange and interdependence. Finally, Niall Ferguson rounds out the volume by arguing that a new cold war is very much under way. He believes that the Trump administration has actually done fairly well in positioning the United States to win it, yet he reminds us that the choices of lesser powers ultimately did much to determine the outcome of the US-Soviet Cold War. Ferguson warns that many of America's allies are contemplating nonalignment in the present rivalry. If that happens, America will find it nearly impossible to prevail in a long competition with China—or sustain its concept of world order.

Themes and Insights

The authors cut across disciplinary lines and deal with subjects that inevitably overlap; they offer both complementary and contrasting viewpoints. The chapters cluster around a variety of themes and debates that bring together the volume as a whole. Here, we highlight a few issues of particular importance.

Will COVID-19 Remake World Order?

It is undeniable that COVID-19 is shaking up the world and laying bare the weaknesses of existing arrangements and institutions. But will COVID mark the end of one world order and the emergence of another? The answer, we believe, is not so simple.

It is not a coincidence that the biggest, most epochal shifts in world order often occur in the wake of major wars. Such cataclysms fatally rupture existing relationships and institutions; they reset the global distribution of power. By leveling the architecture of one world order, they create new possibilities for construction.

That COVID will have a similarly transformative effect seems unlikely. The pandemic has been monumentally traumatic, of course, and all bets are off if the world faces multiple, increasingly lethal outbreaks before a vaccine is developed. But short of that happening, COVID will probably not dramatically change the distribution of material power. To be sure, the United States has fared poorly from a public health perspective and has suffered a severe diminution—in the near term, at least—of its credibility and reputation for competence. Yet several aspects of the crisis—the role of the US Federal Reserve in stabilizing the world economy, the flight to the dollar, and others—actually testify to America's immense structural power. Moreover, it is far from clear that America's foremost challenger—China—will see its own long-term position enhanced, in part because of the way that the crisis has underscored that country's authoritarian pathologies and in part because one result of the pandemic may be a more concerted counterbalancing effort from the world's democracies.

When it comes to institutions, the pandemic has undoubtedly revealed deep-seated weaknesses within many prominent international bodies, from the WHO and WTO to the G7. The need for reform has become clear to all; so has the absence of well-developed institutional structures to deal with a variety of emerging challenges. This should not surprise us: much of our global governance architecture was created at a different time, in a different world, to deal with different challenges. Some of it is now out of date or ill-fitted for new global threats.

Those with long memories understand that there have been previous periods of institutional underperformance, failure, and adaptation within the context of particular orders. The roles and responsibilities of the International Monetary Fund and World Bank have shifted considerably since their creation; the General Agreement on Tariffs and Trade gave way to the World Trade Organization after the Cold War; ad hoc arrangements have often emerged to complement, rather than replace, existing bodies on issues such as nuclear proliferation. Viewed against this precedent, COVID may simply spur a period of much-needed institutional reform and evolution rather than a new start. Indeed, in several chapters in this volume, the authors indicate that, far from destroying the existing order, COVID could spur its reform and renewal. Perhaps that order will be somewhat narrower than it was after the Cold War: a number of contributors argue that the key is to lessen dependence on China while deepening cooperation among the democracies, a reversion to something like the "two worlds" approach of the postwar era. Although that change would be a significant departure from the post–Cold War era of global integration, it would actually take the United States back to its order-building roots, so to speak.

Could the crisis nonetheless force a significant change in our approach to world order by fundamentally altering how the United States and other countries perceive and prioritize key international threats? If COVID ends up killing, just within the United States, a number of people that is orders of magnitude higher than the number that died on 9/11, then surely "soft" security threats will rise in importance relative to "hard" security challenges such as terrorism and geopolitical rivalry. Perhaps the military balance of power is becoming passé—perhaps it simply is not that relevant in a world where small states have often done better than large states in suppressing the pandemic and where grave threats to human prosperity and flourishing do not respect geopolitical divides.[18]

Here too, though, the story is not so simple. COVID-19 may have elevated the threat posed by pandemics and other nontraditional threats. But the threat posed by more traditional dangers remains. COVID has created new temptations for authoritarian actors to undermine the politics and cohesion of democratic societies; it could well exacerbate state failure and instability in fragile regions throughout the world, including the always volatile greater Middle East. And the pandemic was accompanied by a marked increase in Chinese assertiveness, from Hong Kong to the South China Sea to South Asia and beyond, using tools from "wolf warrior" public diplomacy to outright military coercion.[19]

The real takeaway from COVID may be that hard and soft threats often work in tandem, potentially mixing and combining in powerful ways. Geopolitical rivalry may make transnational threats harder to combat; transnational threats can sharpen geopolitical rivalries and instability. America and other countries will not be able to ignore hard or soft threats in a post-COVID world because those challenges are so deeply interrelated.

Balancing Competition and Cooperation

This relates to a second theme: the uncertain balance of competition and cooperation. We may look back on COVID as the crisis that crystallized a protracted, high-stakes competition between the world's greatest powers—much as crises in Greece and Turkey in 1946–47 crystallized an emerging Cold War. The pandemic underscored that the world is fracturing rather than converging; great-power politics are taking on an increasingly zero-sum logic.[20] Yet we may also look back on COVID as the event that threw into relief the mutual vulnerability of even bitter rivals and the need for positive-sum cooperation between them. How—and whether—this balance between competition and cooperation gets struck will be a defining challenge of world order in the 21st century. It will pertain not just to pandemics, but to climate change, food security, migration, information and biotechnology, and other issues with the potential to fundamentally upset the human experience.

There are contrasting perspectives on how to address this dilemma. Some analysts argue that the world's democratic states should first focus on waging and winning the competition with China, because a favorable balance of power is the best guarantee of securing cooperation with rivals on favorable terms. It would be unwise, in this view, to mute Sino-American rivalry in hopes of gaining Chinese cooperation on pandemics or climate change. Rather, America and its allies should compete vigorously, confident that cooperation on shared interests can be compartmentalized, just as the superpowers managed to cooperate on arms control and smallpox eradication during the Cold War.[21]

Or perhaps this first view is too sanguine. US-Soviet cooperation on arms control and global disease emerged only after two decades of Cold War and early moves toward a superpower détente. Perhaps it will be necessary to limit Sino-American rivalry before positive-sum behaviors can take root. If this is the case, a determined effort to seize the geopolitical and ideological high ground could simply ensure that *all* issues come to be seen in zero-sum terms—as happened in the early stages of the COVID crisis.[22] And while the threat that China poses is very real, it remains somewhat more abstract than the human and economic carnage COVID has been wreaking on both countries and around the world. For some, the changed nature of the international system means that a failure by the great powers to subsume their differences to work on shared and potentially catastrophic global challenges will lead the world to ruin.

This book will not fully resolve which approach is best.[23] But the debate reminds us that the challenges of sustaining a peaceful, flourishing world in this century are particularly daunting, because the world is increasingly dividing along geopolitical and ideological lines even as it requires cooperation across them. And it shows that a form of American statecraft that is purely competitive in nature—one that does not feature a leading US role in catalyzing action on transnational challenges—will not meet the demands of global leadership.

The Future of Globalization and Innovation

COVID-19 is not simply a crisis of public health. It is an economic crisis—a self-induced coma, as it has been termed—unparalleled in modern history. Quarantines, shelter-in-place orders, and other restrictions caused growth to collapse and unemployment to surge. These measures also raised sharp questions about how long the resulting damage would last, which industries and countries would emerge with a competitive advantage, and what prospects there are for vibrant equitable economies—at the national and global levels—in the years to come.

Complicating matters is the fact that COVID occurred amid a growing dissatisfaction with the effects of globalization and interdependence. In the years after the Cold War, globalization had intensified and deepened. The process connected the world as never before, generated massive wealth, and pulled individuals around the world out of poverty. Yet domestically, offshoring also exacerbated de-industrialization and the loss of manufacturing jobs in the United States. Globally, massive increases in trade and financial flows generated turbulence and occasional crises, and left countries vulnerable to powerful global forces outside of their control. It was hoped that globalization would bring along with it liberal democracy, transparency, tolerance, and openness, but authoritarian governments—China's being the clearest example—cleverly found ways to capture economic benefits without making political or social sacrifices.

Anxiety about openness went hand-in-hand with anxiety about technological innovation. Much growth and even more interconnectedness have been driven by profound changes in technology, especially in the information sector. Only a decade ago, this technological revolution was viewed as almost entirely beneficial to humanity, but since then, we have seen some of its dark sides. Disinformation campaigns have deepened polarization within democracies while new technologies, such as facial recognition tools, empower authoritarian governments.[24] Artificial intelligence, robotics, machine learning, and biotechnology promise extraordinary benefits for humanity while also raising the threat of potentially vast dangers.[25]

We can take some comfort in the fact that we have been here before. Technological innovation has always been a source of danger as well as opportunity. The postwar economic order was never as smooth or seamless as we sometimes believe. The vaunted Bretton Woods system was prone to crises and collapsed altogether in the early 1970s, leading to years of ad hoc efforts to stabilize a turbulent system. When the Cold War ended, many countries around the world reduced trade barriers, liberalized their economies, and allowed foreign investment; the decades that followed witnessed impressive growth but also debilitating crises. The story of the post–World War II global economy is one of fantastic prosperity and severe, recurring challenges.

In this crisis, there is bad news and good news. The bad news is that globalization proved surprisingly fragile in the face of a raging pandemic—even countries within the European Union barred exports of critical goods and shut their borders. The good news is that certain aspects of the system have worked fairly well. Similar to the 2007–9 global financial crisis, the US Federal Reserve acted as the banker to the world during the pandemic, providing much-needed liquidity to avoid a depression (albeit with less global coordination). National governments, including the United States, initiated massive stimulus programs; the results were mixed but the outcome was surely better than it would have been absent these injections. There are also certain indications that governments may still respond to the crisis in mostly constructive ways. If the outcome of the pandemic is a reduction of specific dependencies on authoritarian regimes, an emphasis on economic resilience that nonetheless encourages deep integration between democracies, a greater pooling of resources among like-minded nations to develop and master the technologies of the future, and enhanced efforts to address inequalities both within and between countries—all possibilities to which authors in this volume point—then the crisis could be a source of renewal rather than a harbinger of a dark new age.

Politics, At Home and Abroad

One reason the COVID-19 crisis has been so jarring is that it seemed to worsen the deepening global crisis of governance. Fraying democratic norms, increased populism and nationalism, overmatched and in effective government bureaucracies, and the growing reach of autocratic leaders have menaced the global order for several years.[26] The pandemic has, at least in the short term, accelerated many of these worrisome trends. American statecraft has long held that world order should be based on liberal ideas and democratic values. If so, reinvigorating and rethinking democratic politics at home may be a prerequisite to sustaining the influence of those values on the global stage.

While there are different views in the book on how the battle between democratic forms of governance and authoritarianism will play out, the future may not be as foreboding as some of the early indicators make it seem. As some contributors note, democracies such as New Zealand, Taiwan, Iceland, and Germany implemented especially effective measures to limit the coronavirus's spread. Countries with illiberal populists or authoritarian leaders in charge—Brazil, Iran, Russia, North Korea, Belarus—saw cases, hospitalizations, and deaths surge. Unfortunately, the world's leading democracy—the United States—fared poorly, due to the erratic presidency of Donald Trump as well as the disappointing performance of the federal bureaucracy. The contrast to the autocratic efficiency of China seems, at first glance, quite striking.

But the story is not all bad. The extent to which China's system has truly done better against COVID is hard to confirm with any precision, given the regime's systematic suppression of reliable information. Whatever progress Beijing has made has come at a high cost in violations of human rights and basic liberties, and failing to honestly communicate the severity of the virus's spread to other states and global authorities.[27] In the United States, the absence of national oversight has allowed certain state and local governments to demonstrate competence and vision. Elements of the nonprofit and private sector have exhibited qualities of nimbleness and adaptation. The extraordinary effort, ongoing as we write this, to develop both effective therapies and a mass-produced vaccine in record time is breathtaking.[28] America's deep, diverse, and innovative civil society provides a degree of resiliency, even in the face of federal underperformance, that autocracies find hard to mimic.

A number of contributors to this volume also point out that COVID-19 may force democracies to confront their limitations, as crises often do. COVID will equip democratic governments around the world with a greater understanding of the dangers of authoritarian disinformation campaigns. The pandemic has highlighted lingering issues of inequality and racial injustice in the United States and other democratic societies. Not least, it has revealed how deep political polarization and tribalism has too often gotten in the way of wise, coordinated policies.[29] It is clear that the United States and other democratic societies face a crisis of politics and governance. We must escape a terrible cycle: the worse our institutions and politics perform, the more people lose faith in governance and the more our politics becomes poisoned. If we are looking for something that will provide an impetus to the slow, messy, incremental process of reform needed to avert such an outcome, a global pandemic seems as good a candidate as any.

Crisis as Opportunity

We are living through a dark time. The world confronts overlapping national and global crises. Governments and international institutions often seem inadequate to the task. Aggressive authoritarianism and illiberalism often seem to be on the ascent. Aspects of the postwar and post–Cold War orders appear worn and outdated.

Here history can provide both consolation and inspiration. The world has seen other periods of great disorder and turbulence—even since World War II—that were arguably worse than our own. The current crisis has even revealed underlying strengths of the current world order. For example, the unprecedented sharing of scientific information and the drive for therapies and a vaccine remind us of the breathtaking economic, intellectual, and scientific advances that have occurred in recent decades.[30] Finally, history reminds us that times of crisis provide opportunities for creativity and reform. Innovation and technical breakthroughs often emerge from economic depressions (the bicycle was invented in Germany during an epidemic among horses in 1815!). Moments of crisis break inertia and create a fluidity that can be put to good purpose; they can foster the political will needed to confront entrenched pathologies. The extraordinary protests over racial injustice in June 2020, which rapidly spread around the world, reflect a collective national and global desire to bring real change. Proposals to reform global governance, enhance the solidarity of democratic nations, and invest in new efforts to confront looming threats reflect a similar impulse.

Can we make the most of the moment? The starting point is to think creatively about how we arrived at our current juncture and how we can make our way out of the accompanying uncertainty. Our hope is that this volume can guide decision makers in this endeavor.

Notes

1. See appendix B: "2019 Global Security Forum Scenarios," in Samuel J. Brannen, Christian S. Haig, Katherine Schmidt, and Kathleen H. Hicks, "Twin Pillars: Upholding National Security and National Innovation in Merging Technological Governance," *CSIS*, Jan. 2020, https://csis-website-prod.s3.amazonaws.com/s3fs-public/publication/200123_Brannen_TwinPillars_WEB_FINAL. pdf; and Samuel Brannen and Kathleen Hicks, "We Predicted a Coronavirus Pandemic: Here's What Policymakers Could Have Seen Coming," *Politico Magazine*, March 7, 2020, https://www.politico.com/news/magazine/2020/03/07/coronavirus-epidemic-prediction-policy-advice-121172. The Johns Hopkins Center for Health Security, in partnership with the World Economic Forum and the Bill and Melinda Gates Foundation, held a global pandemic simulation, "Event 201," in October 2019, https://www.centerforhealthsecurity.org/event201/.
2. For up-to-date data on global COVID-19 cases, see the Johns Hopkins University COVID-19 Tracking Map, developed by Dr. Lauren Gardner and the Center for Systems Science and Engineering at JHU, https://coronavirus.jhu.edu/map.html.
3. Robert Kagan, *The Jungle Grows Back: America and Our Imperiled World* (New York: Borzoi Book, 2018); Hal Brands, *American Grand Strategy in the Age of Trump* (Washington, DC: Brookings Institution Press, 2018); Francis J. Gavin, "Pandemic and the Plight of American Public Policy," *War on the Rocks*, April 2, 2020, https://warontherocks.com/2020/04/pandemic-and-the-plight-of-american-public-policy/; G. John Ikenberry, *A World Safe for Democracy: Liberal Internationalism and the Crises of the Global Order* (New Haven, CT: Yale University Press, 2020); and G. John Ikenberry, "The Next Liberal Order," *Foreign Affairs* (July/August 2020), https://www.foreignaffairs.com/articles/united-states/2020-06-09/next-liberal-order.
4. Hal Brands and Charles Edel, The *Lessons of Tragedy: Statecraft and World Order* (New Haven, CT: Yale University Press, 2019); Henry Kissinger, *Diplomacy* (New York: Simon & Schuster, 1994); and G. John Ikenberry, *After Victory* (Princeton, NJ: Princeton University Press, 2001).
5. Henry Kissinger, *A World Restored* (Gloucester, UK: Peter Smith, 1973); and John Bew, *Castlereagh: A Life* (Oxford, UK: Oxford University Press, 2012).

6. Sally Marks, *The Illusion of Peace: International Relations in Europe 1918–1933* (New York: St. Martin's Press, 1976); and Adam Tooze, *The Deluge: The Great War, America and the Remaking of the Global Order, 1916–1931* (New York: Penguin Books, 2014).
7. Robert Dallek, *Franklin Roosevelt and American Foreign Policy, 1932–1945* (Oxford, UK: Oxford University Press, 1979; Henry Kissinger, *Diplomacy* (New York: Simon & Schuster, 1994); and Benn Steil, *The Battle of Bretton Woods: John Maynard Keynes, Harry Dexter White, and the Making of a World Order* (Princeton, NJ: Princeton University Press, 2013).
8. John Lewis Gaddis, *We Now Know: Rethinking Cold War History* (New York: Oxford University Press, 1997).
9. Harold James, *International Monetary Cooperation since Bretton Woods* (Washington, DC: International Monetary Fund, 1996); and Barry J. Eichengreen, Arnaug Mehl, and Livia Chitu, *How Global Currencies Work: Past, Present, and Future* (Princeton, NJ: Princeton University Press, 2018).
10. Marc Trachtenberg, *A Constructed Peace: The Making of the European Settlement, 1945–1963* (Princeton, NJ: Princeton University Press, 1999).
11. John Lewis Gaddis, *The Long Peace: Inquiries into the History of the Cold War* (New York: Oxford University Press, 1987); Francis J. Gavin, *Nuclear Statecraft: History and Strategy in America's Atomic Age* (Ithaca, NY: Cornell University Press, 2012); James Cameron, *The Double Game: The Demise of America's First Missile Defense System and the Rise of Strategic Arms Limitation* (Oxford, UK: Oxford University Press, 2017); and Hal Brands, "Non-Proliferation and the Dynamics of the Middle Cold War: The Superpowers, the MLF, and the NPT," *Cold War History* 7, no. 3 (2007): 389–423, https://doi.org/10.1080/14682740701474857.
12. Francis Fukuyama, "The End of History?" *The National Interest,* no. 16 (Summer 1989): 3–18, www.jstor.org/stable/24027184; Samuel P. Huntington, "The Clash of Civilizations?" *Foreign Affairs* 72, no. 3 (Summer 1993): 22–49, https://doi.org/10.2307/20045621; Charles Krauthammer, "The Unipolar Moment," *Foreign Affairs* 70, no. 1 (1990); and John J. Mearsheimer, "Back to the Future: Instability in Europe after the Cold War," *International Security* 15, no. 1 (Summer 1990): 5–56, https://doi.org/10.2307/253898.
13. James Addison Baker and Thomas M. DeFrank, *The Politics of Diplomacy: Revolution, War, and Peace, 1989–1992* (New York: G. P. Putnam's Sons, 1995); Hal Brands, *Making the Unipolar Moment: U.S. Foreign Policy and the Rise of the Post–Cold War Order* (Ithaca, NY: Cornell University Press, 2016); George H. W. Bush and Brent Scowcroft, *A World Transformed* (New York: Vintage Books, 1999); and Phillip Zelikow and Condoleezza Rice, *To Build a Better World: Choices to End the Cold War and Create a Global Commonwealth* (New York: Twelve, 2019).
14. Brands, *Making the Unipolar Moment*; and G. John Ikenberry, *Liberal Leviathan: The Origins, Crisis, and Transformation of the American World Order* (Princeton, NJ: Princeton University Press, 2011).
15. Adam Tooze, *Crashed: How a Decade of Financial Crises Changed the World* (New York: Viking Press, 2018).
16. Henry Kissinger, "The Coronavirus Pandemic Will Forever Alter the World Order," *Wall Street Journal,* April 3, 2020, https://www.wsj.com/articles/the-coronavirus-pandemic-will-forever-alter-the-world-order-11585953005.
17. Robert D. Kaplan, "A New Cold War Has Begun," *Foreign Policy*, January 7, 2019, https://foreignpolicy.com/2019/01/07/a-new-cold-war-has-begun/; "A New Kind of Cold War: How to Manage the Growing Rivalry between America and a Rising China," *The Economist*, May 16, 2019, https://www-economist-com.proxy1.library.jhu.edu/leaders/2019/05/16/a-new-kind-of-cold-war; Kevin Rudd, "The Coming Post-COVID Anarchy: The Pandemic Bodes Ill for Both American and Chinese Power—and for the Global Order," *Foreign Affairs*, May 6, 2020, https://www.foreignaffairs.com/articles/united-states/2020-05-06/coming-post-covid-anarchy; and "The New Scold War: The Pandemic Is Driving America and China Further Apart," *The Economist*, May 9, 2020, https://www-economist-com.proxy1.library.jhu.edu/leaders/2020/05/09/the-pandemic-is-driving-america-and-china-further-apart.
18. Richard Haass, "A Cold War with China Would Be a Mistake," *Wall Street Journal*, May 7, 2020, https://www.wsj.com/articles/dont-start-a-new-cold-war-with-china-11588860761; and Lawrence Summers, "Covid-19 Looks Like a Hinge in History," *Financial Times,* May 14, 2020, https://www.ft.com/content/de643ae8-9527-11ea-899a-f62a20d54625.
19. Tom McTague, "The Pandemic's Geopolitical Aftershocks Are Coming," *The Atlantic*, May 18, 2020, https://www.theatlantic.com/international/archive/2020/05/coronavirus-pandemic-second-wave-geopolitics-instability/611668/; and "China's 'Wolf Warrior' Diplomacy Gamble," *The Economist*, May 28, 2020,

https://www.economist.com/china/2020/05/28/chinas-wolf-warrior-diplomacy-gamble; and Minxin Pei, "China's Coming Upheaval," *Foreign Affairs*, May/June 2020, https://www.foreignaffairs.com/articles/united-states/2020-04-03/chinas-coming-upheaval.

20. This is not to say that the US-China rivalry is the same as the Cold War, a debate that continues to play out at greater length in many other forums.
21. See Thomas Wright's and Elizabeth Economy's contributions to this volume (chapters 17 and 20, respectively).
22. In an interview in late January, US Commerce Secretary Wilbur Ross predicted the coronavirus would "help to accelerate the return of jobs to North America." Ana Swanson and Alan Rappeport, "Wilbur Ross Says Coronavirus Could Bring Jobs Back to the U.S." *New York Times,* January 30, 2020, https://www.nytimes.com/2020/01/30/business/economy/wilbur-ross-coronavirus-jobs.html.
23. Hal Brands, "Coronavirus Hasn't Killed the Global Balance of Power," *Bloomberg*, May 27, 2020, https://www.bloomberg.com/opinion/articles/2020-05-27/china-wants-coronavirus-to-destroy-the-global-balance-of-power; and Hal Brands, "Cooperate with China on Coronavirus but Don't Trust It, *Bloomberg*, April 12, 2020, https://www.bloomberg.com/opinion/articles/2020-04-12/china-can-t-be-trusted-in-fight-against-coronavirus.
24. On the impact of disinformation campaigns on Western democracies, see Alina Polyakova and Spencer Phipps Boyer, *The Future of Political Warfare: Russia, the West, and the Coming Age of Global Digital Warfare*, Brookings Institution, March 2018, https://www.brookings.edu/research/the-future-of-political-warfare-russia-the-west-and-the-coming-age-of-global-digital-competition/. China has deployed facial recognition software on a large scale in Xinjiang province to monitor the Uyghur population; see Paul Mozer, "One Month, 500,000 Face Scans: How China Is Using A.I. to Profile a Minority," *New York Times,* April 14, 2019, https://www.nytimes.com/2019/04/14/technology/china-surveillance-artificial-intelligence-racial-profiling.html.
25. Henry A. Kissinger, Eric Schmidt, and Daniel Huttenlocher, "The Metamorphosis," *The Atlantic*, August 2019, https://www.theatlantic.com/magazine/archive/2019/08/henry-kissinger-the-metamorphosis-ai/592771/; and Henry A. Kissinger, "How the Enlightenment Ends," *The Atlantic*, June 2018, https://www.theatlantic.com/magazine/archive/2018/06/henry-kissinger-ai-could-mean-the-end-of-human-history/559124/.
26. The latest Freedom House report found that 2019 marked the 14th consecutive year of net decline in global freedom. Sarah Repucci, *Freedom in the World 2020: A Leaderless Struggle for Democracy* (Washington, DC: Freedom House, 2020), www.freedomhouse.org/report/freedom-world/2020/leaderless-struggle-democracy.
27. Derek Scissors, "Estimating the True Number of China's COVID-19 Cases," American Enterprise Institute, April 2020, https://www.aei.org/wp-content/uploads/2020/04/Estimating-the-True-Number-of-Chinas-COVID-19-Cases.pdf; Emily Feng and Amy Chang, "Restrictions and Rewards: How China Is Locking Down Half a Billion Citizens," *NPR*, February 21, 2020, https://www.npr.org/sections/goatsandsoda/2020/02/21/806958341/restrictions-and-rewards-how-china-is-locking-down-half-a-billion-citizens; and Lin Zhu et al., "China's Cities Lock Up Residents to Prevent Spread of Virus," *Bloomberg*, February 11, 2020, https://www.bloomberg.com/news/articles/2020-02-11/china-s-cities-lock-up-residents-to-prevent-spread-of-virus.
28. Former FDA commissioner Scott Gottlieb predicts the United States will have a better vaccine sooner than China. See "U.S. is Ahead of China in Vaccine Race, Former FDA Chief Says," *Politico,* May 24, 2020, https://www.politico.com/news/2020/05/24/coronavirus-vaccine-china-gottlieb-276763. For a discussion of state and local government responses to COVID-19, see Rebecca L. Haffajee and Michelle M. Mello, "Thinking Globally, Acting Locally—the U.S. Response to Covid-19," *New England Journal of Medicine* 382, no. 22 (May 2020): e75, https://doi.org/10.1056/NEJMp2006740.%2010.1056/NEJMp2006740.
29. A Pew Research Center Coronavirus report, released in June 2020, reported 61% of Republicans felt the worst problems the country was facing from coronavirus were behind us, while 76% of Democrats felt that the worst was still to come. See "Republicans, Democrats Move Even Further Apart in Coronavirus Concerns," Pew Research Center, June 25, 2020, https://www.pewresearch.org/politics/2020/06/25/republicans-democrats-move-even-further-apart-in-coronavirus-concerns/; and Ronald Brownstein, "Red and Blue America Aren't Experiencing the Same Pandemic," *The Atlantic*, March 20, 2020. https://www.theatlantic.com/politics/archive/2020/03/how-republicans-and-democrats-think-about-coronavirus/608395/.
30. Matt Apuzzo and David D. Kirkpatrick, "Covid-19 Changed How the World Does Science, Together," *New York Times,* April 1, 2020, https://www.nytimes.com/2020/04/01/world/europe/coronavirus-science-research-cooperation.html.

www.ingramcontent.com/pod-product-compliance
Lightning Source LLC
LaVergne TN
LVHW080635011026
849160LV00014B/1222